THE ORGANIC PHILOSOPHY
OF EDUCATION

By

Frank C. Wegener

Guide for Students in History and Philosophy of Education
Problems and Principles of School and Society: An Outline.

THE ORGANIC PHILOSOPHY OF EDUCATION

By

FRANK C. WEGENER

PROFESSOR OF HISTORY AND PHILOSOPHY OF EDUCATION
COLLEGE OF EDUCATION AND GRADUATE SCHOOL
UNIVERSITY OF TEXAS

GREENWOOD PRESS, PUBLISHERS
WESTPORT, CONNECTICUT

Library of Congress Cataloging in Publication Data

Wegener, Frank Corliss, 1908–
  The organic philosophy of education.

  Reprint of the ed. published by W. C. Brown,
Dubuque, Iowa.
  Includes bibliographical references.
  1. Education—Philosophy. I. Title.
LB885.W4 1974   370.1   73-9213
ISBN 0–8371–6979–8

Originally published in 1957 by Wm. C. Brown Company,
Dubuque, Iowa

Reprinted with the permission of Helen D. Wegener

Reprinted in 1974 by Greenwood Press,
a division of Williamhouse-Regency Inc.

Library of Congress Catalogue Card Number 73-9213

ISBN 0-8371-6979-8

Printed in the United States of America

To My Mother

FOREWORD

Whatever may be the truth about the educational situation, the public and many members of the teaching profession think there are two kinds of education. One of these they consider conservative, formal, and subject-centered, and the other they consider progressive, informal, and pupil-centered. They write and speak as if it is necessary to take sides. They seem to think that one has to be a conservative or a progressive and take opposing positions on every important educational issue, regardless of how such attitudes may be designated. The underlying assumption of such empirical, common-sense, educational theorizing is that the world allows only one kind of education.

Professor Wegener with his broad knowledge of philosophy and interest in education cannot accept an either-or position. Neither can he accept the indefensible, compromising, eclectic, middle-of-the-road position to which some practical minded educational leaders subscribe; that is, that there is some good in both positions, and one has only to select the good and reject the bad in each. He knows that such eclecticism is philosophically indefensible.

Still, he is quite aware that in educational practice both the so-called conservative and the so-called progressive theories are operating side by side. In the same school system, in the same school, and even in the same classroom under the direction of the same teacher, both attitudes are clearly exemplified in specific programs and activities. In some situations the two kinds of education are clearly distinguished and each assigned its own place. Moreover, Professor Wegener knows that the most conservative, formal, and subject-centered schools often find some place for what has been called progressive education, and the most progressive, informal, and pupil-centered schools likewise find some place for conservative education. The qualified observer must realize that something is wrong with the current assumption that the character of the world of nature and of man justifies one and only one of these two alternatives. Since in practice the implications of both conservatism and progressivism are everywhere very much in evidence, the character of the world must be such as to support both positions in spite of the apparent inconsistency involved.

With such an idea in mind, Professor Wegener explores the whole history of Western philosophy to see whether or not the nature of the world and of man is such as to permit, justify, or require the two kinds of education. There he finds that such philosophers as Plato, Aristotle, and Whitehead among others have, to a considerable degree, verified the results of his own analysis, that the metaphysical world of reality is such as to make the two kinds of education not only possible but also necessary, and even desirable. Such a conception of the world he calls the organic philosophy, which is as different from idealism, realism, and experimentalism as they are different from each other. According to this philosophy the great opposites of the world are exemplified in nature itself. The world is both one and many, eternal and temporal, permanent and dynamic, structure and process, determinate and indeterminate, rational and irrational. Such distinctions are real, and so are their relationships. Such metaphysical opposites are interdependent as well as independent and dependent. Neither could exist without the other. This bi-polarity is characteristic of reality, out of which all experience emerges.

Therefore, experience itself, which, when most broadly conceived, may be identified with the educative process, contains many opposites corresponding to the nature of the world itself. Here we have the explanation of why both conservative education and progressive education, in their various aspects, are found everywhere in school practice. In the very nature of nature both are necessary and each is indispensable to the other. Improvement of the one contributes to the improvement of the other. A balance of the practices which both conservatism and progressivism emphasize is therefore theoretically desirable. Although some higher synthesis may yet be possible, the best philosophical thought up to the present time requires "a school within a school," the formal within the informal.

Whatever may be the school of thought to which teachers of philosophy and philosophy of education may subscribe, they will find

Professor Wegener's approach new and refreshing. To profit from a study of the book, neither they nor their students have to subscribe to the organic philosophy or its correlative bi-polar theory of education, as Professor Wegener has explained them. The significance of any new approach to philosophy does not lie in its validity or its invalidity, but in the new meanings which it provides. Both instructors and students who use this book will see many things in a new light. Those who, without prejudice, read it with attention and a desire to understand will be indebted to the scholarship and insight of the author for a very valuable experience. For class use it is the best statement available of a point of view that should not be neglected in courses in either philosophy or philosophy of education.

(Signed) J. P. WYNNE

Longwood College
Farmville, Virginia
May 7, 1957

PREFACE

There have been numerous approaches to the statement of systematic philosophies of education in fairly abbreviated form. There have been notably few attempts at a thoroughgoing philosophical reconstruction in educational theory in the first half of the 20th Century. John Dewey's writing in this field has been the most influential work of this kind, since he was one of the few philosophers in this country who turned his attention to the subject of education in a systematic and creative manner. Impressed with the need for philosophical reconstruction in education, the author has applied his full efforts to the task.

This comparatively short book is an exposition of some of the propositions and conceptions which are necessary in developing *The Organic Philosophy of Education*. It represents a direct presentation of some of the essential conceptions of this new educational philosophy in condensed and abridged form. It is the writer's hope that this work will contribute something to the fulfillment of the present need until a more thoroughgoing and complete reconstruction of educational philosophy can be accomplished.

The approach is 'systematic' in that the writer has worked from philosophical foundations into the problems of educational philosophy and theory. This procedure has resulted from the conviction that one must not work only at the level of operational expedience, but that it is necessary to ground one's educational conceptions in carefully delineated philosophical propositions. Hence, in this book there has been an effort to proceed from such philosophical propositions into their educational equivalents, and from there into applications to the central issues of educational theory.

The philosophical orientation is 'organic' in the tradition from Plato and Aristotle to the contemporary thought of Alfred North Whitehead. Although this book is substantially overlapping with the philosophy of organism of Whitehead, it is not merely the attempt to translate Whitehead's philosophy into its educational equivalent. Primarily, it represents the formulation of the writer's own philosophy of education, and, secondarily, it utilizes many of the penetrating conceptions of Whitehead's thinking and creativity.

The book is divided into four parts. The Introduction of Part I utilizes one of the writer's earlier articles, "A Proposal . . . The School Within A School," from *Educational Theory*. Also reprinted is a very short article, "The Organic Philosophy of Education," from *School and Society*. Part II presents a synopsis of the writer's foundational propositions, both philosophical and educational. Although these are very broad conceptions presented in fairly abbreviated form, it is believed that they will provide the reader with an overview of the organic philosophical orientation before subsequent analyses of crucial problems of the educational process. In Part III where the problems of the educational process are considered, there have been deliberate attempts to apply organic propositions and principles to crucial issues. Although the analysis is largely theoretical, the author contends that the practical implications for curriculum, methods, role of the teacher, nature of the learning process, the problem of discipline and the like, are very much in evidence. In Part IV, attention is turned to the all important topic of the functions of man and education. It has been the author's endeavor to provide a coherent pattern of organic education in terms of two dimensions. One dimension is provided by the formulation of the ten basic functions of man. The other dimension is provided by an analysis of the needs, values, knowledge, arts, aims, and respective institutional functions of education.

The book necessarily utilizes technical terminology of both philosophy and education. To assist the reader with the technical philosophical terms drawn from the writings of Alfred North Whitehead, the writer has prepared and included a special glossary. Other terms are explained largely in the context of the book. The writer's own terminology necessary to the Organic Philosophy of Education has been explained in context also.

The book has not been written as a conventional textbook. Rather, it has been the intention to state as directly and concisely as possible the basic conceptions and principles which are essential to a resolution of the crucial problems of philosophy of education. There has been no particular attempt to dilute the subject matter or to 'talk down' .to the reader, for it was believed unnecessary. The writer is of the opinion that readability is not so much a matter of simplified wording as it is of having something to say which in itself is intelligible.

It is hoped that serious minded persons who realize that the problems of educational philosophy cannot be easily resolved by simple generalizations will find this effort worthy of their consideration. The book should be of interest to the general reader who is concerned with philosophy as applied to education as well as the educators who are deeply concerned with anything pertaining to the problems of educational theory and practice.

Although it has not been written as a conventional textbook, students and professors in the foundational areas of professional education might find it useful in courses in educational theory, philosophy of education, and principles of education. The author's experiences with both graduate and undergraduate students have led him to believe that students can read this content with understanding and interest. College students who have been confronted with the formidable special terminologies of the physical and social sciences should find no insurmountable obstacle or difficulties in mastering the terminology employed here.

It appears that this work might be used in the college classroom in one of several ways. Many of our 'Philosophy of Education' courses are devoted to a study of comparative philosophies or theories of education in such categories as those of Realism, Idealism, Pragmatism, and the like. One or more textbooks are used with appropriate references. This book, although brief, might be used as a second textbook in such a course. Other courses are devoted to the study of one or more systematic educational philosophies, such as those of John Dewey, H. H. Horne, the Catholic Philosophy of Education, the Herbartian, or others. The systematic character of this work might make it useful as a contrast with one or more of these systematic treatments. Then, too, it might be utilized as one of several books in the study of 'organic philosophies.' Used with various works from Whitehead, such as *Science and the Modern World, Adventures of Ideas,* and *Aims of Education,* this book might prove valuable as a central textbook.

Although the author has endeavored to do a creative and original project in writing *The Organic Philosophy of Education,* he is conscious of his indebtedness to a wide variety of persons and books as well as his own efforts and experiences. It is most difficult to determine just where one has derived the most of his inspirations and ideas. To name certain persons and books is to slight others, perhaps just as deserving.

Nevertheless, I should like to acknowledge my indebtedness for philosophical guidance and inspiration to my former professors, Leonard Eslick, now at St. Louis University; William Weedon, Lewis Hammond, and Albert G. A. Balz, all at the University of Virginia. My original interest in philosophy, particularly the classic philosophies of organism, was generated by these teachers. Dr. M. M. Thompson, now retired from the University of Southern California, contributed much to my understanding and appreciation of the educational philosophy of John Dewey. In this respect, I should be remiss if I did not mention the influence of Dr. Herbert Blackhurst and the late Professor Luther Stalnaker, both of Drake University.

At the University of Texas, I have enjoyed the companionship and philosophical influence of my esteemed colleague, Professor Frederick Eby. His own books and conjoint writings with the late Professor Charles Flinn Arrowood have been a continuing source of inspiration and knowledge to me in the field of history and philosophy of education.

More specifically, with respect to the philosophy of organism of Whitehead and related conceptions of polarity and process, I am happy to acknowledge the helpful writings of Professor Archie J. Bahm, University of New Mexico, and Professor W. H. Sheldon of Yale. Professor Bahm's writings on his philosophy of 'Organicism' and my personal conversations and correspondence with him have been especially clarifying and reinforcing with respect to certain conceptions more or less common to us both. I have profited considerably from Professor W. H. Sheldon's writings, too, particularly on his conceptions of *Process* and *Polarity*.

I am deeply indebted to my friend, Dr. Gus John Craven of Austin College, at Sherman, Texas, for his substantial assistance and cooperation in this enterprise. He has been good enough to read my entire manuscript at various stages of progress, and to provide me with his helpful suggestions for clarification and correction in many places. His assistance in the interpretation of Whitehead has been most valuable to me. His own outstanding dissertation, "A Comparative Study of Creativity in Education in Whitehead and Others," University of Texas, 1952, has been my chief source of inspiration and understanding of the creative process in Whitehead. With Dr. Craven's generous permission I have included substantial excerpts from his dissertation in my discussion of "Organic Conceptions of the Creative Process," in Chapter 14. I am gratified to include these excerpts for I know of no one who is more devoted to the works of Alfred North Whitehead than Dr. Craven. His scholarship and enthusiasm on this subject have been the inspiration for many persons to become vitally interested in the philosophy of organism. I am glad to acknowledge that my friendship with Dr. Craven has done much to add to my personal appreciation and understanding of Whitehead. I am most appreciative of his sympathetic support and encouragement throughout this undertaking.

Other than the works of Plato and Aristotle, the books that have influenced me most are those of Alfred North Whitehead. His *Science and the Modern World*, *Adventures of Ideas*, *Process and Reality*, *The Function of Reason*, and *Religion in the Making*, have been of most assistance and inspiration to me.

Dorothy Emmet's book on *Whitehead's Philosophy of Organism* and A. H. Johnson's recent book, *Whitehead's Theory of Reality*, were most helpful in their interpretations of organic conceptions and in the definition and re-definition of Whitehead's special terminology. One of my favorite books is that of William P. Montague, *Ways of Thinking*. W. M. Urban's works on *The Intelligible World*, and, *Beyond Realism and Idealism*, were both stimulating to my line of thought. Professor W. H. Sheldon's *Process and Polarity* cast additional light upon the nature of polarity as a means of philosophical synthesis. Dr. Archie Bahm's book, *Philosophy: An Introduction,* has been of distinct interest and aid to me because of its chapter on "Organicism." Many other books might well be mentioned, but they will be referred to in the context of the book.

ACKNOWLEDGMENT

The following publishers have been very generous in granting permissions to use substantial quotations from their books: Beacon Press, Columbia University Press, Dial Press, Free Press, Great Books Foundation, Henry Holt and Company, Inc., Harper & Brothers, D. C. Heath and Company, Macmillan Company of New York, Macmillan & Company Ltd. of London, National Society for the Study of Education, New American Library, Oxford University Press, Inc., Philosophical Library, Inc., Prentice-Hall, Inc., Princeton University Press, Ronald Press Company, Routledge & Kegan Paul, Ltd., of London, Charles Scribner's Sons, St. Martin's Press, Inc., University of Chicago Press, and John Wiley & Sons, Inc. I am very appreciative of the co-operation of these publishers and their editors and extend my personal thanks to them.

I should like to acknowledge permissions from Dr. Mortimer Adler and the Bruce Publishing Company on reprinted excerpts from an article, "The Order of Learning," *Catholic School Journal,* (Dec., 1941). I am also indebted to the *Saturday Review* for permission to quote from Lawrence S. Kubie's, "Freud and Human Freedom," (May 5, 1956). The honorary society, *Kappa Delta Pi,* through Editor E. I. F. Williams, of *The Educational Forum,* kindly permitted quotations from their copyrighted work, John Dewey, *Experience and Education,* 1938. My thanks are also extended to the professional journals, *Educational Theory* and *School and Society,* for their respective permissions to reprint some of my earlier articles. Also may

ACKNOWLEDGMENT

I acknowledge Dr. Gus J. Craven's, "A Comparative Study of Creativity in Education in Whitehead and Others," in reprinted form in this book.

The development of a philosophy of education is influenced by so many friends, colleagues, and students that it is impossible to mention all of them by name. I am sorry that it is impracticable to list the many names that bring reminiscences of congenial as well as controversial exchanges of viewpoints concerning the issues of philosophy and education.

I do also want to acknowledge the friendship and encouragement offered by Professor John Wynne, of Longwood College, in Farmville, Virginia. I am also indebted to him for writing the foreword to this book.

My wife Helen has been a constant source of assistance as sounding board and consultant on many of the issues involved as well as helper on editorial and technical tasks in the completion of the book.

FCW

University of Texas
Austin, Texas
July, 1957

TABLE OF CONTENTS

PART I *INTRODUCTION*

PART II *SYNOPSIS OF FOUNDATIONAL PROPOSITIONS*

PART III *THE EDUCATIONAL PROCESS*

PART IV *THE FUNCTIONS OF MAN AND EDUCATION*

LIST OF FIGURES

PART I
Introduction

1

"A PROPOSAL...THE SCHOOL WITHIN A SCHOOL"

T H E reader may not be familiar with the reference which provides the title of this introductory chapter and a necessary orientation to this effort to formulate a new philosophy of education. The original proposal of the "School Within A School" was an hypothesis. It recognized the need for the formulation of a completely reconstructed philosophy of education for our times. It recognized certain validities and shortcomings of conflicting philosophies of education and educational theories. The proposal called attention to the one-sided character of some of these schools of thought with respect to educational theory. Lacking a clearly formulated philosophical basis for such needed reconstruction of educational theory the writer proposed an hypothesis until such time as we were able to articulate thoroughgoing philosophical and educational propositions.

Since writing this proposal the writer has worked toward the formulation of an Organic Philosophy of Education based largely upon propositions consistent with a *philosophy of organism.*[1] In retrospect it is now evident that the proposal served as a point of departure for the present reconstruction. It follows that the reader might well begin with this proposal as a general introduction to this point of view. The original proposal is duplicated here in its entirety.

At the outset then there are several questions to be answered in this chapter. *What was the original proposal? How did it provide a point of departure for working toward an organic philosophy of education? What is the present status of this proposal?*

* * *

"A Proposal . . . The School Within A School"[1]

One of the most fundamental and difficult tasks of educational philosophy is the reconciliation of the valid elements of formal and informal doctrines of education. During the last fifty years we have witnessed the Herculean efforts of John Dewey and his pragmatic followers in their diversified attempts to achieve a theoretical and functional unity of educational doctrines. Prior to the rise of this educational philosophy in the Twentieth Century other eminent educational reformers such as Comenius, Pestalozzi, Froebel, Herbart, Spencer, and G. S. Hall made similar attempts to integrate or synthesize the varied elements of the formalistic tradition and the emergent principles of growth, development, and experience in respect to the nurture of the growing child. Each philosopher of education tried to weld these diverse elements into a unity within his own particular philosophical Weltanschauung.

In retrospect it is clear that each successive attempt at a new integration of these vital but unwieldy components of form and function has enjoyed acceptance for a brief duration. The advances of science and philosophy have made revisions of these philosophies necessary. Also, each educational philosophy has contributed something of lasting value to ensuing philosophies and doctrines. But despite these valuable residual elements which result from the flow of educational developments, the problem of relating the valid elements of formal and informal doctrines of education remains with us for re-examination.

John Dewey has provided us with a pragmatic and naturalistic philosophy of education which has dominated educational thought for most of the Twentieth Century. Despite the weaknesses inherent in pragmatic doctrine, Dewey has achieved a remarkable synthesis of diverse elements derived from such men as Darwin, Hegel, Rousseau, Pestalozzi, Froebel, Herbart, and Peirce. He has artfully subordinated the elements of formal education, with its attendant philosophy and logic, to the predominant demands of his own biological, psychological, and sociological concerns. He has given us a pragmatically oriented philosophy.

It now appears that this pragmatic solution must also pass on. As we view in retrospect the developments in educational philosophy during the last fifty years, we see that the pragmatic revolution has not resulted in a satisfactory solution of educational problems. Despite the advances of the empirical sciences and the accumulations of educational experimentation, we still have considerable confusion in education today. Without denying the many positive contributions ensuing from the educational theories and practices within pragmatic education, we can safely say that the particular philosophical orientation and integration given to us by John Dewey and his followers has not proved satisfactory in solving our problems. Thus by one of its own criteria, that of successful consequences, the pragmatic or instrumental philosophy can be criticized. Once again we are in serious need of a new philosophical synthesis which is more suitable for our times. Since pragmatism and its associated doctrines have proved to be inadequate, we must continue our quest for another orientation. This view does not mean that desirable elements of Dewey's thought should not be continued. Neither does it mean that all that he has suggested is false or wrong. Much of what he has written is a kind of distilled wisdom from diverse sources. It does argue that just as Dewey found it necessary to recast and reconstruct principles of earlier philosophies in his peculiar mold of instrumental thought, that the time has come for a comparable reconstruction of educational philosophy in view of the developments of the first half of the Twentieth Century.

The task of reconstructing our educational thinking to form an adequate philosophy of education is not simple. It involves the tremendous challenge of co-ordinating the valid elements of older philosophies with the complex advances of recent science, philosophy, political ideology, and all that goes into our knowledge of human experience. The persistent problems of metaphysics, epistemology, ethics, and logic within philosophy must be faced; the rapid developments in the physical and social sciences must be considered; these disciplines along with the actual experiences of education must be evaluated and co-ordinated in the formulation of an adequate educational philosophy. To enumerate merely the profound problems which must be faced in such an integration furnishes one with a startling realization of the extensive scope of the philosophic undertakings which have occupied John Dewey during his long and productive life; such efforts and accomplishment command our utmost respect even though we may not agree with all of his philosophical conclusions. Yet in all humility and truth it does appear that we need a philosophical reconstruction to achieve greater educational efficiency.

3

It is not the purpose of this essay to undertake a consideration of the diverse problems mentioned in the previous paragraph. It is the purpose of this writing to propose a vision of the school within a school for both theoretical and practical consideration. It is entirely possible that the plan outlined will evoke theoretical considerations which will result in further reconstruction of our educational philosophies—and perhaps a greater unity. It is conceivable that practical administrators will find the plan suggestive in resolving certain conflicts of educational doctrines.

The Basic Proposal

Until such time as a new synthesis of educational philosophies can be achieved, it is proposed that the hypothesis of a school within a school be adopted. The hypothesis can be formulated basically as follows:

(1) An adequate philosophy of education must accept and co-ordinate the valid elements of two doctrines of the educational process, that of directed growth and that of intellectual and moral development.

(2) The doctrine of education as a process of directed growth, development, and experience of the total personality is valid when applied in an appropriate context.

(3) The doctrine of education as a process of systematic intellectual and moral development is valid when applied within an appropriate context.

(4) Neither one of the doctrines of education should be regarded as inferior or subordinate to the other; each has its rightful sphere.

(5) These two doctrines should be applied within *the school within a school;* they should be co-ordinated and balanced in execution; the related principles and concepts should be applied within the respective spheres of these valid doctrines.

The School Within a School

It is proposed that these two principles be expressed operationally as "the school within a school." The sphere of the conception of education as growth and experience might be termed the "outer school." The sphere of the conception of education as a process of systematic intellectual and moral development could be identified as the "inner school." Thus the whole school, although a unity of educational experiences, consists of a polarity between two different educational doctrines which complement and supplement one another. All of the supporting principles and concepts associated with education as growth and experience can and should be implemented whole-heartedly in the domain of the outer school. Principles of maturation, participation, democratic sharing, intellectualization of activity, problem solving, socialization, and the functional learning typical of modern education should be utilized to their full extent. Similarly, the valid elements of training, instruction, vicarious education, symbolic communication, conceptualization, developments of intellectual skills and understandings, transfer of conceptual learnings, and learning through discovery are applicable to systematic learning; they should be applied rigorously to the units of study within the inner school.

The Fundamental Conception

A fundamental conception of the school within a school includes a vision of the school itself as a miniature democratic community within which boys and girls learn the ways of democratic living by complete and well-rounded curricular participation in the diverse segments of life deemed political, social, economic, aesthetic, re-creational, physical, as well as the intellectual, moral, and spiritual. However, it is considered essential to provide boys and girls with one area of this total pattern of living which might be termed *systematic education.* Thus the systematic education with intellectual and moral emphasis becomes the *inner school* which in a sense is a nucleus of the non-academic or experiential centered *outer school.* Although separated in a theoretical sense in terms of underlying principles, and in an administrative sense for organization and execution, the two spheres of curricular activity, experiential and systematic, are intended to cross-fertilize and support one another educationally in both process and product. Furthermore, this conception embraces the whole community, or society, as a third sphere which both contains and supports the educational community. (See Figure 1) Visualized in terms of concentric circles one sees then the *inner school* of systematic education, supported and contained by the emergent experiences of the *outer school,* which in turn is sustained and reenforced by the whole democratic community. Dependent upon one's philosophy, particularly with respect to a metaphysics, is the real possibility of another concentric circle representing those forces beyond the society of man. The sum total of these spheres of educational activity, or life itself, provides us with the concept of "total education."

Figure 1. *The School Within A School*

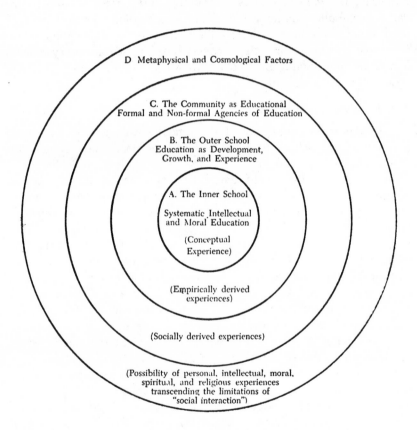

Explanation: These concentric circles represent a hierarchy of educational levels of experience. The "school within a school" or the "school proper" is represented by the two innermost circles, one the "inner school" and the other the "outer school." The school itself is contained by the community, which is also educational. Dependent upon one's philosophy and religion are the transcendent experiences which might be deemed possible beyond social interaction. Each level of experience has its particular kind of educational values, validities, and processes.

Practical Values of the Conception

It would appear that there are both practical and theoretical values to be gained from this conception. A clear-cut recognition of the two doctrines by administrators and teachers should assist them considerably in the clarification of their educational endeavors. By delineating the responsibilities and obligations of systematic education which the teacher should fulfill, a wholehearted devotion to the task could be achieved, without frequent interruptions of conscience in respect to the just demands of experiential education. Likewise, a definitely planned program of experiences to meet the needs of growing youngsters, as well as room for emergent and unanticipated educational needs, should provide the teacher or counselor with time for experiential education.

It is entirely plausible to presume that teachers themselves possess wavering allegiances in respect to educational theories and philosophies involving both progressive and conservative principles. To the extent that this is the case the implementation of the school within a school idea should assist the teachers in resolving their problems in a practical way.

Administrators should find the plan practical and helpful in at least two ways. One way is that of doing justice to both doctrines of education. Another is that of satisfying both conservative and progressive doctrines. Still there is the difficult administrative problem of doing justice to each view within the school program. Secondly, there is the obligation to provide a program of education which will satisfy the community. The school within a school idea should be of direct assistance in helping to meet these trying problems.

Values for Educational Theorists

The hypothesis of a school within a school embodying the recognition of the validities of two diverse doctrines of education should have considerable value for educational theorists. Its particular value should be found in its posing of the fundamental hypothesis for further examination and experimentation. There are at least two alternatives for the theorist interested in this hypothesis. In the first alternative it is conceivable that a synthesis of the two components could be achieved. The challenge to reduce the two doctrines to a monistic philosophy of education is a formidable one. John Dewey has accomplished this task in terms of instrumental-naturalistic concepts of philosophy. However, it is assumed that this philosophical

7

integration in its pragmatic orientation is inadequate, and that the time is now ripe for a re-formulation on different philosophical principles. The formulation of the "dualistic" hypothesis provides needed assistance in the delineation of the problem which faces educational philosophers. In addition to posing this hypothesis, it suggests possible areas for further educational experimentation. Some of the emergent problems are as follows: How can the valid elements of *systematic* and *experiential* doctrines of education be synthesized in terms of educational philosophy? How can doctrines of experience and growth be best applied in the curricula of the outer school? How can the doctrines and principles of systematic education be best utilized within the inner school?

Only the broad philosophical vision is suggested here. Prescriptions as to the specific curricular and methodological implementations are not within the scope of this article. It is hoped that specialists in the various aspects of professional education will be sufficiently interested in this hypothesis to translate its broad principles and concepts into blueprints for educational application within the two spheres. The hypothesis itself can be empirically and experimentally verified as to its workability. Experimentation itself may lead the way to a more satisfactory integration of the two complementary components.

The second alternative suggests that it is entirely feasible from a theoretical point of view that the two components are not capable of further resolution. Educational philosophers may contend that these doctrines in themselves constitute a permanent bipolarity. It is the assumption of this writer that either of these alternatives is genuinely possible and feasible.

Until such time as a new synthesis or integration might be achieved, it would appear necessary to apply the doctrine of the school within a school.

The Failure to Recognize the Validities of Both Doctrines

In a very real sense there has been a continued failure to recognize the legitimacies and validities of both doctrines of systematic and developmental education. Despite the early warnings advanced by John Dewey with respect to the necessity of maintaining a balance between formal and informal aspects of the educational process, progressive educators have proceeded frequently as if all vestiges of formal or systematic education had been banished once and for all, and that *functional education* had assumed the role of the only education worth having. Some have regarded subject matter organizations in secondary education, for example, as completely incompatible with modern theories of education. The partisanship toward *functional education* has carried many educators to the point that they virtually recognize no validity within doctrines of formal or systematic education. Likewise, some conservative educators have tended to depreciate and ridicule the theories and practices of "progressive" and "functional" education. Extreme conservatives have castigated progressive theory and practice as utilitarian, materialistic, pragmatic, and superficial. Again there has been the tendency to overlook the validities of the other view. In short, it is the old bugaboo of "either-or" thinking with respect to progressive and conservative doctrines of education. Fortunately there have been some indications of a willingness to make concessions to contrary doctrines. Progressive and pragmatic educators have tried to appease their critics by pointing out their continued concern with conservative elements and concepts such as organized subject matter, vicarious learning, genuine discipline, orderly procedures, and moral and spiritual values. John Dewey himself went out of his way in such writings as *Experience and Education* to indicate an impatience with those who would overthrow everything labeled "conservative" or "traditional" despite the availability or unavailability of adequate and suitable substitutions. It is to the credit of Dewey, and some of his followers, that they have so vigorously denounced such an irresponsible educational procedure. Illustrative of his view on this matter is the following quotation:

> I do not wish to close, however, without recording my firm belief that the fundamental issue is not of new versus old education nor of progressive against traditional education but a question of what anything whatever must be to be worthy of the name education.[3]

Conservatives likewise have made concessions to modern education. For instance, the Harvard Report, *General Education in a Free Society*, recognizes the role of experimentation, social reconstruction, novelty, change, and special education within the educational processes and curricula of the American secondary schools. Truly, the report does retain a large measure of emphasis upon the conservative functions and the academic concepts in education, but by and large the philosophy expressed is dualistic in its recognition of the twin

9

functions of our schools. Although the willingness to make doctrinal concessions to opposing philosophies is not widespread it does appear that some progress is being made by way of a great dialectic between the advocates and forces of the older and newer theories of education.

Validities Evident in Both Doctrines

Reduced to their very essentials we must grant the existence of validities within each doctrine. The related concepts of education as a constant process of growth, development, and experience, so essential to modern educational theory, possess evident and demonstrable validities. That humans do learn through "experience" and through the "reconstruction of experience" is reasonably evident. With caution we can say that this *is* at least *one mode of human learning*. This observation is hardly questionable. The very feasibility of the whole educational doctrine built upon the conception of the total growth of the human organism in its process of biological and sociological interactions with nature and man is extremely compelling. It is difficult indeed to conceive of any adequate philosophy which neglects the respective truths of these views. The related concepts of modern education such as growth, development, experience, interaction, maturation, and the like must not be rejected, nor neglected.

However, at the same time it is difficult to see how formal and systematic doctrines of education can be completely discounted. That human beings can learn by systematic means of direct communication, by planned instruction, by appropriate training, and by intellectualized education, is equally demonstrable and evident. Given a fair chance, demonstrations of these conventional types of teaching and learning prove their respective effectiveness. Even though we have observed that formal education has often degenerated into verbalism, memoritor emphasis, and downright failure to educate, it must be granted that there have been thousands of successes as a result of intelligent and artistic applications of these conventional modes of teaching and learning.

It therefore appears that both *experiential* and *systematic* doctrines and principles of education have practical validities when properly oriented and utilized within their own respective spheres of efficiency. If we grant that in its broadest sense education is virtually synonymous with life itself, then it is not too difficult to believe that

10

there is ample ground for the two doctrines of education. With the experientialist we can say that human growth means intellectualization of the manifold activities of man and the development of his total personality. With the devotee of systematic education we can agree that since each human cannot possibly experience the centuries of the actual growth of the whole of humanity in a direct manner, it is evident that a large proportion of our education must be attained through vicarious, conceptual, and symbolic modes of communication. Thus we may conclude that the total education of the individual must be a blending of immediate and vicarious experience, a coalescence achieved through a balance of experimental and systematic learning processes.

Since the processes of life are in themselves educative, an equitable proportion of our school activities should be of this type; however, since direct and systematic modes of education are equally feasible and effective, it would appear necessary and desirable to provide an allocated part of the school program to this type of curriculum, where each growing youngster may have the experiences as a pupil and student. Our difficulty seems to stem from previous insistences upon one type of school or the other. Such an insistence on the parts of conflicting parties has resulted in a confusing conglomeration of curricular practices and corresponding confusions of means and ends.

Justification of an Apparent Dualism

At this point it may be objected that the weakness of the proposal of the school within a school lies in its manifest dualism. (It is entirely possible that the alleged dualism is only apparent.) There are at least two philosophical justifications which can be advanced to meet the objection. First, educational philosophers may find that it is advantageous to utilize hypothetical doctrines, however diverse, while working toward a synthesis, as the scientists have demonstrated. Second, it may be that the two doctrines are complementary and incapable of further synthetic reductions.

We are told that in physics scientists sometimes find it fruitful to hold two hypotheses which, although seemingly incompatible in theory, are actually very useful in explaining two types of physical phenomena. For example, it is popularly known that physicists in previous decades maintained two rival hypothetical doctrines with respect to the nature of light. One hypothesis was based upon the corpuscular explanation of the phenomenon of light; the other hypothesis was based upon the undulating or wave explanation of light. Both hypotheses were useful in the operational explanation of two sets of data. At one time each one appeared to be a contradiction of the other. Despite the apparent dualism or theoretical incompatibility, the hypotheses contained validities and values with respect to certain facts and operations and were used despite the differences. We are told now that both of these hypotheses can be successfully synthesized by the more recent advances in physics by Einstein and others.

The analogy to our position in educational philosophy is evident. We are in possession of two contradictory doctrines of education, which, in their respective spheres, seem to possess considerable validity and usefulness. Yet, we have bogged down in our efforts to prove the superiority of one doctrine or the other, and in the felt necessity of subordinating one to the other. We have not made a frank acceptance of the two doctrines as valid within their own respective spheres. If the analogy is valid, we should do well to apply both conceptions until such time as a genuine philosophical synthesis can be achieved, despite the apparent incompatibility of the two hypotheses.

It may be the case that the two doctrines are not capable of synthetic resolution as desired in a monistic philosophy of education. There are numerous philosophical precedents for such a position. For example, the recent New Realism in education, as advocated by Prof. Frederick Breed, insists upon the necessity of the bipolar theory. Dichotomies such as authority and freedom, for example, are not considered dualistic in an objectionable manner, but are regarded as bipolar, or complementary relationships. As he says in the *41st Yearbook* of the NSSE:

> The bipolar view proposed as a guide to education is proposed as well for our orientation throughout the general area of social relations. It begins with respect for individual demands, but it includes respect for social demands. It accepts the spirit of the doctrine that man proposes, but God disposes . . . It believes that democracy maintains itself in a flexible middle ground, where it seeks the most effective balance between two complementary factors.[4]

Also, within the philosophical works of Benedetto Croce, the modern idealist, we find an interesting explanation of the philosophical

12

attempt to achieve syntheses of opposing concepts. Whereas Hegel held that the relationships of thesis and antithesis could always be realized in a higher synthesis, Croce advanced the contention that such syntheses are not always possible. Croce maintained that "abstract opposites" could be further synthesized. But he further contended that no "distinct concept" stands completely antithetical to another "distinct concept." They were incapable of further synthetic reduction or resolution because they were "distinct concepts." For illustrative purposes, we observe that Croce says that "intuition" is not the opposite of "thought," nor is "thought" the antithesis of intuition; nor do "thought" and "intuition" require reconciliation.[5] In the philosophy of Croce some concepts, as those illustrated above, are complementary to one another and cannot be further reduced or resolved.

In fact, polarity is a common concept in various philosophies and need not be considered dualistic. "Philosophies that make the concept of polarity one of the systematic principles according to which opposites involve each other when applied to any significant realm of investigation," is the definition cited in one philosophical dictionary.[6] Cusanus, Schelling, and more recently, Morris R. Cohen, are some of the philosophers who have used polarity.

Spinoza's utilization of physical and mental modes of being or manifestations of one substance provides another interesting approach to the problem of dualism. What we call "dualism" may be the dual manifestation of one substance or process. Thus what appears to be "dualistic" is actually but the two sides of the same coin.

These random illustrations of polarity, bipolarity, and dualism are mentioned only to suggest possibilities by way of justification of the use of two doctrines. The problem of philosophical justification of the use of complementary doctrines or principles, such as those involved in experiential and systematic education, does not seem to be too formidable. In the meantime, let us turn to operational considerations with respect to the proposal of the school within a school.

Functions of the Outer School

By and large the *outer school*, or the *experiential school* as it might be called, should invoke and implement those doctrines of education associated with growth, development and nurture of the self-realization of the individual in and through society, which have developed through the successive contributions of such great educational reformers as Comenius, Rousseau, Montaigne, Pestalozzi, Froebel, Herbart, G. S. Hall, and John Dewey. Principles well known to educational theorists such as "education as life," "democratic participation," "interaction," "problem-solving," "life adjustment," "self-realization," "self-discipline," "purposeful activity," "socialization," "first hand experiences," "experiential learning," "communication through shared means and ends," "many-sidedness," "assimilation of learning," "intrinsic interest," "maturational learning," "moral development," "learning by doing," "education as learning how to live," and many more principles culled from the "modern movement" in education would be the guiding tenets of the outer school.

These principles and concepts are representative of educational doctrines rooted in biological, psychological, and sociological phases of life sciences and philosophies. As manifestations of these roots the principles and concepts are compatible and harmonious. Together they provide an orientation for one of the valid areas of human education.

The activities of the outer school should be characterized by their approximations to the regular round of human activities in the well balanced life, which involves facets usually termed social, political, economic, moral, intellectual, domestic, vocational, aesthetic, practical, and even re-creational. Educationally conceived, the activities should be designed to incorporate learnings which are derived from experiences which might be termed "life-like" as opposed to "academic." Desirable social and political habituations and understandings, for example, should be nurtured through student participation in actualizing a miniature democratic community and the problems and activities inherent in such situations. Although a few primary educational learnings would be attained, there would be numerous concomitant learnings involved. For example, a consistent policy of allowing students to participate in graduated political control of school activities with their teachers and counselors, would not only assist them in gaining valuable political experiences and insights, but would at the same time provide opportunities for such developments as self-control, self-discipline, and total personality growth. We know that intellectual conceptions alone will not result in successful assimilation or modification of patterns of behavior, but that specific experiences must be provided which will permit gradual assimilation or habituation. By way of further illustration, the democratic doctrine may be grasped intellectually as a theory, but if it

14

is to be genuinely learned as part of the behavior pattern there must be ample provision for application and use. One of the prime functions of the outer school, therefore, should be the utilization of such principles and the organization of specific activities, experiences, and problem situations to insure meaningful assimilation. Here we see how the outer school could provide an insurance against the neglect of behavioral assimilation of learning, which has been the case with too many formal schools.

If the outer school strives to become the "miniature democratic society" with all of its problems and complex modes of human relationship, then the young people who take part in these diverse activities will be learning through direct experience and participation. Thus we should visualize the outer school as composed primarily of those community activities and experiences most suitable for school emulation. Within the limitations of the school the artificial life of the community should be realized. That is to say that although students cannot actually live the problems of homemakers and breadwinners as parents, they can be concerned with typical problems of the home as they experience them.

The "inner school" should devote itself to the task of doing the best job possible with the teaching of systematic and organized fields of human knowledge which are deemed "essential" to the needs of liberal men and liberal societies. The inner school should protect and preserve that which is crucial in the academic tradition of the West. This does not mean that it should invoke all of the naïve stereotypes which are used to characterize "traditional education." In short, it should be dedicated to the job of meeting the existing need in any complex culture for the insurance of a systematic and essentialistic education.

Some may be surprised at this insistence upon the protection of systematic education, in view of the fact that so many of our American schools have never gone beyond the most conservative kind of education. However, this writer believes that such a stand can be justified. Even though we grant that numerically most of our schools are weighted on the traditional emphasis, it must be granted also that some educators have expressed themselves for a future education which is completely "pragmatic" and "functional" and devoid of any subject-matter demarcations and content organization. Numerous theorists predict that the progressive transformation of subject-matter curriculum to a life activities basis which has taken place in the elementary grades of many schools will gradually pervade secondary education and higher education until they too have been functionalized. Thus, if these theorists are right in their prognostications, systematic education based upon units of learning within organized subject fields will then be replaced by *functional education.*

Therefore those who believe that pragmatic and functional doctrines of education should be limited in their application to the education of the future, will not be surprised at the deliberate formulation of respective roles and limitations of both systematic and functional conceptions of educational procedure. If the role of systematic education, in terms of logically oriented subject matter, is not preserved, it is possible that youngsters of the future might grow up in blissful ignorance of anything approximating systematic and logical education.

Certainly one of the main functions of the inner school should be that of direct teaching. Direct teaching involves concepts of direct communication and the use of the abstract symbols of language and mathematics of the culture. This process of direct teaching should be considered as an art, which it is. It is unfortunate that older forms of teaching have been so slandered and stereotyped by advocates of "modern" methods. From such literature one would assume that all conservative educators see teaching as a dull process of preaching, drill, memorization, and authoritative regimentation. Dr. Jacques Maritain, a Neo-Thomist and classicist, refutes this notion by stating that the art of teaching is like the art of medicine in that the teacher works with the dynamic agent, the child, just as the doctor of medicine works with nature in exerting cures for his patients. The true conception of the teacher-student relationship is not one in which the teacher does all of the activity with the child remaining passive. There is a sense in which the learner in the pupil-teacher relationship must be docile. However, "docile" has come to be a word of opprobrium in education today, even though at one time it had the legitimate meaning of "teachability." To learn from a teacher the youngster as a pupil must be docile or teachable. He must have a modicum of respect for his guide or teacher and exert a certain amount of attention and effort i nthis direction. Still "docility" does not mean a continued "passivity" during the learning process. Without "activity" in terms of mental effort, concentration, judging, remembering, and the like, we know learning cannot take place.

Despite the present trend to replace the older notion of "teacher" with the current term "guide" or "counselor," the school within a school idea includes an important role for the "teacher *qua* teacher" and the "pupil *qua* pupil." Even though we grant that it is not the primary function of our public schools to turn out "scholars, students, and pupils," but rather to develop all around growth of balanced personalities, we should recognize the need for a student teacher relationship within the total educational structure. One of the ways of insuring a balance between desirable experiences of an informal nature and more formal teacher-student relationships is through the maintenance of the inner school along with the outer school.

This entire concern of education as direct communciation versus pragmatic theories of "shared experiences" is, of course, one of the crucial problems of educational philosophy. Thorough analysis and review of the issue is not possible at this time. Nevertheless, it should be recalled that John Dewey turned the tide against "education as instruction" in his *Democracy and Education*, of 1916, by his denunciation of teaching by direct "communication." Here Dewey calls attention to the educational evils resulting from the common belief in the possibility of education through direct teaching, telling, lecturing, or other direct verbal modes of communication commonly associated with traditional or formal education. Over and over again Dewey emphasizes the necessity of controlling the learning process by the adult control of the environment of the learner. Learning is then a matter of life adjustment through the progressive utilization of subject matter to resolve the problems met by the human organism in attaining his ends or the ends shared with others in conjoint social activity. "Communication" is not then a process of transmission of ideas from one to another through symbol in the conventional sense of the word *communication,* but rather the "sharing of ends and means of conjoint activity."

Had there been time for the analysis, it would become clearer that the educational arguments on the nature of teaching and learning resolve finally into theories of experience. Theories of experience in turn involve not only different schools of psychology from Connectionism to Gestalt, but even more basically they involve different philosophical explanations from Socrates to Dewey. Our philosophies determine our understanding of such terms as "experience," "nature of the learner," "nature of knowledge," and "communication."

Hence, an alleged "traditionalist" or "formalist" does not adhere necessarily to beliefs in the validity of direct teaching and communication merely on the basis of blind allegiances to the *status quo*, but very conceivably because of his philosophical grounding. Dr. Mortimer Adler, for example, as a classical humanist, vehemently defends the concept of education through "the arts of communication." His defense of education as a process of learning the arts of communication through reading, writing, and speaking is in opposition to the previously mentioned contentions of Dr. Dewey. Whereas Dewey believes in "experiential education" Dr. Adler advocates a type of education based upon "formal learning" or an education of direct communication. Dewey's emphasis is upon experience, living, problem-solving, and shared activities, while Adler's emphasis is upon the liberal arts.

Whereas Dewey stresses the "guidance function" of the teacher and the "activity" of the learner, Adler defends the "teacher *qua* teacher" and the requisite "docility" on the part of the student if he is to complete the true teacher-student relationship.

No doubt when properly qualified within their respective philosophical contexts, one could find force to both the arguments of Dewey and Adler and their philosophical interpretations of experience and communication. Dewey's words of caution concerning excesses of formalism and verbalism in educational practices are no doubt justifiable. Formalistic teachers can very easily degenerate into excesses of verbalism which provide little real learning for the students. Instances of verbalism, memoritor emphasis, student passivity, and other such evils are not difficult to find in the history of education, particularly where formalistic doctrines have predominated. On the other hand, it is just as likely that comparable evils have existed where functional doctrines have held sway. Failures to develop efficiency in basic tools of learning, neglect of content, inabilities in fundamental skills, and the like, may be the outcomes of some progressively dominated institutions. Neither school of thought when translated into action has any corner upon success or failure.

Thus the school within a school idea recognizes the plausibility of teaching and learning through direct communication, *if ample precautions have been taken to assure the requisite learning readiness for symbolic and abstract communication via the direct life experiences of the outer school.* This is another way of stating the two basic principles previously enunciated: first, that learning by direct reconstruction of experiences is valid; and second, that learning through a process of direct communication is also valid. Learning through direct communication is possible and desirable, if the requisite sense experiences have been achieved. As Immanuel Kant suggested, "Percepts without concepts are blind, but concepts without percepts are empty." A formal education stressing conceptual relationships is quite meaningless without experience, but experiential education too needs the guidance of a structured, conceptual type of education. Hence the school within a school insists upon the balanced interactions and contributions of both types of education.

Checks and Balances

Another principle of the school within a school is the well known principle in political science of "checks and balances." Essential to the American theory of representative government is the principle that the tripartite division of government into executive, legislative, and judicial branches of political function and jurisdiction affords a co-ordinate system of checks and balances. No single division of the government then becomes overpowerful and excessive in its function because it is checked and balanced by another. The effectiveness of the principle has been well demonstrated throughout our political history.

The underlying principle of checks and balances is also expressed in the two party system of political functioning that has emerged in our political history. There are numerous examples in our history to illustrate how the elements of conservatism and progressivism as manifested in the two parties have been checked and counter-checked or balanced by the political swing to one party and then the other.

There appears to be an analogous conflict in education between conservative and progressive forces. Even without deliberate implementation the constant working of these forces can be discerned in manifold ways. The politics of school and society in many communities and school districts, as well as the theoretical controversies of professional journals bear evidence of this observation.

Still there is a need for a deliberate application of the principle of checks and balances in the school within a school. To achieve the desirable balance, order, and harmony of concepts and principles of conservative and progressive doctrines and theories there must be adequate precaution against the potential excesses of historic and contemporary movements.

The inner school should provide needed checks and balances upon the excesses actual or latent in progressive or modern theories of education. Modern education has been criticized with some justification both in its theory and practice for immoderate emphasis upon doctrines of vocationalism, utilitarianism, anti-intellectualism, empiricism, functionalism, psychologism, scientism, nominalism, instrumentalism, and pragmatism. Even the leader of progressive thought, John Dewey, was moved during the 1930's to criticize and admonish the educators of the "Progressive" movement for their misinterpretations of his educational philosophy and their far-fetched and extreme applications of so-called modern educational theory.

Therefore in the school within a school it should be the function of the inner school, or systematic school, to check and balance the activities of the outer, or experiential school, as follows:

(1) To provide a check upon the modern tendency to make *instrumentalism* the sole philosophy of educational practice.

(2) To provide a check upon the inherent tendency of the *activity movement* to gradually defeat and eliminate the logical organization of subject matter.

(3) To provide a realistic check upon those educators who believe that a completely internal discipline can be successfully substituted for all external control with the immature.

(4) To insure adequate emphasis upon organized *conceptual thought* as a check against the limitations of a purely perceptual level of learning.

(5) To insure adequate emphasis on *intellectual* and *moral development* in a systematic order and the defeat of any real anti-intellectualism which might dominate the schools.

(6) To insure all youngsters of their right to *experiences as students* in good formal education and the avoidance of an education which is completely "experiential" and "functional."

Adequate Checks and Balances on the Systematic School

Since modern education is not the only kind of education subject to error and excess, a definite check on the workings of the inner or systematic school is necessary. Schools devoted to formalistic and systematic instruction have become notorious in terms of educational criticism by their excesses in respect to formalism, grammaticism, logicism, mathematicism, historicism, authoritarianism, verbalism, intellectualism, erudition, and a general neglect of concern for the principles of child nature or the principles of learning. In short, the major criticism of traditional and /formal education has been the excessive concern with the content taught and the virtual neglect of the growth and development of the whole child with respect to his diverse needs. Granted that most of these criticisms have been warranted at one time or another, and that these excesses may be repeated again and again in the future, it becomes imperative that we set up a definite system of checks and balances to prevail against such pedagogical mistakes. Therefore it is the function of the "outer" or "experiential" school to check and balance the "inner" or "systematic" school as follows:

(1) To provide sufficient *experiences* and *life activities* to avoid excesses of *vicarious* and *academic* education.

(2) To provide an educational environment which will nurture *total growth* of the person to balance *intellectual development*.

(3) To provide a direct experiential basis for learning which will insure concrete substance to the *academic abstractions* of formal learning.

(4) To provide experiences affording opportunity for educational *assimilation* and habituation in terms of behavior patterns as contrasted with *theoretical learning*.

(5) To insure *experiences in democratic living* which will insure a meaning in concrete terms of the *abstract principles* of the democratic philosophy.

(6) To provide a gradual development of self-discipline and self-control through participation as a check against excesses of external discipline and adult control.

Mutual Reinforcement

A corollary of the principle of checks and balances is that of *mutual reinforcement*. A rigorous application of the philosophy of the school within a school requires a careful planning of the two curricula so that they provide a mutual reinforcement of learnings. The outer school with its emphasis upon growth and experience, and the inner school with its stress on systematic development of intellectual and moral powers, should furnish mutual reinforcement in the total learning process. The concrete experiences of the outer school, and those of the regular community life, should furnish a perceptual basis for the abstractions necessary for systematic learning in the inner school. Those experiences variously termed empirical, aesthetic, concrete,

21

emotional, interactive, environmental, and experiential should prove to be mutually reinforcing of those experiences termed rational, conceptual, abstract, cognitive, universal, immanent, and intellectual. For example, the direct experiences derived through student government and other related democratic participations, typical of the outer school, should motivate and stimulate the conceptual understandings required in the study of political science and history. Reciprocally the concepts and principles derived from a conceptual understanding of the political conflicts and struggles of history should prove valuable in meeting the emergent problems of student government. One mode of experience and thought supplements and complements the other. Thus the experiences typical of experiential education and conceptual education are not held here to be exclusive, but rather interdependent and interactive.

It should be understood that this writer is not maintaining that the two curricula with their respective principles of experience and system are completely exclusive. An empirical kind of intellectualization, conceptualization, and abstraction must certainly be encouraged in the experiential school. Certainly the formal classroom itself cannot be and should not be devoid of perception, visualization, student participation, and first hand experience, with a completely abstract level of thought maintained at all times. But by and large the emphasis should be different in the two schools. Whereas the experiential school devotes most of its time and energies to growth through the meeting of the emergent problems of living, the formal school dedicates itself to systematic procedures of training, instruction, and education. Anyone who has thought about this problem and has experienced in addition the kind of learning which takes place in an "experience" school in contrast to a "formalistic" one, will probably agree that there is a decided difference in the type of mentality produced. Each has its merits and demerits. The empirical mind thrives on the practical problems as they emerge in typical life activities. The same mind is apt to be at a distinct loss when confronted with purely abstract or conceptual problems of logic, mathematics, science, or philosophy. Powers of generalization and adeptness with universal conceptions seem to be weak. On the other hand, the rationalistic mind is likely to be perplexed when suddenly confronted with specific, practical problems. We may conclude that both types of minds are desirable. Yet, educationally speaking we need to produce a fusion of the two types of intelligence, the practical and concrete, and the universal and abstract. The school within a school program should do much in ₊accomplishing this end.

Summary. The proposal for a school within a school recognized the need for a more adequate integration of educational philosophies than we have had in the past. Indeed the pragmatic philosophy of education formulated by the eminent John Dewey has been a notable attempt at such an integration, but it appears to have theoretical and practical shortcomings together with certain virtues. As a solution to the problems of education it is an inadequate philosophy. Despite Dewey's insistence on the importance of a balance between formal and informal aspects of education, it has not been forthcoming within pragmatic education. Therefore, in our quest for a new synthesis of educational philosophies we should recognize the validities of two diverse doctrines of education: first, education as growth, development, and experience should be accepted; second, education as a process of systematic intellectual and moral education should be accepted.

For practical purposes these two doctrines should be co-ordinated and applied to educational practice in our schools. It is here proposed that the *school within a school* be recognized as a means of applying these two doctrines. This school within a school visualizes the school and community as follows: (1) The *inner school* which is the nucleus of the school itself with its core of systematic units of study and learning. (2) The *outer school* which is that part of the school devoted to the nurture of the activities, experiences, and needs in the growth and nurture of the whole child. (3) The *community itself* provides the over-all environment within which something approaching total education can take place. The actualities of social living in the community provide diverse opportunities for learning from life itself. Dependent upon one's philosophy of life, particularly one's metaphysics, is the possibility of adding another periphery beyond the social life of the community—metaphysical or spiritual forces of the cosmos.

It is presumed that one of the sources of present educational confusion has been the unwillingness or inability on the part of many to see the respective merits and validities of both experiential and systematic doctrines of education. Hence there has been the tendency to promote one or the other doctrine at the expense of the other. Actually we must be willing to admit the possibility of the two doctrines, both valid in certain areas of education, and that these doctrines are bipolar or dualistic in their relationship. Until such time as educational philosophers and theorists can achieve a satisfactory synthesis of the two doctrines, it appears wise and feasible to apply both sets of principles in educational practice.

Consequently there is proposed the idea of the school within a school as a means of implementation of the philosophy. The outer school should be guided by principles of development, growth, experience, democratic participation, and self-realization, while the inner school should be guided by principles of systematic education and appropriate applications of training and instruction along with artistic modes of education.

❃　❃　❃

Status of the Proposal

In retrospect it is clear that this proposal had a number of values in the gradual formulation of the organic educational theory. It furnishes a sharply defined focus on some of the central problems of educational philosophy; the hypothesis provided the necessary impetus and direction for further philosophical and educational inquiry; it provides a tentative statement of underlying principles and propositions for later expansion and development; it furnishes a definite perspective and orientation for coming to grips with the essential problems of educational philosophy.

Although it might be well to alter some of the terms and impressions associated with the diagram of concentric circles, by and large the fundamental conceptions and principles advanced in the proposal are still valid. There were some questions raised earlier concerning the interpretation of the concentric circles; some felt that the *inner* and *outer schools* should be reversed in the diagram. Others contended that dotted lines should have been used rather than solid lines; they felt that the solid lines suggested too much rigidity of demarcation. However, aside from some minor questions of interpretation of this sort, the proposal has been very well received by the students and educators who have made their evaluations known.

In developing a more extended explanation of an organic philosophy of education, no particular brief is held for the demarcations between *inner* and *outer schools* as such; nor is there a wish to defend any particular representation of concentric circles in diagramatic form. Experience has taught that it is dangerous to use diagrams of this sort, for many persons project their own subjective views upon such diagrams, often without careful reading and understanding of one's explanations. In the main the earlier proposal is completely harmonious with the later extensions.

The enthusiastic acceptance of the proposal by many students and educators of my acquaintance encouraged the writer to undertake the long term project of formulating and constructing an Organic Philosophy of Education. Such a project demands working in two directions: first, one must endeavor to ground such a working hypothesis in sound philosophical conceptions; second, one must work through the thorny problems of educational theory in the application of these philosophical and educational principles and conceptions. Philosophical roots must be established before sproutings and buddings can be nurtured in one's more detailed educational theories and applications. The proposal then made this two-way project feasible.

Following this consideration of the original hypothesis, the introductory outlines of an organic educational philosophy are now presented.

FOOTNOTES

1. 'Philosophy of organism' means an underlying general philosophy based upon principles of organism comparable to Alfred North Whitehead's writings.

2. Frank C. Wegener, "A Proposal . . . The School Within a School," *Educational Theory*, III, No. 1, (January, 1953), pp. 14-30. Reprinted with permission of the publisher.

3. John Dewey, *Experience and Education* (New York: The Macmillan Company, 1938), p. 115. Reprinted with permission of the publisher.

4. Frederick Breed, "The Realistic Outlook," in *Philosophies of Education,* ed. Henry Nelson (Chicago: National Society for the Study of Education, 1942), Forty-First Yearbook, Part I, p. 137. Reprinted with permission of the publisher.

5. See Wildon Carr, *The Philosophy of Benedetto Croce.*

6. See 'polarity' in the *Dictionary of Philosophy,* ed. Dagobert Runes (New York: Philosophical Library, 1942).

2

THE ORGANIC PHILOSOPHY OF EDUCATION

THERE are certain questions which students and educators usually raise when the *organic viewpoint* is mentioned.[1] What is "The Organic Philosophy of Education"? What is meant here by the term "organic"? Is it a "dualistic" philosophy? Is it a "middle-of-the-road" philosophy? Is it "eclectic"? Persons familiar with the various conflicting philosophies and theories of education frequently ask the following questions: How is organic philosophy related to other schools of thought? Is it a form of realism, idealism, or pragmatism? Is it progressive or conservative? What is its relationship to A. N. Whitehead's *philosophy of organism*? What is its relationship to the Platonic-Aristotelian tradition?

Since these are the exploratory questions which are usually asked by persons interested in philosophy of education when this systematic point of view is proposed, they might well be questions of interest to a reader of this synoptic presentation. It is apparent that these questions can be answered only in a cursory and fragmentary manner in this single chapter, for they quickly carry one into the vast complex of philosophical and educational issues of our times. More thorough and satisfactory answers to these and other questions about an Organic Philosophy of Education will have to be postponed until a later and more extensive work.[2]

To answer certain of these questions a short article is reprinted from *School and Society;* other questions are dealt with directly.

* * *

The Organic Philosophy of Education[3]

Education needs a reconstructed philosophy of education which synthesizes the valid elements from conflicting philosophies of education. The Organic Philosophy of Education represents a deliberate attempt to formulate such a systematic, coherent theory of education built around the core of a philosophy of organism.

Some of the distinguishing beliefs of a philosophy of organism are as follows: the principle of bipolarity is fundamental to all thought and reality; the universe is organic; all of reality is connected and related, not truly bifurcated; entities are possessed of a complex structure comparable to that of living beings; reality is to be understood in terms of whole-part and "one and many" relationships. Through the sustained application of such postulates and principles we hope to achieve an educational synthesis beyond the stage of contemporary eclecticism.

In an earlier statement, it was suggested that "until such time as a new synthesis of educational philosophies can be achieved, it is proposed that the hypothesis of a school within a school be adopted."[4] The present Organic Philosophy of Education represents an effort to move from the former hypothesis to a philosophically formulated theory of education. The principle of bipolarity, along with other organic principles, is requisite to the task of reconciliation.

Organic Bipolarity

Such a proposal might be interpreted as an unfortunate "dualism" by many educators, which was not intended. Consequently, it has been necessary to set forth the principle of bipolarity, which is one of the primary postulates underlying the organic viewpoint.

Bipolarity in essence means "a unity of opposites." It is not a new principle by any means, but is found in various forms in the early Greek philosophers, namely Pythagoras, Heraclitus, Empedocles, Plato, and Aristotle. Plato was perhaps a bipolarist in his exposition of the "unity of opposites" in such seeming bifurcations as the One and Many, Identity and Difference, Same and Other, True and False, Being and Non-Being, Rest and Motion, Permanence and Change. The conception of the unity of opposites is truly a metaphysical conception, and necessarily manifests itself on the observational level.

Bipolarity is found eminently in such historical philosophers as Cusanus, Schelling, Hegel, and Croce. Among contemporary philosophers we find various interpretations of the conception in A. N. Whitehead, Charles Hartshorne, William Reese, David Bidney, Morris R. Cohen, W. H. Sheldon, A. J. Bahm, and undoubtedly many others. Professor Frederick Breed has made some application of the

27

principle in educational theory, but not extensively. To the writer's present knowledge, there has been no extensive and deliberate application of this important principle to the problem of education.

It has been my sustained effort to formulate the postulate of bipolarity, along with other postulates, and to apply these conceptions systematically to the problems of education. Consequently, we are now able to justify the co-ordination of the two spheres of the educational process in terms of the philosophical principle of *bipolarity*, or the intrinsic unity of opposites. Plato's principle of unity and diversity is a means of solving this problem.

Organic Postulates

Further insight into the organic viewpoint can be obtained by reviewing some of the outstanding postulates very briefly.

1. Reality is organic rather than singularly materialistic or idealistic. Hence, organic reality possesses distinct parts which are integral parts of the whole; the relations of the whole-part unities, as actual entities and ideal entities, are intelligible and reciprocal. Reality is complex and therefore cannot be completely identified as unity or plurality, except in a qualified sense; it is both one and many.

2. Man is a microcosmic organism embodying the essential elements of the macrocosm; he is a whole being constituted of distinct parts which are intrinsically integrated with the whole of his organic being and of organic reality. Society itself is in a sense organic. Man is not merely an organic part of society, he is intrinsically a part of the organic cosmos. Thus, man's self-realization necessarily transcends social ends, although social being is necessary to self-realization.

3. Most of what Plato said is still philosophically sound, although many conceptions must be reconstructed in harmony with certain advancements of modern cultures, particularly with respect to scientific, social, and political modifications. Plato was undoubtedly very wrong about some things. Hence, we must enter into the difficult task of philosophical reconstruction, which means participation in the great dialectic of philosophy from Plato to Whitehead.

4. Professor Alfred N. Whitehead's philosophy of organism provides us with most of the requisite modifications of the Platonic-Aristotelian Tradition up through contemporary thought, scientifically and philosophically. This does not mean that we shall accept all that Whitehead asserts either. Yet it does mean that, by and large, his principles of organism, as advanced particularly in *Science and*

the Modern World and *Adventures of Ideas,* provide us with most of the requisite reconstructions of Greek theories of organism.

5. There is much of positive value in the educational doctrines of John Dewey. Yet it is necessary to modify and reconstruct many conceptions in his educational theory. Most of the Dewey methodology is valid when reconstructed within the philosophical system of organism.

Man and Education

In previous writings the writer has asserted "The Ten Basic Functions of Man" as a basic framework for an organic educational theory. Man, though evolved as a species, does exist as a relatively enduring structure. Despite cultural diversity, mankind possesses the following universal and generic capacities or functions: Intellectual, Moral, Spiritual, Social, Economic, Political, Physical, Domestic, Aesthetic, and Re-creational (renewal).[5] These functions, although delineated here separately, are actually organically and intrinsically interrelated. Like the organs of the body, they are in a sense separable in structure and function, but they are essentially interdependent and organic.

It is the task of education to assist in the actualization of these common functions in what might be termed the education of man *qua* man. Each person, despite individual differences, must be educated to the optimum level of his human capacities. Yet, within this general education of man as man, there must also be emphasis on the development of the person as an individual. Granting that there are individual differences in terms of capacities, propensities, aptitudes, and inclinations or interests, education must seek to assist the individual in his self-determination as an individual as well as self-realization as a human being.

Organic Principles and Educational Conflicts

The organic principle of bipolarity and related principles are essential to the reconciliation of the valid elements of the conflicting theories of education. Existent conflicts between educational theories—formal versus informal, conservative versus progressive, classic versus subjective, liberal versus practical, realistic versus idealistic, academic versus pragmatic, logical versus psychological, external versus internal, and many others—are really complementary and reciprocal when viewed organically. As set forth originally in the proposal of the spheres of the inner and outer schools in co-ordinate, reciprocal relationship, we now see that these relationships are truly bipolar, or unities of opposites. It has been the writer's task to analyze and synthesize the valid and invalid elements of these conceptions in terms of the educational process.

Organic Conceptions of Experience

Using the principle of bipolarity we see that there are two legitimate spheres of educational experience: ordinary life experience, and ordered, systematic, conceptual, and intellectual experience, sometimes called "academic learning." School cannot actually be "life" in the full meaning of that term. We cannot approximate full life experiences in a laboratory sense in the schools. But, by the very nature of *schooling*, it must in large part be vicarious. Only through maturation, adulthood, and all of the varied life experiences that come with increasing age can we truly learn through ordinary life experience.

When we realize that school, then, is in one sense a process of ordinary experiences, and systematic intellectual experiences, we see the importance of bipolarity in the educational process. Learning is likened to Plato's 'Analogy of the Prisoners of the Cave.' Ordinary life experience is being in the cave and viewing the particulars and the many; when we are led out of the cave into the light, we are figuratively and educationally learning in the abstract, ideational realm. These phases of the total learning experience are reciprocal.

By the same token we must realize that education is not simply a social process. Education truly is an *organic process* to be understood in the complex interactions of the *ten basic functions of man*. The total process is intellectual as well as social, moral as well as economic, spiritual as well as political, physical as well as aesthetic, re-creational as well as domestic.

Democracy and Education

Organic education, although rooted in the Platonic Tradition, is thoroughly devoted to the democratic ethos. Plato's philosopher kings in our ethos must be reconstructed to mean that *all citizens* are philosopher-rulers. Democracy means a guarantee of freedom in the pursuit of happiness—or the Good. Democracy is not so much an end in itself as it is a means to the end, or the pursuit of the Good. This places a tremendous responsibility on education to assist the individual in his quest for self-realization, self-determination, and the pursuit of happiness.

Every person in a democracy must be a philosopher in actuality for he holds intellectual, moral, spiritual, social, economic, and political responsibilities. He must make decisions with respect to means and ends and with respect to values. He must make decisions in terms of a world-wide ideological struggle. He must make decisions which affect the whole social organism as well as his own family's well-being. No responsible citizen can escape these philosophical problems. He must be educated for freedom and responsibility.

The organic philosophy holds that the Good is both immanent and transcendental. The lure of the True, Good, and Beautiful moves mankind. Educationally, then, we must assist each other in our continued quest for the good life. Democracy provides us with the freedom to enter into this great dialectical, unceasing quest. It also requires that we be philosophers in this quest.

❀ ❀ ❀

Coherence versus Eclecticism

The Organic conception is not *eclectic,* anymore than are other doctrines such as *instrumentalism, idealism,* and *realism.* Rather, it represents a systematic and coherent viewpoint. That is to say, organic ideas and principles are coherent in that they are not only harmonious in character, but they require each other for their existence and significance.

Eclecticism implies that one holds ideas and principles drawn unsystematically from a variety of sources, and organizes them loosely so that they tend to form a mosaic of diverse conceptions rather than a genuine integration of thought. *Eclecticism* is frequently a forerunner of a unified philosophy—it is a preliminary stage of development. *Eclecticism* in its relationship to a *systematic* or *coherent* philosophy is analogous to the relationship of mixture and compound in chemistry. One is merely a mixture of elements, while the other achieves a new unity.

It is a commonplace observation that students of comparative philosophies of education are attracted by each doctrine successively. The typical student is attracted by the merits of *realism, idealism, pragmatism, existentialism* and the like. Unable to choose between the various systems he frequently arrives at an eclectic collection of ideas and beliefs from the various sources. The beliefs are often sadly torn from their original contexts. The ideas as held may be incompatible. The desire to hold divergent beliefs is quite understandable. Yet the task of reconciliation is truly a philosophical enterprise of some proportions. Unless the student can carry through with a high degree of substantial philosophical reconstruction, he is likely to conclude with a very confused outlook upon "the principles of his educational philosophy."

The Organic Philosophy of Education endeavors to overcome an eclectic approach to validities in various philosophies and educational theories by including the construction of the system within the very groundwork of philosophy—in a *philosophy of organism.* Such a philosophical groundwork refers to the organic principles and propositions with respect to the perennial problems of philosophy such as the nature of reality, knowledge, value, ethics, logic, and beauty.

The Organic Philosophy of Education endeavors to achieve a system based upon basic propositions and principles which are inherently *logical* and *coherent.*[6] The *logical* aspect implies that all of the conceptions in the philosophy are consistent and not contradictory. The aspect of *coherence* implies that all of the developing ideas are meaningful in relation to one another; they require each other and are harmonious.

Whitehead suggests that such a philosophy also has the tests of *applicability* and *adequacy.*[7] On the actual level of experimentation the general concepts of the philosophy should prove to be valid in their application and adequate in treating facts and findings on the level of observation.

The main conceptions of this educational philosophy have been drawn from organic thinkers. However, all of the conceptions which have become a part of the system have been judged by their coherence with organic criteria and primary conceptions.

For these reasons then it is clear that the Organic Philosophy of Education is not intended to be eclectic in nature, but rather a coherent system.

Not Deliberately Middle-of-the-Road

It has not been my intent to seek a flaccid "middle-of-the-road" philosophical position. A middle-road position usually depends on others to take a definite stand and thereby to determine the limits, and then one tries to find a moderate position between them. This may be expedient, but it is not truly philosophical.

The organic philosophy in effect does seem to approximate such a middle position on many issues. But this position derives largely from the basic principles and propositions of the philosophy, and not from expediency. First, the organic principles of *relatedness* and *wholeness* prevent our standing completely on one side or another of a basic issue. We cannot make these sharp divisions of reality; the effect is that of finding valid elements in these seeming divisions.

Organic philosophy is also rooted in certain Greek ideals which result in an apparent middle position. Some of these ideals include balance, proportion, ratio, *Sophrosyne*, harmony, unity, and wholeness.[8] It would be quite inconsistent with such accepted ideals in working out an Organic Philosophy of Education if there were glaring examples of one-sidedness, imbalance, disregard for harmony and proportion, or other such deviations.

Admittedly the organic philosopher consciously seeks to maintain a just balance and sense of right proportion with respect to the many contending doctrines and philosophical orientations. It is recognized that the history of philosophy is marked by striking examples of action, reaction, and counteraction in the struggle of ideas. Many philosophies have resulted, obviously, from a sharp reaction to another contrary point of view. Then there are the inevitable reactions and attempts at syntheses which in turn become new theses. Something similar to the Hegelian story of the triadic pattern of thesis, antithesis, and synthesis, seems actually to occur.

The organic philosopher is, however, by no means limited to seeking balance and proportion, for this is only one part of his mind-set. He is seeking philosophic truth as far as it is humanly possible with the aid of all contributing sources of human knowledge and experience. In this quest for a kind of truth and understanding, which he admits is an unending process, he recognizes that all philosophers and philosophical points of view worthy of the name possess some partial validities in terms of their various perspectives. Every contending school of thought is respected as having something positive to offer as a check against human error in the extensive enterprise of philosophical inquiry. Whether old or new philosophy, metaphysical or positivistic, realistic or idealistic, or empirical or rationalistic, that philosophy must contain some validities. Consequently, when one persistently strives to squeeze out of the competing doctrines all of the validity which can be logically and coherently reconstructed with one's organic presuppositions, or organic core, a philosophy of education emerges which appears to be middle-road.

Also, the *principle of bipolarity,* which is one of the basic principles of this position, asserts that fields of reality and experience necessarily involve diverse forces which are essentially *unities of opposites.* This principle by its very nature tends to mediate extremes rather than to make actual divisions.

Thus when we apply *bipolarity* and other related organic principles to the familiar dichotomies of educational theory, such as formal and functional, logical and psychological, objective and subjective, conservative and progressive, we find that they comprise *a unity of opposites.* Hence our *whole-part* interpretation of the educational enterprise *appears* to be a middle-of-the-road compromise position, when it actually stems from basic principles.

The writer's disdain for such middle positions results from his belief that the holders of such views have located their contentions superficially from the top of the philosophical structure, and have not taken the trouble to ground their beliefs consciously at the bottom of the philosophical foundation.

It is quite possible that some "middle-of-the-road" advocates, who have not taken the trouble to search for metaphysical moorings for their beliefs, might find many of the conclusions and recommendations of the Organic Philosophy of Education seemingly coincident with their own. This philosophy of education as formulated here is not merely such a middle-road doctrine, for it possesses its own distinctive presuppositions and principles. Hence it has the structure of a coherent philosophy, and is not dependent upon arbitrary midpoints between extremes. Rather it strives to achieve a higher synthesis.

Whitehead's Philosophy of Organism

The Organic Philosophy of Education is in substantial agreement with Whitehead's philosophy of organism. Yet this statement needs clarification so that it is not misunderstood. This writer's knowledge and understanding of the profound works of Whitehead are admittedly limited and incomplete; there is no intimation here that were it desirable and possible to convert the philosophy of organism directly into an equivalent educational philosophy, that this writer claims such an ability.

In this project it has been the writer's honest endeavor and intent to formulate his own convictions and conceptions of the educational process upon philosophical propositions which were essentially 'organic.' In laying down his own philosophical propositions and in pursuing this inquiry this writer became convinced that the long development of a philosophy of organism from the Hellenistic philosophers down through modern thought, through such modern thinkers as Descartes, Locke, Hume, Berkeley, Spinoza, Leibniz, in the pre-Kantian group, and in part through Kant, Hegel, and other post-Kantian thinkers, and through more recent thinkers such as Bergson, Alexander, James, Peirce, and Dewey, has been best formulated and synthesized by Alfred N. Whitehead. It appears to many that he has been the unique person in philosophy who has been able to synthesize the valid elements of the classical philosophical tradition with the most modern scientific advances of recent centuries into the most logical and coherent philosophy of our age.[9]

Anyone with a strong predisposition toward the Platonic-Aristotelian tradition in general philosophy, who is also impressed with the idea that philosophies actually develop and advance through the centuries with cultural epochs, might well raise this question: If Plato and/or Aristotle were reincarnated today in the fullness of our present knowledge of the 20th Century, what modification would they of necessity make in their philosophies?

Since it is recognized frequently that Plato's philosophy was not a closed system, in contrast with that of Aristotle, we might well focus our question more in terms of Plato, although not entirely.

Many persons believe that Whitehead's *philosophy of organism* represents the best answer to the foregoing hypothetical question. Whitehead with his enormous and comprehensive knowledge of such varied fields as history, religion, mathematics, physics, and science in general, along with philosophy, has successfully synthesized the valid elements of these fields of knowledge into a coherent philosophy rooted in conceptions of an organic universe.

Students of Whitehead know that he found it necessary to formulate a new philosophical vocabulary consistent with an organic outlook and in contrast to terminology associated with traditional "substance" philosophies. In thinking through an Organic Philosophy of Education, then, we are indebted to Whitehead not only for philosophical orientation but also for a new working vocabulary. (See Glossary of Whitehead's Terminology in the back of this book prepared by this author, pages 453-60.)

Turning the question around it might be asked, "To what extent would the Philosophy of Organism be in agreement with the 'Organic Philosophy of Education'?" It should be clearly understood that discrepancies of interpretation, application, and emphasis would no doubt be very evident. There has been no effort here to "translate" Whitehead's philosophy into its exact educational counterpart.

The sources of one's philosophy of education are of necessity diverse; they include the multiple influences of all of one's studies and experiences. On the theoretical side one's educational views are colored by his study of various philosophers and educators. On the practical side one is influenced by his own peculiar educational experiences, by one's own perspective.

More concretely principles such as those of *bipolarity, process, order,* and the like, are perhaps differently emphasized and interpreted than they might well be by some one else who embraced an organic philosophy. Although admitting a profound debt to Whitehead and other organic thinkers, the writer must take the responsibility for the Organic Philosophy of Education as it is formulated here. Formulations of such educational principles as illustrated by *bipolarity, reversibility, logical-psychological continuity,* and the like, as incorporated here, may be immanent in Whitehead's writings, but they may

36

well be quite removed from his original intention in education. Since Whitehead did not apply his philosophy to the formulation of a systematic philosophy of education, this is problematic.

Organism Contrasted with Other Views

It may be helpful to the reader if the organic viewpoint is contrasted with opposing doctrines or philosophies. Philosophies are usually derived from strong reactions to objectionable views of others, or from efforts to reconcile opposing viewpoints. Before presenting the writer's own reactions in philosophy of education, let us briefly review Whitehead's objections to certain prevalent habits of thought. In the preface to *Process and Reality* he sets these views forth very succinctly as follows:

> These lectures will be best understood by noting the following list of prevalent habits of thought, which are *repudiated*, in so far as concerns their influence on philosophy.
>
> (i) The distrust of speculative philosophy.
>
> (ii) The trust in language as an adequate expression of propositions.
>
> (iii) The mode of philosophical thought which implies, and is implied by, the faculty-psychology.
>
> (iv) The subject-predicate form of expression.
>
> (v) The sensationalist doctrine of perception.
>
> (vi) The doctrine of vacuous actuality.
>
> (vii) The Kantian doctrine of the objective world as a theoretical construct from purely subjective experience.
>
> (viii) Arbitrary deductions in *ex absurdo* arguments.
>
> (ix) Belief that logical inconsistencies can indicate anything else than some antecedent errors.
>
> By reason of its ready acceptance of some, or all, of these nine myths and fallacious procedures, much nineteenth-century philosophy excludes itself from relevance to the ordinary stubborn facts of daily life.[10-11]

The Organic Philosophy of Education is in substantial agreement with the foregoing quotation from Whitehead.

Relation to Other Philosophies

In discussing modern philosophies and philosophies of education, categories such as realism, idealism, and pragmatism are frequently used. The question then arises in the student's mind as to the proper categorical allocation of "the Organic Philosophy of Education" or the general "philosophy of organism." The feeling is that it must be realistic, idealistic, pragmatic, or even existential.

It has been my firm conviction that the *philosophy of organism* is a philosophical category which is not subordinate to any of the aforementioned schools of thought. It is not limited to realism, idealism, or pragmatism *per se*. It is a philosphical orientation in its own right which from its own unique conceptions includes validities that are found partially in these other philosophical positions. One works from organic propositions in his organic philosophy rather than from the established lines of demarcation between these other philosophies. Hence with A. N. Whitehead, Charles Hartshorne, and W. M. Urban, we believe it is quite necessary to go "beyond realism and idealism," and pragmatism.[12] This view does not carry with it the idea that an organic philosopher builds eclectically with fragments derived from other philosophies. Rather, it is that the philosopher of organism works both inductively and deductively from the postulations of an organic world. Thus in following through the various comparative philosophies which have appeared from ancient to modern times one's constant quest is for the organic core which is found expressed in philosophers of systematic persuasion who are more or less realistic, idealistic, pragmatic, existential, or the like.

It is the contention here that a new educational epoch is burgeoning forth which will be characterized by higher syntheses of the conflicting elements of older philosophies and educational theories. The older and equivocal issues of naturalism versus supernaturalism, relativism versus absolutism, realism versus idealism, and progressivism versus conservatism, and their respective solutions, need to be reformulated at a higher level of philosophical analysis.

It has been recognized by many modern philosophers that there is no flat 'either . . . or' solution open to us in terms of the older delineation of these issues. The present philosophical problem is one of securing a higher synthesis which contains the respective validities of these older conflicting schools of thought. We have cited the philosophical progress made by such men as A. N. Whitehead, Wilbur M. Urban, Charles Hartshorne, and W. P. Montague, in terms of their reconstructions of the issues and their resolutions, although certainly other philosophers have made such reconstructions which we cannot review here. Whitehead, Urban, and Hartshorne, for example, have made notable attempts to reconcile elements of realism and idealism, while Montague is well known for his reconciliations of the various ways of knowing.

A. N. Whitehead said in the preface to his *Process and Reality* that he sought to place Absolute Idealism on a realistic base.[13] There are those who prefer to call Whitehead "a realist," while others maintain his "idealism" or even his "agreement with Dewey" thereby implying a pragmatism. Since Whitehead was so ingenious in his philosophical constructions, it is possible to see strong elements of these various schools of thought in his thinking. Yet it is extremely doubtful if anyone can properly reduce his philosophy of organism to one of these categories, for his whole effort was to carry out the consequences of an organic conception of the world—to do justice to the competing demands of realism and idealism, of reality and process. A philosophy of organism is then a philosophy which represents a blending of the elements of realism, idealism, pragmatism, and similar categories. The Organic Philosophy of Education seeks then to follow in this category of organism and not realism, idealism, pragmatism or any other '-ism' *per se.*

Organic Philosophy Opposed to "Dualism"

Neither Whitehead's philosophy of organism nor this writer's formulation of an Organic Philosophy of Education is meant to be "dualistic" in character. In fact Whitehead has been most critical of those philosophies which make actual "bifurcations" of reality. The concept of organism itself emphasizes continuity, connectedness, and relatedness. The story of the organic world in constant process is largely the story of entities emerging and perishing. The *concrescence* of any given entity results from its becoming "one" by an integration of the "many" contributing elements within the total process.

René Descartes, to whom Whitehead so often refers, is not eulogized with respect to his "dualism" of mental and physical substances. Here is metaphysical dualism in its clearest form. Yet Whitehead does not for an instant countenance this "dualism" of substances, but he rather corrects the Cartesian metaphysics with organic conceptions of process and reality. He does commend Descartes for his recognition of the subjective principle, which he considers one of the most important of modern advances. Although we can see the world conjunctively and disjunctively, its being is actually organically related. Mental and physical poles are related integrally.

In the Organic Philosophy of Education the frequent references to the *principle of bipolarity* do not imply an acceptance of "dualism." As it has been repeatedly indicated, *bipolarity* illustrates *unity and diversity*, or the union of opposites. At no time has it been said that aspects of reality or of the educational process were completely or absolutely independent; on the contrary, pains have been taken to emphasize the co-ordinate and interdependent character of certain separable elements of reality and the educational process.

Relation to Platonic-Aristotelian Tradition

The Organic Philosophy of Education reflects in many aspects the abiding influences of the Platonic-Aristotelian tradition in Western philosophy and education. Perhaps this is necessarily true of anyone who has taken the dialectic of western philosophy from the Greeks to the present seriously; however, the point is that the organicist is glad to acknowledge the inspiration and insights which have been provided by this rational tradition, and is not openly antagonistic toward this great tradition, as some of the modern schools of thought seem to be toward anything which originated with Plato and Aristotle.

The richness and depth of the speculative thought of these notable Greek thinkers has provided organic philosophy with much of its inspiration and motivation for further inquiry into new questions as well as concern with perennial problems of man. Both Whitehead and Dewey, for example, have paid tribute to the contributions of Plato in particular. Whitehead has frequently called attention to the fact that Western philosophy is largely a series of footnotes to Plato.[14] He has added that Plato's philosophical intuitions have for the most part been reinforced by recent developments philosophically and scientifically. Here Whitehead may have had in mind the cosmology suggested in Plato's *Timaeus* in its metaphorical form; Whitehead frankly admits that his own cosmology has been greatly influenced by Plato's thought, particularly in the dialogue the *Timaeus*.[15] Whitehead, although respectful of Plato's lasting contributions, states unequivocally that Plato was very wrong about some things and that some rather drastic revisions are necessary before we can make the early Platonic thought square with our present developing outlook. Yet with all of these observations, it is clear that organic philosophers in general, and Whitehead in particular, reflect the lasting influences of the speculations of both Plato and Aristotle.

For those who are accustomed to thinking of John Dewey as an opponent of the Greek contributors to the Great Tradition the following quotation from Dewey on Plato may come as a surprise:

> Were it possible for me to be a devotee of any system, I still should believe that there is greater richness and greater variety of insight in Hegel than in any other single systematic philosopher—though when I say this I exclude Plato, who still provides my favourite philosophic reading. For I am unable to find in him that all-comprehensive and overriding system which later interpretation has, as it seems to me, conferred upon him as a dubious boon. The ancient sceptics overworked another aspect of Plato's thought when they treated him as their spiritual father, but they were nearer the truth, I think, than those who force him into the frame of a rigidly systematized doctrine. Although I have not the aversion to system as such that is sometimes attributed to me, I am dubious of my own ability to reach inclusive systematic unity, and in consequence, perhaps, of that fact also dubious about my contemporaries. Nothing could be more helpful to present philosophizing than a 'Back to Plato' movement; but it would have to be back to the dramatic, restless, co-operatively inquiring Plato of the Dialogues, trying one mode of attack after another to see what it might yield; back to the Plato whose highest flight of metaphysics always terminated with a social and practical turn, and not to the artificial Plato constructed by unimaginative commentators who treat him as the original university professor.[16]

This tribute, of course, does not mean that Dewey was a Platonist by any means, but it does indicate a significant respect for the inspirational and suggestive qualities of Plato's works to a modern pragmatist.

The task of modifying and reconstructing some of the fundamental philosophical propositions laid down by Plato and Aristotle has occupied western philosophers for these many intervening centuries. It is this continuing task which some have called 'the great dialectic' which in turn marks the cultural development in the west and today affects the whole world.

Many philosophers would no doubt agree that Whitehead has accomplished a most remarkable philosophical synthesis in this very reconstruction of valid elements from this great tradition of the past and those emerging valid elements of modern thought in science, philosophy, and religion. All of us who have professed an admiration for Hellenistic thought and philosophy in turn face this problem: What validities are to be retained from the organic traditions of the early philosophers, and how are they to be reconstructed with the advances and contributions of modern thought? Unless one wants to follow such men as Whitehead, Peirce, Bergson, James, or Dewey as their complete disciples, and most of us don't, one must make his own decisions on all critical issues of philosophical and educational importance.

Hence it follows from this difficulty that in acknowledging sources of inspiration and imagination for an Organic Philosophy of Education, it is almost impossible to state with final precision one's relative degree of commitment to Whitehead's present philosophy of organism or to the earlier doctrines of Plato and Aristotle. By and large the agreement lies with Whitehead's philosophy of organism. Questions of interpretation of 'eternal objects,' 'universal values,' 'the nature of thought,' 'the categories of thought,' and similar problems arise. Only in time with further elaborations of the organic educational philosophy will these distinctions appear more sharply. For example, Plato's allegory of the cave as oriented in the full complexity of his dialogues has been a constant source of inspiration and imagination in the formulation of an organic conception of the educational process.[17] Also, although Whitehead does advance the notion of dipolarity, his writings or essays on education do not amplify or apply dipolarity or bipolarity to the educational process. In this case the analogy of the cave had more direct influence on organic educational theory than Whitehead's writings alone; it became necessary to amplify Whitehead's creative process in terms of this analogy.

Other conceptions which are more or less direct influences of the Hellenistic thinkers could be cited. Plato's concern with the ultimate categories of being and thought have had a lasting impact on this writer's philosophizing.[18] It seems that there is still much validity in the notion of such categories if slightly modified in terms of our organic bipolar relationships.

This writer is in full agreement with Whitehead's transformation of Aristotle's category of Primary Substance in terms of process and reality.[19] As Whitehead contends, we must give up materialistic conception of extended substances floating in a world of absolute time and space.[20] Yet it does not follow that this means a complete abandonment of any kind of 'substance' or 'structure' in the philosophy of organism. Whitehead's ontology recognizes actual entities not only in their fluency and in their becoming, but he also recognizes their determinacy as 'actual objects.' Thus this writer finds 'substance' in the philosophy of organism along with process. He finds 'structure' as the other side of 'function' or process. This recognition of 'structure' and 'function' is essential to the line of argument of the organic educational philosophy.

Summary. The Organic Philosophy of Education is a newly formulated educational philosophy based upon principles and conceptions of a philosophy of organism. These conceptions are derived from the organic tradition of philosophy from Plato to Whitehead. Although many of the validities of the Platonic-Aristotelian tradition are retained, the philosophical position defended here is not strictly one of ancient or classical organism, but one which has been modified and reconstructed in terms of modern developments of science and philosophy as expressed largely in Whitehead's philosophy of organism. The organic educational philosophy stated here is not necessarily Whitehead's educational theory, but it is rather a fusion of this writer's educational conceptions with many of Whitehead's conceptions, along with other conceptions derived from the long history of organic thought in western philosophy and education. Although Whitehead did write and lecture on aspects of education, he did not apply his basic philosophical conceptions in the overt formulation of a systematic organic philosophy of education.

The term 'organic' is used in its philosophical sense to characterize a living world as opposed to a materialistic or mechanistic world. An organic world is one which is characterized by continuity, connectedness, relatedness, togetherness and interaction of its elements in process. An organic world is one which is not dualistic or bifurcated; rather it is characterized by its great bipolarities of "conjunctiveness and disjunctiveness," "unity and diversity," "being and becoming," "permanence and novelty," and "'joy and sorrow."[21]

In this educational philosophy man is depicted as a microcosm of the macrocosm, exemplifying the essential bipolarities of the world in his evolving but relatively persistent nature. Man is essentially ambivalent in his makeup, and it is the task of man and education to achieve a proper harmonization of these components. Man is also a many-sided creature who manifests his complexity in what has been called here the ten basic functions of man. It is the task of education to give systematic development to these functions.

The organic principle of bipolarity and the related principles are essential to the reconciliation of the basic conflicts of contemporary educational theory and practice. The organic educational philosophy represents an attempt to systematically resolve these issues between conservative and progressive, classical and modern, liberal and practical, realistic and idealistic, and academic and pragmatic doctrines of education.

This educational philosophy is not 'dualistic' for it is based upon organic principles. Yet it differs from other contemporary educational philosophies in that it respects the principle of 'unity of opposites' or the recognition of 'duality' as the principle of diversity within unity. Thus the valid element of 'dualism' is retained within organic unity without commiting the error of monopolarity.

It is not an eclectic philosophy in the sense of being unsystematic or incoherent. Since the organic educational philosophy represents a systematic conception of educational theory, grounded in coherent principles of philosophies, it is systematic rather than eclectic.

Neither is it intended to be a 'middle-of-the-road' philosophy. The mediating characteristics are not derived from expediency and compromise on the operational level of educational practice, but they are derived from their grounding in coherent philosophical propositions.

It is not essentially realistic, idealistic, or pragmatic. Organism as a philosophical category is distinguishable from the foregoing categories *per se*. Certainly the organic philosophy overlaps with what are believed to be valid elements of realism, idealism, and pragmatism, in its existence as a logical, coherent, adequate, and applicable philosophy. Neither is it exclusively progressive or conservative in its tenets. These views are held to be parts of the whole.

FOOTNOTES

1. For several years this writer has taught an advanced graduate course in philosophy of education at the University of Texas entitled, "The Organic Philosophy of Education."

2. Manuscript in process.

3. F. C. Wegener, "The Organic Philosophy of Education," *School and Society*, Vol. 81, No. 2031, (June 11, 1955), pp. 177-80. Reprinted with permission of the publisher.

4. *Educational Theory*, Vol. III, No. 1, p. 15.

5. F. C. Wegener, "The Ten Basic Functions of Man," *School and Society*, Vol. 80, pp. 17-21, (July 24, 1954). Also, *Educational Theory*, Vol. V, No. 2, (April, 1955), pp. 110-17.

6. A. N. Whitehead, *Process and Reality* (Cambridge: Cambridge University Press, 1929), pp. 1-2 . Reprinted with permission of Macmillan Company, copyright in U.S.A., 1929.

7. A. N. Whitehead, *Process and Reality*, pp. 5-7.

8. Frederick Eby and Charles F. Arrowood, *The History and Philosophy of Education, Ancient and Medieval* (New York: Prentice-Hall, Inc., 1940, copyright by publisher 1940), pp. 228-33.

9. See Schilpp, P. A. (ed.), *The Philosophy of Alfred North Whitehead* (The Library of Living Philosophers, Vol. III). Evanston, The Library of Living Philosophers, Inc., 1941.

10. A. N. Whitehead, *Process and Reality*, p. viii. Reprinted with permission of the Macmillan Company, copyright in U.S.A., 1929.

11. This reference to 19th century philosophers is interpreted as referring to the German idealists. Whitehead, although agreeing in part with idealism, believed it needed a strong realistic base.

12. W. M. Urban, *Beyond Realism and Idealism* (London: Geo. Alen & Unwin Ltd., 1949), pp. 66-67. Se also Charles Hartshorne, *Reality as Social Process* (Glencoe, Illinois: The Free Press, 1953), p. 69 ff.

13. A. N. Whitehead, *Process and Reality*, Preface.

14. Lucien Price, *Dialogues of Alfred North Whitehead* (Boston: Little, Brown and Company, 1954), p. 132.

15. A. N. Whitehead, *Process and Reality*, p. ix.

16. John Dewey, "From Absolutism to Experimentalism," in *Contemporary American Philosophy*, Vol. II, Edited by George P. Adams and William P. Montague (New York: The Macmillan Company, 1930), p. 21. (Printed in Great Britain by Unwin Bros. Ltd., Woking.) Reprinted with permission of the publisher.

17. Plato, *The Dialogues of Plato*, trans. by B. Jowett, Third Edition (New York: Random House, 1937), Republic, Book VII, p. 773.

18. The writer interprets Plato's Categories as expressing the fundamental character of bipolarity implicit in human thought processes. This notion will be expanded in subsequent writings.

19. See an excellent article by Ivor Leclerc, "Whitehead's Transformation of the Concept of Substance," *The Philosophical Quarterly*, July 1953, Vol. 3, No. 12.

20. Alfred North Whitehead, *Science and the Modern World* (New York: The American Library, A Mentor Book, by arrangement with The Macmillan Company, 1949), pp. 121-23.

21. See A. N. Whitehead, *Process and Reality*, pp. 482-83.

PART II

Synopsis of Foundational Propositions

3

FOUNDATIONAL EDUCATIONAL PROPOSITIONS

I N this chapter some of the foundational educational propositions of the Organic Philosophy of Education are set forth. These propositions stated in relatively brief form should provide the reader with an overview of this educational viewpoint. The brevity of the exposition in many cases will leave a number of questions unanswered. However, the general orientation and direction of thought will have been provided. These propositions are necessarily in very generalized form and require considerable explanation and qualification in other contexts. Some of these propositions are explained further in the essays of this brief work. The remaining propositions, although implicit in the formulations of this viewpoint thus far, will be necessarily expanded in a later work. The following propositions then characterize the foundations for an Organic Philosophy of Education. They represent the guiding principles of this viewpoint.[1]

The Organic Philosophy of Education holds:—
General Co-ordinates
(1) *That education is essentially a creative process.* It is 'creative' on the metaphysical plane in the sense that all human beings are involved in a process of *becoming*, unconsciously or consciously. On the educational plane 'creativity' becomes deliberate and conscious to the maximum degree in terms of selected means and ends by all those directly involved in the educational process. 'Creativity' here means deliberate human development in the broadest sense of the word ontologically, and it does not mean that creative education is primarily concerned with the making or production of things.

In the most general terms education is characterized as a deliberate process of harmonizing and integrating the many contrasting elements. The vast and complex potentialities of man and total cosmic environment, in terms of actual and ideal potentialities, present the raw materials and forms for successful harmonization or human determination. The diverse elements of reality and man's ambivalent nature must be creatively unified and determined. The contrasting elements such as the emotional and intellectual, the conative and cognitive, the aesthetic and theoretic, the prehensive and the apprehensive, the passional and the rational, and all similar contrasts that burgeon forth in man's nature, challenge the educational enterprise to achieve a harmonious reconciliation of such elements.[2] Other contrasts are man and man, man and society, man and nature, man and the divine power, man and cosmos, and man and all reality. Education and life together cannot be expected to remove fully all degrees of contrast and conflict between opposing elements; it can only be hoped that an optimum balance and proportion between the dynamic factors of organic life in a continual cycle of birth and perishing of actual entities can be achieved.[3]

(2) *That 'creativity' is exemplified in education in terms of the unification of bipolarities in the developing person.* A corollary of the foregoing proposition is that education organically conceived is characterized by the co-ordination of *bipolar* and complementary elements and forces. The very structure of thought and existence causes us to comprehend *ideal objects* or *actual entities* in terms of *sameness* and *otherness, similarity* and *dissimilarity, unity* and *diversity, conjunctiveness* and *disjunctiveness,* and in many derived pairs of opposites. These *bipolarities* or *unities of opposites* are not merely forms of thought; they emerge in the actual organic relationships of *entities* in the *time-space continuum.* They are *existential* as well as *ideational;* there is then a correlation between the ideal forms of thought as *possibles* and the embodiment in *actual entities* in shifting dynamic relationships.

Let me illustrate with just a few selected *co-ordinates.* Education must not be *monopolar,* or one-sided in its perspective. On the contrary it must realize the *bipolar* character of such *co-ordinates* as: *theoretical* and *practical, structural* and *functional, formal* and *informal, objective* and *subjective, logical* and *psychological, rational* and *aesthetic, cognitive* and *emotional, external* and *internal, rational* and *irrational, conceptual* and *observational, rational* and *empirical,* and *speculative* and *experimental.* These *co-ordinates* are exemplifications of *organic categories* of thought and actuality which are in their highest form of generalization *one* and *many, true* and *false, same* and *other,* and *being* and *non-being.* They are *bipolar co-ordinates* because they are diverse in the disjunctive sense of *otherness,* but they are also unified in the conjunctive sense of *sameness* or relatedness. *Theoretical,* for instance, is logically and actually related to the co-ordinate *practical.* Their *sameness* is that they imply each other; their *otherness* is that they are in a sense contrasting elements to one another. In one sense they are separable terms, and in another sense inseparable or *interdependent* terms. Hence they are *bipolar* or a *unity of opposites.*

It is the constant task of organic education, therefore, in the light of the organic conception of thought and reality, to seek unification of such *bipolar* and complementary elements and contrasts.

In terms familiar to educational theorists, then, it is the task of education to *co-ordinate* elements and forces termed conservative and progressive, individual and social, academic and experiential, structural and functional, theoretical and practical, and formal and informal.

(3) *That education requires the co-ordination of knowing and doing, or Science and Art.* Education is not exclusively a process of knowing, or obtaining knowledge, nor is it simply "doing," or learning through "purposeful activity." Properly conceived, education is constituted by both in co-ordination. As *bipolar co-ordinates,* "education as science" and "education as art" are again both separable and inseparable in qualified respects. They are reciprocal and complementary. It is an error of *reductionism* or *monopolarity* to reduce the educational process to one or the other; all knowing should not be reduced to a subordinate and incidental role as contributor to

51

"doing." Likewise, all doing should not be made a mere appendage to abstract knowledge. Organic education involves the co-ordination of the realms of science and art in the educational process.

In the realm of organized knowledge it follows that students must become familiar with the structures of human knowledge which have been slowly built by the combined intelligences and experiences of persons in succeeding cultures over the many centuries of human development. Using "science" broadly we refer to the necessarily structured conceptual patterns of natural and physical sciences, social sciences, humanities, and all branches of human knowledge. We hold that these vast *structured intelligibilities* cannot be neglected in the educational process, nor can they be sufficiently learned through "education as art" or "education as doing and discovery."

However, education as art (as doing, experience, creativity) is a co-ordinate of education as science. Neither co-ordinate should completely replace the other. Hence it is indispensable to an organic conception of education that education as art have its rightful role as a part of the total process.

(4) *That education includes harmonization of feeling and reason.* Education has as one of its deepest obligations the harmonization and development of those sides of man characterized as "feeling" and "reason." Man's nature is profoundly *bipolar* and ambivalent; as a *concrescence* of an organic world, man exemplifies the ideal opposites and the *metaphysical bipolarities* of the universe. In what Whitehead terms "the final opposites" man exemplifies "joy and sorrow," "good and evil,'" and the other previously cited opposites, and intimate community with God and the World.[4]

On one side the organic viewpoint agrees with Charles S. Peirce in emphasizing the obligation of education to develop "ratiocination" or the rational process of thinking.[5] It is here, too, that we agree in large part with the classical viewpoint which holds that education should develop man's reason. This does not mean that the development of reason is to be limited to formal and academic modes; we believe wholeheartedly in a pluralistic approach to ways of knowing and ways of thinking. Education needs to "return to reason" as professor Isaac Kandel and others have suggested.[6]

However, the knowledge of man which has developed in the last seventy-five years biologically, psychologically, sociologically and in other disciplines cannot be ignored. With Whitehead we must recognize man's continuity with all of organic nature; man feels, prehends, senses, and intuits the existent entities and forces about him.[7] Man in a very real sense is the product of centuries of evolution and "creative advance." Man like other entities has emerged from the dynamic world of process and reality; this conception is contrary to the Kantian conception which would make man's world a product of his subjectivity.[8]

It is the task then of education to nurture right feelings as well as right reason.

With the rise of modern scientific knowledge of man's behavior, principally from biological and psychological theories, a profound controversy has arisen with respect to the validities of man's reason. The Aristotelian conception of "man as a rational animal" has been severely challenged. Freudian and related psychologies, for example, have called attention to the predominant role of the unconscious processes in influencing the behavior and happiness of normal individuals as well as of the mentally ill.[9] Evolutionists of the mind, such as G. S. Hall in the latter part of the 19th Century, called attention to the genetic story of man's being and pointed out that the emotional life was far more fundamental than the intellectual, for intelligence had developed comparatively late in human evolution.[10] He indicated further that the motivation for intellectual development was furnished by the emotions and that the emotions contributed to the origins of consciousness and thought.

At the present vantage point it is now evident that the classical emphasis upon the education of man as a rational animal was in part deficient in its knowledge of the unconscious motivations and aberrations of man's behavior; it also lacked the knowledge we now have of man's long evolution. Yet the intuitions and inquiries of philosophers and theologians into the deeply rooted conflicts of man's passions and reasoning power were not too far from the mark. On the other hand the devotees of the modern theories of non-rational explanations of man's behavior have no doubt exceeded the limits of prudence in their claims. It is significant that there are psychologists and students of Freud and others who call attention to the fact that the hope of psychiatry today is to help man free himself from the neurotic compulsions of the unconscious and to guide him to the rational controls of his *conscious and preconscious spiritual forces*.[11]

> The hope which psychiatry holds out for Man's future is that the light that it sheds on the earliest steps in human development will gradually help us to find out how to avoid entering the prison cell in which Everyman now lives his life. It gives us the right to look forward to a time when we will know how to influence the development of each human being so that as he grows the empire which is under the control of his conscious and preconscious spiritual forces will expand, while that darker empire of irresponsible, rigid, insatiable, and inaccessibly unconscious control will shrink.[12]

Man like the universe is shot through and through with both rational and irrational forces. Man and reality are constituted by mixtures of these opposing elements. An education devoted only to the rationality of man is one-sided; an education devoted only to the psychological elements of the unconscious is also one-sided. The task of education is the co-ordination of (a) the aspects of man termed rational, cognitive, volitional, evaluative, and conscious, and, (b) those aspects of man termed irrational, emotional, sensate, sensual, and unconscious.

Educational Co-ordinates

(5) *That education involves systematic schooling and life experience.* Education in public schools should consolidate and embrace "education as systematic schooling" and "education as life experience." It is clear that it is not a matter of *either* "systematic schooling" *or* "experiential education" *per se.* The Organic Philosophy of Education opposes the idea that all "academic education" or "systematic teaching of subject matter" should be altered or subordinated into channels of education as emergent life experience. We oppose also the notion that formal education or academic education does not need that aspect or realm of education termed "ordinary experience." Academic education without the complementary assistance of ex-

perience is susceptible to degeneration in terms of pedantry, verbalism, and separation from life. Experiential education without the guiding light of formal education is susceptible to degeneration in terms of disorder, conceptual chaos, disorganization, and intellectual confusion.

Schooling in the best sense needs to be a component part of the educational process in formal education. Young men and women should not be deprived of the distinctive experiences which accompany schooling in terms of systematic study, intellectual experience, and organized subject matter. However, it is now clear that the burdens and responsibilities of our schools today are such that schooling must be harmonized with the full dimensions of human development.[13]

(6) *That 'creative education' embraces both the formal and informal aspects of teaching and learning.* The previous proposition is supported by the organic conception of 'creative education.' All types of human experience contribute to the 'self-creativity' of the developing person. Hence 'creative education' within the province of deliberate institutions of education includes both formal and informal teaching and learning experiences. This interpretation is in contrast to the popular notion that 'creative education' necessarily involves overt acts of creation, or 'self-expression.'

The conception of 'creative education' advanced here holds that formal procedures are broadly 'formative' or 'creative' of the developing person. Formal procedures include direct teaching, direct communication, vicarious learning, training, habituation, imitation, study of subject matters, and utilization of external controls. Informal procedures include learning through ordinary experience, problem-solving, discovery, and socialization. These formal and informal procedures are equivalents of our earlier 'inner and outer schools' of the original proposal. We are contending here that all education, formal or experiential, is creative.

The error of traditional education has been the one-sidedness of the notion that teachers and parents should 'form' or 'create' the growing young person as their product. This was the error particularly of 'education as formation.' There was not enough allowance for participation in degrees of 'self-determination' or 'self-creativity' by the immature.

Likewise the error of progressive or modern education has been the one-sidedness of their notion that youth should be given freedom from authority and external direction for 'self-creativity.' This was the error of 'education as experience.' 'Creativity' from this viewpoint was taken too literally as the right of the young to control their development. There was insufficient recognition of the role of adults in external creativity and external direction.

As it is indicated in terms of the organic theory of control, the organic viewpoint recognizes the bipolarity of these external and internal factors of control. By the same token we must avoid the error of monopolarity in our interpretation of creative education. There is a sense in which the teacher is creative in directing and influencing the direction of development, as well as guiding and nurturing the deliberate creativity of the learner. The teacher 'forms' the young by the use of direct teaching, communication, and control (or formal methods) as well as encouraging participation of the young in their own self-creativity.

(7) *That education requires co-ordination of progressive and conservative forces.* Education should not be predominantly progressive nor conservative in its emphasis; it should not be one-sidedly retrospective or prospective. Conservative forces tend toward a philosophy of permanence, stability, and perennial values; progressive forces tend toward a philosophy of change, mobility, and temporal values; organicists believe in the harmonization of these conservative-progressive forces. The school itself is most democratic when it strives to harmonize these forces, instead of throwing its educational influence predominantly with either side philosophically, morally, politically or otherwise. The creative advance of the society as well as of the world itself moves through the unity of such ideal opposites as permanence-novelty, unity-diversity, stability-change, transmission-reconstruction, and conservation-progression. Education should co-ordinate the forces of the conservative and progressive.

(8) *That education is both preparation and life.* Modern educational theorists have frequently challenged and defied the older notion of

"education as preparation."[14] They have insisted that "education is life" and not mere preparation for adult life or the life hereafter. This has been the cry from Rousseau[15] to Kilpatrick.[16] The implicit notion was, of course, that such education for life would really in the long run be the best "preparation" anyway. The Organic Philosophy of Education contends that formal schooling must include both "education as preparation" and "education as life experience" both in concept and in spirit. In terms of the realistic component we must recognize the fact that the complex character of education and the tremendous obligations and responsibilities placed upon it by modern life make it mandatory that the educational process must in large part be interpreted as "preparation for adult life." This emphasis is to be harmonized with "present experiences of the learner" to an optimum degree.

Many of the followers of the progressive movement in education seem to regard the choice between "education as preparation (or "academic education") and "education as life experience" (or "functional education") as an exclusively "either-or" choice; they choose the latter. The reverse is also true with many conservatives. By using the *principle of proportionate bipolarity* the two conceptions can be harmonized effectively both in theory and practice. Both conceptions have some validity when co-ordinated through *bipolarity*. To the extent that learners are *immature* and require systematic training, instruction, habituation, and education for later anticipated needs, the educational process must be in terms of preparation. To the extent that learners are actually *mature* and can profit by the progressive notions of learning through present experiences, purposeful activities, genuine problem-solving, and self-direction (and sharing in increasing degrees of self-determination), the educational process must be in terms of life experiences and the reconstruction of experience. This organic reconciliation of complementary conceptions of the educational process is not accomplished arbitrarily and eclectically, but such harmonization follows from the application of other organic principles such as *proportionate bipolarity, theory of control, immaturity-maturity,* and *organic field of educational experience.*

The Educational Process

(9) *That education is an organic process.* Education in its broadest sense is coextensive with life experiences; it is an organic process. Education within the limitations of the formal school can only approximate the full experiences of life; as Dewey has pointed out the school must provide a special environment which is 'balanced, ordered, and purified.'[17] However, organicists differ from Dewey's conception and that of some of his followers with regard to the respective conceptions of the educational process within formal schooling. By the same token our conception differs sharply with traditional and conservative views of the formal school program. The organic theory holds that we cannot conceive of the school realistically as life itself in the fullness of that term. The very nature of the educational institution in society limits its scope and possibilities.

Education in the broadest sense demands the cultivation of all of man's proper functions.[18] Education cannot be limited properly to any one of these functions. Organicists disagree with the progressive theory that "education is a social process." This doctrine makes the whole of education "socialization." Actually the social process is only a part of the whole of the human development. When you take education as a social process you produce a topsy-turvy conception of education with everything else in the process *subordinated* to the social function. Although organicists agree to respect the vital role of education and the social process within the totality of organic education, it is believed here that Dewey and the progressives have erred in *superordinating* this function of education and the *subordination* of all others.

Conservatives by the same token have often erred in their exclusive emphasis upon education as strictly an intellectual process, subordinating all other aspects of education. To the extent that intellectual development is a unique and primary function of the schools, especially within the notion of education as schooling, organicists do agree in the forthright recognition of the importance of education in terms of the intellectual function. Education is organic in its overall conception, however, and should not be reduced to single conceptions of intellectuality, socialization, or aesthetic creativity.

(10) *That the educational process is characterized by stages of development termed Exploration, Analysis, and Synthesis.* By and large organicists are in agreement with Whitehead on this formulation in what he has termed the three stages of *"Romance, Precision,* and *Generalization."*[19] The first stage is marked by its "vividness of novelty"; the second stage is marked by "exactness of formulation"; the third stage is that of generalization comparable to Hegel's synthesis. Education is a constant repetition of such cycles; educational processes are marked by these cycles within cycles and "eddies of cycles."[20] One may see the cycles in terms of elementary education, secondary education, and higher education, or even within a given study within a given semester of study.

(11) *That learning takes place in an organic field of experience.*[21] Actually the field of learning is that of the individual and reality in its wholeness. However, for our purposes we have simplified the "field of experience" in terms of bipolar aspects of experience. The field illustrates the *bipolar hemispheres* within an organic unity. We see the exemplification of organic relationships in terms of *independence* (separability), *dependence* (incompleteness *in se*), and *interdependence* (togetherness or reciprocity) in the hemispheres. In this field we see diverse exemplifications of such organic principls as *unity-diversity, sameness-otherness, structural-functional relations,* and the like.

(12) *That organic education is characterized by a continual process of interweaving of opposites or contrasts.* Elements of unity and diversity, conjunctiveness and disjunctiveness, interdependence and independence must be recognized throughout life and the educational process. With the recognition of these strands in their separateness and in their togetherness it is the task of the organic teacher to nurture an interweaving of the elements.

(13) *That education requires coherence and continuity.* The educational process in terms of schooling should be characterized by *coherence* and *continuity.* The evils of gaps in experience, fragmentation of learning, and the confusions of discontinuity and incoherence of studies and experiences, are well known to students of educational theory and practice. Progressives have in too many instances

59

sacrificed the logical continuities of organized subject matters in their zealous efforts to achieve continuity and coherence in terms of "life experiences." Emphasis upon "core curricula" and "experience curricula" has subordinated and subjugated and in fact destroyed the logical continuities of subject matters. Conservatives frequently have continued to place emphasis solely upon subject matter continuities to the neglect of experiential interweavings of continuities.

The Organic Philosophy of Education recognizes (a) the continuities of subject matters (our "Logical Order"); (b) the continuities of functions and experiences (our "Psychological Order"); and (c) the continuities resulting from an interweaving of these *logical* and *psychological continuities*.[22] Single strands of subject matter form more *complex continuities* in correlated subject matters. Also, there are the continuities of functions and experiences of the individual as correlated with subject matters. The point is that *logical continuities* should not be destroyed in the actualization of *experiential continuities;* nor should psychological and functional continuities be completely sacrificed to the single-tracked continuities of subject matters. Although separated at times for practical purposes in the educational process these continuities must be interwoven in the long run.

The teacher should at all times seek to maintain coherence both in terms of relations of subject matters studied and in the various experiences of the students. The teacher of astronomy, for example, should present a comprehensive and coherent study of this subject; but in addition to the internal coherence of the facts and concepts of astronomy itself, in good time it is the responsibility of the teachers to show the coherence and relationships of the study of astronomy in its external relations to the other sciences and in fact to the other fields of knowledge and experience. Then too there is the matter of coherence of the units of study of astronomy and the actual experience and understandings of the students. (Fields of knowledge are in varying senses both internally and externally related.) Although continuities and coherences of logical studies and student experiences (psychological continuities) are in a sense distinguishable and separable, one should not be continually separated from the other; they must be interwoven. Yet in this *interweaving process* of organic education these orders should not be subordinated to one another, nor should one be sacrificed or destroyed for the other.

Multiple Types of Experiences

(14) *That organic education requires multiple types of experience.* All types of experience must be included in the full life; no mode of knowing should be rejected. Whitehead's poetic appeal for a variety of experiences is emphasized as follows:

> In order to discover some of the major categories under which we can classify the infinitely various components of experience, we must appeal to evidence relating to every variety of occasion. Nothing can be omitted, experience drunk and experience sober, experience sleeping and experience waking, experience drowsy and experience wide-awake, experience self-conscious and experience forgetful, experience intellectual and experience physical, experience religious and experience skeptical, experience anxious and experience care-free, experience anticipatory and experience retrospective, experience happy and experience grieving, experience dominated by emotion and experience under self-restraint, experience in the light and experience in the dark, experience normal and experience abnormal.[23]

Whitehead is speaking in the most general terms of life, and we need not take it literally in terms of the schoolroom, which must necessarily be balanced, ordered, and purified experience. Yet the substance of the contention is valid. By and large education should encourage the multiple types of experience for the total development of the learner. Paraphrasing Whitehead's statement we might say that the learner should be nurtured in contrasting types of school experiences, academic experience and life experience, rational experience and emotional experience, authoritative experience and democratic experience, instructive experience and creative experience, theoretical experience and practical experience, cognitive and aesthetic experience, and formal and functional experiences.

The teacher who realizes the values of these multiple types of experiences will feel a new freedom in teaching. He will not feel restricted to the confined limitations of traditional formalisms nor to the equally confining limitations of "education as life experience."

There is a danger in this conception which this writer has tried to avoid in formulating the Organic Theory of Education. Without a clear-cut conception of the field of teaching-learning experiences and the relationships of these diverse modes of experience, their very diversity may cause confusion. Hence it is important that we understand the organic principles whereby reconciliation of such contrasting elements can be accomplished with both unity and diversity. (15) *That education involves multiple ways of thinking.* Education necessarily involves the learning of various ways of thinking. Too often educators have declared that the aim of education is to teach people to think, only then to presume that there was one fixed solution to this problem. Traditionalists have spoken of training the mind through formal discipline. Dewey wrote of "training people to think" through the method of scientific problem-solving in his book, *How We Think.*[24]

The Organic Philosophy of Education accepts the notion that there is an underlying unity to the thought processes of mankind. However, this writer suggests that there are diverse ways of thinking on the operational level. Thus our educational task is not simply to teach any one mode of thought, but rather we should teach a plurality of ways of thinking and a variety of types of experience.

These ways of thinking are not to be divorced from their respective functions, contents, purposes, and settings. Thus in learning a way of thinking, one should also learn to see things in a perspective, to comprehend these associated functions, contents, and purposes of a given field of study or endeavor.

These ways of thinking can be approached from the perspectives of different contexts. One might well utilize the typical and predominant ways of thinking associated with the various fields of study: the scientific method of the sciences; the speculative and logical methods of philosophy and other humanities; the analytical and interpretative methods of languages and literature; the deductive and inferential methods of mathematics; the creative methods of the arts; the observational and experimental methods of experimental sciences; and the practical utilization of problem-solving methods in *ad hoc* problems of interdisciplinary studies and ordinary life.

The proposition here advanced then is that students should become familiar with as many of these diverse ways of thinking and experiencing as possible, both in methodology and related contents and purposes. The reverse of this proposition is that all educational curricula should not be reduced to the melting pot of the "experience curriculum." In doing this we should be destroying the individuality of the various ways of thinking and reducing the rich variety of modes of thinking to one of pragamatic *ad hoc* problem-solving.

Another approach to modes of thought is that of the validities in the various theories of knowledge (epistemology).[25] Assuming that, aside from the question of which theory of knowledge is ultimately the true one, there are educational merits to these various theories of knowledge, and students should then be provided with experiences in the following types of knowing and thinking: (a) *Empirical experience;* (b) *Rational experience;* (c) *Intuitional experience;* (d) *Authoritative experience;* (e) *Pragmatic experience;* (f) *Skeptical experience;* and (g) *Organic experience.*[26]

(a) In *empirical experience* the student is taught by methods of observation, induction, generalization, experimentation, and the like, presumably largely through the physical and social sciences susceptible to such emphasis.

(b) In *rational experiences* the student is nurtured in the methods of abstract reasoning, conceptual relationships, symbolic reasoning, deductive methods, mathematical reasoning, logical reasoning, both formally and dialectically. The subjects which lend themselves most easily include: languages, grammar, logic, rhetoric, semantics, philosophy, literature, poetry, mathematics and speculative sciences.

(c) *Intuitional experiences* and modes of thought associated with them involve the stimulation and guidance of feelings, intuitions, and efforts to realize those aspects of experience which temporarily or consistently transcend cognitive experience. These "intuitions" or "feelings" frequently seem to precede intellectualization or cognition. They also include recognition of the limitations of language, and they exercise efforts to extend man's experiences, feelings, emotions, prehensions, and valuations beyond the regular channels of ordinary scholastic intellectual experience. This can be done particularly through the arts, music, literature, religion, aesthetics, and philosophy.

(d) Students should have *authoritative learning experiences.* They should have an opportunity to learn directly from others as well as through their own experiences. They should learn the arts of communication in the direct terms of speaking, listening, writing, and reading. Much of the world's work must be done expeditiously and efficiently through direct authority and communication. Thus students should learn to follow the reasoning of another person, to follow the arguments of the others, to interpret the objective meanings of the words of others.

Perhaps there are no subjects where such experiences are exclusive. Certainly in fields of study where there are vast amounts of materials to be covered, or where the views of experts are to be taken at face value, such as in history, law, and the like, we might well find exercise for the authoritative method.

To the extent that students are immature in certain respects, or where they must necessarily accept expert opinion and interpretations of matters which are at the moment not susceptible to the student's reflective powers, there certainly is a place for some authoritative instruction and direction. With time and adequate maturity there should, of course, be recourse to reflective and critical inquiry and analysis by the learner.

The five year old child, for example, does have to accept many things on the basis of authority of parents, teachers, and officials which are beyond his maturity. The high school student cannot resolve those complexities of subject matter which are of the university level; the undergraduate college student cannot at his level of maturation solve the problems of advanced graduate study. Hence where opinions are needed pre-maturationally by students, there must be some concession to learning from rightful authorities.

(e) By the same token students should be nurtured in the *pragmatic approach to experience.* All students should be taught the rudiments of the problem-solving approach to both academic and life problems where most suitable and adaptable. Abilities and skills should be nurtured with respect to self-initiated inquiries, formulation of means-ends relationships, formulation of problems, setting forth of hypotheses, collecting pertinent data, analysis and selection of tentative solutions, and the actual or logical application of these tentative solutions to practical consequences. The valuable and rich doctrines with respect to pragmatic methodologies advanced by such men as Charles S. Peirce, William James, and John Dewey should not be neglected in terms of applications to ways of thinking and learning. Peirce's notion that abstract ideas are clarified and given added meaning through a conception of their consequences is undoubtedly a valuable educational proposition.[27]

William James' notion that our beliefs should be formed in terms of choices between live options is another valuable pragmatic notion for educational use.[28] John Dewey's whole elaborate exposition and interpretation of the *reconstruction of experience* through reflective inquiry and problem-solving is a most valuable contribution to educational theory and practice.[29] Students should be afforded opportunities to experience these ways of thinking and acting.

The point is clear that neither the pragmatic methodology nor any other methodology should be used exclusively in the vast and complex business of the educational process. When one accepts the notion that there are educational values to be derived from the diverse ways of knowing and thinking, one sees how the various methodologies supplement and complement each other. The authoritative method used alone becomes vicious and limiting in its effects; likewise the pragmatic method becomes equally partial and one-sided when used to the exclusion of other methodologies. *Organically we hold that all of these approaches to life, all these ways of thinking, all of these types of experience should be afforded to the student.* To limit educational experience to one or two of these types of human experience is a distinct error in educational theory and practice. Organically it is contended that these diverse methods and types of experience should be planned for and encouraged.

In this larger organic sense it is apparent that empirical and rational experiences are complementary; likewise the experiences of authority and of pragmatism are certainly complementary; authority emphasizes the direction of the immature by the mature in direct forms; pragmatism emphasizes the control and direction of the immature through the actions inherent in given environmental situations; at least in the educational sense we can see the values which flow from the various experiences and approaches. The strictly epistemological problem of obtaining a genuine synthesis of the alleged validities from this *federation of methodologies* is one of the most intricate and challenging problems of contemporary philosophy.[30] Many of the authorities in this field appear to be quite modest about their claims to any final solutions of this problem; they concede the problem to be so complex as to forestall any quick solution in the near future.

This writer does not mean to imply a pessimistic or agnostic conclusion with respect to the epistemological problem in the long run. He is merely calling attention to the present attitude which some of the authorities in this field seem to hold. Very formidable theories of knowledge have been advanced in recent times. Perhaps in the future further advances can be made in further reconstruction of existing epistemological theories.

The philosophy of organism as set forth by Whitehead does possess a sound epistemology in terms of its ontology and cosmology. In fact the epistemology is dependent upon the ontology here. This organic educational philosophy is in substantial agreement with the organic ontology and epistemology. However, there are rather obvious validities in the various theories of knowledge as indicated by Professor William P. Montague in his 'federation of methods.'[31]

On the practical level of educational experience these validities should not be lost in the endeavor to maintain epistemological nicety and precision. There are discernible educational implications of the organic theory of knowledge—to be sure. Yet it needs to be emphasized *that there are educational values in terms of human development which can be accomplished through the utilization and exploration of the multiple modes of human experience and ways of knowing.* Rigid restriction to one or two ways of knowing and thinking on the practical level of teaching-learning results in an impoverishment of the educational process. An educational theory, for example, which restricts itself to the pragmatic method of thinking and learning is quite as inadequate and narrow as an educational theory which restricts itself to the method of authority.

W. P. Montague's argument that the various ways of knowing have special provinces of human experience in which they are the most effective, certainly has important implications for education. We agree then that on the practical level of education these various ways of knowing and learning in terms of special provinces of each method should be applied.

(f) *Skeptical experience*: It might seem indefensible to include *"skeptical experiences"* as a way of experiencing and thinking. However, the utilization of a Humean type of skepticism in moving toward the problem of truth and the attainment of genuine human knowledge can be a very worthwhile aspect of total educational experience in the life of the student. David Hume is well known in the history of modern philosophy for his agnostic attitude and conclusions with respect to the possibility of attaining either rational knowledge or any real empirical knowledge about reality itself. His skepticism was "double-edged." His philosophy stands as a continual challenge to the claims of "knowledge" made by the opposing theories of knowledge. What educational value then might accrue by the utilization of "skeptical experience and approach"?

It appears that the Humean skepticism might well afford the student with a healthful antithesis to the claims made by *authoritative experiences* and others. Teachers utilizing this method would no doubt challenge the easy convictions, solutions, and knowledge claims made by students who have derived such beliefs from their diverse modes of experience. Students would be schooled in the limitations of language, the ambiguities of communication, the fallacies of logical thought, the dangers of verbalism, and the illusory character of truth. The whole round of studies could be used by teachers employing the skeptical approach; sciences, social studies, humanities, philosophy all would come under the critical eye of skeptical experience. The student would become more cautious in his generalizations and in his thinking. He would be less likely to accept easy truths without considerable analysis and doubt. He would in the end, perhaps, be a much more thoughtful person. In the end his beliefs would come much closer to being authentic than if the *experiences of skepticism* had been omitted from the curriculum.

(g) *Organic experience*: *Organic experiences* should certainly be included in these many modes of thinking and experience; in fact, *organic experience* might well be the capping stone of the means of integrating the validities of the other modes of experience, because of its very nature. *Organic experiences* would emphasize those principles which organicists have frequently expounded and emphasized of wholeness, relatedness, connectedness, togetherness, and of conjunctiveness. *Organic experience* is further an emphasis upon those harmonizations of feeling and thinking, of body and mind, of the aesthetic and the theoretic, the experiential and the rational, the deductive and the inductive, and the many other double aspects of experience.

Organic experience would by and large include the theories of the educational process that have been advanced in this work. To expand the meaning of organic modes of learning would be only to repeat what has been said throughout these writings. The harmonization of the functions of man, the development of the functions of man, in relation to all aspects of society, nature, and cosmos is the end of organic experience.

(16) *That these multiple types of experience and ways of knowing are exemplified in the various fields of knowledge and experience.* They are *exemplified* in the established fields of knowledge which are most intimately associated with these distinctive types of experience. This does not mean that they are restricted by any means to these fields, but they are well exemplified there. As we have seen, the physical and natural sciences are most susceptible to ways of empirical and pragmatic experience, but not exclusively so. The humanities lend themselves particularly to rational and authoritative experiences. Art and religion certainly employ intuitional and authoritative experiences. Depending on one's view, philosophy utilizes both rational and skeptical experience. On the operational level of

everyday problems the pragmatic methods seem to apply. All in all we seem to employ organic experiences.

Each distinctive field of study has educational values in terms of its methods, mode of thought, content, values, and ways of looking at the complex of life. It is well known that the artist in painting or literature makes us see the world through his eyes and in his perspective through his medium. The artist gives us new insight into the commonplace; we see beauty through his eyes where once we saw only the mundane. The poet does likewise; he makes us see the world either simply or in metaphor as we had never quite viewed it before. Life becomes more interesting, valuable, and understandable through their arts.

Likewise the scientist with his knowledge, methods, and perspective makes us see life quite differently from the artist or the commonplace. We see the object then in its essence, or quantitatively, or in objective form. Again we are richer and more intelligent in our way of looking at things.

The philosopher initiates us to his speculative methods of reason; we see the world through vast conceptual networks and systems; we secure new perspective on the particular and the immediate; we see the fragmented holistically; we see the world in new perspective when we learn to think philosophically.

The historian teaches us to see things and events in temporal sequence; we view things genetically as they have developed over centuries and epochs; we obtain the feeling of time as we never have before. We comprehend temporal causality as it works with humanity.

The mathematician shows us how to think in the purest terms of symbolic thought. He shows us the meaning and feeling of what it means to think objectively, quantitatively, and with utter precision; he teaches us the meaning of proof in thinking; he shows us how long chains of mathematical reasoning are possible; he shows us how it is possible to transcend particulars, unimportant appearances, trivial differences and to penetrate to the very core of conceptual relationships; he impresses with the sheer precision of cognitive thought; he illustrates the cogency of sharp reasoning, the importance of inference, and of accuracy. He shows us ways of using symbols and

69

symbolic relations to transcend the limitations of ordinary experiential problem solving. He shows us a way of thinking, a way of learning, which is found in its purest form in mathematics.

The grammarian, semanticist, and logician show us the power of logical analysis and precision in the utilization of ideas and symbols in words. Each makes us see that language is capable of a precision which we never suspected before; he also shows us the limitations of language and the deceptiveness and equivocal character of language and thought. We gain insight into the strengths and weaknesses of verbal expression; we acquire the power of language and literature in terms of human communication and rhetorical persuasion; on the other hand there are the numerous fallacies of thought to which humans are prone without logical, dialectical, and grammatical education. Through meticulous attention to the structure and function of verbal and logical relationships the student becomes sensitive to the whole realm of symbolic thought—its strengths and weaknesses.

The organic defense of these various disciplines is not to be confused with the older formal discipline or faculty psychology. The values of experiencing different disciplines are summarized as follows:

(1) Values in the unique methodology and content;

(2) Values in modes of thought ;

(3) Values in varying perspective on life and events;

(4) The accumulative values to be derived from the blending of these other values into an approach to life's complexity.

All of these approaches to life enter into a fusion of thought in the realm of complex problems of life; this area is commonly called the "experience curriculum" or the "core curriculum." Students should experience cross-fertilization of methods, concepts, tools, *et cetera*, of heterogeneous disciplines, too, in the solution of life problems. But the whole curriculum need not be limited to this complex form.

Thus the rationale is that of subject areas, homogeneous subjects in a given field, such as social science, then combination of fields, such as physical sciences and social sciences, and finally "life problems" which virtually cut across all fields. The over-all picture of curriculum includes all of these areas, both subject and experience; the whole curriculum is maintained in terms of logical-psychological continuities and the various intelligibilities.

FOOTNOTES

1. Many of these propositions are utilized or developed further in later contexts of this book; the reader should consult index for related discussions and extensions. See also glossary on page 453.

2. See Figure 13, p. 351.

3. A. N. Whitehead, *Process and Reality* (Cambridge: Cambridge University Press, 1929), p. 40. Page numbers vary with different editions of *Process and Reality*. The writer's references are derived from the edition printed in Great Britain by the Cambridge University Press and copyrighted in the U.S.A. by the Macmillan Company.

4. A. N. Whitehead, *Process and Reality*, pp. 482-83.

5. George S. Maccia, "A Comparison of the Educational Aims of Charles Peirce and John Dewey," *Educational Theory*, Vol. IV, (October, 1954), pp. 289-96.

6. Isaac Kandel, "Humanism and the Return to Reason," *The Cult of Uncertainty* (New York: The Macmillan Company, 1943), pp. 96-129.

7. See A. N. Whitehead, "Science and Philosophy," *Science and the Modern World* (New York: The American Library, A Mentor Book, by arrangement with the Macmillan Co., 1949), p. 149.

8. See A. N. Whitehead, *Process and Reality*, pp. 99-100.

9. Lawrence S. Kubie, "Freud and Human Freedom," *Saturday Review*, May 5, 1956, p. 37.

10. Frederick Eby and Charles F. Arrowood, *The Development of Modern Education* (New York: Prentice-Hall, Inc., 1942, copyright 1934 and 1952 by Prentice-Hall, Inc.), p. 854.

11. L. S. Kubie, *op. cit.*, *Saturday Review*, May 5, 1956, p. 37.

12. L. S. Kubie, *op. cit.*, *Saturday Review*, May 5, 1956, p. 37. Reprinted with permission of the publisher.

13. See Figure 14, page 400.

14. See Dewey's rejection of 'education as preparation.' John Dewey, *Democracy and Education* (New York: The Macmillan Company, 1916), pp. 63-64.

15. Frederick Eby and Charles F. Arrowood, *The Development of Modern Education*, pp. 467-69.

16. William Heard Kilpatrick, *Philosophy of Education* (New York: The Macmillan Company, 1951), pp. 222-35.

17. John Dewey, *Democracy and Education*, p. 27.

18. See Figure 13, page 351.

19. Alfred North Whitehead, "The Rhythmic Claims of Freedom and Discipline," *The Aims of Education* (New York: The New American Library, A Mentor Book, 1949, by the Macmillan Co.), pp. 40-52.

20. A. N. Whitehead, *The Aims of Education*, p. 49.

21. See Figure 6, page 183.

22. See Figure 8, page 222.

23. Alfred North Whitehead, *Adventures of Ideas* (New York: The Mac-Millan Company, 1933), pp. 290-91. Reprinted with permission of the publisher. See also A. H. Johnson, *Whitehead's Theory of Reality* (Boston: The Beacon Press, 1952), p. 74.

24. John Dewey, *How We Think* (Boston: D. C. Heath and Company, 1933), pp. 205-80.

25. Wm. Pepperell Montague, *The Ways of Knowing* (New York: The Macmillan Company, 1925), p. 34.

26. *Organic Experience* is formulated from the author's point of view.

27. See also Charles S. Peirce, "How to Make Our Ideas Clear," *Popular Science Monthly*, November, 1877, and January, 1878.

28. See William James, "The Will to Believe," *Essays in Pragmatism* (New York: Hafner Publishing Company, 1949), pp. 88-90.

29. John Dewey, *Democracy and Education*, pp. 163-78.

30. W. P. Montague, *Ways of Knowing*, pp. 311-15.

31. W. P. Montague, *Ways of Knowing*, pp. 311-15.

4

FOUNDATIONAL EDUCATIONAL PROPOSITIONS-cont.

CONTINUING *the educational propositions the organic educational philosophy holds:*—

(17) *That education involves the harmonious development of the functions of man.* It is the business of *general education* to nurture the harmonious development of the functions of man. Man possesses generic functions and potentialities in our present epoch which the writer has formulated as: Intellectual, Moral, Spiritual, Social, Economic, Political, Physical, Domestic, Aesthetic, and Re-creational. As generic functions and potentialities of mankind they should be developed as universal functions of education. Admittedly these universal functions and potentialities of man are developed through the specificities of cultures which exist in profusion and diversity. Although it is apparent that individuals are educated through the media of their given cultures, education need not stop here. Educational development should continue through comparative cultures both contemporaneously and historically in the constant effort to achieve greater understanding and the optimum way of life for peoples of all cultures through interchange of ideas.

Such harmonious development of man's proper functions is then to be accomplished through the ten functions of man. These ten categories provide us with a valuable pattern for the envisionment of general education. The ten categories furnish us with a pattern in terms of *Educational Needs, Values, Organized Knowledge, Arts and Experiences, Functions and Aims,* and *Respective Institutional Responsibilities.*[1]

73

The subsequent developments of the functions of man are to be viewed *conjunctively* and *disjunctively*. Disjunctively we see each function of man separately in terms of its peculiar needs, values, knowledge, arts and experience, aims, and institutional responsibility. Conjunctively we see the organic relationships of these ten functions as they interact and as they must be interwoven, if we are to attain harmonious development of the individual with his world.

(18) *That education involves development of man qua man and man in his individuality.* Education requires the development of man *qua* man as well as the development of man in his unique individuality. An education which neglects either of these twofold requirements is destined to be one-sided and inadequate. The education of man *qua* man emphasizes the development of man's common functions and potentialities as *Homo sapiens*. The similarities of man are emphasized here; the need for a common education is stressed.

Man's diversity is expressed in terms of his unique propensities, capacities, and desires. Education also has a responsibility to develop these powers of individuality. By and large the one is in terms of general education, and the other in terms of special education. The two are not antithetical but complementary. Ideally the common functions of man should be developed to an optimum; actually and realistically much of the educational process of becoming demands the nurture of individuality in the realization of powers.

(19) *That the ten basic functions of man provide the pattern for the functions of general education.* Education has for its task the systematic development of the functions of man. These ten categories are to be analyzed in terms of educational *Needs, Values, Knowledge, Arts and Experiences, Functions and Aims,* and *Institutional Responsibilities.*[2] Education is responsible particularly for the systematic aspects of these functions and their development; the experiential aspects are residual in character. That is to say the school should not duplicate unnecessarily those common experiences which are derived from the diverse sources of social life. However, the school should include those necessary experiences of the *experiential realm* which are not in the backgrounds of the learners.

74

(20) *That education involves determination of being.* Education is in a very profound sense a process of determination of one's *being.* The process is partly determinate and partly indeterminate in the perspective of the learner. Education in a real sense is an answer to this question, "What am I going to *be?*" Or, "What am I to *become?*" One's whole life cycle from birth to death is the constant attempt to answer this question and to do something about it. One can do nothing about the completed past. The constitution and complex environment which one inherits is the given. Long before conscious and deliberate self-determination takes place in the individual organism the complex internal and external factors have been forming his being. With the dawning of the self-consciousness and self-powers of direction and valuation, the individual can exert feelings, desires, understandings, and powers in behalf of his own "self-determination."

Within the given potentialities of the organism and the environment determinations can be made. The actual entities and the ideal possibles (forms of definiteness) furnish the materials and forms for such determinacy. The being of a given subject is determined by its mode of becoming through positive and negative prehensions, and physical and conceptual prehensions. Positive prehensions or feelings consist of positive appropriations of data. Negative prehensions are constituted by consideration of data and final rejection of them. Thus the entity as subject is internally constituted by its prehending of the available data in the light of its subjective aims.

In a real sense one *becomes* according to these choices and actions. Yet we must not overlook the fact that this *becoming* is not completely flexible and completely free, for the choices of the organism are always in a measure determined by previous stages of being and previous determinations. Man's constitution as man is a stubborn and realistic fact; he is the product of millions of years of evolution. To a remarkable extent man is flexible and educable. Yet in our enthusiasm for self-determination through conscious becoming, we must not overlook these stubborn facts. Another word of caution: to say that man *becomes* by what he does is a limited truth; he becomes also by what he feels and what he thinks; actions are also determined by feelings and ideas.

(21) *That teachers should seek to nurture wisdom as well as knowledge in the learners.* Knowledge as well as 'know-how' is a legitimate objective of education. However, a higher goal of organic education is the unification of abstract knowledge and concrete experience in wisdom.

(22) *That education involves concrescence.*[4] Education is a process of *concrescence* whereby the learner as *subject* literally absorbs the *data* of his environment, of which he is a continuous extension, into the complexity of his life as a new unity.[5] This process of *concrescence* or bringing together of diverse elements into a new unity of the individual *entity* or *organism* is marked by *prehensions*.

The *organism* as a learner, in this case, is organized through physical and conceptual *prehensions*.[6] The *subject* or learner physically prehends concrete data from the other *actual* entities of the environment. *Conceptual prehensions* refer to the *prehension* or *apprehension* of *eternal objects* as *forms of definiteness* which may be utilized in the experience of the *actual entity* or learner in this case.[7] As Whitehead says the *eternal objects ingress* into the *actual entity*.[8] In lower order organisms this ingression takes place solely by *prehension* or *feeling* for the *eternal objects*, whereas with high grade human organisms non-cognitive prehension or cognitive apprehensions might well characterize the process.

Prehensions are both positive and negative. The learning process is characterized by *positive prehension* when the learner actually absorbs the data into the real internal constitution of his being.[9] External facts are no longer external when they have been absorbed into the private being of the learner. This absorption of data from other entities by the subject in concrescence is prehension or feeling. However, from the standpoint of the actual or completed entities (objects) it is a process of objectification, for they make their objective data available for the use of other prehending entities. Whitehead's terminology is used deliberately in terms of the respective standpoint of either subject or object. Hence we must understand the term 'ingression' from the standpoint of the eternal objects or 'forms of definiteness,' as the way in which they make themselves available for definiteness in the concrescence and prehensions of entities in their becoming.

These 'forms of definiteness' are said to subsist in God's primordial conceptual being as envisagements; they are not created for they are 'eternal objects' which simply come and go in temporal exemplifications. It has been suggested that from the standpoint of the eternal objects, the way they make themselves available for definiteness in the absorbing process of the subject is described as ingression; this is to emphasize that they are torn out of their subsistence in God's nature and that they are not created, but rather that they simply appear, disappear, and re-appear (are eternal) in the physical world.[10]

Whitehead contends that *negative prehensions* are as important as *positive prehensions*. *Negative prehensions* refer to the decisions made in the consideration and rejection of data. The learner as a *subject* is experiencing a process of *becoming;* he is also *superject* in that he has an achieved being as the result of prior processes of *becoming.*[11] What we are, at any given time, as a total product, is the result of prior *decisions*, or *positive* and *negative prehensions.* One's decision to go to college instead of going into some line of employment, for example, gains for him the positive data of college education, but rejects the data which might have been derived from the other course of action and experience.

Thus the development of the internal constitution of the learning organism is a result of a process of concrescence and prehension. The *being* of the learner is formed through complex interactions between his own actualities and potentialities and those of the entities, forces, and conditions of his environment. The active process of *becoming* of the *subject* involves constant prehensions, positive and negative, ideal and actual, in an over-all *concrescence.*

(23) *That education requires harmonization of authority and freedom.* Education is a process of harmonizing the forces of authority and freedom in mankind and in the individual. One must constantly reckon with the diverse authorities of fact, science, human experience, reality, nature, society, reason, truth and their opposites. One must strive for intelligent use of freedom. It is evident that freedom

is always relative to existence and ideal possibilities. Thus, since education deals largely with those who are relatively immature and relatively mature, it is necessary that the educational process be carried on in clear cognizance of the dynamic ratio of factors of authority and freedom. Immaturity demands more authority and less real freedom; increasing maturity earns more real freedom and decreasing authority. However, the increased power and freedom that come with maturity and wisdom continue to be relative to reality.[12] Even the sage and saint are never completely free from the limitations of reality.

(24) *That educational discipline should be obtained through the organic theory of control.* This theory of discipline asserts that control of the human being is always a ratio or *proportionate bipolarity* equated with existent levels of maturity and immaturity, internal and external factors, idealistic and realistic components, degrees of freedom and reality, and elements of *indeterminism* and *determinism.* It is based upon the assumption that man is relatively determined and undetermined, and that with increasing maturity, power, and knowledge one gains more freedom, but never absolute freedom.

(25) *That the motivation of learners is pluralistic rather than monistic.* It is contended here that human motivation is *pluralistic* rather than *monistic,* and that motivations may be both external and internal, extrinsic and intrinsic, directed and non-directed, remote and immediate, and compulsory and voluntary. These terms must be understood in the context of the Organic Philosophy of Education as interpreted here, for they may be used somewhat differently in the contexts of other systems.

(26) *That education requires external and internal control and direction.*[13] Education is never a matter of *either* external control and direction *or* internal control in the larger sense of these terms. Progressives and followers of Dewey and Kilpatrick have tended for the most part to minimize the need for "external controls" and to maximize the need for "internal controls." Conservatives and traditionalists have tended to reverse this emphasis. The 'organic theory of control' and direction asserts that external and internal forces and factors are two aspects of organically related factors.

Learners engaged in the educational process are always relatively immature and relatively mature in various respects. To the extent that they are relatively immature they are in need of mature guidance, instruction, training, control and direction. To the extent that they are relatively mature they should be encouraged and nurtured in the development of their own powers through gradually increasing use of self-direction, discovery, learning through experience, and purposive behavior.

Control of the young then is to be achieved by a proportionate bipolarity (or shifting ratio of complementary factors) of external and internal factors of discipline. The proportion shifts from infancy through adulthood. External controls and internal controls vary in proportion through the levels of educational growth and development. By and large the external controls can be decreased and internal controls increased with the achievement of successive levels of maturational development.

The *direction* of educational development is also a problem of the fusion of external and internal forces and objects. In one sense direction is determined by realistic factors such as the actual environment which exists, school and community conditions, public and professional opinion, the potentialities of the learner, established practices, customs, expectations of parents, and the like. In another sense direction can and should be determined by the developing ambitions, desires, feelings, beliefs, values, and purposes of the individual learner. Loosely speaking we may refer to these as external and internal forces, although they are in the end intrinsically related.

The direction of one's educational development then is partly self-determined and partly determined by "other" considerations. Realistically we cannot and must not neglect the acknowledgment and recognition of these "other" factors. Idealistically and pragmatically we must acknowledge the validity of personal determination in terms of one's increasing degree of self-direction. This distinction then is relative and not absolute in character. Humans find themselves in situations which are partly determined and partly undetermined. They have relative degrees of *self-determinacy* and *other-determinacy*.

79

Organic education then is composed of co-ordinations of realistic and idealistic factors, of external forces of discipline and internal forces of discipline, of determinate elements and indeterminate choices. The teacher or parent must then realize the *proportionate bipolarity* of external and internal forces. Adult control and direction should be administered in proportion to the actual capacities and powers of the learners at the various levels of development and maturation.

(27) *That education demands the co-ordination of reason and experience.* Education should be characterized by its co-ordination of the functions of reason and the realm of ordinary experience. *Reason* has diverse functions and manifestations; in one sense reason has a *contemplative function*—that of seeking Truth, Goodness, Beauty, or understanding. Whitehead has called our attention to this function using the figure of the Greeks, *"the reason of Plato."*[14] In another sense, using the Greek figure further, there is the *prudential function* of intelligence, or the *"reason of Ulysses."* Education has an obligation to develop both types of thinking. Thus one function of education derived from the *contemplative function* is that of development of scientific and philosophical inquiry in pursuit of truth and understanding. It is also a function of education to develop *prudential intelligence* in the *means-ends processes* of deliberate and purposeful behavior.

The realms of *rational inquiry* and *prudential intelligence* are in one sense susceptible to disengagement; in fact truly rational and objective inquiry requires such temporary disengagement from practical interests. However, the separability is only qualified; for in the long run there is a necessity of seeing the interaction and the complementary relationship of the two functions. Thus organic education requires *interweaving* of these functions in the long run.

(28) *That the educational process must embrace (a) the realm of reason, and (b) the realm of ordinary experience.*[15] These two realms of learning are analogous to Plato's *Parable of the Prisoners of the Cave.* Students must be led from the cave of ordinary experience to the light of reason and inquiry and back again to enlightened experience.

(29) *That logical continuities must be respected within the teaching-learning processes.*[16] Logical continuities are to be interwoven with psychological continuities (orders of experience). Neither one is to be subordinated to the other; they are to be co-ordinated.

(30) *That the logic of subject matter must be respected within the educational process.* Subject matters provide the necessary frameworks for *structural intelligibility.* As such they should not be treated incidentally and subordinated to psychological or experiential continuities. Vitalized teaching can take place within such frameworks.

(31) *That education in terms of schooling should follow the logical-psychological continuity.* The *logical order* is determined by objective factors; the *psychological order* is determined by subjective factors; the logical-psychological continuity is the resulting interweaving order of the two.[17] They constitute a *dynamic bipolar relationship.*

(32) *That aspects of the educational process are subject to the principle of reversibility. Reversibility* is a basic principle of the Organic Philosophy of Education, not explicitly stated in other educational philosophies to my knowledge, which states that the educational process is characterized by the *reversibility* of certain co-ordinate principles—namely: *abstraction-concretion, objectification-subjectification, structuralization-functionalization,* and *ratiocination-personalization.*

(33) *That objectification and subjectification are essential phases of the whole educational process.*[18] By *objectification* is meant that process in knowing or learning whereby the peculiarly unique and personal understandings, perceptions, feelings, and values are developed to an objective status or level. By *subjectification* this writer means that process in knowing or learning whereby the knower or learner formulates one's personal orientation in terms of understanding, appreciation, values, or purposes. Organic education is characterized by the movement through these two phases of the educational process by means of the *principle of reversibility.*

(34) *That the theoretical and practical aspects of the curriculum are bipolar in nature.* Theory and practice in school studies are independent and interdependent; they are disjunctive and conjunctive. For clarity in the mind of the learner there is a necessity that

81

theoretical inquiries be separated from practical projects. The student should see the conceptual relationships clearly and distinctly in their own intelligibility. At another stage of the learning process he should see the practical applications and significances. Hence, it is a fundamental error of recent progressive practices in education which frequently treated all "theoretical aspects of the curriculum" as incidental to and subordinate to "the experiential curriculum." The *experiential curriculum* is a legitimate part of the whole, but it is wrong to reduce all aspects of total learning to the *experiential curriculum.*

(35) *That organic education recognizes the role of diversity within unity, but it does not countenance dualism.* "Dualism" allows for absolute distinctions between substances or processes, whereas, the distinctions made within the philosophy of organism are not *absolute* but *relative.*

(36) *That John Dewey was right in his constant endeavor to unify the dichotomies and bifurcations of former philosophies and educational theories; however, that he erred in overlooking the legitimate diversities and bipolarities in actuality and the educational process.* Dewey rightly inveighed against "gaps in experience" and absolute "either-or" bifurcations.[19] He constantly sought to unify mind and body, the individual and society, feelings and thought, interest and effort, methods and subject matter, and school and life. However, the effect of his strong reaction against "bifurcations" has been to blur the legitimacy of *bipolarity,* or the *diversity* (separableness) as well as the *unity of opposites* (*togetherness*). The Organic Philosophy of Education seeks to correct the older error of "dualism" as well as the more recent error of "monism." For example, this writer holds that "theory and practice" can and must be disengaged, as well as engaged.

(37) *That Whitehead is quite right in saying that we should teach fewer subjects and to teach them more thoroughly.*[20] In his *Aims of Education,* Whitehead has said: "Let us now ask how in our system of education we are to guard against this mental dryrot. ('inert ideas') We enunciate two educational commandments, "Do not

teach too many subjects," and again, "What you teach, teach thoroughly."[21] The direct quotation from Whitehead is given because it supports the writer's feelings on this matter. One evil of recent education has been the superficiality and fragmentation of learning resulting from the efforts to teach everything at once. It is high time that we recognize the wisdom of Whitehead's commandments on fewer subjects and thorough teaching.

(38) *That the educational process includes complex and simple intelligibilities.* Complex intelligibility is defined here as that intelligibility which is found in problems or situations requiring concepts, principles, and skills derived from two or more strands of subject matter; that type of intelligibility exemplified in "fused curriculum," "core curriculum," and "interdisciplinary studies."

Simple intelligibility is defined here as that intelligibility which is found in single strands of subject matter; that type of intelligibility found in the logical continuity of a given strand of subject matter, such as arithmetic.

It is contended here that the curriculum shall include the *simple* and *complex intelligibilities.* Students must not be expected to learn only from *complex intelligibilities;* they need the clarification to be derived from the study of *simple intelligibilities* and *logical continuities,* too.

(39) *That the educational process properly involves the recognition of both structural and functional intelligibilities.* These *intelligibilities* when interwoven result in *organic intelligibilities;* that is, the learner exemplifies the unification of both.

(40) *That education should nurture structural intelligibility.* *Structural intelligibility* is defined here as the comprehensibility of anything in its formal aspects; it refers to the knowability of something intrinsically. *Structural intelligibility* is complemented by *functional intelligibility* in the organic educational process.

(41) *That education should nurture functional intelligibilities.* One aspect of education has to do with intelligent doing, acting, making, and creating. This involves *functional intelligibility* or "know-how."

83

This phase of the educational process is complemented by the nurture of *structural intelligibility*.

(42) *That organic intelligibility is a constant objective of organic education.* The term is used here to denote the unification of *structural* and *functional intelligibilities* in the learner. When the "why, what, and how" aspects of *diverse intelligibilities* are exemplified in the being of the learner, *organic intelligibility* has been achieved.

(43) *That those engaged in the educational process must constantly seek to obtain the validities of objectivity and subjectivity and to avoid the one-sidedness of objectivism or subjectivism.* One of the most intricate problems of all philosophy and science is that involving the discernment of elements of objectivity and subjectivity—especially in the educational process. In one's enthusiasm for a scientific approach or in one's concern for personal and subjective factors it is easy to fall into the error of *monopolarity*.

(44) *That education requires harmonization of reality and freedom.* Education is constituted by deliberate harmonization of factors of reality and freedom in the developing individual. The individual human organism is never completely free; he is not absolutely free; he is only relatively free. His development necessarily involves his relationships to reality and growing degrees of freedom. He must adjust to reality, but to the extent that actuality in the process of becoming is partly indeterminate he has degrees of freedom. Freedom is increased with the development of one's powers and capacities and understandings. However, this freedom involves the truth and understandings of reality. Hence, it is the continuing task of education to assist the individual in understanding the scope and limits of his freedom and the possibilities and limitations of reality. The ratio is a shifting one, but it is always a dynamic, existential ratio.

(45) *That education involves realization of responsibility and freedom.* Education is a process of realization of human responsibility and freedom to optimum degrees of possibility. It is commonplace to note that responsibility implies freedom and that freedom implies responsibility. In a democracy we value the rights of

individual development according to our own preferences and values. It should be noted that the individual also has a deep responsibility to the society which nourished him, and to humanity at large, and that therefore the educational process must develop one's social responsibilities as well as one's rights and freedoms.

(46) *That education involves the process of harmonizing the individual with the seven factors of process and reality.* In a sense education is also a process of harmonizing the individual in his concrescence with the seven factors of process and reality. With Whitehead we should agree that Plato's thought was largely concerned with the interweaving of seven notions: The *Ideas,* The *Physical Elements,* The *Psyche,* The *Eros,* The *Harmony,* The *Mathematical Relations,* and The *Receptacle,*—and that these notions are as important for us now as they were then.[22]

If these are the factors with which we must deal in relationship to the macrocosm, then certainly it follows that we must deal with them in the microcosm of man.

(47) *That education involves the process of realization of beauty.* Education is also a process of realization of beauty. "Beauty is the mutual adaptation of the several factors in an occasion of experience."[23] Again Whitehead sees beauty in terms of abstract or ideal possibilities and as exemplified in *actual objects.* Beauty is characterized by harmony and "absence of mutual interference."

> In addition there are striking contrasts of content. This set of conditions results in an increased intensity and issues in a higher form of beauty. There is *harmony of patterned contrasts* in which the various distinct elements contribute to the total effect and also are enhanced by the totality of which they form a part.[24]

Education then involves the realization of such harmonies of patterned contrasts both in man himself and in his creations. Education requires the fusion of actual and ideal possibilities in beauty as well as in value.

(48) *That education is a process of realization of truth.* Education is also a process of realization of truth. In Whitehead's sense truth may be defined as the conformation of appearance to reality.[25]

The concrete data which actual entities prehend from other actual entities constitute reality (in Whitehead's special, technical use of the term), and the novel use which the new actual entity makes of these data, in accordance with its own *subjective aim,* constitutes what Whitehead calls appearance.[26]

There are several truth relations which are to be realized in the educational process. The most common conception of truth is perhaps that of the conformation of a proposition to objects described. Another truth relation is that of sense perception and accurate conformity with external events. Another relationship is that of symbolic truth, or the relation of symbols and non-inherent meanings.

Although there are elements of pragmatism within Whitehead's epistemology, his theory of knowledge is by no means limited to the pragmatic viewpoint. A. H. Johnson observes that since Whitehead defines truth as the conformity of appearance and reality, he is committed to a kind of correspondence theory of truth, modified by his conception of coherence; despite the fact that Whitehead's theory is partly pragmatic in its recognition of consequences, it is not pragmatic in the ultimate sense; his theory contains other essential elements and it is by no means limited to the pragmatic doctrine of consequences.[27] Johnson underscores this distinction as follows, "However, the pragmatist is like Hamlet, continually postponing a final decision. Whitehead contends that intuition (immediate experience) in at least some instances removes the need for this tentativeness."[28]

(49) *The problem of knowledge has important consequences for philosophy of education.* This proposition need not imply that the problem of knowledge is more important than problems of reality and value. However, a familiarity with the problem of knowledge and the existing theories of knowledge does provide the student of educational theory with rewarding insights into the dimensions of the educational process. It does make a difference to one's conception of the educational process, what his theory of knowledge is. It makes a difference whether one is devoted to one or more theories of knowledge. The *philosophy of organism* takes the position that all modes of human experience should be utilized in achieving maximum human *concrescence.*

(50) *That philosophy of education is educational theory in its most general phases.* The complexities of educational practice require that sound educational practices must be grounded in right theory. Theories of the educational process, human development, curriculum, methods, administration, educational psychology, counseling, and the like are apt to be very inharmonious and incoherent if they are not co-ordinated. This co-ordination and harmonization of theories of education is to be found in the undergirding philosophy of education. Hence educational philosophy is educational theory in its most general phases.[29]

(51) *That education involves the maximization of good and the minimization of evil.* Education is a process whereby humans seek to maximize the good and to minimize the actualization of evil. This proposition follows from the belief that the ideal contrasts of good and evil in the universe are always with us and that absolute goodness or absolute evil are impossible states of organic achievement. Education in its effort to achieve positive valuation of Good, True, and Beautiful can only hope to maximize such values and to reduce opposites to a minimum.

(52) *That education requires a process of realization of value.* In a sense education is a process of deliberate realization of value. This organic theory agrees with Whitehead in saying that "value is inherent in actuality" and that it is not an artificial construct.[30] Values exist in entities and are enjoyed by all actual entities. This is true of the high-grade human entity or organism too. Hence the educational process becomes a deliberate attempt to realize values in the becoming and being of the learner.

The process of self-realization and the creation of selfhood is in large measure the acquisition of value. As the learner *becomes* through the process of *concrescence* he experiences *positive* and *negative prehensions* in appropriating data from his environment. These appropriations are necessarily determinate and selective; some data must be accepted and some rejected. Thus the *becoming* learner accepts and rejects values to be incorporated in his *being;* values are co-ordinated in his unique being.

87

It is important to note that according to Whitehead there are *value ideals* and *actual values*.[31] The *value ideals* are the abstract possibilities or *eternal objects*. The *actual values* are those existent values in actual entities. Human development then necessarily involves constant *valuation*.[32] The educational process is characterized then by the determination and realization of ideal values and existing values through *becoming* of the learner in actual *being*.

It is important in this connection to note that value should not be merely interpreted in terms of interest. Value arouses interest rather than being the result of interest.[33] This twist has striking implications for educational theory in that the problem of values holds a priority over the problem of interests. Instead of asking constantly about students' "interests," it is more important to determine their values. Values in turn are rooted in the reality of existence and in the ideality of *abstract possibilities*. Valuation in Whitehead's terms also involves the complex role of God and the lure of the True, Good, and Beautiful.[34] Time does not permit discussion of this part of his philosophy.

(53) *That education is a fusion of potentialities and possibilities.*[35] Education is a process whereby there is a deliberate fusion of *actual potentialities* of the learner and existing conditions and *ideal possibilities*. The learner and his environment represent the existential state of being at a given moment in a certain epoch. The learner as one among many entities of this epoch has achieved *being* in terms of his *organized internal constitution*. Thus there are actually existent determinate factors, and ideal possibilities (*eternal objects*). The learner's being is then determined by a process of *concrescence* as he unifies aspects of the data about him; his being becomes formed or determined by the *ingression* of ideal forms in fusion with actualization of potentialities. Learning then in a very real sense requires that the learner move from present existence into actualization of the ideal as well as *existential potentialities*.

(54) *That education involves maximum realization of the potentialities of man qua man and man's unique individuality through democracy.* Education is the maximum realization of the potentialities of man *qua* man and in man's unique individuality through democracy. The optimum degree of freedom and responsibility is furnished

by a truly democratic environment; this democratic way of life then is the means whereby man can realize his potentialities with respect to the totality of reality and not merely social environment.

(55) *That educational theories cannot exist in a philosophical vacuum or in atomistic independence.* Theories advanced by specialists in Curriculum, Instruction, Administration, Educational Psychology, Counseling and Guidance, or other divisions of Education, must be grounded in a philosophy of education which in turn is rooted in general philosophy. A given educational theory requires an underlying philosophical orientation either explicitly or implicitly. A standing danger in professional education is that specialists in these various areas of education will put forth theories of education which are not properly grounded in a coherent philosophy of education.

The next chapter presents an overview of some of the philosophical foundational propositions which provide the ground for these educational propositions.

Summary. The Organic Philosophy of Education is characterized by selected foundational educational propositions. In most general terms education may be characterized as a deliberate process of creativity and the integration of contrasting elements. A corollary of the foregoing proposition is that education organically conceived is marked by the co-ordination of bipolar and complementary elements and forces. It seeks to avoid the error of monopolarity which results in a one-sidedness of both conservative and progressive theories. Education requires the fusion of knowing and doing, or science and art. The subordination of one to the other must be avoided through the principle of bipolarity.

Education has as one of its deepest obligations the harmonization and development of those sides of man termed 'feeling' and 'reason.' Since man is fundamentally bipolar and ambivalent, exemplifying the great ideal opposites of all reality, it is the function of education to harmonize these components.

Education involves the blending of systematic 'schooling' and 'life experience' in the total educational process. In this sense education as carried on by the schools is both preparation for life and life in its immediacy.

Education requires both systematic learning from another and the nurture of originality through direct experience. This follows from the organic insistence upon the utilization of pluralistic modes of human experience in the total educational process.

Organic education depends upon the co-ordination of progressive and conservative forces; these two sets of forces contribute to the wholeness of the educational process which we seek to achieve. The school itself is thus more democratic than when devoting itself more or less to the beliefs of progressivism or conservatism. The educational process and product are sounder when following the organic conception.

Education is most comprehensively conceived as an organic process. The organic process includes all of the functions of man. It is an error of reductionism to conceive of 'education as a social process,' 'intellectual process,' or 'moral process' *per se.*

The educational process is cyclical in nature and is characterized by three stages of development: (i) Exploration, (ii) Analysis, and (iii) Synthesis, as Whitehead has indicated.

The field of learning is that of the individual and reality in its wholeness. Such an organic field of experience is marked by various manifestations of bipolarity, which have to be taken into consideration in our understanding of the teaching-learning processes.

Organic education is then characterized by a continual process of interweaving various kinds of opposites, contrasts, components, and co-ordinates. In short it involves bringing the many into the one; this is concrescence.

The organic field of experience exemplifies the bipolar hemispheres with their conjunctiveness and disjunctiveness. In my terms they are related through (i) Relative Separability, (ii) Relative Incompleteness *in se,* and (iii) Relative Togetherness, or Reciprocity; in Professor Bahm's terms the relations are similar: (i) Relative Independence, (ii) Relative Dependence, and (iii) Relative Interdependence.

Elements of unity and diversity, conjunctiveness and disjunctiveness, interdependence and independence must be co-ordinated and harmonized in the educational process.

Coherence and continuity are essentials of the teaching-learning process. Logical and psychological continuities must be recognized as separate strands, which are interwoven within the learning process. Neither is subordinate to the other.

Education must utilize all of the multiple types of human experience. Reason, experience, intuition, authority, doubt, and problem-solving are components of the total process. No single methodology is sufficient for education in the larger sense. It follows that in teaching students 'how to think,' the diverse modes of thought open to mankind should be encompassed in the education of our youth.

These multiple types of experience and ways of knowing are exemplified in the various fields of knowledge and experience. These modes of knowing are more or less exemplified in the established fields of knowledge and curriculum. From the organic point of view it would be a mistake to reduce all subject matter demarcations to the emergent, mixed problems of life, in the teaching-learning process.

It is the business of general education to nurture the harmonious development of the ten basic functions of man. These generic functions are Intellectual, Moral, Spiritual, Social, Economic, Political, Physical, Domestic, Aesthetic, and Re-creational. A pattern for general education is secured when we combine these ten dimensions with the horizontal dimensions of Educational Needs, Values, Organized Knowledge, Arts (Experiences), Functions and Aims, and the Respective Institutional Responsibilities.

Education requires the development of man *qua* man, as well as the development of man in his unique individuality. There is the two-fold obligation of education: to man in his common denominators, and in his individuality with its individual differences.

Education is in a very profound sense a process of the determination of one's being. One's being is determined by the great bipolarity of nature-nurture—considered conjunctively and disjunctively. Essentially education assists the individual in realizing the answer to this question: "What am I going to be?" In this process teachers should assist individuals in the acquisition of wisdom as well as practical 'know-how.'

Education is a process of concrescence whereby the learner as subject literally absorbs the data of his environment, of which he is a continuous extension, into the complexity of his life as a new unity.

Education is also a process of harmonizing the forces of authority and freedom in mankind and in the individual. One's degree of freedom is relative to the facts of reality. Hence the problem of control of the immature depends on our recognition that the human being is always an exemplification of the ratio or proportionate bipolarity equated with existent levels of maturity and immaturity, internal and external factors, idealistic and realistic components, freedom and reality, and elements of indeterminism and determinism.

It follows that human motivation and control are pluralistic. Education is never a matter of either external control or internal control in the larger sense of these terms. The teacher must always strive for the ratio of realistic and idealistic components in the direction of the young.

Since man has both contemplative and prudential intellectual functions, it follows that education should seek to co-ordinate reason and experience. It requires scientific inquiry as well as pragmatic experience. It follows as a corollary that logical continuities must be respected within the learning process. Subject matter continuities are necessary to avoid fragmentation. Objectively determined logical orders should be blended with subjectively determined psychological orders. One should not be subordinated to the other.

Organic theory introduces a new principle: reversibility. The teaching-learning process should be marked by moving from the respective spheres of the organic field of experience. Thus through reversibility the teacher achieves abstraction-concretion, objectification-subjectification, structuralization-functionalization, and the like. One's experiences become objectified during one sustained movement, only to be subjectified during the deliberate reversal of that process.

Education has theoretical and practical components which are learned in disjunction and conjunction at different stages. One is not subordinated to the other. Likewise, the organic conception of education seeks to realize both principles of unity and diversity in the process. Dewey and his followers were right in seeking to close gaps in experience, but their revolt against dualism led them to overlook the validity of bipolarity, or the unity of opposites.

Practically we are in need of teaching fewer subjects, but more thoroughly. Within the educational process it is necessary that we sustain simple intelligibilities as well as complex intelligibilities; there must be recognition of the respective roles of structural and functional intelligibilities as they contribute to the synthesis—organic intelligibility. In working toward the realization of these intelligibilities the respective validities of objective and subjective phases of human experience are to be recognized.

Education requires the harmonization of reality and freedom and the realization of the right ratio between responsibility and freedom. Since man is a microcosm of the macrocosm, education involves the process of harmonizing the individual with the seven factors (metaphysically) of process and reality, namely: the Ideas, Physical Elements, Psyche, Eros, Harmony, Mathematical Relations, and the Receptacle.

It should go without saying that the education of man requires the deliberate realization of Truth, Beauty, and Goodness to the highest of man's capacities. Hence studies of reality, truth, and value have tremendously important implications for the educational process. Education then involves the maximization of good and the minimization of evil in human experience. It requires a deliberate realization of value. In this sense educational philosophy is educational theory in its most general phases.

Education is a process whereby there is a deliberate fusion of actual potèntialities with ideal possibilities. Hence education involves the maximum realization of the potentialities of man *qua* man and man's unique individuality through democracy. In conclusion it should be noted that educational theories within Education—such as educational psychology, educational administration, curriculum and instruction—cannot function in a philosophical vacuum or in atomistic isolation. Consciously or unconsciously an educational philosophy is implied.

FOOTNOTES

1. See Figure 14, page 400.

2. See also Figure 14, page 400.

3. Alfred North Whitehead, *Process and Reality* (Cambridge: Cambridge University Press, 1929), copyright U.S.A. by Macmillan Co., pp. 33-34, 71, 123. Also, A. H. Johnson, *Whitehead's Theory of Reality* (Boston: The Beacon Press, 1952), pp. 126-27, 21 and 18.

4. See index and glossary. The term *concrescence* is adapted from A. N. Whitehead; see his *Process and Reality*, p. 299; A. H. Johnson, *Whitehead's Theory of Reality*, p. 18.

5. See index and glossary. A. N. Whitehead, *Process and Reality*, p. 123; A. H. Johnson, *Whitehead's Theory of Reality*, pp. 47-48.

6. See index and glossary. Alfred North Whitehead, *Science and the Modern World* (New York: The American Library, A Mentor Book, by arrangement with the Macmillan Company, 1949), p. 101; A. H. Johnson, *Whitehead's Theory of Reality*, pp. 22-27.

7. See index and glossary. A. N. Whitehead, *Process and Reality*, pp. 29, 54, 56, 60; A. H. Johnson, *Whitehead's Theory of Reality*, pp. 19-20.

8. See *ingression* in index and glossary. A. N. Whitehead, *Process and Reality*, pp. 31, 54, 56; A. H. Johnson, *Whitehead's Theory of Reality*, pp. 21, 24.

9. See index and glossary. A. N. Whitehead, *Process and Reality*, pp. 31, 32, 56, 71; A. H. Johnson, *Whitehead's Theory of Reality*, p. 21.

10. Suggested by Prof. G. J. Craven in our personal correspondence of 1956.

11. See *subject-superject* in index and glossary. A. N. Whitehead, *Process and Reality*, pp. 39, 96, 117, 121-23; A. H. Johnson, *Whitehead's Theory of Reality*, pp. 42-43.

12. See Figure 11, page 280.

13. See Figure 11, page 280.

14. See Alfred North Whitehead, *The Function of Reason* (Princeton: The University of Princeton Press, 1929).

15. See Figure 6, page 183.

16. See Figure 8, page 222.

17. See Figure 8, page 222.

18. This writer's use of 'objectification' differs from Whitehead's philosophical use of this term. Here it means development of common understandings of objective subject matter; in Whitehead it refers to an entity's realization in other entities.

19. Melvin C. Baker, *Foundations of John Dewey's Educational Theory* (New York: King's Crown Press, Columbia University, 1955), p. 116, *et passim.*

20. Alfred North Whitehead, *Aims of Education* (New York: The New American Library, A Mentor Book, by arrangement with The Macmillan Company, 1949), p. 14.

94

21. A. N. Whitehead, *Aims of Education*, p. 15.

22. See A. N. Whitehead, *Adventures of Ideas*, p. 188.

23. A. H. Johnson, *Whitehead's Theory of Reality*, p. 104. Reprinted with permission of the publisher.

24. A. H. Johnson, *Whitehead's Theory of Reality*, pp. 104-05. Reprinted with permission of the publisher.

25. See A. H. Johnson, *Whitehead's Theory of Reality*, p. 100.

26. See A. H. Johnson, *Whitehead's Theory of Reality*, p. 100. Reprinted with permission of the publisher.

27. See A. H. Johnson, *Whitehead's Theory of Reality*, p. 101.

28. See A. H. Johnson, *Whitehead's Theory of Reality*, p. 101. Reprinted with permission of the publisher.

29. The writer is indebted to John Dewey for his original notion that "philosophy is education in its most general phases"; this proposition is analogous to his observation.

30. See A. H. Johnson, *Whitehead's Theory of Reality*, p. 98. Reprinted with permission of the publisher.

31. See A. H. Johnson, *Whitehead's Theory of Reality*, p. 98.

32. See A. H. Johnson, *Whitehead's Theory of Reality*, pp. 98-99; see A. N. Whitehead, *Process and Reality*, pp. 25, 32, 36.

33. See A. H. Johnson, *Whitehead's Theory of Reality*, p. 98.

34. See A. H. Johnson, *Whitehead's Theory of Reality*, pp. 99-118; see A. N. Whitehead, "God and the World," *Process and Reality*, Chapter II, Part V, pp. 484-501.

35. See Figure 7, page 194.

5

FOUNDATIONAL
PHILOSOPHICAL PROPOSITIONS

THE previous chapter has set forth the foundational educational propositions of this educational philosophy. These educational propositions are in turn based upon the foundational philosophical propositions that are set forth in this chapter. These philosophcial propositions are necessarily brief; the exposition of these propositions in adequate form would require a complete volume in itself. The comparative brevity of these propositions makes it possible to provide the reader with an overview and a general understanding of the philosophical orientation of this educational philosophy. Those propositions which have been the most significant and influential in the formulation of this educational theory have been selected for the purposes of this book.

All of these propositions are either explicitly or implicitly utilized in the later formulations of this book. Some of the propositions are expounded in later contexts, while others are merely implicit. For the most part these philosophical propositions *per se* will require more extensive exposition and defense in a later work devoted to these purposes. Many of these propositions are either directly or indirectly related to Whitehead's philosophy of organism. However, there are many of the propositions which are not necessarily an integral part of Whitehead's philosophy and which are essential to this writer's own philosophy as derived from his own experiences as well as a variety of sources in the history of philosophy—particularly from Plato, Aristotle, and the organic tradition to the present.

FOUNDATIONAL PHILOSOPHICAL PROPOSITIONS

The Organic Philosophy of Education holds as follows:

(1) *That we live in an organic universe.* Our universe is organic in character throughout. It is characterized by its elements of feeling, thinking, moving, creating, purposing, evolving in the organic sense as opposed to the conception of the world as mechanical, inert, materialistic, and atomistic. As Whitehead has indicated we live in a living universe as opposed to a dead universe.[1] As organic, the world is further characterized by its continuity, connectedness, relatedness, coherence, and internal relationships. It is like a seamless coat in that it admits no real *bifurcation*.[2] Because of the reality of its conjunctiveness and disjunctiveness, however, the universe is conceived of in its *organic-atomistic relations, whole-part relations, one-many relations*, in *unity and diversity*. Its permanent *creative factors* are constantly in process in the *temporal-spatial continuum*.[3] The world is a mixture. Hence it is both being and becoming as it evolves in *the creative advance*.[4]

(2) *That reality is best characterized by a philosophy of organism.* In other words a *philosophy of organism* is ultimately a better characterization of the world than those philosophies termed realism, idealism, pragmatism or the like. This does not for a moment imply that systems of philosophy other than organism lack substantially valid conceptions. The writer merely raises the time honored philosophical question as to which philosophy is most adequate and coherent. A *philosophy of organism* overlaps with philosophies of other systems. However, a *philosophy of organism* is not eclectic in this overlapping. It possesses its own core of coherent conceptions and propositions. Hence, organism is found to have principles in common with parts of realism, idealism, pragmatism, existentialism, and other views. It strives for a higher synthesis. By the same token there are important deviations and distinctions between all of these views.

(3) *That the ultimate entities of nature, though governed by mechanical principles, are not inert, but are enduring structures of activity, and that the nature of each reflects its organic relations with the larger structures of nature in which it enters.*[5] The *entities of*

nature are in whole-part relationships where the unity of any given whole provides orientation for the parts which are mutually dependent and intrinsically related.[6] An analogy may be drawn between the relationships of the human body and those of nature. All of the organs of the body, for example, are related in whole-part structures and functions; the various organs derive their respective functions from their relation to one another and to the whole of which they are a part. They are all related to the environment with which they are continuous.

(4) *That there is a stubborn persistency in the nature of things.* An organic world is characterized by permanence as well as novelty; by *endurance* as well as *fluency;* and by *structure* as well as *process.*[7] A philosophy of process and reality does not mean giving way to a one-sided notion of the world as flux and novelty. To correct this erroneous conception which some seem to have, the reader's attention is called to the proposition that there is a stubborn persistency of the evolved entities of nature.

Organisms which have achieved their being through long ages of evolution are indeed the product of recurring *concrescences* and *evolution.* There is a sense, however, in which their becoming approaches a plateau of *becoming.* It approaches the end of a cycle of development, and a persistent factual *being* is the result. Thus it may well be that man as *Homo sapiens* has approached such a plateau. Within the organic philosophy, it is important that we acknowledge his formal structure within the context of *process.*

(5) *That the world is both a process of becoming and a product in its being.* The cosmology underlying the Organic Philosophy of Education is comparable to Whitehead's *philosophy of organism.* Since, however, Whitehead's cosmology has been inspired by Plato's thought, particularly in his *Timaeus,* there are roots in Plato's fundamental conceptions too.[8] According to Raphael Demos, Plato said that the organic creature which we know as the world of experience is a mixture formed by the creative factors.[9] The latter Plato held as the *realm of being,* known only through reason and speculation, or dialectic. These *creative factors* for Plato included *God,* the *Pattern,* the *Receptacle,* the *Good,* and the *Eros.*[10] God was the maker or father,

98

the cause, the teleological source. The pattern was the element of structure and order, or the limiting principle. It included the mathematical basis for all explanations of nature; it included the *forms*, the *mathematicals*, the *categories*, and *reason*.[11] The *receptacle* represented the *primordial chaos*, or the principle of the *unlimited*. To us today it is the *space-time continuum;* in another sense it represents passion, the irrational, and brute fact. The *Good* is the principle of the best; it is equivalent to beauty and perfection. The other creative factor is that of *Eros*, which provides the link between the *creative factors* and the *creature of existence*. It might well be the *élan vital* of Bergson's modern philosophy. It is the vital urge toward perfection.

With the modifications made by Whitehead we come to a modern cosmology of organism. The actual world is composed of entities in the process of *birth* and *perishing*, who through *prehension* and *concrescence* contribute to the *creative advance* of that world.[12] Each event in coherence with others contributes to the *being* and *becoming* of the world in the total process.

Actual entities are *events* in the *extensive continuum*. They constitute *reality*. Eternal objects, entities or *forms of definiteness*, are eternal and universal like Plato's *eternal forms*, and transcend time; they are the *possibles* or *abstract potentials* capable of characterizing or informing different actual entities in time-space. As defined by Whitehead, "Any entity whose conceptual recognition does not involve a necessary reference to any definite actual entities of the temporal world is called an eternal object."[13] They subsist in God's primordial conceptuality.

God is also necessary to this cosmology. He has *primordial* and *consequent being* and *becoming;* he is conceptually *primordial* and consequently realized in a process of creation. *God* is the bond between the *conceptual* and the *existential*. *God* is *bipolar* in his *mental* and *physical poles*, and all entities share in this *bipolarity*. As Whitehead says, "The things which are temporal arise by their participation in the things which are eternal."[14]

Whitehead has salvaged much of Plato's cosmology in his modern modification. He does not hold that there is one set of archetypal forms which form the inevitable pattern for the world of becoming. The *eternal objects* are infinite in number; they are *possibles* for *ingression* into actual entities in process. They are not *vacuous entities* floating outside of space, but rather they are the *conceptual envisagements* of God.[15]

Whitehead's world is not *bifurcated* into a world of *being* and *becoming;* the world is *constituted* in its being by its *becoming.* "One principle is that the very essence of real actuality—that is, of the completely real—is *process.* Thus each actual thing is only to be understood in terms of its becoming and perishing."[16]

As noted earlier Whitehead is consistently concerned with *Plato's Seven Notions* in any adequate philosophical explanation.[17] "I mention them because I hold that all philosophy is in fact an endeavour to obtain a coherent system out of some modification of these notions."[18] They are The Ideas, The Physical Elements, The Psyche, The Eros, The Harmony, The Mathematical Relations, and The Receptacle. These metaphysical considerations then figure prominently in the *philosophy of organism.*

It is important to note that Whitehead speaks of *process and reality.* There is *becoming* and *being.* Process is the expression of *creativity* in the world. Yet the *entities* which emerge are the products of that process. Although entities do emerge in time, they are both *fluent* and *enduring.* All entities are exemplifications of *forms.* As temporally enduring entities with forms, they do *possess structure.* Mankind as an evolved species of *Homo sapiens* is both *fluent* and *enduring;* within given epochs he possesses the evolved structure and form of his *being.* As a product of millions of years of evolution he represents evolved structure as well as the fluency of process. Thus, even though a *philosophy of organism* admits the *processual aspects of reality,* for practical purposes it is important that we recognize the existence of temporally enduring structures in relation to other enduring factors in a given *epoch.* In this qualified sense we can rightfully speak of the "nature of something."

(6) *That there are ideal opposites which pervade the world.* As Whitehead says,

In our cosmological construction we are, therefore, left with the final opposites, joy and sorrow, good and evil, disjunction and conjunction—that is to say, the many in one—flux and permanence, greatness and triviality, freedom and necessity, God and the World."[19]

The world is not dual in the sense of absolute divisions or *bifurcations* of *reality;* the world is characterized, however, by contrasting ideals in dynamic relationships which are elsewhere termed "bipolar" or a "union of opposites." Essentially there is a *sameness* and *otherness* which characterizes all thought and existence. The world then is male and female, physical and mental, permanent and novel, and eternal and temporal. As Plato said the world as an organic creature is a mixture.

(7) *That the universe is characterized by bipolar opposites.* Some of the bipolarities are rationality-irrationality, determinacy-indeterminacy, *logoi* and existence, ebb and flow, good and evil, birth and death, eternality and temporality, permanence and novelty, stability and flux, organic and atomistic relations, externality and internality, co-operation and competition, and God and the World and the World and God.[20] Thus the separableness and otherness of things are relatively so and not absolutely so.

(8) *That the organic world is characterized by the principle of bipolarity both metaphysically and in its apparent manifestations.* Essentially *bipolarity* refers to the *unity of opposites* which seems to characterize both thought and existence.[21] *Bipolarity* manifests itself constantly in *sameness* and *otherness, unity* and *diversity,* and *conjunctiveness* and *disjunctiveness.* Bipolar fields of existence or experience are marked by contrasting poles which are not *dualistic,* but are respectively (a) dependent, (b) independent, and (c) interdependent.[22]

(9) *That the principle of unity and diversity is one of the foremost bipolarities of the organic viewpoint.* The significance of this proposition lies in the fact that a definitive stand is taken here on the perennial problem of the "one and the many." Philosophers throughout history have been concerned with this problem. In their speculations

they have been concerned with the question of unity and diversity as it applies to thought and existence. Some philosophers have held that reality is "one" and therefore are known as "monists." Others deny this viewpoint and hold that reality is characterized by diversity; they are known as "pluralists." Plato and other philosophers of the organic tradition have argued that the world is both one and many in different senses. The "one-many" was one of Plato's highest categories and he held that there was an affinity between the one and many as expressed in the laws of thought and its manifestation in the world creature itself.[23]

In the Organic Philosophy of Education there is firm agreement with Whitehead when he says that the problem of the one and the many continues to be the main problem of contemporary philosophy. Indeed his explanation of the concrescence of actual entities is largely the story of how "the many" elements enter into "the unity" of a given entity. In fact most of Whitehead's cosmology is an effort to explain how the actual world is in one sense a unity and another a diversity or plurality.

We cannot here enter into the philosophical ramifications of the problem of the *one and the many.* It should be noted, however, that the *one and many,* or the *principle of unity and diversity,* is one of the foremost bipolarities of this viewpoint. Hence one of the main efforts of this organic formulation has been the correction and reconstruction of educational theories through the application of the *principles of unity and diversity* and other organic principles.

The applications of such principles are many. For example, it is the commonplace contention of some progressive theorists that in view of the "doctrine of individual differences" all educational procedures should be adjusted to individuals. Such proponents allege "that there are no two persons alike, and therefore procedures must be tailored to the individual." Here then is a clear case of a half-truth and an exclusive reliance on the principle of diversity, of "manyness" in Plato's terms. They one-sidedly see only the diversity and differences of their students.

How should this error be corrected in terms of the "one and the many"? Organically we should see persons in virtue of the principle of unity and diversity—in their sameness and in their diversity. The "one and many" category of Platonic organism is but a corollary of another category, "identity and difference." Thus we must see not only the unity or identity of persons or things of a class, such as *Homo sapiens*, but we must correctly see the principle of diversity or difference as well. Consequently it is clear that an educational philosophy cannot be soundly based upon either exclusive view (a) that all persons are alike, or (b) that all persons are different; rather the organic doctrine recognizes both common elements, and individual differences in its view of man.

The doctrine of the one and many has an infinite number of applications from the broadest philosophical conceptions to the most common identification of commonplace things of everyday life. It is the intent of this work to show the significance of this principle in diverse applications to problems of educational theory throughout this presentation.

(10) *That God is an actuality in the organic cosmology.*[24] The organic conception of God as evidenced in both Plato and Whitehead is "panentheistic" and not "theistic" or "pantheistic." A monopolar theism, such as Aristotle's theism, conceives of God as "the supreme as eternal consciousness, not knowing or including the world."[25] Another version of emphasis on the one pole is that of pantheism which recognizes "the supreme as eternal consciousness, knowing and including the world," as in Spinoza and Royce. Panentheism is bipolar in that it recognizes "the supreme as eternal-temporal consciousness, knowing and including the world," as in Plato, Schelling, Fechner and Whitehead.[26]

Speaking of the 'Law of Polarity' as it applied to the panentheistic conception of God, Hartshorne and Reese summarize the three views as follows:

> A principal aim of this sourcebook is to exhibit a pattern in the history of rational reflection about God. . . . What we propose to call 'classical theism' is, in the West, the chief product of this method; in the Orient, its chief product is pantheism. The difference between the two is that theism admits the reality of plurality, potentiality, becoming—as a secondary form of existence "outside" God, in no way constitutive of his reality; whereas

103

pantheism, properly so called, supposes that, although God includes all within himself, still, since he cannot be really complex, or mutable, such categories can only express human ignorance or illusion. Thus, common to theism and pantheism is the doctrine of the invidious nature of categorical contrasts. One pole of each contrary is regarded as more excellent than the other, so that the supremely excellent being cannot be described by the other and inferior pole. At once the dilemma results: either there is something outside of deity, so that the total real is deity-and-something-else, a whole of which deity is merely one constituent; or else the allegedly inferior pole of each categorical contrast is an illusory conception. Theism takes one horn of the dilemma; pantheism, the other. The dilemma, however, is artificial; for it is produced by the assumption that the highest form of reality is to be indicated by separating or purifying one pole of the ultimate contrasts from the other pole.[27]

A *panentheistic* view of God then includes five aspects according to the description given by Hartshorne and Reese:

(1) Eternal: in some aspects of his reality devoid of change . . .
(2) Temporal: in some aspects capable of change . . .
(3) Conscious: Self-aware . . .
(4) Knowing the world or universe, omniscient . . .
(5) World-inclusive, having all things as constituents . . .

It is significant then that the Organic Philosophy of Education is grounded in a *philosophy of organism* which in turn provides a sound basis for a modern cosmology and source of religious as well as philosophical belief. We are deeply indebted to Whitehead and his interpreters for these valuable formulations of organic thought.

(11) *That the laws of nature are to be explained largely through the Doctrine of Law as Immanent.*[29]

By the doctrine of Law as immanent it is meant that the order of nature expresses the characters of the real things which jointly compose the existences to be found in nature. When we understand the essences of these things, we thereby know their mutual relations to each other. Thus according as there are common elements in their various characters, there will necessarily be corresponding identities in their mutual relations. In other words, some partial identity of pattern in the various characters of natural things issues in some partial identity of pattern in the mutual relations of those things. These identities of pattern in the mutual relations are the Laws of Nature. Conversely, a Law is explanatory of some community in character pervading the things which constitute Nature. It is evident that the doctrine involves the negation of "absolute being." It presupposes the essential interdependence of things."[30]

(12) *That the world has an intelligible nature.*[31] It is not without permanent characteristics even though it is in creative process. The world is not mere flux, novelty, chance, precariousness, and unpredictability. Despite its organic character which includes dynamic processes, it does have a nature. It includes principles of stability, endurance, regularity, permanence, purposefulness, abiding values, eternal forms, intelligibility, rationality, as well as the inevitable opposites of these.

Complete and final knowledge is not possible for the finite intelligence of man. Yet if the world were not essentially and theoretically intelligible in its nature, there could be no progress in science, philosophy, religion, or in any branch of human knowledge and wisdom. If all is precarious and unpredictable flux, then any semblance of scientific knowledge is impossible.

(13) *That the temporal world is composed of mixtures, the rational and irrational, the intelligible and the sensible, and the like.* Our theories about the temporal world can only be probable because it is in a constant process of flux and therefore knowledge about it must be hypothetical.

Thus, the world is a stage for conflict; there is the process of determining the indeterminate, the stress between these opposites, the relative success in the adjustment, the constant failure. The duality in the mixture is the source of the moral problem.[32]

(14) *That the rational principle may be defined as an organic principle which holds that there is a source of rationality in the universe; the universe is characterized by elements of rationality and irrationality; this matrix of rationality manifests itself in the potentialities and actualities of human reason and science. It is also exemplified in the actual processes and entities of the Extensive Continuum.*

Organism contends that there is a fundamental affinity between the rational structure of thought itself and the ratios or forms expressed in the entities and forces of the actual world. Here is the rationalistic conviction that intelligence is one of the creative factors of the universe. Here is the conviction which has appealed to organic rationalists from Pythagoras and Plato to Descartes, Leibnitz, Spinoza, and Whitehead.

What is the significance of this belief? This belief in a rationalistic element or creative factor cosmologically signifies an organic faith in an intelligible world. Philosophically it indicates a kind of world in which we can obtain meaning, science, value, order, causality, and purpose. It provides the basis for a life of intelligence. Educationally it signifies a basis for the pursuit of intelligibility and understanding in terms of scientific or philosophical inquiry, as well as the prudential and pragmatic concern with intelligence as applied to problem-solving in the affairs of everyday living. The postulation of a rationality which permeates our real world lifts us out of the life in a philosophical quandry which characterizes those schools of thought who deny or seriously doubt this rational faith.

The rational principle undergirds the organic conception of the field of teaching-learning experiences discussed elsewhere. The organic belief in the actuality of stubborn fact has been indicated. Despite the fluency of actual entities as subjects of the developmental process, they achieve being through concrescence—they become actual objects. Man is in one sense a developing subject; in another sense he has a discernible nature as product or object. This embodiment of forms even in fluency makes for the intelligibility of actual entities. The eternal forms are clearly objects of intelligence. Yet it must be recalled that a philosophy of organism insists upon the concomitant recognition of the 'reformed subjective principle.'

> The reformed subjectivist principle adopted by the philosophy of organism is merely an alternative statement of the principle of relativity . . . This principle states that it belongs to the nature of a 'being' that it is potential for every 'becoming.' Thus all things are to be conceived as qualifications of actual occasions.[33]

That is to say that there is an "objective-relativism" in organic philosophy which says that in one respect objects exist independently or disjunctively, but in a very fundamental sense they are interdependent in their constant interplay.

The reader should not presume that we are affirming a position of pure rationalism. Far from it. The rationalistic element of organism is more than counterbalanced by the role of "feeling." In organism Whitehead has virtually presented a "critique of pure feeling" in paraphrase of Kant's *Critique of Pure Reason.* The aesthetic component is crucial and fundamental in the *philosophy of organism.* Likewise there is the recognition of limits of human rationality, and the acknowledgment of the irrational.

(15) *That the world of the time-space continuum is a mixture of the creative elements.* The metaphysical elements are immanent in the world of phenomenal actuality. As Demos suggests *in re* Plato's *Timaeus,* which furnishes a substantial point of departure for the organic cosmology:

> Finally, the world is a mixture of the creative factors. This makes the relation of the creative factors and the creature immediate; the metaphysical elements are ingredients of the world, they enter into its composition; they are immanent. The world is the creative factors in their togetherness.[34]

(16) *That there are actual entities.* Whitehead has said that he intended to place idealism on a realistic base.[35] In so doing he emphasized the reality of *actual entities* as follows: "'Actual entities'—also termed 'actual occasions'—are the final real things of which the world is made up. There is no going behind actual entities to find anything more real."[36] The *actual entities* have emerged from the world of the *extensive continuum* very concretely in time-space. They become through *prehension* and *concrescence* in interaction with other entities. Each entity has a mental and physical pole. Through its mental pole it has conceptual prehensions of ideal forms. Through its physical pole it prehends or appropriates data from other entities of its environment. Each such actual entity is a *subject-superject.*

(17) *That there is always the embodiment of form within existing entities.* It should not be overlooked that a *philosophy of organism* does not postulate *process* as formless flux. Entities and societies of entities have *being* as well as *becoming.* A bar of steel is an entity

107

and it is an event. It is in the process of *becoming* from its birth to its death. Its atomic elements are in motion. Yet it does have *endurance* as well as *fluency*. It *is* a bar of steel with certain definite characteristics during its lifetime. It does possess *structural intelligibility*. It is the exemplification of forms which can be known scientifically. For all practical purposes we can treat such entities or structures as "substances," as long as we remember the metaphysical qualifications. Mankind as evolved *Homo sapiens* then has structure and function; he has an enduring nature in this sense.

(18) *The actual world is involved in creativity.* All entities are involved in constant creativity. The very process of becoming in terms of *prehension* and *concrescence* is that of *creativity*. Creativity itself is an eternal object as is exemplified in the activity of actual entities. God as an actual entity is creative; he weaves his primordial conceptuality upon his temporal consequent becoming. All entities in their complex interactions contribute to the *creative advance* of the world through the joint processes of creativity.

(19) *That the qualitative elements of the world are characterized by mathematical harmonies.* Greek philosophers were impressed with the harmonies and proportions of all reality. Plato in particular emphasized the harmonies of the spheres which characterized both realms of being and becoming.

> In respect to Harmony, the Greeks made a discovery which is a landmark in the history of thought. They found out that exact Mathematical Relationships, as they exist in Geometry and in the numerical proportions of measurements, are realized in various outstanding examples of beautiful composition.[37]

The Greek discovery of the relationships between the vibrations of stringed instruments and mathematical ratios was an immense one. To the philosophical mind of Plato it meant that mathematical proportions and ratios characterized the world. Science seeks the exact ratios exemplified in entities and events; man seeks harmonious adjustment to his world.

(20) *That there are eternal objects.* These *eternal objects* as recognized by Whitehead are similar to Plato's *eternal forms* or *ideas*,

but with some significant differences; the *eternal objects* are synonymously *possibles, pure potentials,* or *forms of definiteness.* Whitehead defines them as, "Any entity whose conceptual recognition does not involve a necessary reference to any definite actual entities of the temporal world is called an 'eternal object.' "[38]

Whitehead's *eternal objects* are infinite in number; they do not constitute a single model or ideal architectonic for the world of becoming; they represent an infinite number of *possibles* or *ideal forms* which may or may not ingress into *actual entities.* Furthermore they do not subsist as vacuous entities in nothingness; they are the envisagements of the primordial conceptuality of God; in this sense they are internally related and possibles for exemplification in actual entities in the *extensive continuum.*

(21) *That the forms of thought and existence emanate from a common matrix.* The conceptual forms which are manifest in the cognitive processes of the high-grade human organism are not alien to the forms which are exemplified in other actual entities and objects. They are derived from a common matrix. Thus there is a genuine intelligibility between theoretical inquiry and the forms discovered in existing entities. Entities are intelligible to the extent that they exemplify forms of definiteness. For example, the highest categories of thought manifest the bipolarities of *unity and diversity, being and non-being, identity and difference,* and *truth and falsity.* These categories are essential to human thought and predication. They are also inevitably manifest in the *being* and *becoming* of actual entities in the temporal-spatial continuum. They are manifest in our description of the nature of things, or in statements of human knowledge. When we say "The chair is heavy," we assert it is one object of many; we assert that it has *being* and *non-being;* we see its identity with other chairs as well as its differences; we utter a partial truth and a partial falsity. If we take our statement too seriously, we have made the error of "misplaced concreteness." The "chair" is also many other things we have not mentioned.

(22) *That man is an ambivalent organism because of his exemplification of the bipolar opposites of the world itself.* As a microcosm

of the macrocosm man exemplifies the deeply rooted ideal opposites of the universe. As a high-grade organism the existence of a bipolarity of physical and mental poles in man is most significant. The contrary attractions of physical pleasures and the ideal lures of the mental pole contribute to man's ambivalence. Excessive pursuit of physical pleasures can result in the rejection or diminution of the intellectual, moral, and spiritual life. Man's appetites and passions may contradict his desire for higher experiences. The educational significance of this ambivalent nature is that education should assist man in harmonizing and co-ordinating these contrasting forces of his being. Man, although a temporal creature in one sense, has a longing for and a participation in the eternal. Man is not "dualistic" in nature according to a *philosophy of organism.* He is an organic mixture and embodiment of such contrasts as permanent and novel, spiritual and physical, mental and physical, rational and emotional, comprehension and prehension, intellectual and aesthetic, joy and sorrow, birth and death, the eternal and the temporal. There is no thought of dualistic separations of mind and body. Our whole continuity of human experience convinces us that the relationship between human body and human intelligence is so intimate, interwoven, and intrinsic, that the question of intercommunication between body and mind does not emerge. The body itself is important in the *philosophy of organism.* The body with its subtle feelings, sensations, prehensions, intuitions, emotions, appetites, hungers, and rhythmic demands, is the vital link between external reality and the more cognitive and intellectual functionings of the human intelligence. Since existence is continuous in the organic outlook, it is most difficult to distinguish between so-called external and internal realities.

(23) *That man as Homo sapiens has a discernible and enduring nature as well as a fluent nature.* Man today is a product of the creative advance of the world. Although organicists do not speak of man's nature in terms of the older *substance* theory, this fact does not mean that there is no enduring pattern of man's being which we may call "nature." In terms of this epoch it can be said that man has achieved a relatively stable pattern of characteristics of his being through a process of becoming. Man's present nature as an endur-

ing entity is a stubborn fact. Despite certain apparent plasticity and modifiability of man's nature, it is clear that his being, which is the product of untold millions of years of evolution, represents a patterned concrescence. Although subject to further evolution, man as man today is a relatively enduring product with intelligible characteristics.

(24) *That man is an organic microcosm of the macrocosm.* Man is an evolved product of the *creative advance* of the world; as such he is really a microcosm of the macrocosm; he is a *concrescence* of the multiple creative factors which in process and reality have produced the *entities* of the present *epoch.* Figuratively man is a drop of water of the ocean of the universe. He is the epitome of its ideal and actual possibilities as determined by past events up to the present moment. Man then must be understood as a product of all the complex forces and events of the past. He is the product of prior events and interactions of entities which were in part determined and in part undetermined—but which inevitably became determined.

As such, man must be understood only in part as the product of given cultures. In a larger context man is the product of the totality of forces—which might well be termed metaphysical, physical, biological, as well as cultural.

FOOTNOTES

1. Alfred North Whitehead, *Science and the Modern World* (New York: The American Library, A Mentor Book, by arrangement with the Macmillan Company, 1949), p. 80.

2. A. N. Whitehead, *Process and Reality* (Cambridge: Cambridge University Press, 1929, copyright U.S.A. by Macmillan Co.), pp. 410-11.

3. See A. N. Whitehead's notion of 'extensive continuum,' in *Process and Reality,* pp.. 84-115; see also A. H. Johnson, *Whitehead's Theory of Reality* (Boston: The Beacon Press, 1952), pp. 56-57.

4. A. N. Whitehead, *Process and Reality,* pp. 48, 147, 180.

5. See definition of 'organism' in Webster's *New International Dictionary,* Unabridged, Second Edition.

6. See index and glossary. Also, A. H. Johnson, "Introduction to the Theory of Actual Entities," *Whitehead's Theory of Reality,* Ch. 1, pp. 3-16.

7. A. N. Whitehead, *Process and Reality,* pp. 46, 47, 190, 295 and 305; A. H. Johnson, *Whitehead's Theory of Reality,* pp. 43, 51, 64, and 75-76.

8. A. N. Whitehead, *Process and Reality,* Preface, p. ix.

9. Raphael Demos, *The Philosophy of Plato* (New York: Charles Scribner's Sons, 1939), p. 11.

10. Raphael Demos, "The Creative Factors," in *The Philosophy of Plato*, Part I, pp. 3-129.

11. R. Demos, "The Fundamental Conceptions of Plato's Metaphysics," *The Philosophy of Plato*, Ch. 1, *et passim*, pp. 3-24.

12. See A. N. Whitehead's 'perpetual perishing,' in *Process and Reality*, pp. 40, 83, 113, 118; A. H. Johnson, *Whitehead's Theory of Reality*, pp. 28-29.

13. See 'eternal objects' in A. N. Whitehead, *Process and Reality*, p. 60. Reprinted with permission of Macmillan Company. See also, A. H. Johnson, *Whitehead's Theory of Reality*, pp. 19-20.

14. A. N. Whitehead, *Process and Reality*, p. 63. Reprinted with permission of Macmillan Company.

15. See Dorothy Emmet's discussion of, "Are Eternal Objects Platonic Ideas?" in *Whitehead's Philosophy of Organism* (London: The Macmillan Company, 1932), Ch. V, pp. 102-39. She offers the interpretation that the eternal objects are envisagements in the Primordial Nature of God, pp. 116-17.

16. Alfred N. Whitehead, *Adventures of Ideas* (New York: The Macmillan Company, 1933), p. 354. Reprinted with permission of the publisher.

17. A. N. Whitehead, *Adventures of Ideas*, p. 354.

18. A. N. Whitehead, *Adventures of Ideas*, p. 354. Reprinted with permission of the publisher.

19. A. N. Whitehead, *Adventures of Ideas*, pp. 482-83. Reprinted with permission of the publisher.

20. A. N. Whitehead, "The Ideal Opposites," *Process and Reality*, Ch. 1, Part V, pp. 477-97. See also, A. N. Whitehead, *Adventures of Ideas*, pp. 244-45.

21. This writer's views are partly Platonic in origin as are many of Whitehead's philosophical conceptions. "That is to say, he (Whitehead) is claiming to follow the Platonic intellectualistic tradition, that there is a real affinity between Reason in us, and the structure, which is an objective *logos*, in the nature of things." From D. Emmet, *Whitehead's Philosophy of Organism*, p. 46. Reprinted with permission of the copyright holder, St. Martin's Press, associates of publisher, Macmillan & Company Ltd. of London.

22. See A. J. Bahm, "Organicism," in *Philosophy: An Introduction* (New York: John Wiley & Sons., Inc., 1953, copyright by publisher (1953), Ch. 20, pp. 234-54.

23. See R. Demos, *The Philosophy of Plato*, for amplification of this subject.

24. This proposition is derived directly from Whitehead's conception of God as an actual entity, exemplifying metaphysical principles.

25. See Charles Hartshorne and William Reese, editors, *Philosophers Speak of God* (Chicago: University of Chicago Press, 1953, copyright 1953 by

the University of Chicago), p. 1. Reprinted with permission of the publisher.

26. C. Hartshorne and W. Reese, *Philosophers Speak of God,* p. 1. Reprinted with permission of the publisher.

27. C. Hartshorne and W. Reese, *Philosophers Speak of God,* p. 1. Reprinted with permission of the publisher.

28. C. Hartshorne and W. Reese, *Philosophers Speak of God,* p. 1. Reprinted with permission of the publisher.

29. A. N. Whitehead, *Adventures of Ideas,* pp. 142-44.

30. A. N. Whitehead, *Adventures of Ideas,* p. 142. Reprinted with permission of the publisher.

31. Wilbur Marshall Urban, *The Intelligible World* (New York: The Macmillan Company, 1929).

32. R. Demos, *The Philosophy of Plato,* p. 11. Reprinted with permission of the publisher.

33. A. N. Whitehead, *Process and Reality,* p. 233. Reprinted with permission of the Macmillan Company.

34. R. Demos, *The Philosophy of Plato,* p. 6. Reprinted with permission of the publisher.

35. See Preface to A. N. Whitehead, *Process and Reality,* p. vii.

36. A. N. Whitehead, *Process and Reality,* p. 24. Reprinted with permission of the Macmillan Company.

37. A. N. Whitehead, *Adventures of Ideas,* p. 190. Reprinted with permission of the publisher.

38. A. N. Whitehead, *Process and Reality,* p. 60. Reprinted with permission of the Macmillan Company.

6

FOUNDATIONAL PHILOSOPHICAL PROPOSITIONS—continued

CONTINUING the basic propositions the organic educational philosophy holds:—

(25) *That speculative and experimental modes of inquiry are necessary to one another.* Exclusive dependence upon modes of speculation or experimentation is deplorable. Scientific inquiry needs the fruits of speculative thought, and philosophical speculation needs the facts of scientific inquiry. Likewise, the conceptual order complements the observational order.

> Our co-ordinated knowledge, which in the general sense of the term is Science, is formed by a meeting of two orders of experience. One order is constituted by the direct, immediate discriminations of particular observations. The other order is constituted by our general way of conceiving the Universe. They will be called, the Observational Order and the Conceptual Order. The first point to remember is that the observational order is invariably interpreted in terms of the concepts supplied by the conceptual order.[1]

(26) *That human beings should utilize all modes of experience open to them in prehending and comprehending their world.* Whitehead has called attention to the varieties of human experience and the necessity of utilizing all types of experience.[2] The methods of introspection, intuition, literature, humanities, sciences, and ordinary experience should be included. This writer adds that in view of the apparent validities existing in the various "ways of knowing"[3] (theories of knowledge), we should avail ourselves of all types of experiences, including the empirical, rational, intuitional, authoritative, pragmatic, and skeptical.

114

The value theory is both ideal and actual, or transcendent in one sense and immanent in another. To the extent that there are ideal values in the eternal forms which defy perfect or final embodiment in actual things in process, we can say that the ideal values are in this sense transcendent. To the extent that ideal values have been exemplified in the creative advance of the world, that is they have contributed to the determination of actual entities, there is said to be an immanence of norms or values. Thus to the extent that actual entities have exemplified certain forms and values in their real internal constitutions, and to the extent that they have achieved determined being, these values in actual entities are immanent.

(27) *That human thought processes necessarily involve concepts of contrast.* There is a profound unity undergirding human rational thought. Human thought necessarily involves forms of contrast; these forms of contrast are inherent in thought and are thereby universal for *Homo sapiens.* The writer refers here to the proposition that thought necessarily involves such implicit or explicit contrasts as suggested in the *categories* of Plato. Thought involves *Sameness* and *Otherness, Identity* and *Difference, Truth* and *Falsity,* and *Being* and *Non-Being.* Rational thought requires predication, which in turn contains these contrasts. If we say, "This is a book," we assert that it has been perceived as a book and not something else. We assert a kind of being and non-being. We utilize similarity and difference in our perception. The proposition about the book is partially true in a sense, and partially false—it is also other things. There is a sense in which Plato was right in saying that there is a natural metaphysics of thought itself.

(28) *That there is an immanence of oughtness in the very nature of things.* Man in his evolved nature embodies an inherent oughtness for his living. His actualized being contains the generic requisites for his living. Man ought to act intelligently, morally, spiritually, and according to his nature. In this sense there is an immanence in his very being. Furthermore, man should actualize ideal values in the existing conditions of his epoch.

(29) *That values are both ideal and actual.* Values are not merely subjective; they inhere in the very nature of things; they are part of

the objective constitution of entities. As Whitehead says, the flower that blooms in the desert has its own beauty and is dimly appreciated by the life about it.[4] *Concrescence* involves the appropriation of value from other actual entities. There are also ideal values or abstract possibilities of value. These ideal values are not complete in themselves, for they are only possible values for *exemplification* in *actual entities*. *Ideal values* need this exemplification in actual entities through ingression to complete their possibility of realization. We have referred elsewhere to the fact that God serves as the binding element for the translation of abstract values into concrete entities.[5] Organic values then are not assigned to some transcendental realm beyond attainment; as ideal values they are possibles for exemplification in our actual existence as real entities. They are transcendental in that they may not be perfectly embodied *per se*.

(30) *That man can experience eternal values in his temporal existence.* In large measure the traditional dichotomy between "other worldliness" and "this worldliness" can be overcome through the realization that man can experience *eternal values* in his *temporal existence*. As Plato suggested the temporal musical instrument can play eternal harmonies while it enjoys its existence. Values derived from *eternal objects* can be enjoyed in the particular conditions of a given temporal epoch and through the media of the existing entities of that time and place. Thus the eternal values are exemplified and objectified in the concreteness of the given entities of an epoch. Justice, for example, is an eternal object; yet as actualized in the relations of concrete entities it becomes a relative value as felt and conceived in a determinate situation. In the situation it is relative and not absolute; it is this complex situation with combinations of justice and other eternal objects that makes the problem on the practical level so difficult.

(31) *That the spiritual function of man is largely his identity with the world.* Man in his many-sidedness is very much a part of the cosmos as well as the human society. Leaving the social side of man's existence for a moment, the spirit of man is also concerned with his solitariness and his place in the world.

In its solitariness the spirit asks, What, in the way of value, is the attainment of life? And it can find no such value till it has merged its individual claim with that of the objective universe. Religion is world-loyalty.[6]

(32) *That the existence of evil in the world is one of the tragic truths of reality.* Evil cannot be wished away, for it is part of the creative advance of the world. The fluctuating ratios of good and evil are inevitable. The very processes of concrescence of entities in the determination of their respective beings involve good and evil.[7] Humans can reduce evil in their lives, but they can never completely eliminate it from existence. "No religion which faces facts can minimize the evil in the world, not merely the moral evil, but the pain and suffering."[8]

(33) *That the quest for universality is motivated by the desire for some connection with permanence in the world.* Man does not want to be lost in the hurly-burly of immediate detail.

The reason of the connection between universality and solitariness is that universality is a disconnection from immediate surroundings. It is an endeavour to find something permanent and intelligible by which to interpret the confusion of immediate detail.[9]

(34) *That doubt about the divinity of the universe does not in itself make one irreligious.*[10] Most thinking persons have evolved in their conceptions of God and the universe. During the time of this evolution they have had conflicts and doubts within their complex experiences of life. During periods of personal loss and deep bereavement many have no doubt experienced an all pervasive feeling of loneliness in the sea of reality. Many have felt forsaken even by God. Whitehead with his usual penetration has divined this too and said: "It belongs to the depth of the religious spirit to have felt forsaken, even by God."[11]

(35) *That one's religious life may or may not be furthered through institutional rituals.*[12] Since religion is largely a matter of what one does with his solitariness, it is quite possible that one can be devoutly religious in his own right.

Thus religion is solitariness; and if you are never solitary, you are never religious. Collective enthusiasms, revivals, institutions, churches, rituals, bibles, codes of behaviour, are the trappings of religion, its passing forms. They may be useful, or harmful; they may be authoritatively ordained, or merely temporary expedients. But the end of religion is beyond all this.[13]

(36) *That "religion is what man does with his solitariness."*[14] One of the most succinct and meaningful definitions of religion in my opinion is that furnished by Whitehead. Religion is man's feeling of his relationship as an individual with the universe. The completely socially oriented person is afraid to be alone; he is lost when he is not part of the crowd. Man should cultivate his powers of solitariness as well as his social being. "Accordingly, what should emerge from religion is individual worth of character."[15]

(37) *That we must not make the error of reductionism in conceiving of man narrowly as a social product.* Man is necessarily a social being, but he is more than that.

You cannot abstract society from man; most psychology is herd-psychology. But all collective emotions leave untouched the awful ultimate fact, which is the human being, consciously alone with itself, for its own sake.[16]

Man must find his place in the cosmos.

(38) *That the development of man is not limited to his social environment; human development requires individualistic internal nurture and an intimate feeling of community with those elements of permanence in the world.* Man is a product of the cosmos as well as of his immediate culture. Hence the importance of religion in man's development.

Religion is the art and the theory of the internal life of man, so far as it depends on the man himself and on what is permanent in the nature of things.[17]

(39) *That one's character is fundamentally dependent upon his beliefs.* To believe at all one must have faith in something whether it be reason, experience, or revelation. One's religion in the final analysis is a matter of his faith.

Your character is developed from your faith. This is the primary religious truth from which no one can escape. Religion is force of belief cleansing the inward parts. For this reason the primary religious virtue is sincerity, a penetrating sincerity.[18]

(40) *That modern man is suffering from the loss of religious moorings.* Some of the modern existentialists have correctly pointed out that for modern man the statement that "God is dead" is a very real one.[19] Hence man is alone; he feels a sense of homelessness in his modern world. As Whitehead says, "The modern world has lost God and is seeking him."[20]

(41) *That God is necessary to the actual world, and that the actual world is necessary to God.*[21] Whitehead's explanation of the reciprocal role of God and the actual World is indeed a fundamental one. God is the necessary binding element between abstract forms (possibles) and actual entities (exemplifications in time-space).

Apart from God, there would be no actual world; and apart from the actual world with its creativity, there would be no rational explanation of the ideal vision which constitutes God.[22]

(42) *That God and the World need each other.* "It is as true to say that God creates the World, as that the World creates God."[23]

God and the World are the contrasted opposites in terms of which Creativity achieves its supreme task of transforming disjoined multiplicity, with its diversities in opposition, into concrescent unity, with its diversities in contrast. In each actuality there are two concrescent poles of realization—'enjoyment' and 'appetition,' that is, the 'physical' and the 'conceptual.' For God the conceptual is prior to the physical, for the World the physical poles are prior to the conceptual poles.[24]

God is that function in the world by reason of which our purposes are directed to the ends which in our own consciousness are impartial as to our own interests.[25]

He is the binding element in the world.[26]

He is not the world, but the valuation of the world.[27]

(43) *That an organic world is a fusion of elements of permanence and flux.*

The vicious separation of the flux from the permanence leads to the concept of an entirely static God, with eminent reality, in relation to an entirely fluent world, with deficient reality. But if the opposites, static and fluent, have once been so explained as separately to characterize diverse actualities, the interplay be-

119

tween the thing which is static and the things which are fluent involves contradiction at every step in its explanation.[28]

(44) *That God moves the world by the lure of the true, good, and beautiful.*

He does not create the world, He saves it: or, more accurately, He is the poet of the world, with tender patience leading it by his vision of truth, beauty, and goodness.[29]

(45) *That God has a consequent nature which binds him with all actual entities.*

But God, as well as being primordial, is also consequent. He is the beginning and the end. He is not the beginning in the sense of being in the past of all members. He is the presupposed actuality of conceptual operation, in unison of becoming with every other creative act. Thus, by reason of the relativity of all things, there is a reaction of the world on God. He shares with every new creation its actual world; and the concrescent creature is objectified in God as a novel element in God's objectification of that actual world. This prehension into God of each creature is directed with the subjective aim, and clothed with the subjective form, wholly derivative from his all-inclusive primordial valuation. God's conceptual nature is unchanged, by reason of its final completeness. But his derivative nature is consequent upon the creative advance of the world.[30]

(46) *That God is bipolar in nature.*[31] He has mental and physical poles; they are manifest as a *primordial* and *consequent nature;* God's primordial nature represents the *conceptual unification* of all *eternal objects;* God is an *actual entity* expressed in his consequent nature as constituted by prehensions of other actual entities. God weaves his primordial conceptual being upon his actuality in the *creative advance* of the world. God is *"panentheistic"* in that he is constituted by a bipolarity of his primordial and consequent nature.

Viewed as primordial, he is the unlimited conceptual realization of the absolute wealth of potentiality. In this aspect, he is not *before* all creation, but *with* all creation. But, as primordial, so far is he from 'eminent reality,' that in this abstraction he is 'deficiently actual'—and this in two ways. His feelings are only conceptual and so lack the fullness of actuality. Secondly, conceptual feelings, apart from complex integration with physical feelings, are devoid of consciousness in their subjective forms.[32]

He is the lure for feeling, the eternal urge of desire.[33]

(47) *That God is an exemplification of metaphysical principles.*[34] God is not an exception to metaphysical principles; he is the chief exemplification of such organic principles.

(48) *That philosophy is the handmaiden of religion.* History offers ample proof of the proposition that philosophy is the handmaiden of religion. Certainly the rise of the great religions of the world shows a close kinship with philosophical conceptions and inquiries. If we are to nurture religion in our own lives, we must also nurture the spirit of philosophy. "The peculiar position of religion is that it stands between abstract metaphysics and the particular principles applying to only some among the experiences of life."[35] Furthermore religion in its intuitions has need for philosophy in its rational articulation. "The rational religion must have recourse to metaphysics for scrutiny of its terms."[36]

(49) *That conflict between science and religion is unnecessary.* There is no necessary antagonism between these respective fields of inquiry and experience. As Whitehead says of this conflict between science and religion:

> In one sense, therefore, the conflict between science and religion is a slight matter which has been unduly emphasized. A mere logical contradiction cannot in itself point to more than the necessity of some readjustments, possibly of a very minor character on both sides. Remember the widely different aspects of events which are dealt with in science and in religion respectively. Science is concerned with the general conditions which are observed to regulate physical phenomena; whereas religion is wholly wrapped up in the contemplation of moral and aesthetic values. On the one side there is the law of gravitation, and on the other the contemplation of the beauty of holiness. What one side sees, the other misses; and *vice versa.*[37]

Conflict occurs only when dogmatic stands are taken by the protagonists of each field and an unwillingness exists on the part of one or both to work toward continual development and reconciliation.

> Religion will not regain its old power until it can face change in the same spirit as does science. Its principles may be eternal, but the expression of those principles requires continual development. This evolution of religion is in the main a disengagement of its own proper ideas from the adventitious notions which have

121

crept into it by reason of the expression of its own ideas in terms of the imaginative picture of the world entertained in previous ages. Such a release of reᴿgion from the bonds of imperfect science is all to the good. It stresses its own message. The great point to be kept in mind is that normally an advance in science will show that statements of various religious beliefs require some sort of modification . . . The progress of science must result in the unceasing codification of religious thought, to the great advantage of religion.[38]

(50) *That there is no necessary conflict between philosophy and science.*[39] The organic viewpoint acknowledges our indebtedness to both science and philosophy in their respective contributions and in their reciprocal interplay. Scientific facts and observations are meaningless without an over-all philosophical framework for interpretation. Science is in part dependent upon philosophical speculation with respect to the concepts within a cosmology of such topics as space, time, causation, form, matter, organism, function, or structure. Philosophy on the other hand with its important speculative tasks cannot function in isolation from science; the experimentation, empirical verification, the factual observations, and other advances of science and scientific method are necessary aspects of philosophical inquiry and generalization.

Science on its empirical and experimental side is indispensable to an adequate philosophy. The purpose of science is to search out exemplifications of conceptually designated laws of nature or the universe. Philosophy profits from the findings of science; the relationship is reciprocal. Without the imaginative speculations, the dialectical inquiries, the penetrating flights of reason in the ideational realms of philosophy and mathematics, science would be limited indeed.

Our organic orientation then is found in a tradition of organic thinkers from Plato to Whitehead. We cannot limit ourselves to the religious, scientific, or philosophical viewpoints. We entertain an organic world which is both one and many, permanent and changing, determined and undetermined, and both rational and irrational, as well as manifesting what we in varying perspectives term good or bad. It is a world in which there is an actual God, but he is not

122

everything; he is a representation of the sources of good, value, intelligibility, order, beauty, and purpose.[40]

(51) *"That philosophy always buries its undertakers."*[41] Etienne Gilson points out in his *Unity of Philosophical Experience* that the history of philosophy indicates that with the rise and fall of particular philosophical systems there recurs an attempt to do away with philosophy. "The so-called death of philosophy being regularly attended by its revival, some new dogmatism should now be at hand. In short, the first law to be inferred from philosophical experience is: *Philosophy always buries its undertakers.*"[42] Despite the recent attempts to destroy philosophy, it is very much alive. The Organic Philosophy of Education is dedicated to the important role of philosophy throughout human affairs.

Summary. The foregoing educational propositions are grounded in foundational philosophical propositions. In summary form, the Organic Philosophy of Education holds the following beliefs:

(1) That we live in an organic universe.

(2) That reality is best characterized by a philosophy of organism.

(3) That the ultimate entities of nature, though governed by mechanical principles, are not inert, but are enduring structures of activity, and that the nature of each reflects its organic relations with the larger structures of nature in which it enters.

(4) That there is a stubborn persistency in the nature of things.

(5) That the world is both a process of becoming and a product in its being.

(6) That there are ideal opposites which pervade the world.

(7) That the universe is characterized by bipolar opposites.

(8) That the organic world is characterized by the principle of bipolarity both metaphysically and in its apparent manifestations.

(9) That the principle of unity and diversity is one of the foremost bipolarities of the organic viewpoint.

(10) That God is an actuality in the organic cosmology.

(11) That the laws of nature are to be explained largely through the Doctrine of Law as Immanent in the Organic cosmology.

(12) That the world has an intelligible nature.

123

(13) That the temporal world is composed of mixtures, the rational and irrational, the intelligible and the sensible and the like.

(14) That the rational principle may be defined as an organic principle which holds that there is a source of rationality in the universe; the universe is characterized by elements of rationality and irrationality; this matrix of rationality manifests itself in potentialities and actualities of human reason and science. It is also exemplified in the actual processes and entities of the Extensive Continuum.

(15) That the world of the Extensive Continuum is a mixture of the creative elements.

(16) That there are actual entities which emerge in the world of process.

(17) That there is always the embodiment of form within existing entities.

(18) That the actual world is involved in creativity.

(19) That the qualitative elements of the world are characterized by mathematical harmonies. See also, Friedrich Nietzsche, "Zarathustra's Prologue," *Thus Spake Zarathustra*.

(20) That there are eternal objects as pure potentials.

(21) That the forms of thought and existence emanate from a common matrix.

(22) That man is an ambivalent organism because of his exemplification of the bipolar opposites of the world itself.

(23) That man as *Homo sapiens* has a discernible and relatively enduring nature as well as an evolving fluent nature.

(24) That man is an organic microcosm of the macrocosm.

(25) That speculative and experimental modes of inquiry are necessary to one another.

(26) That human beings should utilize all modes of experience open to them in prehending and comprehending their world.

(27) That human thought processes necessarily involve concepts of contrast.

(28) That there is an immanence of oughtness in the very nature of things. (There is also a sense of transcendency of ideal forms.)

(29) That values are both ideal and actual.

(30) That man can experience eternal values in his temporal existence.

(31) That the spiritual function of man is largely his identity with the world itself.

(32) That the existence of evil in the world is one of the organic truths of reality.

(33) That the quest for universality is motivated by the desire for some connection with permanence in the world.

(34) That doubt about the divinity of the universe does not in itself make one irreligious.

(35) That one's religious life may or may not be furthered through institutional rituals.

(36) That 'religion is what man does with his solitariness.'

(37) That we must not make the error of reductionism in conceiving of man narrowly as a social product.

(38) That the development of man is not limited to his social environment; human development requires individualistic internal nurture and an intimate feeling of community with those elements of permanence in the world.

(39) That one's character is fundamentally dependent upon his beliefs.

(40) That modern man is suffering from the loss of religious moorings.

(41) That God is necessary to the actual world, and that the actual world is necessary to God.

(42) That God and the World need each other.

(43) That an organic world is a fusion of elements of permanence and flux.

(44) That God moves the World by the lure of the true, good, and beautiful.

(45) That God has a consequent nature which binds him with all entities.

(46) That God is bipolar or 'panentheistic' in nature.

(47) That God is an exemplification of metaphysical principles.

(48) That philosophy is the handmaiden of religion.

(49) That conflict between science and religion is unnecessary.

(50) That there is no necessary conflict between philosophy and science.

(51) "That philosophy always buries its undertakers."

FOOTNOTES

1. Alfred North Whitehead, *Adventures of Ideas* (New York: The Macmillan Company, 1933), p. 198. Reprinted with permission of the publisher.

2. A. N. Whitehead, *Adventures of Ideas,* pp. 290-91.

3. Wm. Pepperell Montague, *Ways of Knowing* (New York: The Macmillan Company, 1925), pp. 292-94. Montague shows how the respective validities of various epistemological methods can be reconciled.

4. A. H. Johnson, *Whitehead's Theory of Reality* (Boston: The Beacon Press, 1952), p. 106.

5. A. N. Whitehead, "Religion in the Making," chapters I, II, III, IV, *Alfred North Whitehead: An Anthology,* selected by F. S. C. Northrop and Mason W. Gross (New York: The Macmillan Company, 1953).

6. A. N. Whitehead, "Religion in the Making," *Alfred North Whitehead: An Anthology,* p. 489. Reprinted with permission of the publisher.

7. A. N. Whitehead, "Religion in the Making," *Alfred North Whitehead: An Anthology,* pp. 484-85.

8. A. N. Whitehead, "Religion in the Making," *Alfred North Whitehead: An Anthology,* p. 484. Reprinted with permission of the publisher.

9. A. N. Whitehead, "Religion in the Making," *Alfred North Whitehead: An Anthology,* p. 484. Reprinted with permission of the publisher.

10. A. N. Whitehead, "Religion in the Making," *Alfred North Whitehead: An Anthology,* pp. 472-73.

11. A. N. Whitehead, "Religion in the Making," *Alfred North Whitehead: An Anthology,* p. 473. Reprinted with permission of the publisher.

12. A. N. Whitehead, "Religion in the Making," *Alfred North Whitehead: An Anthology,* p. 472.

13. A. N. Whitehead, "Religion in the Making," *Alfred North Whitehead: An Anthology,* p. 472. Reprinted with permission of the publisher.

14. A. N. Whitehead, "Religion in the Making," *Alfred North Whitehead: An Anthology,* p. 472. Reprinted with permission of the publisher.

15. A. N. Whitehead, "Religion in the Making," *Alfred North Whitehead: An Anthology,* p. 472. Reprinted with permission of the publisher.

16. A. N. Whitehead, "Religion in the Making," *Alfred North Whitehead: An Anthology,* p. 472. Reprinted with permission of the publisher.

17. A. N. Whitehead, "Religion in the Making," *Alfred North Whitehead: An Anthology,* p. 472. Reprinted with permission of the publisher.

18. A. N. Whitehead, "Religion in the Making," *Alfred North Whitehead: An Anthology,* p. 472. Reprinted with permission of the publisher.

19. Ralph Harper and Robert Ulich, "Significance of Existence and Recognition for Education," in *Modern Philosophies and Education* (Chicago: The National Society for the Study of Education, 1955), Part I, *Fifty-fourth Yearbook*, p. 217.

20. A. N. Whitehead, "Religion in the Making," *Alfred North Whitehead: An Anthology*, p. 494. Reprinted with permission of the publisher.

21. A. N. Whitehead, "Religion in the Making," *Alfred North Whitehead: An Anthology*, p. 526.

22. A. N. Whitehead, "Religion in the Making," *Alfred North Whitehead: An Anthology*, p. 526. Reprinted with permission of the publisher.

23. Alfred North Whitehead, *Process and Reality* (Cambridge: Cambridge University Press, 1929, copyright in U.S.A., by Macmillan Co.), p. 492. Reprinted with permission of the Macmillan Company.

24. A. N. Whitehead, *Process and Reality*, pp. 492-93. Reprinted with permission of the Macmillan Company.

25. A. N. Whitehead, "Religion in the Making," *Alfred North Whitehead: An Anthology*, p. 527. Reprinted with permission of the publisher.

26. A. N. Whitehead, "Religion in the Making," *Alfred North Whitehead: An Anthology*, p. 527. Reprinted with permission of the publisher.

27. A. N. Whitehead, "Religion in the Making," *Alfred North Whitehead: An Anthology*, p. 527. Reprinted with permission of the publisher.

28. A. N. Whitehead, *Process and Reality*, pp. 490-91. Reprinted with permission of the Macmillan Company.

29. A. N. Whitehead, *Process and Reality*, p. 490. Reprinted with permission of the Macmillan Company.

30. A. N. Whitehead, *Process and Reality*, p. 488. Reprinted with permission of the Macmillan Company.

31. A. N. Whitehead, *Process and Reality*, p. 486.

32. A. N. Whitehead, *Process and Reality*, p. 486. Reprinted with permission of the Macmillan Company.

33. A. N. Whitehead, *Process and Reality*, p. 487. Reprinted with permission of the Macmillan Company.

34. A. N. Whitehead, *Process and Reality*, p. 486.

35. A. N. Whitehead, "Religion in the Making," *Alfred North Whitehead: An Anthology*, p. 478. Reprinted with permission of the publisher.

36. A. N. Whitehead, "Religion in the Making," *Alfred North Whitehead: An Anthology*, p. 496. Reprinted with permission of the publisher.

37. Alfred North Whitehead, "Religion and Science," *Science and the Modern World* (New York: The New American Library, A Mentor Book, by arrangement with The Macmillan Company, Second Printing, 1949), Ch. 12, p. 184. Reprinted with permission of the publisher.

38. A. N. Whitehead, *Science and the Modern World*, pp. 188-89. Reprinted with permission of the publisher.

39. A. N. Whitehead, *Science and the Modern World*, p. 184.

40. A. N. Whitehead, "Religion in the Making," *Alfred North Whitehead: An Anthology*, pp. 523-28.

41. Etienne Gilson, *The Unity of Philosophical Experience* (New York: Charles Scribner's Sons, 1937), p. 306. Reprinted with permission of the publisher.

42. E. Gilson, *The Unity of Philosophical Experience*, p. 306. Reprinted with permission of the publisher.

PART III

The Educational Process

7

BACKGROUNDS OF BIPOLARITY

IN Part III we shall move from our previous survey of foundational propositions to a consideration of some of these conceptions as they apply to crucial problems of the educational process. Some of the questions with which we shall be concerned in this part are: What do you mean by the *principle of bipolarity?* How does it apply to the educational process? How do you propose to reconcile *realms of reason* and *experience?* What is the role of *intelligibility* in the educational process? How are the valid elements of *objectivity* and *subjectivity* to be reconciled in the educational process? What is the organic conception of *creativity* in the educational process? What is the *organic theory of control?* What is the *organic theory of creativity?* What are the *types of creativity?*

In this chapter we shall probe further into the *principle of bipolarity.* We need to know something of its historical treatment as well as contemporary interpretations. Some of the questions to be considered are as follows: What are some of the "'opposites" to be considered? What are some of the historical sources of the bipolar problem? What were the views of Plato and Aristotle? What were some of the medieval views? What were the views of the German idealists? What are the evaluations of these views by this organic philosophy?

Introduction

One of the perennial problems of philosophy is that of contraries, opposites, contradictions and contrasts. Problems of reality, knowledge, logic, and value are inevitably involved with the explanations of various types of oppositions. Schools of thought such as *monism,*

131

dualism, pluralism, and *organism* have flourished in their respective responses to these problems.[1] It is no overstatement to say that one of the enduring challenges to philosophy is that of explaining these subtle and complex relationships of seemingly opposing elements and principles. Much of one's philosophical orientation depends upon his explanation of such elements.

Some of the "opposites" which have formed the issues of the long history of western philosophy are as follows:[2]

(1) *Permanence and Change*
(2) *Eternal and Temporal*
(3) *One and Many*
(4) *Ideal and Sensible*
(5) *Being and Becoming*
(6) *Ideal and Material*
(7) *Knowledge and Opinion*
(8) *Form and Matter*
(9) *Absolute and Relative*
(10) *Rational and Empirical*
(11) *Universal and Particular*
(12) *Identity and Difference*
(13) *Continuity and Discontinuity*
(14) *Substance and Function*
(15) *Infinite and Finite*
(16) *Indeterminate and Determinate*
(17) *Internal and External*
(18) *Intrinsic and Instrumental*
(19) *Organic and Atomistic*
(20) *True and False*
(21) *Good and Evil*

It is the writer's contention that one's philosophical propositions with respect to problems of reality, knowledge, and value should be intimately related to one's educational propositions. Hence, before we can turn to some of the major conflicts of educational theory, the organic approach to these perennial oppositions must be set forth. In other words the resolution of such oppositions as *formal* and *informal, structural* and *functional, logical* and *psychological, rational* and *empirical, objective* and *subjective, academic* and *experiential, cognitive* and *conative, theoretical* and *practical, conservative* and *progressive, general* and *special, cultural* and *vocational,* and the like, requires a philosophical orientation of adequate propositions.

It would not be appropriate in this writing to engage in a long survey of philosophical resolutions of this problem of opposites. However, the *principle of bipolarity* as later developed in this educational philosophy can be understood better, if some of the historical and contemporary sources of *bipolarity* are briefly indicated.

We are particularly concerned with any philosophers or educators who have been concerned with the concept of polarity itself, especially those who are concerned with the polar aspects of opposites. One dictionary defines *philosophy of polarity* as follows:

> Philosophies that make the concept of polarity one of the systematic principles according to which opposites involve each other when applied to any significant realm of investigation. Polarity was one of the basic concepts of Cusanus and Schelling. Morris R. Cohen made use of the principle of polarity in scientific philosophy, in biology, in social and historical analysis, in law and in ethics.[8]

It is the purpose here then to provide a brief sketch of some of the notable philosophers and educators who have dealt with the problem of opposites in such a way as to approximate one form or another of polarity or duality. The selection of illustrative philosophers is arbitrary and incomplete. A few of these notable thinkers have been chosen to indicate the variety of sources available to one interested in the problem, from ancient, medieval, modern, and contemporary times. A complete analysis of this problem would lead one through the entire history of philosophy.

Historical Instances of "Opposites"

One does not find clearly formulated instances of "bipolarities" in the long history of philosophy. Instead one finds philosophers in ancient, medieval, and modern times wrestling with the problem of "opposites" in their various ways.[4] Pre-Socratic Greek philosophers such as Pythagoras, Anaximander, Empedocles, and Heraclitus, for example, had their diverse and respective conceptions of the opposing forces of the cosmos. Plato and Aristotle too had their conceptions of the nature of "opposites" and "contraries."[5] Their diverse views contribute to our own appreciations of the problem of opposites and to the nature of bipolarity as viewed today.

Pythagoras, for example, produced "The Table of Ten Opposites" out of his view of the "dyadic" relations of things. They included:

> Odd and Even, Right and Left, Male and Female, Limited and Unlimited, One and Many, Rest and Motion, Square and Rectangle, Straight and Crooked, Light and Darkness, and Good and Bad.[6]

In the far east the Indian and Chinese philosophers formulated the "Binary Wheel of Yang and Yin" which shows they too were cognizant of the bipolar forces of reality as expressed poetically in the conceptions of Heaven and Earth, Light and Darkness, Masculine and Feminine, Good and Bad, and Life and Death.[7] These historical examples are cited as evidence of their concern with the problem of opposites and not necessarily as legitimate bipolarities with which we are bound to agree today. The history of philosophy illustrates the perennial quality of the interest in this problem of opposites. Virtually every philosophical system illustrates some explicit or implicit solution to this problem of opposites, whether it be a monism, dualism, pluralism, or organism in its solution. The problem is perennial; its solution within a given system depends on the presuppositions of that system.

Plato: "Dualist" or "Bipolarist"?

Some philosophers would argue that Plato was not a believer in the *principle of bipolarity*, or "the unity of opposites." Accordingly they would say that since Plato emphasized the ultimate reality of the *realm of being*, as opposed to the *realm of becoming*, that in effect he "bifurcated" his world and gave *being* a superior role in the hierarchy of reality or "great chain of being."[8, 9] Many would say that Plato was a "dualist" in separating the ideal and actual worlds and that therefore he could not have been seriously interested in bipolarity.

On the other side, however, it can be argued that Plato's conceptions seem to reinforce a bipolar principle. Although Plato did

134

make distinctions between the ideal and the actual realms, his whole outlook is organic. As we have noted earlier the actual world is an organic creature which is composed of the mixtures of the creative factors, *God*, the *Mathematicals*, *Pattern*, the *Forms*, the *Good*, the *Eros*, and the *Receptacle*.[10] Thus actual entities are mixtures in the realm of becoming as they embody these creative factors. Actual entities then are mixtures of "forms" and matter," or a unity of opposites.[11]

Only a few of the conceptions in Plato are mentioned here briefly that might be cited in the direction of a bipolarity. Plato's concern with the interdependence of "being" and "becoming" is shown many times in his criticism of those who would defend one to the exclusion of the other.

In the *Sophist*, for example, Plato criticizes the "friends of the forms" or apparently the idealists.[12] As A. E. Taylor says very pointedly,

> From the statement of their theory, it is clear that they are extreme dualists, who regard 'being' and 'becoming' as absolutely sundered. They then identify 'becoming' with the sensible world, and consequently hold that the sensible world has no real existence. To state the same thing from the epistemological standpoint, they deny that sensation has *any* cognitive value, or plays any part in the apprehension of truth. This shows that the reference cannot be to the type of theory ascribed to Socrates in the *Phaedo* and *Republic*. The whole point of the doctrine of 'participation' of sensible things in forms was just to break down the absolute severance between a real world of 'being' and an illusory world of 'becoming,' by ascribing a partial and secondary reality to the sensible. So the doctrine of 'recollection' was intended to assign a genuine, if a humble, part in the process of reaching truth; sensation is, on that theory, just what 'suggests' or 'calls into our minds' the thought of the forms.[13]

Many such evidences could be brought to bear on the contention that Plato's later thought tended more and more toward a "unity of opposites" in terms of being and becoming, one and many, rest and motion, and other fundamental bipolarities. It seems incredible that Plato should really have contended that the ideal realm could exist in absolute independence from the realm of becoming; it is even more obvious that he would never have argued that the realm of becoming could have any existence without the metaphysical creative factors. From this line of argument it would seem that one could find strong evidence for a bipolar conception of dependence, independence, and interdependence in Plato's works.

Aristotle and Contraries

Although Aristotle does not speak directly of bipolarity he does speak pointedly of the relationship of contraries:

> Again, in the list of contraries one of the two columns is privative and all contraries are reducible to being and non-being, and to unity and plurality. And nearly all thinkers agree that being and substance are composed of contraries; at least all name contraries as their first principles—some odd and even, some hot and cold, some limit and the unlimited, some love and strife. And all others as well are evidently reducible to unity and plurality and the principles stated by other thinkers fall entirely under these as their genera. It is obvious then from these considerations too that it belongs to one science to examine being *qua* being. *For all things are contraries or composed of contraries,* and unity and plurality are the starting-points of all contraries. And these belong to one science, whether they have or have not one single meaning.[14]

Although there are certainly important distinctions between the systems of Plato and Aristotle on this very principle, it can be said that they both approximate a doctrine of bipolarity. Some of the relationships in Aristotle which appear to be virtually bipolar in character are the following: the form-matter relationship, the entelechy of potentiality and actuality, the active-passive concept of mind, the Golden Mean in his ethical outlook, the structure-function principle, and man as knower and doer. Although Aristotle does not overtly state that these are "bipolarities" or "unities of opposites" with the characteristics of "dependence, independence, and interdependence," in retrospect from our present position it would not be difficult to project these terms into Aristotle's exposition.

Historically it has been maintained that despite certain common beliefs of Plato and Aristotle, that they represented two divergent philosophies, idealism and realism. It is contended that Aristotle objected to the Platonistic "dualism" of the realm of ideal forms and the realm of becoming, or the bifurcation of the realms of Being and Becoming. This view would make Plato a "dualist" in place of an "organic bipolarist." Perhaps this theory is the more feasible, but there are reasons for believing this answer to be too pat. However, the historian of philosophy, Dr. W. Windelband, has this to say about Aristotle's *Logic* and *Metaphysics*:

> As such, however, it has its roots in the Socratic-Platonic doctrine of ideas. That which truly *is*, is the *general* or *universal*, and knowledge of this is the *conception*. In this respect Aristotle always remained a Platonist. What he combated in the system of his great predecessor was only the *Eleatic assumption of absence of relation,*—absence of relation between general and particular, between Ideas and phenomena, between conceptions and perceptions; *an absence of relation which, in spite of all his efforts, Plato had not overcome, even in the later phase of his teaching.* (italics added) Even as the final cause of occurrence the Ideas remained a world by themselves beside the phenomena. This tearing apart of essence and phenomenon, of Being and Becoming, is, in addition to special dialectical objections, the object of the chief reproach which Aristotle brings against the doctrine of ideas. *While Plato had made two different worlds out of the general which is known by the conception, and the particular* which is perceived, the entire effort of Aristotle is directed toward removing again this division in the conception of reality, and discovering that relation between Idea and phenomenon which shall make conceptional knowledge able to explain what is perceived.[15] (italics added)

The problem resolves itself to this: Did Plato in the later stages of his philosophical development make an absolute separation of realms of Being and Becoming, or was this separation "bipolar" in that it was conceived of as a "unity of opposites"? Would Plato say that Being and Becoming were unified in one respect, but diverse or separable in another respect? Consensus seems to be on the side of the dualistic interpretation; however, it does remain as an interesting problem for further inquiry and resolution. However, regardless of the question of Plato's dualism or organism, the writer's own conviction is that the creative factors (realm of being) of the universe are organically related to the entities in the space-time continuum of process and reality (realm of becoming); hence it is more accurate to speak of "Becoming-Being" of actual entities as bipolar.

Medieval philosophers' views

If space permitted here it would be most interesting to make an analysis of the great philosophical controversy of the 12th Century with respect to the nature of concepts, the joint problem of epistemology and metaphysics. Particularly significant in the light of our previous observations on Plato and Aristotle would be the comparative analysis of the views of the well known philosophers of this period: Anselm, William of Champeaux, Roscellinus, and Abelard. Although the famous controversy over Universals of this period would carry us far afield, it would also contribute significantly to our particular interest in the principle of bipolarity, which in turn involves the problem of relations.

It will be recalled that the dispute at first was largely between the extreme realists, such as William of Champeaux, who insisted upon the reality of individual substances. Abelard endeavored to mediate between the extreme realism of William of Champeaux and the nominalism of Roscellinus.[16] He could not agree that universals were mere words or sounds; nor could he agree that only the individual substances constituted the real. He came to believe that universals had three modes of "being" or existing: (a) in the mind of God, (b) in things, and (c) after things in the human understanding.

> Even Abelard, however, explains this likeness of character in a multiplicity of individuals upon the hypothesis that God created the world according to archetypes which he carried in his mind (*nous*). Thus, according to his view, the universals exist firstly, *before the things*, as *conceptus mentis* in God; secondly, *in the things*, as likeness of the essential characteristics of individuals; thirdly, *after things*, in the human understanding as its concepts and predicates acquired by comparative thought."[17]

Abelard had unified the thinking of the time on universals; his view came to be accepted by the Arabian philosophers (Avicenna) according to Windelband in the formula:

> *Universalia ante multiplicatem, in multiplicitate et post multiplicitatem*; to universals belongs equally a significance *ante rem* as regards the divine mind, *in re* as regards Nature, and *post rem*

as regards human knowledge. And since Thomas and Duns Scotus in the main agreed in this view, the problem of universals, which, to be sure, has not yet been solved, came to a preliminary rest, to come again into the foreground when Nominalism was revived.[18]

It is interesting to note that Charles S. Peirce in his Pragmaticism approximated this position in his philosophy according to Feibleman:

> Making due allowance for the language of the scholastics, *ante res* became for Peirce the logical possibility of ontology; *in rebus* became the knowledge relation of epistemology; and *post res* became the mental concepts of psychology. But the solution was not confined to the level of metaphysical problems only; it became a leading canon for Peirce and stands implicit behind all his other writings. For by scholastic realism Peirce understood that "general principles are really operative in nature."[19]

It is evident that the problem of opposites in relation to our problem of bipolarity takes us through the mainstream of the perennial philosophical issues. Pursuit of this problem systematically would involve us in virtually every philosophy of importance.

In later contexts it will be noted that these three relations are reflected in Whitehead's philosophy of organism, too. His "eternal objects" or possibles envisaged by the primordial aspect of God, his "actual entities" which embody or exemplify these forms, and his "prehension" and comprehension of these "eternal objects" in human beings, approximate the older triadic explanation of conceptualism in universals *ante res, in rebus,* and *post res.* The organic view sees these distinctions as relatively *conjunctive* and *disjunctive,* and not as absolute distinctions or bifurcations of reality. Again there is no absolute distinction between realms of being and becoming for organism; they represent bipolar relations.

German Idealism and Notable Treatments of Opposites

During the period of the late 18th Century and early 19th Century we find the rise of German Idealism. If time permitted we should like very much to pursue the notable treatment of opposites by such men as Kant, Fichte, Hegel, Schelling, Schlegel, Krause, Schiller, Herbart, Froebel, and many others of note. Kant, for example, is notable for his effort to reconcile the rival contentions of empiricism and rationalism, as well as the objective and subjective elements. His vast influence on those who were to follow him is well known. Hegel's famous dialectical idealism is of course one of the most outstanding expositions of the relationships of opposites in the dynamics of the triadic pattern of thesis, antithesis, and synthesis. Friedrich Schiller's *Aesthetic Education of Man* exemplifies another influential contribution of a German idealistic philosopher in dealing with the dynamics of the interweaving of opposites in the educational process of man. The various influences of Krause, Schiller, Schelling, and others upon the organismic educational philosophy of Froebel also is most significant.[20] A few brief observations of the way in which these philosophers and educators treated the problem of opposites are in order in our review of concepts and bipolarity.

Friedrich W. J. Schelling and Polarity

In the period of the development of German Idealism the name of Friedrich Schelling stands out as a contributor to the notion of polarity. A member of the famed University of Jena group, along with Fichte and Hegel, he is known mainly for his *Transcendental Idealism.* According to Windelband his development as a philosopher includes five periods: (1) Philosophy of Nature; (2) Aesthetic Idealism; (3) Absolute Idealism; (4) Doctrine of Freedom; and (5) his Philosophy of Mythology and Revelation.[21]

Schelling was an organic philosopher with idealistic emphasis and interpretation. For him *"Nature is the ego, or self, in process of becoming."*[22] This is his theme in his philosophy of nature. He opposed the "Democritic-Galilean principle of the purely mechanical explanation of nature."[23] Speaking of Schelling's philosophy Windelband says:

> As a result its central conception is *life,* and it makes the attempt to consider Nature from the point of view of the *organism,* and to understand the connection of its forces from the ultimate end of the production of organic life.[24]

This emphasis on the perspective of the organism is certainly an important part of the modern philosophy of organism.

His notion of polarity was expressed in his conception of the manner in which objective reason struggles its way upward through the material modes of manifestation and expression in the entities of nature.[25]

> In particular, it was the conception of *duality*, of the opposition of forces which negate each other in a higher unity, that formed the fundamental schema of his "construction of nature," —a conception due to the Science of Knowledge,—and from this point of view the *polarity* in electric and magnetic phenomena which busied Schelling's contemporaries as a newly found enigma was particularly significant for him.[26]

It would be interesting and revealing indeed to pursue the question of how much influence he had upon his contemporaries: Krause, Hegel, and perhaps Froebel. We cannot pursue that inquiry here.

Friedrich Schiller and Aesthetic Idealism

Educationally speaking, one of the most significant philosophers was Schiller. This writer is impressed with Schiller's explanation of the aesthetic process in education as expessed in his *Letters on the Aesthetic Education of the Human Race*, because he saw the important role of the interweaving and fusing of the theoretical and the practical in the aesthetic.[27] Since references have been made to Schiller elsewhere in some detail it is unnecessary to repeat here. Yet it should be remembered that Schiller found the principle of unification in human development in the artistic impulse and in the fusing of intellectual and moral elements with the sensuous and emotional elements through the aesthetic expression. In contrast to Kant's almost stoical devotion to the life of moral duty in terms of his categorical imperative, Schiller contended that it is the quest for the beautiful which unifies man's development and in time brings him to the realization of the good.

> From this Schiller concluded in the first place that wherever we have to do with educating man, subject to his sensuous nature, to a condition where he shall will morally, the aesthetic life offers the most effective means to this end.[28]

Thus where Kant offers religion as an aid to man's moral life, Schiller offers art. Art in turn is an interweaving or fusion of the spiritual and sensuous, and the cognitive and the emotional. This fusion is certainly a dynamic educational bipolarity.

Again it would be most interesting and enlightening to pursue the whole of Schiller's educational theory with its emphasis upon the role of play and the notion of education as art. His influence upon educational theory in general, and on Froebel in particular, has been admirably revealed by the writings of my esteemed colleague, Professor Frederick Eby, in his *Development of Modern Education.*[29] We can only note this relationship in passing.

Organic Comments on Schiller's View

Here we have an excellent example of the overlapping of two varying philosophical systems on the role of the aesthetic in the education of man. The *philosophy of organism* is not an idealistic system *per se; it places idealism on a realistic base.* With the difference of philosophical context in mind, we can note the mutual insistence upon the role of the aesthetic in human development. Whitehead comes very close to Schiller in his emphasis on the role of the aesthetic. It is quite remarkable how much of the thinking of such men as Hegel, Schiller, and Froebel is approximated by Whitehead, who certainly has much more realism in his theory of organism. Hence within the context of the present educational theory of organism there would be some agreement with Schiller's concept of the role of the aesthetic in education.[30] This writer finds much merit in Schiller's confidence in the role of the aesthetic process in achieving the good life. However, "education as art" is only a part of the whole complex process of education and life.

Kant, Hegel, Pestalozzi, and Froebel.

If space permitted we should certainly want to investigate and discuss the problem of opposites, as treated by Kant, Hegel, Pestalozzi, and Froebel, very thoroughly. Kant's dictum, "Percepts without concepts are blind, and concepts without percepts are empty,"[31] which grew out of his endeavor to reconcile the valid elements of Empiricism and Rationalism, is indicative of the pertinence of his thought to the problem. Kant was certainly well involved in the problem of opposites. His works in this subject are considered by many to be the most eminent in the history of philosophy.

Hegel stands out as one of the notable exponents of idealistic dialectics in his now famous triadic pattern of thesis, antithesis, and synthesis. His enormous philosophical contribution with its idealistic logical system certainly bears upon the problem of opposites with unusual clarity. Any thorough-going analysis of philosophers of polarity would have to include Hegel.

In another context analysis of the views of Pestalozzi and Froebel as educational philosophers would certainly be in order. Pestalozzi's devotion to organic principles is particularly intriguing to this point of view. The fact that he took seriously Kant's dictum quoted above on the relation of percepts and concepts is proven by the emphasis which he placed upon "object lessons" in moving from the concrete to the abstract in the educational process. Also, as Eby points out, Pestalozzi became entangled in difficulties of educational theory because he never realized the significant differences between logical and psychological continuities.[32]

Friedrich Froebel stands out also as an educational philosopher very much concerned with the dynamics of opposites. In setting forth his *law of development* Froebel apparently went beyond the views of Fichte and Hegel. Froebel was concerned with the actual forces of organic processes in addition to the processes of thought emphasized in the Hegelian dialectic.

> Froebel also searched for a single principle that would explain the process of the creative activity of the universe. This creative activity is, as previously indicated, the same in the inorganic as in the organic world; it is also the same power that is known in human willing and thinking. According to Froebel, it is not pure thought or idea, as Hegel taught; nor physical force, as the materialists believed. It is a spiritual, creative energizing that shows itself alike in the force of the physical world and in the will power and thought of the mental world.[33]

It is most significant that Froebel deviated from the Absolute Idealism of Hegel to the extent that he did not restrict his notion of dynamics of opposites to the dialectic of ideas, but extended his conception into the physical forces of nature. It should be noted too that in extending the concept of creative activity from the organic world into the inorganic, Froebel was in large part anticipating Whitehead's philosophy of organism. As we have noted, Whitehead's theory of organism extends through all entities; *all entities* are said to participate in the organic processes of *prehension* and *concrescence.* Here then is a very interesting similarity between Froebel and Whitehead.

Froebel's Law of Opposites

Froebel is well known in the history of education for his conception of education as "Cosmic Evolution and Organic Education."[34] In stating his theory of development he formulated the "law of opposites" as a dynamic principle of action, reaction, and equilibrium. Although similar to Hegel's triadic pattern of thesis, antithesis, and synthesis, Froebel's principle was intended for broader application.

As Froebel conceived it, the law, according to which spiritual activity or creative energy evolves, is the law of opposites, or of unity. It is similar to the law of thesis, antithesis, and synthesis, except that the latter dialectic process is a process of logical ideas or meanings. Froebel's law is a dynamic principle. It is the law of activity, the law of action, reaction, and equilibrium. It is, therefore, broader in application than the process of thesis, antithesis, and synthesis, which is applicable only to thought. Froebel's law includes and explains this dialectic process of thought, but his law is universal in scope. It explains the creation of all things in the physical and spiritual worlds. Its greatest value is in explaining the course of development of human conduct, skill, and thought.[35]

From this brief exposition of Froebel's Law of Opposites it can be seen that further penetration into his writings would be very pertinent to our line of inquiry on the nature of opposites and their implications for the educational process. Such an analysis will also have to be postponed for a later work.

Organic Response to these Theories

In referring to these idealistic thinkers—Kant, Hegel, Pestalozzi, and Froebel—it should be remembered that the organic philosophy has its differences as well as its agreements with these views. It has been noted that whereas for Kant the world emerges from mind, Whitehead insists in his philosophy of organism that entities emerge from the world. Whitehead is deeply both empirical and rationalistic. Yet organically the driving force of realism—the objectivity of the world —and the driving force of idealism—the important role of subjectivity —are combined in the organic philosophy.

Hegel and the others in German Idealism made magnificent contributions to the development of philosophical thought. The similarities of organic concepts of creative processes and some of the idealistic concepts are striking. Yet the reader should not equate the philosophy of organism, or the organic educational philosophy *per se*, with these 18th and 19th Century idealistic theories. The strong realistic and existential aspects of organic philosophy along with many other qualifications distinguish these philosophies, despite similarities.

Summary. It has been the perennial problem of philosophy to deal with the nature of opposites, contraries, and contradictions. Various philosophical schools of thought have emerged in their attempts to reconcile such opposites as permanence and change, the eternal and temporal, the one and the many, and being and becoming. The present organic conception of bipolarity is understood better in the context of its long historical development.

Ancient philosophers of East and West wrestled with the problem of opposites. Pythagoras was one of the first to recognize the dyadic relations of things. Indian and Chinese philosophers formulated the doctrine of Yang and Yin which recognized certain complementary forces of nature. Although Plato is usually interpreted as a dualist in his philosophy of Being and Becoming, there is some evidence of the basis for an organic bipolarity in his later writings. Aristotle dealt with the problem of contraries and opposites at some length in his works. Although he did not state bipolarity in the sense that we have described it, he did achieve a unity of Being and Becoming in his system, which was in turn based upon the Category of Substance. Aristotle found essences exemplified in the realm of particulars.

Medieval philosophers in their famous controversy over the nature of universals contributed further to the problem of opposites. Abelard endeavored to mediate between the extreme realism of William of Champeaux and the nominalism of Roscellinus. He concluded that the disputed universal has three modes of being: (a) in the mind of

God, (b) in things, and (c) after things in the human understanding. Charles S. Peirce, American Pragmaticist of the 19th Century, seems to have approximated this conclusion *in re* universals.

Notable treatments of opposites are also to be found in 18th and 19th Century philosophies of German Idealism. Friedrich Schelling, organic and idealistic philosopher, contributed to the notion of polarity through his emphasis on the opposition of forces which negate each other in nature's process of becoming. Friedrich Schiller in his Aesthetic Idealism contributed to the bipolar notion in his exposition of the interweaving or fusion process which takes place through aesthetic creativity in bringing together the spiritual and the sensuous, the cognitive and the emotional.

The problem of opposites received eminent treatment at the hands of Kant, Hegel, Pestalozzi, and Froebel too. Kant saw the polarity of perception and conception. Pestalozzi was devoted to organic principles in the education of man. He applied Kant's dictum on percepts and concepts. Froebel formulated the 'law of opposites' as a dynamic principle of action, reaction, and equilibrium. He saw the principle as applying to all the dynamic forces of nature and not merely to abstract levels of human thought.

Hegel's exposition of the dialectical process of being and becoming in terms of thesis, anti-thesis, and synthesis is, of course, one of the most penetrating treatments of the problem of opposites in the history of philosophy. His influence philosophically and educationally has been far-reaching, especially in the work of W. T. Harris and other American educators of the 19th Century.

The Organic Philosophy of Education is not in complete agreement with these 19th Century conceptions of idealistic philosophy and its resolution of the problem of opposites. Certain overlappings are indeed evident. However, the organic conception of bipolarity and the resolution of the problem of opposites defended here is more in line with the contemporary viewpoints expressed in the next chapter.

FOOTNOTES

1. See glossary and index.

2. Whether these pairs of terms are to be properly designated as opposites, contradictories, contrasts, contraries, or complementaries, depends upon

one's philosophical framework. The foregoing illustrations may well illustrate different kinds of relations, even within a given philosophy.

3. *The Dictionary of Philosophy*, 4th ed., ed. Dagobert D. Runes (New York: Philosophical Library, 1942), p. 241. Reprinted with permission of the publisher.

4. This writer has made a more extended analysis of this topic in another manuscript, "The Organic Philosophy of Education."

5. Seymour G. Martin, and others, *A History of Philosophy* (New York: F. S. Crofts & Co., 1941).

6. S. G. Martin. *A History of Philosophy*, p. 27.

7. Ralph Tyler Flewelling, *The Things That Matter Most* (New York: The Ronald Press Company, 1946, copyright by publisher), pp. 74-75.

8. It is acknowledged herewith that Plato is usually interpreted as "Dualist" or "Absolutist."

9. This phrase is derived from Arthur O. Lovejoy's book, *The Great Chain of Being*.

10. Raphael Demos, *The Philosophy of Plato* (New York: Charles Scribner's Sons, 1939), pp. 3-129.

11. Raphael Demos, *The Philosophy of Plato*, pp. 11-12.

12. See Plato's Dialogue, *The Sophist*.

13. A. E. Taylor, *Plato: The Man and His Work* (New York: The Dial Press, Inc., 1936), pp. 385-86. Reprinted with permission of the publisher.

14. Aristotle, *Basic Works of Aristotle*, ed. Richard McKeon (New York: Random House, 1941), "Metaphysics," Bk. IV, Ch. 2, p. 735. Reprinted with permission of the publisher, Oxford Univ. Press, Inc.

15. W. Windelband, *A History of Philosophy*, trans. James H. Tufts, 2nd ed. (London: The Macmillan Company, Ltd., 1893, 1901), p. 133. Reprinted with permission of the publisher, and associates St. Martin's Press.

16. W. Windelband, *A History of Philosophy*, p. 298.

17. W. Windelband, *A History of Philosophy*, p. 299. Reprinted with permission of the publisher.

18. W. Windelband, *A History of Philosophy*, p. 299. Reprinted with permission of the publisher.

19. James Feibleman, *An Introduction to Peirce's Philosophy, Interpreted as a System* (New York: Harper and Brothers Publishers, 1946), p. 59. Reprinted with permission of the publishers.

20. Frederick Eby, *The Development of Modern Education*, 2nd Ed. (New York: Prentice-Hall, Inc., 1952, Copyright 1934, 1952, by Prentice-Hall, Inc., Englewood Cliffs, N. J.), pp. 414-30.

21. W. Windelband, *A History of Philosophy*, pp. 598-601.

22. W. Windelband, *A History of Philosophy*, p. 597. Reprinted with permission of the publisher.

23. W. Windelband, *A History of Philosophy*, p. 598. Reprinted with permission of the publisher.

24. W. Windelband, *A History of Philosophy*, p. 597. Reprinted with permission of the publisher.

25. W. Windelband, *A History of Philosophy*, pp. 599-600.

26. W. Windelband, *A History of Philosophy*, p. 600. Reprinted with permission of the publisher.

27. W. Windelband, *A History of Philosophy*, p. 601.

28. W. Windelband, *A History of Philisophy*, p. 601. Reprinted with permission of the publisher.

29. Frederick Eby, *The Development of Modern Education*, pp. 496-532.

30. See Chapters 14 and 15.

31. See Frank C. Wegener, "Perception and Conception in Education," *School and Society*, 70: 37-39, July, 1949. See also, Frederick Eby, *The Development of Modern Education*, p. 450.

32. F. Eby and C. F. Arrowood, *The Development of Modern Education*, 2nd ed. (New York: Prentice Hall, Inc., 1942, copyright, 1934, 1952, by publisher), p. 650.

33. F. Eby and C. F. Arrowood, *The Development of Modern Education*, p. 803. Reprinted with permission of the publisher.

34. F. Eby and C. F. Arrowood, *The Development of Modern Education*, p. 790.

35. F. Eby and C. F. Arrowood, *The Development of Modern Education*, p. 803. Reprinted with permission of the publisher.

8

CONTEMPORARY CONCEPTIONS OF BIPOLARITY

T H E foregoing historical background should provide us with a better appreciation and understanding of some of the contemporary conceptions of bipolarity. Various expositions and interpretations of 'bipolarity,' 'polarity,' and 'dipolarity,' in recent philosophical literature have come to the attention of the writer. In this chapter we shall review some of the other conceptions of polarity; comparisons and contrasts of these conceptions with this writer's viewpoint contribute to the formulation and clarification of bipolarity in the Organic Philosophy of Education.

Numerous contemporary and recent philosophers have utilized polarity or bipolarity significantly in their writings. The most notable expression is perhaps that of the late A. N. Whitehead in his organic theory of reality. He speaks both of 'bipolarity' and 'dipolarity' in various contexts. Charles Hartshorne and William Reese have made extensive expressions of the Law of Polarity in their recent work, *Philosophers Speak of God.* Professor W. H. Sheldon devotes considerable attention to the notion of polarity, particularly in his book, *Process and Polarity.* Professor Archie J. Bahm has made some excellent articulations and formulations of the bipolar principle in his writings on 'Organicism.' In his *Reason and Nature* Morris Cohen recognizes the important role of polarity. In the field of Anthropology Professor David Bidney in his book, *Theoretical Anthropology,* makes distinctive use of the principle of polarity. This writer has been able to find only one instance of utilization of the principle of bipolarity among recent or contemporary educational philosophers; Professor Frederick Breed, writing on the "Education and the Realistic Outlook," in the *41st Yearbook, Philosophies of Education,* has made definite but brief application of bipolarity to problems of education. No doubt there are many others who have written on aspects of polarity which have not come to the attention of this writer.

John Dewey's stand on bipolarity appears to be a debatable question. His views are included in this chapter in relation to this topic of bipolarity because of the eminent role of his educational philosophy, and because any reconstruction of educational philosophy could hardly be adequate without critical consideration of his views on a given problem.

A number of questions emerge for our consideration in this chapter. What are some of the contemporary views of polarity and bipolarity? What is Professor Bahm's 'organicism'? What is Whitehead's conception of bipolarity? What is the comparative evaluation of these two viewpoints made by the Organic Philosophy of Education? What is Professor Sheldon's conception of 'process and polarity'? What is this organic response to Sheldon's views? What is Cohen's notion of polarity? What is the organic response to Cohen's views? What is Breed's proposal with respect to a 'bipolar theory of education'? What is the organic critique of this proposal? Did John Dewey believe in the principle of bipolarity? What is the organic response to Dewey's views on this subject? What is the theory of bipolarity as formulated and amplified in the context of the organic educational philosophy? What seems to be the educational significance of the principle of bipolarity? What is the error of monopolarity? How expressed in educational theories?

Professor Archie Bahm's Organicism

One of the most ingenious and explicit analyses of the concept of polarity which this writer has encountered is that of Professor Archie J. Bahm in a philosophical viewpoint which he terms "Organicism."[1] Bahm states that it is advanced in a pragamatic spirit "as a tentative proposal to be examined for its relative merits as a general interpretive hypothesis."[2] The student will find Professor Bahm's book a most helpful and clarifying exposition of organic and polar relationships.

Bahm presents his view of "Organicism" by showing and explaining its relationships to eight other theories or philosophies.[3]

150

Figure 2. *Bahm's 'Organicism'*

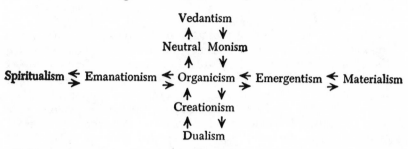

Bahm states,

> For organicism, then, each of the other eight theories expresses a fundamental truth in its positive assertions, but each is inadequate to the extent that its negative assertions deny fundamental truths embodied in the positive assertions of the others.[4]

For example, spiritualism is one-sided because it holds only that spirit exists.[5] Materialism is in error because it holds that only matter exists. Each of the theories contains some validities and some invalidities; organicism seeks to contain these validities of the other theories, but to avoid their invalid claims. Using the very helpful accompanying diagram (see figure 3) Bahm illustrates Organicism's relationship to the other eight theories with respect to each polarity:[6]

Figure 3. *Bahm's Diagram of Types*

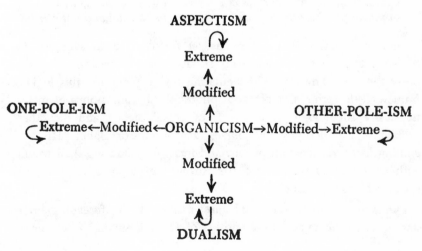

His logical analysis is excellent and is therefore reproduced here quite extensively:

> The meaning of each of these types may be stated generally as follows: 1. Extreme one-pole-ism: One pole of the polarity exists; the other does not exist. 2. Modified one-pole-ism: One pole exists prior to the other pole. The other pole depends upon the one pole for existence, but the one pole does not depend upon the other. 3. Extreme other-pole-ism: The other pole exists; the one pole does not exist. 4. Modified other-pole-ism: The other pole exists as prior to the one pole. The one depends upon the other for its existence, but the other does not depend upon the one. 5. Extreme dualism: Both poles exist independently of each other. Neither depends upon the other for its existence. 6. Modified dualism: Both poles exist, independent of each other for what they are in themselves, but dependent upon each other for what they are in relation to each other. 7. Extreme aspectism: That which is polar exists, but its poles do not exist. Both poles are merely apparent aspects of that which is polar. 8. Modified aspectism: That which is polar exists, and its poles depend upon it for their existence. That which is polar does not depend for its existence upon its poles. 9. Organicism: *Both poles exist and that which is polar exists—interdependently, i. e., partly dependently and partly independently. Each pole is partly independent of and partly dependent upon its opposite pole, and that which is polar is partly independent of and partly dependent upon its poles. That which is polar can be reduced neither to one nor to both of its poles, neither wholly nor partly; a pole can be reduced neither to its opposite pole nor to that which is polar, neither wholly nor partly.*[7]

One sees clearly that Bahm has set forth a logical synthesis in terms of Organicism, which expresses its truths in relation to eight other theories. The task of formulating and expounding this logical framework in terms of substantial philosophical conceptions of metaphysics, epistemology, axiology, ethics, social theory, and the other problems of philosophy, of course, faces Professor Bahm. His beginning has been most auspicious and intriguing, and we shall watch with considerable interest for the further development of his philosophy of "organicism."

The writer is in fundamental agreement with the foregoing brief statement of the logical relationships of Organicism in these polarities. Professor Bahm's writing came as a welcome reinforcement to the expositions of this organic theory of education. This writer had conceived of these relations which Bahm terms "dependent, independent, and interdependent," as relatively separable, incomplete *in se,* and together or connected. Similarly in Whitehead's terms organic relations are "conjunctive and disjunctive," "organic and atomic." Although Professor Bahm and this writer have come to similar conclusions with respect to organic polarities through different routes, acknowledgment of the valuable contribution of Bahm's analysis of the nine theories and the subsequent clarification of thought for many of us interested in organic polar relations is happily made. The extent of our philosophical agreement is not yet clear, and will not be clear until we have both extended our organic writings much further than at present.

Although there are apparent agreements in Bahm's Organicism and Whitehead's philosophy of organism, there are disagreements too.[8] Both are opposed to bifurcations and dualisms in philosophical explanations of reality.

> Both agree that creativity involves the emergence of unique individuals, that each individual is unique, but that somehow each individual involves, and is involved in, every other individual, even if primarily in negative ways. Both agree that value is concrete and that whatever is concrete is value.[9]

We cannot enter into the analysis of agreements and disagreements between Organicism and Organism in this limited context. This writer finds himself sympathetic with many of the criticisms advanced by Bahm toward Organism, but he also believes that there are legitimate answers to Bahm's criticisms within Whitehead's vast writings. For example, Bahm calls attention to Whitehead's rejection of "Aristotelian Substance" in favor of process. He says,

> Whitehead had to reject the notion of substance if he wished to adopt a doctrine of dependence or interdependence. Organicism accepts a more literal definition of "sub-stance" as that which stands under or remains through change. Whenever there is functioning there is that which functions, so whenever there is functioning there is substance. Having defined substance functionally, organicism keeps it as a category of organic existence.[10]

He then calls attention to how this affects Whitehead's criticisms of subject-predicate notions and then concludes:

> Organicism, with its organic logic, finds subject-predicate logic partly true, partly false . . . . Subject and predicate are partly interdependent.[11]

Now this writer is in sympathy with Bahm's desire to utilize "substance" in this qualified manner, and also the partial validity of subject-predicate logic which follows. But it appears that he is doing an injustice to Whitehead when he takes this interpretation of his rejection of substance so finally as to believe that Whitehead saw only "becoming" of actual occasions "in arising and perishing without endurance."[12]

Whitehead does assert "endurance" as well as "fluency"; he asserts elements of permanence as well as novelty in his events and entities. Whitehead speaks of these entities as "enduring societies," in other words as relatively persistent patterns of existence. Each entity as object has both becoming and being; it is both subject and superject in bipolar relations. Whitehead speaks explicitly about the sense in which we can think about and describe these relatively enduring entities. He says that these relatively enduring objects can be treated pragmatically and practically as "substances."[13] Thus he is able to say elsewhere that in a sense the correspondence theory of truth and the coherence theory are both in part utilizable and correct.[14] In this sense then there is the practicability of the "subject-predicate" type of logic within practical limits of Whitehead's philosophy of organism, which Bahm believes is not there.

Bahm also criticizes Whitehead's rationalism and his tendency to accept Plato's notion of the priority of the rational.

> Not only does he assert "the essence of the universe is more than process," but also persistent overtones of statements to the contrary leave the impression that eternal objects constitute the reality in the process. His admiration for Plato, the father of rationalism, reveals a lurking insistence upon the priority of the rational, despite his claim to having found roots for the dynamic aspects of his philosophy of organism in the thought of Plato.[15]

Now whereas Bahm takes this as the most serious defect in Whitehead's system, by contrast this writer finds it to be a distinct virtue.

Here then is a clue to an important difference between Bahm's organic approach and that of this writer. Bahm admittedly makes a pragmatic approach to organicism and is apprehensive of Platonism. This writer is gratified by Whitehead's deep devotion to empirical and rational principles. The thinking here is strongly in the Platonic-Aristotelian tradition; therefore, this organic doctrine is approving of Whitehead's faith in a rationalistic principle in the primordial aspect of God.

The position for the time being then with respect to these two philosophies, "Organicism" and "Organism," is this: the writer finds himself in admiration of Bahm's logical analysis of the nine theories previously expounded as the basis of clarification of the polar relationships. He is quite sympathetic with Bahm's observations of other philosophies, including Whitehead's. However, Bahm's system is relatively new and undeveloped; Whitehead's philosophy of organism has been set forth in its entirety. Until we can read and study Bahm's sustained development of his present ideas, this writer must admit a strong inclination toward the bulk of the philosophy of organism as set forth by Whitehead and his own organic formulations.

Whitehead and Bipolarity

Elsewhere Whitehead's formulations of his bipolar or "dipolar" conceptions have been described.[16] In this context a brief statement of these conceptions is in order with some comments on their relations to this viewpoint and other bipolarists.

We have noted repeatedly that Whitehead's philosophy of organism is a protest against "dualisms" and "bifurcations" of nature. Every actual entity has two poles, the physical and the mental. This applies to all entities: as things, persons, and even God. Thus *bipolarity*, or *dipolarity* which he seems to use interchangeably, is an organic principle which is coherent with other principles of *prehension, concrescence, creativity, becoming, being, conjunctiveness, disjunctiveness*, and the like. Thus the nature of any real entity is not "dualistic" but it is *bipolar*. Processes of prehension and concrescence must be understood in terms of this bipolar structure.

Whitehead speaks of the *dipolarity* of actual entities as follows:

> In each concrescence there is a twofold aspect of the creative urge. In one aspect there is the origination of simple causal feelings; and in the other aspect there is the origination of conceptual feelings. These contrasted aspects will be called the physical and mental poles of an actual entity. No actual entity is devoid of either pole; though their relative importance differs in different actual entities. Also conceptual feelings do not necessarily involve consciousness; though there can be no conscious feelings which do not involve conceptual feelings as elements in the synthesis.[17]

Here then is an expression of the ontological structure of reality; the actual world of entities involves the necessary interdependence of two poles, the physical and mental. The poles are "other" or different in one sense as mental and physical, but they are essentially related in structure and function. They are necessary components of process and reality—of the relations of becoming and being. Here is an idealistic panpsychism blended with a realistic physical pole—inseparably blended or fused.

Speaking of "The Order of Nature" Whitehead clearly states this *bipolarity* as follows:

> Each actuality is essentially bipolar, physical and mental, and the physical inheritance is essentially accompanied by a conceptual reaction partly conformed to, and partly introductory of, a relevant novel contrast, but always introducing emphasis, valuation, and purpose. The integration of the physical and mental side into a unity of experience is a self-formation which is a process of concrescence, and which by the principle of objective immortality characterizes the creativity which transcends it. So though mentality is non-spatial, mentality is always a reaction from, and integration with, physical experience which is spatial.[18]

Bipolarity is not an exclusively important principle for Whitehead, for it is important as coherently related to other organic conceptions. Elsewhere it will be fruitful to inquire into the significance of bipolarity within the context of prehension, concrescence, and the totality of Whitehead's organic cosmology. For our purposes here we note the essential meaning and role of his bipolar conception. A. H. Johnson presents a most succinct summary of the two poles as follows:

This reference to the ultimate bricks of the physical universe serves to emphasize a point briefly mentioned previously. Every actual entity has a physical and mental pole—i. e., every actual entity is composed of physical and mental activities. Physical prehensions have already been discussed at sufficient length. It is important to discover exactly what Whitehead means by mental pole of an actual entity. He claims that the basic operations of mentality are conceptual prehensions (so-called pure mental activity). However, in the broader sense, the term *mentality* is also applied to integrations of conceptual and physical prehensions as in physical purpose and propositional prehensions (so-called impure prehensions). Further, Whitehead seems to be suggesting that by mental he means the subjective side of experience, which is the essential uniqueness of individual reaction to data. Mentality involves the introduction of emphasis, valuation, purpose. In other words, the subjective aim of an actual entity is one phase of its mental pole.[19]

In other words a philosophy of organism contains a bipolarity of objective and subjective poles, or the physical and mental poles. Here is a realistic-idealism. It is important to note that Whitehead's level of generality about the mental pole excludes the notion of always meaning conscious intelligence. This is, of course, why he has chosen the term "prehension." The organism has conceptual prehension of ideal objects through the mental pole; in its physical pole it has prehensions of the data of actual objects. In its subjective aspect it becomes non-temporal; while in the physical pole its prehensions are temporal.

Comments from the Viewpoint of Organic
Educational Philosophy

It is clear that there are similarities and dissimilarities evident in Whitehead's exposition of bipolarity and other bipolarists. There is the common rejection of *dualism* and true bifurcation in the views of Whitehead, Bahm, and our own view. Bahm's conception of bipolarity emerges from his analysis of eight other theories, as we have seen. His results in large part are from logical analysis. Whitehead's view is similar in that he too rejects the one-sidedness of other theories such as realism, idealism, materialism, and dualism. Whitehead's differences, however, seem to grow out of his whole theory of process and reality. Bipolarity, although essential, is only one organic principle out of many coherent principles. His philosophy has mature and far reaching development; it embraces the problems of reality, truth, value, nature, and aesthetics.

It appears that Whitehead's bipolarity in terms of his "conjunctiveness and disjunctiveness" of *organic* and *atomistic* relations is essentially the same as Bahm's meaning of "dependent, independent, and interdependent" relations, and what this writer has meant by separability, incompleteness *in se* of poles, and togetherness of poles. Terminologies vary within the different contexts.

Bahm has indicated his agreements and disagreements between his "Organicism" and Whitehead's "Organism." As we have seen one difference is that Bahm insists on "sub-stance" as he opposes Whitehead's "process" insistence.

The Organic Philosophy of Education is in substantial agreement with Whitehead's formulation of bipolarity. However, this formulation and application of the bipolar principle within the context of this educational theory expands and extends that conception. The treatment of the co-ordinates in terms of structural and functional intelligibilities, logical and psychological continuities, objectification and subjectification of the educational process, and similar applications, is the responsibility of this educational philosophy. It may be that the constructions that have been advanced here are implicit in Whitehead's philosophy of organism; on the other hand it is also possible that another interpreter of the philosophy of organism would not agree with my own formulations. One must admit that these formulations follow only in part from the doctrine of bipolarity; they also result from the writer's own experiences and reasonings with respect to the nature of the educational process.

It should be noted that one does not find a direct and overt expression of these organic principles in Whitehead's essays on education. That is his essays on the *Aims of Education* do not reveal a direct use of such conceptions as bipolarity, concrescence, subject-superject, and the like. One reason is no doubt that his educational essays were written much earlier than his main philosophical expositions. Then too it is the rare general philosopher who makes direct and overt use of his own philosophical constructions in the expressions of his educational views. For some unknown reason they don't seem to use them directly. Locke, Kant, and Descartes are examples. Plato and Dewey, on the other hand, seem to be outstanding exceptions to this rule. Their educational views exemplify their philosophical conceptions directly.

W. H. Sheldon and Bipolarity

Another thinker along bipolar lines who has won this writer's admiration is Professor W. H. Sheldon. In his book, *Process and Polarity*, this writer found much which clarified and reinforced his thinking about polarity. Sheldon's admonition concerning the limitations of any given philosophical principle is most appropriate to our discussion of bipolarity.

> And this suggests a needed caution for every philosophy: let no metaphysician claim to have unearthed the one absolute all-consuming principle that dominates every reality, actual or possible. For polarity can make no such claim. We affirm only that it is a very widespread phenomenon, fertile and suggestive for discovery and indeed, being polarity, indicating a counter-principle (which . . . is process).[20]

It is very important that we keep this admonition in mind as we survey the possibilities and limitations of bipolarity.

Professor Sheldon, too, is concerned with the formulation of a synthesis of surviving types of metaphysical systems. He sees these as idealism, materialism, Scholasticism, process philosophy, and irrationalism. These systems contain the fundamental oppositions which must be synthesized in another philosophy. Polarity must be recognized as essential in this synthesis.

Sheldon, too, sees polarity as involving poles which are both dependent and independent respectively. He does introduce the concept of productive power which results from the asymmetrical and independent status of the poles. Sheldon relates polarity to process very effectively as follows:

> In sum, polarity means a relation between two opposites, each of partly independent status, asymmetrical and productive because of their cooperation, and also just because each has al-

ready a being, power, and efficacy of its own which enables it to contribute something in the cooperation. If polarity did not involve this element of independence, of ultimate *duality*, it would not have the productive power. For to be independent is to have some quality irreducibly one's own, not in the least derivable from the other. This was in fact foreshadowed in the asymmetry of the two poles, for asymmetry points to an irreducible difference. And just this bit of independence is what enables one of the factors—mind—to proceed ahead of the other, to see new possibilities and better ways of ordering man's earthly life. Through this small inlet enters the note of process or progress; a category not included in polarity, yet complementary to it and thereby forming a new polarity.[21]

It is most important that this relationship of polarity and process be grasped. Polarity is not a static relationship; it is dynamic in character, and gives rise to motion and process. Polar differences give rise to productive power. This asymmetry of the two poles is most significant when one considers the mental and physical poles of all entities. In Whitehead's system the conceptual and physical prehensions made possible by these bipolarities are virtually the key to the creative process.

Professor Sheldon's insistence upon the necessity of "structure" as well as "function" in his synthesis is very reinforcing, for we too have been concerned about the "structure-function" bipolarity. This distinction is very important to this viewpoint for some devotees of process philosophies seem to overlook the role of structure. As stated earlier, it appears that Whitehead does allow for such structure within process. Sheldon summarizes his application of polarity to the various systems as follows:

> The many systems *on the whole* tend to condense them into the two types, scholasticism and process. The former conserves the main positive values of both idealism (in its two forms) and materialism; it is the preservative philosophy *par excellence*. The second, being the latest product of reflection, introduces not only a new note but also the motive of harmony between the old and the new, between conservativism and progress. The old order may be expected to change to new orders, but these may and should preserve the elements of the old that have been attested as forces which may contribute to man's good life. It is the incremental factor of process-philosophy that alone enables it to

160

teach this. Nature herself seems to sponsor such a program. She has her laws, and she has her tendency to form ever-new combinations—giving all positive possibles a fair chance. This is her principle of plenitude—let man follow it, guided by his knowledge drawn from experience.[22]

Organic Response to Sheldon's Views

Despite certain differences which obtain between the philosophy of organism and Sheldon's synthesis of types, there are striking similarities in our respective views:

(1) The recognition of the fundamental character of metaphysics in any philosophical formulation; (2) The recognition of partial validities in apparently conflicting philosophies and theories; (3) Emphasis upon the recognition of a structure as well as process; (4) Recognition of the vital role to be played by 'polarity' or bipolarity; (5) Acceptance of the limitations of the polar principle; (6) Acknowledgment of the wide scope of applications of the polar principle; (7) Recognition of asymmetry as well as symmetry in polar relations, or what I have called 'proportionate bipolarity'; (8) Recognition of relative relations of dependence, independence, and interdependence of poles; (9) The danger of over idealization of polarity as some idealists seem to have done; (10) Recognition of the actuality of polarity in process.[23]

Morris Cohen and Polarity

In his *Reason and Nature* Professor Morris Cohen too emphasizes the important role of polarity in resolving the admitted paradoxes of philosophy. Speaking of the wider uses of polarity, he states:

> By this I mean that opposites such as immediacy and mediation, unity and plurality, the fixed and the flux, substance and function, ideal and real, actual and possible, etc., like the north (positive) and south (negative) poles of a magnet, all involve each other when applied to any significant entity. Familiar illustrations of this are: that physical action is not possible without resistence or reaction and that protoplasm, in the language of Huxley, cannot live except by continually dying. *The idea is as old as philosophy.*[24]

These ideas reinforce what has been said throughout this chapter. Granting certain differences, the similarities are striking.

This review of Cohen's views on this topic cannot be extended here. Yet a quotation from Cohen which provides additional insight into the meaning and significance of bipolarity is included. Professor Cohen suggests that the bipolarity of mind and its action on intelligible objects can be compared to the blades of the scissors as they function co-ordinately. He says,

> I am indebted to Professor Felix Adler for the figure of the scissors to denote the fact that the mind never operates effectively except by using both unity and plurality like the two blades which move in opposite directions. Professor Marshall, in his *Principles of Economics*, has used the same figure to express the mutual dependence of the two factors of supply and demand. We may, if we like, also use the figure of the pestle and mortar, of our jaws in mastication or of applying brakes when going down a hill.[25]

Response to Cohen's Analogies of Bipolarity

Cohen's analogy of bipolarity and the scissors is an excellent one; it suggests the power and force of the concept. One has only to look around a bit to find a plenitude of exemplifications of bipolarity in various fields of human endeavor or existence. The human body itself in its structure and functions exemplifies bipolarity. Consider the co-ordinate aspects of such organs as brain, eyes, ears, lungs, and the like. Of course, the physical and mental polarities are most conspicuous, or the psycho-somatic aspects of man's being. Then too there is the fundamental ambivalence of man's being caught between drives toward pleasure and the ideal or spiritual realm. The classical distinction of the Dionysian and Apollonian contrasting drives in man, in his fervent passionate and calm rational aspects of his nature, are illustrative of the bipolarity in poetic and philosophical language.

One sees exemplifications of bipolarity in politics, psychology, history, education—in fact in virtually every field of study. The political process exemplifies bipolarity in contrasting approaches to the very issues of life. Psychology is filled with co-ordinates such as extrovertive-introvertive, psycho-somatic, structure-function, and the like. In the story of history we see numerous exemplifications of conservative-progressive, permanence-change, unity-diversity, being-becoming, and other such co-ordinates. The nature-nurture bipolarity is perhaps one of the most far-reaching and profound co-ordinates. As stated before, one should not treat all such contrasts as "bipolarities" for any principle has its limitations. There are many other shades of distinction and relationship to be considered. Yet the bipolar co-ordinates are evident throughout human experience and the world.

Frederick Breed and "The Bipolar Theory of Education"

To this writer's knowledge there has been no thoroughgoing, explicit development of a philosophy of education utilizing the concept of bipolarity in the 20th Century. However, there was one proposal which briefly advanced the notion of "the bipolar theory of education." Frederick Breed set forth "the realistic outlook" on educational theory in the 41st Yearbook of the NSSE, Part I, in 1942.[26] In this chapter he devoted several pages to the bipolar view.[27] Outside of this exposition this writer has not found any systematic development of bipolarity in recent educational philosophy.

In summary, Breed makes the following proposals: (1) That the educational program should embrace both the *methods* and *content* of knowledge; (2) That *freedom* and *authority* are complementary; (3) That progressive emphasis on content internally produced and conservative emphasis on content externally supplied should be co-ordinated.[28]

Professor Breed attacks instrumentalism from the point of view of Neo-Realism largely on the basis of different epistemological theories. He is strongly devoted to the realistic correspondence theory and its respective corollary, *the principle of independence*. Breed sees the progressive one-sided emphasis upon scientific method without equal concern for scientific content as the result of the instrumental or experimental theory of knowledge. In contrasting realistic and instrumental outlooks on the world, he says:

> Instrumentalism is solipsistic in character, suffering from the rigors of a radical and parsimonious methodology, flouting the intuitions of common sense regarding the existence of an external world, and attributing creative power to the intelligence of man to supply the data of knowledge that an amputated cosmos can no longer supply.[29]

163

Thus throughout his chapter Breed hammers away at the "relative stability of knowledge," the limitation of the operational character of ideas, the importance of acknowledging a realistic objective world as the source of human knowledge, as opposed to instrumental and progressive devotions to experimental methods without the content.

Hence Breed stresses the need for an educational program which incorporates the realistic aspect of knowledge and content and the experimental method. "The writer ventures to propose an educational program in which the chief values of both the method and the material of knowledge will be synthesized and conserved."[30] In other words the psychologically manifested interests of the learners were to be utilized in the educational process, but they were not to be allowed to determine the direction of education.

Professor Breed also believed that authority and freedom should be viewed as complementary poles. His most explicit statement of bipolarity is as follows:

> With regularity the fundamental factors of adjustment boil down to two—organism and environment, individual and society, purpose and possibility, personal interest and external demand, or, if you prefer, freedom and authority. It is the problem of freedom *and* authority rather than of freedom *versus* authority, for the two are complementary. They furnish the basis for a theory of instruction, indeed for a theory of government in the broadest sense, to which the term 'bipolar' seems appropriate.[31]

This Neo-Realist then saw the educational battle as one drawn between the progressive extremists who believed in internally produced mental content and realistic believers in mental content externally provided. As he says it is a battle "between those whose criterion of truth is the satisfaction of man and those whose criterion includes also the satisfaction of the fact."[32] He believed these extremes could be synthesized through a bipolar concept.

Organic Comments on Breed's Concept of Bipolarity

From the organic point of view there are several observations which should be made about Breed's concept of bipolarity and the educational process. There is an obvious agreement concerning the need for a bipolar concept with respect to certain conflicts in educational theory. Many of the concepts advanced here in the Organic Philosophy of Education would substantiate and further Breed's broad contention. On the other hand there are questions which the philosopher of organism would raise with respect to Breed's brief use of the "bipolar concept." It would appear that because of his strong realistic orientation that there would be significant differences with organism.

Some of the questions from this organic viewpoint are: What view of bipolarity would Breed take philosophically and educationally? Would he agree with the criteria which we have set forth as to the relative conjunctivity and disjunctivity of bipolar relations? Would his insistence on the *law of independence* of external objects result in a violation of the organic view of the objective-subjective bipolarity? That is to say, would his realism itself result in a one-sidedness? Would he acknowledge the Reformed Subjective Principle? Would he go beyond realism and idealism? In short, is his view organic?

Broadly speaking, then, it is apparent that Breed's bipolar suggestions are consonant with many of the views advanced here. The insistence on the complementary relations of authority and freedom, for example, is similar. Yet since his bipolar views were not extensively developed, these questions remain. An organicist is particularly perturbed by such a statement as this:

> Modern realism accepts the bipolar interpretation of the philosophy which Dewey offers to educators, rather than the one-sided interpretation offered by those of his followers who are outdoing him in their individualistic emphasis in education.[33]

In the light of the devastating criticism of the instrumentalist doctrine from the Neo-Realistic viewpoint which Breed had previously offered, one wonders at this amazing concession to Dewey on bipolarity. No doubt Breed refers to Dewey's continued endeavors to unify the opposites of body and mind, action and knowledge, method and subject matter, individual and society, and the like. But despite the truth of this endeavor, what about the philosophical distinctions which should be made about bipolarity in terms of theories of reality, knowledge, and value? The Organic Philosophy of Education cannot accept the totality of Dewey's instrumental-naturalistic philosophy here, as Breed seems to do.

Although there are evident similarities between Breed's bipolar conceptions and this educational theory, the Neo-Realistic view has not been developed far enough to answer many questions that have been raised. Bipolarity is not a construct to be used merely operationally in terms of conflicting educational theories; it is a principle which demands philosophical grounding before its operational values can be appraised. Thus until bipolarity is grounded philosophically in a doctrine of realism, and then interpreted educationally, it is difficult to make comparisons with bipolarity within the Organic Philosophy of Education.

John Dewey and Bipolarity

In the writer's judgment Dewey cannot be classified as a believer in the *principle of bipolarity* as it has been described here.[34] It is certainly true that Dewey, like Whitehead, criticized any bifurcations of nature in the general revolt against dualism. It was characteristic of Dewey's line of thinking that he deplored gaps in experience or dichotomies of any kind, such as the well known pairs of mind and body, interest and effort, individual and society, education and life, and the like. In his instrumental way he employed an adaptation of the Hegelian triadic pattern and invariably reduced a thesis and antithesis to a synthesis.

However, Dewey in revolting against the error of "dualism,"[35] failed to place proper emphasis on the factor of *diversity,* or the *unity of opposites.* Bipolarity as we have pointed out repeatedly requires a recognition of the reality of *diversity* as well as *unity.* Organic *bipolarity* preserves the partial truth of "dualism" by recognizing the *relative* but *real* factor of *separability* or *independence.* The organic separability, however, is *relative* and not *absolute.* Thus the Organic Philosophy of Education rests upon a clear recognition of bipolar relations, or the unity of opposites. For example, it has been noted that whereas Charles S. Peirce held that there was a legitimate disengagement of *theory* and *practice* for educational purposes, Dewey would not sanction such a separation.[36] This organic view then is more in agreement with Peirce at this point. However, it has also been noted in research that Peirce did not express *bipolarity* explicitly or overtly; it might have been implicit in much of his thinking.[37]

It is relatively easy for defenders of Dewey's position to argue that Dewey was a believer in *bipolarity* because of his frequent references to such dichotomies. The organic retort is that Dewey did use such dichotomies in his writing, but he was always criticizing the dichotomies as "bifurcations." His emphasis then followed on noting how these two elements should be unified; but one does not find that Dewey was equally concerned with the importance of recognizing and respecting the elements of *diversity* and *separability*, or *independence*. In fact, in one place he speaks of the "duplicity" of such efforts on the part of those who would note this element of diversity.[38] If Dewey were to be classified as a "bipolarist" in retrospect, it would be incumbent upon the one trying to prove such an allegation to find substantial evidences in his writings for emphasis upon the criteria which we have set up for *bipolarity* including "unity of opposites," "separability," "incompleteness *in se*," and "togetherness."

This discussion is far from academic with respect to educational philosophy. This writer contends that Dewey's emphasis upon the unifying factor and the consequent neglect of the factor of *organic separability* has been reflected in the work of his followers; the educational process has become amorphous and confused in large part by running all these separable factors together. The Organic Philosophy of Education hopes to correct this in large part by the recognition of factors of *separability* as well as the factors of *togetherness*. Elements in bipolar relationship are in one sense separable and in one sense interdependent; examples of this are bipolarities of reason and experience, organized subject matter continuities and experience, theory and practice, logical and psychological continuities, and structural and functional elements. Hence we see that the differences are both theoretical and practical.

Bipolarity Restated in the Organic Philosophy of Education

Bipolarity then is a contemporary resolution of the problem of opposites which holds as follows: *that organic process and reality* *are constituted by diverse elements in a unified relationship, such that this unity contains the relations of two poles, which exhibit a diversity within that unity.* This relationship of diverse poles in a unity of opposites exemplifies the relations of togetherness (con-junctiveness) and separableness (disjunctiveness). The two poles exist and the polarity between the poles is existent, interdependently or relatively. In isolation the two poles are incomplete. The separableness (disjunctiveness) is only relative and not absolute.*

Any field of organic *bipolarity* includes a unity of opposites and exhibits other related principles of organism. Such a field of organic bipolarity is important and significant for it illustrates how organically at least some of the perennial problems of philosophy can be resolved: What is the relationship of the "one and the many"? What are the relations of bipolar opposites? Is reality dualistic? How are metaphysical forces manifest on the operational level? How can a higher synthesis be achieved so that older issues may be resolved?

The educational importance of these philosophical questions may not be readily apparent to the student of education. Yet they are involved in the notion of *bipolarity,* and it will be seen subsequently how important the notion is to our educational theory and practice.

It may be of some assistance to the reader to use the example of *Male and Female Components,* or plus and minus symbols, in the interpretation of the figure of *bipolarity.* Plato and others have spoken of the *Male and Female Components* of the universe in the metaphysical sense.[39] The plus and minus symbols are familiar in modern physics. Either of these concepts may be used in illustrating *bipolarity.*

In a *philosophy of organism* reality is not conceived of as one or many. In the perennial dispute and speculation as to the oneness or the manyness of reality itself, the philosopher of organism believes it is both one and many. Reality exhibits both unity and diversity in certain respects. It is a unity of diversities in certain respects— or a *unity of opposites.* The male and female components are such a unity of opposites; they are in one sense the *same* and in another sense *other.* They exemplify the principle of diversity in one sense,

168

and they exemplify the principle of unity in another sense. Together they represent the organic field of experience in a *unity of opposites*. Such a field is not characterized alone by manyness, or pluralism, nor by unity, or monism. The organic field of experience in its bipolar aspects represents relationships of *whole and part, unity and diversity*, and *bipolarity*.

In *bipolar relations* there exists a unity of opposite poles. These poles are in a sense similar and in a sense other. They are in one respect separable, yet not absolutely so. They are in another sense inseparable, for they are incomplete in themselves. They are not absolutely separated, but only relatively so. They are not mutually exclusive in their organic relationships.

Now this duality of the poles does not constitute "dualism." They do not constitute two poles that are *absolutely* independent of one another. They are *relatively independent*. Furthermore they do not constitute a genuine *bifurcation* of nature or field of reality. They characterize a kind of independence or separability.

It should be remembered that although the *principle of bipolarity* has been emphasized as essential to the organic philosophy of education, it is not the only important principle of organism. It is coherent with other principles of a *philosophy of organism*. As such it is logically consistent with organic conceptions of *creativity, conjunction* and *disjunction, relatedness, concrescence*, and *process*. As Whitehead says, "Coherence, as here employed, means that the fundamental ideas, in terms of which the scheme is developed, presuppose each other so that in isolation they are meaningless."[40]

On its rational side it is contended that bipolarity is a logical and coherent principle and ideal of an organic speculative philosophy and metaphysics. On its empirical side it is both "applicable" and "adequate" in Whitehead's terms.

> It means that the texture of observed experience, as illustrating the philosophic scheme, is such that all related experience must exhibit the same texture. Thus the philosophical scheme should be "necessary," in the sense of bearing in itself its own warrant of universality throughout all experience, provided that we confine ourselves to that which communicates with immediate matter of fact.[41]

Summary Statement of Organic View

It is apparent that *bipolarity* has been conceived in various forms by ancient, modern, and contemporary philosophers. The conception of *bipolarity* as formulated in the Organic Philosophy of Education is not derived from any single source. In fact it is most difficult to retrace the steps by which one has come to embrace the idea of *bipolarity*. Perhaps all of these sources have had their respective influences on our own lines of inquiry concerning the relationships of opposites. The conception of bipolarity as formulated here has been derived from historical sources of philosophy and educational thought, and supported and clarified by the writings of contemporary bipolarists. The following propositions then indicate the status of bipolarity in the Organic Philosophy of Education:

(1) That it is a fundamental principle derived from the organic tradition from the ancients to the present;

(2) That bipolarity here refers to a unity of opposite poles, which are related by the characteristics of (a) *separableness*, (b) *incompleteness in se*, and (c) *togetherness*; and that the distinctions are relative and not absolute;

(3) That bipolarity as used here does not indicate genuine "dualism" or "bifurcation," although it does indicate real separability in the organic sense;

(4) That bipolarity does not stand alone as the basis of the Organic Philosophy of Education; it is intrinsically related to other supporting organic principles;

(5) That bipolarity is another way of expressing the organic proposition of conjunctiveness and disjunctiveness;

(6) That the main contribution of the Organic Philosophy of Education with respect to bipolarity is the working out of systematic applications to the crucial problems of educational theory; that these applications had not heretofore been worked out in terms of a thoroughgoing educational philosophy;

(7) That it is a metaphysical principle and that it manifests itself in virtually all aspects of human knowledge and experience;

(8) That on the rational side it is logical and coherent; and on the empirical side it is applicable and adequate;

(9) That it cannot be applied indiscriminately to all dichotomies; it must be subject to organic criteria of bipolarity;

(10) That it is essential to the Organic Philosophy of Education;

(11) That the principle applies to such educational co-ordinates as: formal-informal, structural-functional, logical-psychological, objective-subjective, external-internal, and rational-experiential.

It may be helpful to visualize these many bipolarities through the following figures:

Figure 4. *Bipolarities and the World*

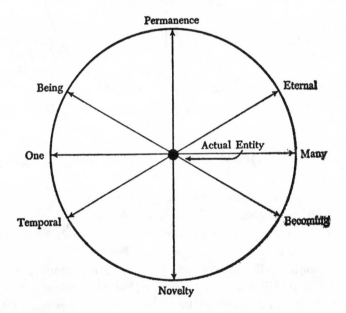

The ideal opposites are actualized in the processes of the world. The actual entities which emerge from the creative processes exemplify such bipolarities as permanence and novelty, being and becoming, and one and many. The world is the realization of these creative factors. They are co-ordinate within the process. These bipolar forces intersect in actual entities.

171

Figure 5. *Bipolarities and the Educational Process*

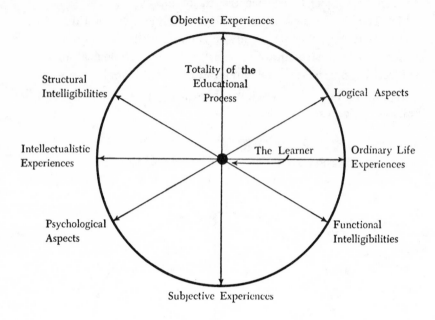

This figure illustrates some of the chief bipolarities as they apply to the educational process. It is apparent that these diverse aspects of the educational process are really co-ordinates. As co-ordinates they are complementary and reciprocal in character. The various sets of co-ordinates in turn are corollaries; each with a slightly different context, meaning and emphasis. They are the many parts of the total unity of the educational process. Other bipolarities could well be included in the figure; for purpose of simplicity they were omitted here. They include theoretical-practical, external-internal, formal-functional, and the like. Thus the educational process is characterized by the harmonization of these co-ordinates.

Educational Significance of Bipolarity

One of the main tasks confronting us has been the reinterpretation and reconstruction of educational theories in the light of bipolarity and other organic principles. Strange as it may seem, little has been done by educational theorists with these specific principles in recent times.[42]

The principle of bipolarity along with other organic principles has far reaching meaning and significance in its application to crucial educational problems. These principles apply significantly to such problems as the nature of man, the educational process, the curriculum, methods of teaching, the role of the teacher, the functions and aims of education, discipline, control, motivation, the individual and society, school and society—in fact to most of the real issues of educational theory.

Most educators now agree that education needs a synthesis of the valid elements of conflicting theories of education.[43] It is clear to them that it is not simply a matter of either progressive or conservative education, but rather that there are indispensable validities within each educational viewpoint and their supporting philosophies. It is easy to say that we should have such a synthesis, but it is quite another task to actually achieve a synthesis. A synthesis worthy of the name is not merely eclectic, experimental, fragmentary, or arbitrary in character. As indicated earlier, one does not secure a synthesis by piecing together the random parts of different philosophical and educational doctrines; it is necessary to obtain a philosophical core of principles and then to re-examine the conflicting theories with respect to the coherence and applicability of valid elements.

The reconstruction of educational theory to achieve a new synthesis is really a philosophical enterprise. It requires the content and methods of philosophy. Such a reconstruction cannot be properly conducted from one of the subdivisions of educational science, such as administration, educational psychology, curriculum and instruction, or the like. Fundamental conceptions must be set forth in terms of the philosophical foundations of the whole educational enterprise. Hence it has been my endeavor to set forth a core of organic principles which would provide the theoretical basis for such an enterprise. The translation of these principles into the various fields within education is, to be sure, a task for the experts in their respective fields.

Without a systematic and theoretical architecture to follow in educational reconstruction, administrators, teachers and others on the practical level must feel their way along in experimental fashion. Even here they must have some philosophy in mind explicitly or implicitly, or unintegrated aspects of many theories. Many teachers have no doubt approximated the principles, which we have theoretically formulated, in their actual practices. Many teachers have told this writer that they do combine aspects of progressivism and conservativism, of the old and the new, in their teaching practices. Although much of what they say about such blendings is true, yet they are unable as teachers to clearly articulate the "why" of the "theory" of what they are doing. At times it seems that teachers who try to incorporate aspects of different "theories" are hesitant and uncertain in their own minds, because of their very lack of a reinforcing and positive philosophy of education which coincides with what they are actually doing through "common sense" or "experience." They may teach quite progressively for part of the school year with emphasis upon "life experience" and "life adjustment" education, only to have pangs of conscience which goad them into a return to old fashioned direct teaching of subject matters. These organic principles should make it possible to formulate sound theoretical doctrines, which will meet these deeply felt needs on the part of the teachers and educators for a philosophy of education, which actually synthesizes the validities of conflicting theories in some coherent pattern.

Monopolarity

Recent educational theories have suffered from the error of monopolarity or one-sidedness. In philosophy this is known as the "error of reductionism," or the attempt to reduce a real complexity of factors requiring multiple explanations to a single concept. Progressives, for example, have erred on the side of such concepts as "life adjustment," "growth and development of the personality," "learning by doing," "socialization," "group dynamics," "functionalism," and the "emergent curriculum." Properly complemented by validities from other theories of education, these concepts are extremely valuable to education. But when they are taken to the exclusion of other conceptions, as they have been so frequently, they result in a one-sided and violent reaction against "academic schooling," "formal education," "subject-matter-set-out-in-advance," and "direct teaching." By the same token certain conservatives have been very one-sided in their defense of the academic, formal, linguistic, literary education, and even memoritor type of learning. In their rejection of the other validities of modern education, they have then failed to keep step with the necessary reconstructions of modern educational theory.

The significance of the principle of bipolarity is that it shows the error of such one-sided thinking and also provides the means of overcoming that kind of error in education.

Quite understandably teachers have followed the lead of some educational theorists in their desire for unity. We romantically idealize unity and in modern times have reacted strongly against what philosophers have termed "dualism." Dewey quite rightly led the protest of educators against the "dualisms" of interest and effort, mind and body, methods and subject matter, the individual and the group, democracy and education, and school and social progress. It was cogently argued that we should do away with the old "dualisms" or bifurcations of nature, and should instead realize the unity rather than the separateness emphasized in the past.

"Fusion" or "integration" has become the word of the moderns. The child is not a "mind" separated from his "body." "Interest" is not opposed to "effort," but it is a unity in terms of "intelligent action"; the school is not divorced from "life," but it is "life itself"; "subject matter" is not something to be studied at school, but is the stuff of life's problems. Subject matters are not to be sharply demarcated into compartments; rather the dividing lines are to be removed and the various subject matters "fused" into the "life activities curriculum" or the "core curriculum" or the "life adjustment" school.

Here then was the emergence of progressive educational theory based upon a great half truth. Certainly "unity" is to be desired; nature should not be split asunder unnaturally and arbitrarily. Logical and analytical distinctions should not obliterate the enduring fluencies and organic unities of nature. The child and his educational program should not be bifurcated beyond reason and fact. All of these desires for unity and the rejection of "dualism" are understandable. But now we can see clearly why they were half truths; we can see from our present vantage point that they were in large part misdirected efforts and why they resulted in the error of one-sidedness in their corresponding educational theories and practices.

Organic principles of unity and diversity as expressed in the *principle of bipolarity* now shows us most graphically why traditionalists and progressives committed the error of *monopolarity* in their struggles over educational theory and practice. We do not have to be "dualists" in order to avoid the error of one-sidedness. Our choice is not between *unity and diversity*. It is clear that in the conception of *bipolarity,* nature and education exemplify the unity of opposites, the *one and the many*. The error of the "dualists" was that they bifurcated nature and the component elements of education. The error of the modernists was that in their desire to eliminate dualism and achieve unity, they unwittingly obscured the *principle of diversity—of separableness*. With the *bipolar principle* and its reinforcing organic concepts, educational theory can be reconstructed along sounder lines—the respective truths of unity and diversity can be reunited.

Summary. Several of the contemporary conceptions of polarity and bipolarity are pertinent to our exposition. Professor Archie Bahm has exemplified a form of bipolarity in his position which he terms 'Organicism.' His Organicism is the logical product of an analysis of the respective validities and invalidities of eight other theories. Bahm objects to positions known as 'Extreme One-Pole-Ism,' 'Other-Pole-Ism,' 'Aspectism,' and 'Dualism.' Bahm's analysis reveals the organic conclusion: that the poles (of a given bipolarity) exist in a three-way relationship, partly independently, partly dependently, and partly interdependently.

To this extent the organic view expressed here and Bahm's views of bipolar relations are in agreement. There are underlying differences though, as revealed in Bahm's critique of Whitehead's philosophy of organism. Bahm criticizes Whitehead's transformation of substance, and his inherent tendency to accept the tenets of rationalism. By and large my own philosophical propositions are more in conformity with those of Whitehead; this writer finds merit in his inherent rationalism.

Bipolarity (or dipolarity) is found prominently in Whitehead's philosophy of organism. It is coherent with his principles of prehension, concrescence, creativity, becoming, conjunctivity, disjunctivity, and the like. All actual entities possess physical and mental poles. God is bipolar. The great ideal opposites of the world are bipolar. Since Whitehead's thought is a protest against dualism *per se,* and all things are connected, the principle of bipolarity plays an important role in his philosophy of organism.

To my knowledge Whitehead has not made direct application of bipolarity and related organic principles to educational theory. The reinterpretation, extension, and application of bipolarity to the fundamental problems of educational theory as expounded here are the responsibility of this writer. The direct applications of philosophical principles to educational theories seem to have been overlooked by most philosophers of renown.

Professor W. H. Sheldon has written significantly of the principle of polarity. He properly warns of the danger of exaggerated use of the polar principle. He holds further that polarity means a relation of two opposites, each partly independent, and that it is the asymmetrical relationship of the poles which contributes to the power and efficacy of the relationship in the resulting process. He holds also to the necessity of 'structure' as well as 'process,' a contention which finds support in the Organic Philosophy of Education, too.

Professor Morris Cohen reminds us the principle is as old as philosophy itself. He uses the figure of the scissors as analogous to the bipolar functioning of the human intelligence. With this analogy in mind one sees numerous exemplifications of bipolar functioning in all fields of human experience.

To my knowledge Frederick Breed has made the only application of bipolarity to educational theory in recent educational literature in

177

philosophy of education. Briefly he asserts that the educational program should embrace both the methods and content of knowledge; that freedom and authority are complementary; and that progressive emphasis on content internally produced and conservative emphasis on content externally supplied should be co-ordinated. The principle of bipolarity is not expounded in terms of its philosophical grounds, nor is it applied extensively to the other problems of education.

The problem rises as to whether Dewey believed in bipolarity. My answer is in the negative. Dewey in his revolt against dualism did seek to unite all bifurcations of experience. Yet it is my contention that in his reaction against dualism he achieved a unity at the expense of the truth of 'duality,' or as I should prefer to call it —the principle of diversity. To my knowledge Dewey emphasized the principle of togetherness of things, but never the principle of bipolarity which also recognizes the 'unity of opposites.' Herein lies much of the existent weakness of his educational theory.

The organic view expounded here then is one which recognizes the bipolar relations of any given poles as exhibiting unity and diversity, or a unity of opposites. Interpreted in terms of an organic field of experience the two poles represent two hemispheres of educational significance which are relatively separable, incomplete *in se*, and together (Bahm's independence, dependence, and interdependence). This relationship does not constitute a 'dualism' for the poles or spheres are relatively conjunctive and disjunctive in the words of Whitehead. The organic world exemplifies bipolarities of such co-ordinates as the one and many, permanence and novelty, being and becoming, and eternal and temporal. From the viewpoint of the Organic Philosophy of Education the educational process exemplifies such bipolarities as objective and subjective experience, structural and functional intelligibilities, logical and psychological continuities, and rationalistic and ordinary life experiences.

The bipolar principle with other organic concepts provides us with the basis for a thoroughgoing reconstruction of educational theories. A genuine synthesis is now possible. With these organic principles we are in a position to avoid the error of monopolarity or one-sideness which has been the case with all too many educational theories. Excesses of theories termed progressive and conservative can now be avoided.

FOOTNOTES

1. A. J. Bahm, *Philosophy: An Introduction* (New York: John Wiley & Sons, Inc., 1953, Copyright 1953 by John Wiley & Sons, Inc.), pp. 234-72.

2. A. J. Bahm, *Philosophy: An Introduction*, p. 234. Reprinted with permission of the publisher.

3. A. J. Bahm, *Philosophy: An Introduction*, p. 235. Reprinted with permission from the publisher.

4. A. J. Bahm, *Philosophy: An Introduction*, p. 237. Reprinted with permission from the publisher.

5. A. J. Bahm, *Philosophy: An Introduction*, p. 235. Reprinted with permission from the publisher.

6. A. J. Bahm, *Philosophy: An Introduction*, pp. 240-41. Figures and exposition reprinted with permission from the publisher.

7. A. J. Bahm, *Philosophy: An Introduction*, p. 241. Reprinted with permission from the publisher.

8. A. J. Bahm, *Philosophy: An Introduction*, pp. 269-72.

9. A. J. Bahm, *Philisophy: An Introduction*, p. 269. Reprinted with permission from the publisher.

10. A. J. Bahm, *Philosophy: An Introduction*, p. 270. Reprinted with permission from the publisher.

11. A. J. Bahm, *Philosophy: An Introduction*, p. 270. Reprinted with permission from the publisher.

12. A. J. Bahm, *Philosophy: An Introduction*, p. 271.

13. A. N. Whitehead, *Process and Reality* (Cambridge: Cambridge University Press, 1929, copyright in U.S.A. by Macmillan Co.).

14. A. N. Whitehead, *Process and Reality*.

15. A. J. Bahm, *Philosophy: An Introduction*, p. 267. Reprinted with permission from the publisher.

16. Described in another manuscript of this writer, "The Organic Philosophy of Education."

17. A. N. Whitehead, *Process and Reality*, p. 339. Reprinted with permission of the Macmillan Company.

18. A. N. Whitehead, *Process and Reality*, p. 151. Reprinted with permission of the Macmillan Company.

19. A. H. Johnson, *Whitehead's Theory of Reality* (Boston: The Beacon Press, 1952), p. 39. Reprinted with permission of the publisher.

20. W. H. Sheldon, *Process and Polarity* (New York: Columbia University Press, 1944), p. 106. Reprinted with permission from the publisher.

21. W. H. Sheldon, *Process and Polarity*, p. 108. Reprinted with permission from the publisher.

22. W. H. Sheldon, *Process and Polarity*, p. 145. Reprinted with permission from the publisher.

23. From another manuscript, "The Organic Philosophy of Education."

24. Morris Cohen, *Reason and Nature* (Glencoe, Illinois: The Free Press, 1935), p. 165. Reprinted with permission of the author's estate.

25. M. Cohen, *Reason and Nature*, p. 165. Reprinted with permission of the author's estate.

26. Frederick Breed, Chapter 3, "Education and the Realistic Outlook," *Philosophies of Education*, Part I (Chicago: NSSE, 1942), Forty-First Yearbook of the National Society for the Study of Education, pp. 87-139.

27. F. Breed, *Philosophies of Education*, pp. 124-37.

28. F. Breed, *Philosophies of Education*, pp. 124-37.

29. F. Breed, *Philosophies of Education*, p. 101. Reprinted with permission from the publisher.

30. F. Breed, *Philosophies of Education*, p. 125. Reprinted with permission from the publisher.

31. F. Breed, *Philosophies of Education*, p. 127. Reprinted with permission from the publisher.

32. F. Breed, *Philosophies of Education*, p. 128. Reprinted with permission from the publisher.

33. F. Breed, *Philosophies of Education*, pp. 132-33. Reprinted with permission from the publisher.

34. In personal correspondence, certain professors of educational philosophy of pragmatic persuasion have contended "that Dewey would agree with your theory of bipolarity." This writer has argued that Dewey did not really accept the bipolar idea.

35. Melvin C. Baker, *Foundations of John Dewey's Educational Theory* (New York: King's Crown Press, Columbia University, 1955), pp. 116-18.

36. George S. Maccia, "The Peircean School," *Educational Theory*, Vol. V, No. 1, (January, 1955), p. 30.

37. James A. Turman, "A Comparative Study of Some Selected Solutions to the Problem of Logical-Psychological Continuity in the Educative Process," unpublished dissertation, University of Texas, 1956, pp. 72-84.

38. Paul Arthur Schilpp, ed., *Philosophy of Alfred North Whitehead*, 2nd ed. (New York: Tudor Publishing Company, 1951).

39. F. S. C. Northrop, *The Meeting of East and West* (New York: The Macmillan Company, 1946), p. 62.

40. A. N. Whitehead, *Process and Reality*, p. 1. Reprinted with permission from Macmillan Company.

41. A. N. Whitehead, *Process and Reality*, p. 4. Reprinted with permission from Macmillan Company.

42. As we have previously noted, Frederick Breed has done something with the bipolar notion in educational theory.

43. Joseph Justman, "Wanted: A Philosophy of American Education," *School and Society*, May 12, 1956, pp. 159-61.

9

THE ORGANIC FIELD OF EXPERIENCE

IN large part the foregoing analysis of bipolarity provides us with the conceptual basis for an understanding of the teaching-learning processes in terms of the organic field of human experience. Conceptions of the creative process from later chapters are also interwoven with the content of this chapter. Diverse aspects of the educational processes are exemplified in the organic field of experience.

Some of the underlying questions proposed for consideration in this chapter are as follows: How does the principle of bipolarity apply to the organic field of experience? How does it apply to the teaching-learning process? What is meant by the organic field of experience? What are the relations of the various aspects of the educational process to the organic field of experience? How are Whitehead's conceptions of creative process exemplified in the organic field of experience? How are these philosophical notions amplified and extended in terms of the educational process? What is the significance of this organic process? What contrasts are evident between the organic theory and progressive and conservative theories of the educational process?

The Organic Field of Experience

The accompanying figure shows graphically the organic field of experience and its exemplifications of the diversities of the teaching-learning process and human development. This figure illustrates how many organic principles and conceptions can be brought to-

182

Figure 6. The Organic Field of Experience

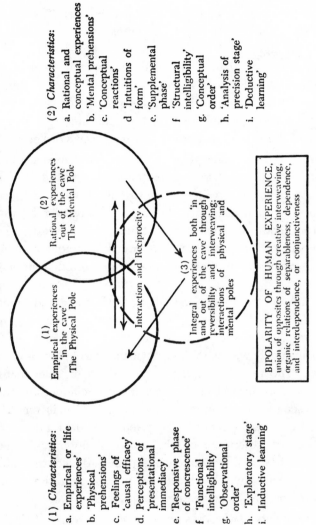

(1) *Characteristics:*

a. Empirical or 'life experiences'
b. 'Physical prehensions'
c. Feelings of 'causal efficacy'
d. Perceptions of 'presentational immediacy'
e. 'Responsive phase of concrescence'
f. 'Functional intelligibility'
g. 'Observational order'
h. 'Exploratory stage'
i. 'Inductive learning'

(2) *Characteristics:*

a. Rational and conceptual experiences
b. 'Mental prehensions'
c. 'Conceptual reactions'
d 'Intuitions of form'
e. 'Supplemental phase'
f. 'Structural intelligibility'
g. 'Conceptual order'
h. 'Analysis of precision stage'
i. 'Deductive learning'

(3) *Characteristics:*

a Unity of empirical-rational experiences
b Unity of physical-mental prehensions
c 'Symbolic reference'
d Unity of aesthetic-theoretic components of experience
e. Phase of 'satisfaction'
f 'Organic intelligibility'
g. Unity of observational-conceptual orders
h 'Generalization & synthesis stage'
i. Interweaving of inductive-deductive learning through reversibility

Labels within figure:

(1) Empirical experiences 'in the cave' The Physical Pole

(2) Rational experiences 'out of the cave' The Mental Pole

Interaction and Reciprocity

(3) Integral experiences both 'in and out of the cave' through reversibility and interweaving; interactions of physical and mental poles

BIPOLARITY OF HUMAN EXPERIENCE, union of opposites through creative interweaving, organic relations of separableness, dependence, and interdependence, or conjunctiveness gether in a unified conception of the organic educational process. This figure with its delineations represents this writer's amplification and extension of organic conceptions of the creative process as fused with his own interpretations of the educational process. The discussion immediately following is largely in terms of an exposition of this accompanying figure.[1]

The three overlapping spheres represent the organic field of experience. The main bipolarity exists between spheres 1 and 2. Sphere 3, indicated by dotted circle, is the resulting product or synthesis of the interactions of the other spheres. Each of the three spheres represents a phase of the educational process, or the process of becoming.

Since a wide variety of conceptions are interpreted here in terms of the three spheres, the designations of the characteristics of these areas should not be taken too literally or strictly. Like most figures it represents a very great simplification of complex relationships derived here from both ontological and educational contexts. The figure with its various characterizations is largely figurative and suggestive for our purposes. A literal interpretation would destroy its value.

These three spheres represent three phases of learning and human experience and can be considered both conjunctively and disjunctively. Conjunctively the spheres represent the total process of development; disjunctively we see the phases of the learning or developmental process. The relations of these spheres are organic, that is complementary and reciprocal. Like other bipolar relationships they exemplify (i) separableness in a relative sense, (ii) incompleteness *in se,* and (iii) interdependence. They represent the fundamental bipolarity of human experience or 'the union of opposites.' They illustrate and emphasize the interactive experiences and the interweaving of experiences in the educational process requisite to the conscrescence of the person or learner.

Relations of elements of the organic field of experience. (a) The initial aspects of the learning process are 'empirical' or 'ordinary life experiences.' These direct experiences are 'in the cave' represented by sphere 1. These empirical experiences are complemented and extended by the 'rational experiences' 'out of the cave' indicated by sphere 2. The 'life experiences' or even 'systematic experiences' are extended conceptually by 'schooling' in the formal sense of organized, vicarious study. The interactions of these two spheres are accomplished by 'interweaving' these two types of experiences and by 'reversibility' which amounts to the 'inductive-deductive' experiences of the third sphere. Here then we see a unification of empirical and rational experiences. This union constitutes one way of looking at the educational process within the organic field of experience.

(b) In terms of concrescence sphere 1 is characterized by the 'prehensions' of the physical pole and sphere 2 by the 'prehensions' of the mental pole; sphere 3 represents the interactions and the integral experiences resulting therefrom.[2] (There are also 'hybrid' prehensions which are not expounded in this simplified version.) In terms of Whitehead's 'creative process' the 'real internal constitution' of a developing organism is integrally constituted by the interactions of its physical poles as they in turn interact with other entities. We see in this figure how these interactions are nurtured within the organic educational process.

(c) Whitehead's three stages of the process of concrescence correspond with the three spheres depicted here.[3] The 'responsive phase' or primary stage is characterized by feelings of 'causal efficacy.' There are vague intuitions of the world of actual objects. This 'responsive phase' coincides with the experiences in sphere 1 as initially experienced. Correspondingly the 'supplemental phase' or secondary stage is marked by the influx of 'conceptual reactions.' These 'conceptual reactions' are illuminations derived from the lure of the 'ideal forms' and 'subjective aims.' This 'supplemental phase' coincides with our sphere 2.

(d) What Whitehead terms the perceptions of 'presentational immediacy' or sense perceptions can be equated with the perceptual experiences of sphere 1 here. Actually it is most difficult to separate perceptions and conceptions for they are so intimately related. Perceptions of actual objects are more discrete while conceptions are more abstract and general. These perceptions of 'presentational immediacy' are extended and clarified on the conceptual level of sphere

185

2, or the 'intuitions of form.' In terms of concrescence of the learner there is also the emergence of 'subjective aims' during the 'supplemental phase' of our second sphere.[4] The 'symbolic reference' (c) is accomplished in the third sphere by the linking of the forms with 'the feelings of causal efficacy' and 'the perceptions of presentational immediacy' of the first sphere. Educationally this means that the learner grasps the relationships of the conceptual level and the perceptual level of ordinary experience. Thus our third sphere represents the unification of the 'aesthetic' and 'theoretic' components of human experience.

(e) The three stages of Whitehead's concrescence harmonize with this schema very nicely: his primary phase coincides by and large with the first sphere 'in the cave'; his secondary phase corresponds with the second sphere 'out of the cave'; and his final phase corresponds with our third sphere or 'product' realized through interweaving and 'reversibility.' Thus there is a movement from indeterminacy to determinacy through these three stages and spheres of experience.

(f) The writer's own terms of 'functional, structural, and organic intelligibilities' in slightly different perspective harmonize with these three spheres. 'Functional intelligibility' coincides with the experiences 'in the cave' or sphere 1; 'structural intelligibility' coincides with the experiences 'out of the cave' in the second sphere; 'organic intelligibility,' or the product of the other two, coincides with the third sphere.

(g) Whitehead also speaks of understanding the facts of 'the observational order' in terms of 'the conceptual order.'[5] This notion also harmonizes with our diagram. The 'observational order' is found in the first sphere; the 'conceptual order' is largely found in sphere 2; the unity of observational and conceptual orders of experience, feeling, and thought is achieved in the third sphere.

(h) It is clear then that Whitehead's three stages of the creative process coincide with our figure. In addition his three stages of the learning process correspond with our figure. The 'exploratory' or 'romantic stage' of any unit of experience is equated here with experiences 'in the cave' or the first sphere. The stage of 'analysis' or 'precision' is patently that of the second sphere. The third stage of 'generalization' or 'synthesis' coincides with the synthesis of our third sphere. This analysis is still another way of interpreting the organic field of experience.

(i) Frequently, it is argued whether or not the educational process is inductive or deductive. A resolution is offered here. It is apparent that the educational process is in one sense inductive, in another deductive, and still in a third, it is inductive-deductive, or an interweaving or reversibility of the two. It is apparent that 'inductive learning' harmonizes with the empirical sphere, and that 'deductive learning' coincides with the rational sphere, and that 'inductive-deductive' learnings coincide with the third sphere of 'integral experience.'

These are the broad outlines of the organic field of experience. If space permitted, further ramifications and qualifications would be advanced. Such expositions will have to be made in other contexts.

The writer contends that the one-sidedness of conflicting theories of education can be corrected largely through the recognition of this organic field of learning, when conceived in the light of the principles which have been set forth. Any doctrine which ignores the organic co-ordination of these hemispheres, and clearly subordinates one pole to the other, as both formal and functional theories have done, violates the intention and spirit of organic education.

In summary form it is clear that the writer conceives of such a *field of teaching-learning experiences* as exemplifying organic principles. There is no intent to see things only in their *disjunctiveness;* there is an intent to see aspects of reality and the educational process both *conjunctively* and *disjunctively.* Likewise there is no intent here to see aspects of the educational enterprise only through the *principle of unity* or the *principle of diversity*—but rather through *bipolarity,* or the *unity of opposites.* There is a distinct advantage to the visualization and conceptualization of two distinct hemispheres of educational experience. There is a proper distinction between the realms of sphere 1 and sphere 2 in their varying relationships. As we apply this organic field to the varying problems of education and the existent controversies, we can see the legitimate and respective claims of *theory* and *practice, form* and *fact, theoretic* and *aesthetic components, eternal forms* and *actual entities, logical* and *psychological elements,* and *structural, functional,* and *organic intelligibilities.* It is clearly evident that these *polar realms* are related through *interdependence, dependence,* and *independence.* It is beyond argument that there is intent here to defend a "dualism." In this figure we see in simplified form the wisdom of Plato's *Parable of the Cave* in terms of the educational process. In short many of the conflicts of educational theory can visually and conceptually be resolved and the valid elements reconciled through this conception.

Interpretations of the Organic Field of Experience

The figure illustrating the *organic field of experience* is subject to a variety of interpretations and applications of organic educational principles. Some of these interpretations are as follows:

(1) *The organic field of experience* in its over-all sense is a unity; it is also characterized by *diversity;* as a given field of experience it is a microcosmic exemplification of organic principles of the macrocosm. Hence it is marked by *whole-part relations, bipolarity,* and *conjunctiveness* and *disjunctiveness.* As a figure it is necessarily incomplete because of its severe simplification.

(2) *The organic field of experience* as illustrated in the figure is a stage where the scenes are rapidly shifted with the varying contexts of educational descriptions of the complex processes. Although the field of experience may at one time be visualized with the triadic relations of *structural, functional,* and *organic intelligibilities* in clarification of one aspect of the educational process, in other contexts it may be necessary to substitute alternately other phases of the educational process such as the bipolarities of *formal-informal, rational-experiential, logical-psychological, scientific experience-personal experience,* and so forth. It should be understood that although there are rough analogies between these various sets of conceptual relationships, one should not make the mistake of believing that they are always exact equations.

(3) The important thing here is for the teacher to realize that although the learner in all of his aspects is continuous with the totality

188

of his experiential environment, there are legitimate *diversities* and *bipolarities* within that totality. The doctor of medicine knows that the organs of the body are vitally related in their totality, but he also knows that one's illness or disease can center in certain organs predominantly.

(4) Now the learning process always involves *unity and diversity*, or sameness and otherness. This can be symbolized by the familiar signs of plus and minus as utilized in physics, mathematics, and in the sciences. They are literally bipolar in nature; they complement one another. In our figure we have used the complementary interactions of *structural* and *functional intelligibilities* to produce the polarity of *organic intelligibility*. We see that they embody the bipolar relations of togetherness, incompleteness *in se,* and separateness. We see also they represent a union of opposites. We see learning in the cave as well as outside of the cave. We see the advantages of disengaging the various types of intelligibility enough so that they can be clear and distinct to both the teacher and students. It is also evident that there is no intention of creating a lasting "dualism" between these aspects of the total learning process.

(5) *The organic field of experience* also makes the *principle of reversibility* and the concept of *interweaving* clear. It is evident that the organic teacher would not stay in one hemisphere or the other, but that he would move from the functional to the structural, and the structural to the functional in terms of reversibility. It is also clear that he would not neglect the experiential phases of the educational process, but neither would he neglect the realms of structured thought and subject matter. The bipolar notion of the educational process makes it clear that such elements would be carefully *interwoven* and *harmonized*; the unity and the diversity of theory and practice, reason and experience, structure and function, academic and life experiences, logical and psychological elements, and the like, would be respected in the educational process.

(6) *The organic field of experience* is a field whereby the *diversities* are seen clearly as parts of *unities*; it is the field wherein the educational process of *interweaving* the *developmental functions of man* with the complexities of his total environment must take place.

189

Education as Organic Process

Organic education means total education. Education, as John Dewey so correctly pointed out, is as broad as life itself.[6] However, the equation of education with the dimensions and complexities of life itself should carry with it an insight into the difficulty or impossibility of reducing the educational process to any partial conception.

Some educational theorists have been prone to reduce education to a single conception. At least in teaching about various educational theories it is common practice to reduce a complex explanation to one or two terms. We are all familiar with such reductionisms as education as unfolding, formation, preparation, experience, development, growth, life adjustment, or formal discipline.[7]

In theoretical analyses of the educational process there are similar reductionisms to instruction, creativity, discovery, habituation, or problem-solving. Likewise we may consciously or unconsciously emphasize the learning process as largely empirical, rational, experimental, linguistic, or authoritative.

All of these expressions, although very convenient, are forms of reductionism, or over-simplification. Since education in the broad sense is as wide as life itself, and as complicated, it defies reduction to any of these foregoing descriptive terms or phrases.

Hence the term *organic education* is used to emphasize the totality and complexity of the educational process. It is the task of a thoroughgoing philosophy of education to describe the various facets of this complex thing called education. An adequate theory of education thus allows for seemingly opposite elements of instruction and discovery, direct and indirect learning, academic and experiential learning, and the utilization of diverse methods.

Organic education must be viewed in terms of man and reality. Man is a *concrescence* of the elements of cosmic reality. We have elsewhere discussed the 'Ten Basic Functions of man.'[8] All of these functions in their internal and intrinsic relationships constitute the dimensions of man's activities and the educational process.

It is evident that the whole of education viewed in terms of these ten categories cannot be reduced properly to any single function, for this would constitute a severe reductionism, the reduction of the whole to one of its parts. For example, we have criticized those progressives who equate education with a "social process." This fact in effect means that the *social function* is utilized as the key to the educational process. It does not mean that other functions are necessarily totally neglected, but it does mean that they are *subordinated* to social interaction. In effect there is a *socialization* of aims, values, curriculum, methods, procedures and outcomes. Certainly we must acknowledge the partial role of education as a social process—a very important part. Yet we should remember that it is only a part and not the whole. Our objection then is to the emphasis given to one function over the others. Education as a social process is cited only as an example of reduction of whole to part, and this conception is not the only offender. Education reduced to the aesthetic, recreational, or intellectual functions would also create a one-sided conception of the total educational process.

By and large then Organic Education means the process whereby there is a deliberate, constructive interweaving of the diverse elements of man and reality as expressed in our ten catgories. There is an organic interplay and interconnectedness of all of these elements. The intellectual and the aesthetic, the moral and the recreational, for example, are interwoven; in fact each element should be nurtured with all of the others.

This over-all view of organic education in the broadest sense does not exclude necessary specializations and concentrations within the total process where such are called for. Admittedly it is obviously necessary to allow for special emphasis upon the intellectual, moral, social, or aesthetic function, for example, in meeting certain objectives. It is not maintained here that each teacher can nurture all ten of man's functions with equal emphasis at all times. On the contrary, in schooling, some fields of study lend themselves quite naturally and inherently to the nurture of some functions more than others. Some of the arts, for example, would lend themselves forcefully to the nurture of the aesthetic capacities and functions of man, and incidentally to the others. The study of mathematics *per se* might well emphasize the intellectual function with other functions to a lesser degree. Participation in religious experiences would nurture spiritual functioning for the most part, although certainly it would involve the other functions in varying degrees.

We have emphasized organic education in terms of the dimensions of the ten functions of man to provide an adequate pattern for education in the larger sense. The main point here then is that our conception of education should not be reduced to any one of the categories. However, it is granted that varying proportions of emphasis in terms of these functions will be realized in the innumerable aspects of the educational environment, be it formal or informal.

It is apparent that a very acute and grave problem of educational theory emerges here: How shall the functions be co-ordinated in the total organic process of education? It is part of our sustained inquiry into an organic conception of education to determine the probable solution to this all important problem.[9]

This problem involves the question of what parts of education can be accomplished best in the schools, and what aspects are better developed through the functions of other social institutions, and through the life experiences of the individual at various maturational levels of his life cycle.

The Significance of Education as an Organic Process

The significance lies in the conception of education, not as simple growth or natural development, but rather in Whitehead's conception of *concrescence*. As an entity *becomes*, it achieves more perfect *being*. It is a process of the *many* becoming integrated in the *one*. In the organic process the entity, or here the learner, becomes both in terms of its *actual potentialities*, and also in terms of ideal potentialities. In the technical terms of the *philosophy of organism*, the entity at any stage of its development is both a *subject* and a *superject*, or an *active agent* and a *product* of that activity. The true being of the entity or organism is not achieved arbitrarily at any point in the development, but at the end of the cycle. The entity also becomes in terms of an interplay between the factors of nature and nurture.

192

The organism comes to be a concrescence of these real and ideal potentialities. The organism or entity in question is an actualization of its organic environment. It cannot help but partake of its environment in the actualization of its becoming and being. However, this latter statement needs to be qualified by the concept of *negative prehension,* which Whitehead uses to indicate *decisions* whereby the ingression of certain forms or possibilities are negated or rejected.

In less technical terms, applied to the child as a learner, the child has actual potentialities as an existent organism. Genetically or biologically, for example, the child has real potentialities for biological development. Mentally there are real potentialities for psychological development. There are multiplicities of real potentialities in the complex environment in which he exists. His very existence at any given time testifies to his continued participation in that environment. We draw no sharp line between the organism and his environment, for as he lives, breathes, and takes on nourishment and the necessities of the life processes, he is a real product of that environment.

We must exercise caution in taking the word environment in too narrow a meaning. We must remember that in this organic view the child is a microcosm of the macrocosm. There are cosmological and metaphysical dimensions to his environment as well as the immediate biological and sociological dimensions. The world is a mixture of creative factors as they operate in the time-space receptacle. Each entity is an exemplification of these creative factors in an organically related world. The child is an exemplification of the potentialities and forces which we have described in terms of the ten basic functions of man. He exemplifies these functions because they exist in an organic world.

What about the *ideal potentialities?* Ideal potentialities such as values, purposes, goods, and understandings are also available to his development. In the actualization of his actual potentialities there will be a fusion with ideal potentialities. Certain possibilities of value will enter into the development rather than others. As Whitehead points out the ingression of these ideal potentialities takes place in all entities, whether low grade non-cognitive organisms, or high grade, cognitive organisms. To the extent that education is considered a deliberate enterprise, we should emphasize the necessity for directing the learner's development in the direction of de-

Figure 7

Fusion of Ideal and Actual Potentialities in the Learning Process

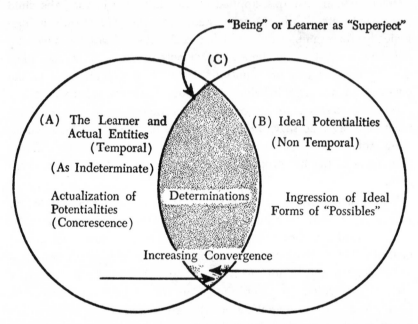

"Being" or Learner as "Superject"

(C)

(A) The Learner and
Actual Entities
(Temporal)

(As Indeterminate)

Actualization of
Potentialities
(Concrescence)

Determinations

(B) Ideal Potentialities
(Non Temporal)

Ingression of Ideal
Forms of "Possibles"

Increasing Convergence

Explanation. Here is a variant figure illustrating the fusion of ideal and actual potentialities in the organic teaching-learning process. The learner as an actual entity in relative state of indeterminacy is represented in Sphere (A). He is in process of concrescence, or moving from indeterminacy to determinacy. Sphere (B) represents the lure of ideal potentialities. From their viewpoint the ideal forms ingress into the actual entity. These ideal forms are 'forms of definiteness.' The overlapping area of the two spheres, represented by (C), represents the determinations which are made through the increasing convergence of the two spheres. It represents the actualization of the potentials; it also represents the 'being' side of the 'becoming' process, or again the 'superject' aspect of the 'subject-superject.' The learner actualizes his potentialities purposefully in terms of the felt 'subjective aims.' He also interacts with other actual entities and ideal entities in his becoming.

194

sired ideal potentialities. Since growth and development of actual capacities must be realized in some intelligible or ideal forms, there is the important matter of selection and direction. Hence the educational process is one of fusing actual potentialities with selected ideal forms or potentialities in what amounts to a creative process.

In the accompanying figure we may see the process represented by two overlapping circles: one represents the learner with his actual potentialities, and the other circle represents his ideal potentialities. The educational process then is realized in the increasing convergence of the two types of potentiality; the ideal potentialities are determined in the actual potentialities of the learner, and the actual potentialities are given form by the ingression of these ideal forms. There is a reciprocal realization through the fusion of actual entities and ideal forms.

This process involves a creative development on the part of the organism. It is not simply unfolding of fixed potentialities in the older way of thinking. On the other hand it is not a denial of the nature of man and his inherent potentialities and functions. Even though we grant that in the ultimate metaphysical sense man's being is evolving, there is the relatively enduring structure of man's being in this epoch which possesses definite characteristics, functions, and capacities in its structure. For all practical purposes of education then, in this qualified framework, we may speak of "the nature of man." Man as man has potentialities in his present epoch, but each man as an individual also has his particular endowment of potentialities and powers.

These potentialities are organic, which means, of course, that they are intimately associated with the structure of the organism and with the environment of that organism. The potentialities are not alien to the environment, for they have been born of that environment. Man's functions, as we have maintained throughout, are not functions alien to an organic universe, but they are functions which exemplify the very potentialities of that universe at its present epochal advanced state.

The organic philosophy disagrees with the existentialist's statement that man begins with absolutely nothing. On the other hand we should disagree with the Aristotelian notion of fixed potentialities of man, in the simple sense of linear development. We cannot suppose man's development to be linear in the sense that the acorn always becomes the oak tree. The interplay of forces and potentialities in the process of concrescence is too complex to presume a linear development.

How then are we to mediate between these two views? We cannot agree that man begins with nothing. Since he has evolved, he begins with an evolved structure with its respective functions. Since he has actual and ideal potentialities, it cannot be said that he begins with nothing. Here we must disagree with the existentialist, for this evolved nature with its immanent functions implies a certain oughtness for the development of man further. He does not have complete freedom, for his very actuality is dictated by the facts of his particular nature; his actual potentiality for intelligent behavior is still a strong argument for the normative development of this potentiality—that is, because man has this unique potentiality, he should develop it. It follows that since man has the ten functions we have enumerated, these should be developed. There is an implicit oughtness to the possession of this kind of structure evidenced in *Homo sapiens.*

On the other side we should agree that human realization does involve *becoming* and *being.* We do not achieve the being of humanity automatically, but rather through effort, struggle, experience, and education. There is a sense, even though we do grant actual potentialities, in which we exist prior to the achievement of our being. We may at one stage of our lives exist as an illiterate, ignorant, rudimentary human being. With the aid of experience, culture, and education we may achieve higher stages of being.

Education as an organic process takes into account the immanence of the many factors in the complex environment, as well as the actual potentialities of the individual and the ideal potentialities.

Contrasts with Conservative and Progressive Theories

Traditional education is characterized by the direct, systematic teaching of subject matter in terms of the teaching-learning process.

Even in the relatively advanced Herbartian notions of the educational process, the teacher was considered the builder of the mentality of the developing youth. The Herbartian viewpoint has been termed "education as formation" largely for this reason. There is no intent to disparage the Herbartian conceptions of teaching for this writer has considerable respect for the contributions which were made with reference to such topics as interest, motivation, Culture-Epoch Theory, systematic procedure, and educational psychology in general. Yet it is true that as a system it exemplified the idea that the teacher is the artist who deliberately forms the mentality of the learner.

What then is the difference between an older view, such as 'Herbartianism,' and the organic viewpoint? The crucial difference is this: Herbartianism, like most forms of traditional education, did not make allowance for the learner's active participation in the process of self-determination and his part in the *creativity* of his own *being* through *intelligent becoming.* In traditional procedure the matured student is the product of the teacher's formation; in the organic view the matured student is a product of diverse forces of control (including those of the teacher, family, community institutions, experiences, etc.) and the gradually increasing degree of self-direction and self-determination by the immature learner.

The organic theory actually deviates from both the conservative and progressive conceptions of control and self-determination. Traditional or conservative theories place too much emphasis upon the one pole of teacher direction and external control with too little concession to self-direction or self-determination. Progressive theories err in the opposite direction in an over-emphasis upon "self-discipline," "self-direction," and "self-determination." What is needed is a philosophical principle which will make possible a genuine co-ordination of the two poles of adult direction and youthful self-direction, or external and internal controls; we believe this is accomplished through the organic principle of *proportionate bipolarity.*[10]

Self-determination is actually shared determination during the formative years of a person's life. The rule of thumb for the organic teacher is stated as follows: allow the student to participate in the educational process and his own self-determination to the maximum

197

extent of his actual powers and propensities at each successive maturational level. By the same token the teacher should accept the responsibility for teaching and training the learner as well as directing the learning process in direct proportion to his level of immaturity of powers and limited experiences.

There are limitations for self-control, self-direction, and self-determination in the necessary degrees of immaturity of youth, which then necessitate a variety of external controls in the form of direct teaching, direct guidance, and even training. At the same time the respective degrees of maturity also allow for an ever increasing amount of self-control, self-direction and self-determination on the part of youth. Concomitant with these gradual increases for self-responsibility are the educational methods advanced by Dewey and others such as sharing instrumentally in the determination of means and ends, pupil-teacher planning, learning through inquiry and discovery, and through problem-solving.

The reason we are able to mediate between the extreme educational conceptions of traditionalism and progressivism is not simply a matter of expediency and compromise, but rather because of the underlying organic principles, such as the *principle of bipolarity,* the *organic theory of control,* and *creative process.*

Summary. The principle of bipolarity is applicable to the organic field of teacher-learning experience. By means of such a conception the organic means of reconciling supposedly conflicting elements of the educational process can be graphically displayed. Such familiar dichotomies as those of reason and experience, logical and psychological aspects, objective and subjective elements, structural and functional elements, organized subject matter and behavioral activity, formal and informal elements, and the like, are not opposing or conflicting theories of education, but they are co-ordinates which function reciprocally within the organic field of teaching-learning experience.

The totality of the learning process is represented by the field of experience which contains bipolar hemispheres which operate both disjunctively and conjunctively. Education in a metaphorical sense requires systematic experience 'in the cave' of immediate experience and 'out of the cave' in terms of rational experience. Experiences in these two spheres allow for contrast and diversity; the result of the interweaving of the contrasting experiences through the process of reversibility is a synthesis or unity in the learning and developing product. Graphically a third sphere represents this synthesis.

Education is more than a social process; it is an organic process in its totality. It contains facets expressed in terms of the ten basic functions of man. It requires the multiple modes of learning and thinking open to human experience. It is a form of reductionism to say that education is simply 'a social process,' 'an intellectual process,' or 'an aesthetic process.'

Education involves concrescence. The learning process represents a fusion of ideal and actual potentialities in the becoming of the learner. The learner absorbs data from other actual entities in his development and self-determination. Through his subjective aims he progressively embodies certain ideal potentialities or forms of definiteness. Eternal objects ingress into the learning entity. Determination results from the increasing convergence of actual and ideal potentialities as they are actualized in the learner.

The organic theory is in contrast with traditional theories because of its emphasis upon the active participation of the learner in his self-determination. It is in contrast with progressive theories in its emphasis upon the bipolar aspects of the educational process in terms of authority and freedom, external and internal controls, direct forms of instruction and discovery through experience, and education as preparation as well as education as life in the immediate sense.

FOOTNOTES

1. For the Analogy of the Cave, see Plato, *Republic*, Bk. VII.

2. See Chapters 14 and 15 on the 'creative process' in relation to this chapter.

3. A detailed exposition of Whitehead's 'concrescence' is given in Ch. 14.

4. See Dr. Craven's 'Five Stages of Concrescence' in Ch. 14.

5. A. N. Whitehead, *Adventures of Ideas* (New York: The Macmillan Company, 1933), p. 198.

6. John Dewey, *Democracy and Education* (New York: The Macmillan Company, 1916).

7. For textbook purposes, such reductionisms may be inevitable.

8. See Ch. 16, "The Ten Basic Functions of Man."

9. See Figure 14 and discussion, page 400.

10. See Figure 11 and discussion, page 280.

10

REASON and EXPERIENCE

CRUCIAL to the conception of the educational process in any given philosophy of education are the relationships of *reason* and *experience*. Classical doctrines have emphasized the rationalistic aspects of the educational process; modern doctrines have repudiated the realm of reason as such and have emphasized experience *per se*. A number of questions emerge then at this point. What is the organic view of the functions of reason? How are the realms of *reason* and *experience* to be reconciled? What is the organic stand on *the logic of subject matter?* What should be the continuity of the teaching-learning process? How is the *logical continuity* defined organically? How is the *psychological continuity* defined organically? What is the organic theory of *logical-psychological* continuity? How does it differ from Dewey's conception of *logical* and *psychological continuities?* What is the *organic analogy of the rope?* What are some of the implications for curriculum and instruction? How is organic education an *interweaving process?* What are some of the implications for teacher education?

The Functions of Reason

In the organic tradition from Plato and Aristotle there has been the recognition of the dual *functions of reason*, (a) the *contemplative*, and (b) the *practical* or *prudential*. The *contemplative function*, or the *theoretic* as it is also called, embraced the highest type of reason, that which was directed toward the inquiry of *truth*, the *good*, and the *beautiful*. The *practical intelligence*, or the *prudential function*, on the other hand embraced the problems of practical action.

201

In modern times the rise of behavioristic theories of intelligence, and bio-social theories, too, have tended to push aside this classical version of the functions of reason. Instrumental, experimental, and functional theories of intelligence, for example, frown upon any deviation from their insistence upon the prudential character of human intelligence and reason. It is significant that not all pragmatists, for example, have insisted upon intelligence as behavioral. Charles S. Peirce, who preferred to call himself a "pragmaticist," dared to make the classic distinction between the functions of reason as (a) having to do with the pursuit of truth, and (b) having to do with intelligent behavior. According to George Maccia's research[1] on this topic this was one of the main differences between Peirce and Dewey. Maccia said that his findings showed that Peirce believed educational aims should include both the pursuit of truth and intelligent behavior, while he found Dewey's thought centered in the behavioral concept of intelligence.

In his work, *The Functions of Reason,* Whitehead makes a similar delineation of *theoretical* and *practical reason.* "The Greeks have bequeathed to us two figures, whose real or mythical lives conform to these two notions—Plato and Ulysses. The one shares Reason with the Gods, the other shares it with the foxes."[2]

From the organic viewpoint reason has a double function of seeking complete understanding and as seeking an immediate method of action. Whitehead calls attention to the dangers inherent in a science which excludes consideration of the final cause. "The evolution of Reason from below has been entirely pragmatic, with a short range of forecast."[3] Here then he is referring to the reliance on the reason of Ulysses which should be complemented by the reason of Plato. "The good life is attained by the enjoyment of contrasts within the scope of method."[4] Reason then in promoting the good life must alternate between the two modes of reason. "Provided that we admit the category of final causation, we can consistently define the primary function of reason. This function is to constitute, emphasize, and criticize the final causes and strength of aims directed toward them."[5]

Speaking of efficient and final causes, he says,

A satisfactory cosmology must explain the interweaving of efficient and of final causation.[6] Meanwhile, we find that the short-range function of Reason, characteristic of Ulysses, is Reason criticizing and emphasizing the subordinate purposes in nature which are the agents of final causation. This is Reason as a Pragmatic agent.[7]

Again there is the recognition of "dipolarity" in the very character of experience.

But every occasion of experience is dipolar. It is mental experience integrated with physical experience. Mental experience is the converse of bodily experience. It is the experience of forms of definiteness in respect to their disconnection from any particular physical experience, but with abstract evaluation of what they *can* contribute to such experience.[8]

These quotations are cited to verify the notion of Whitehead's accession to these dual functions of reason. Although strongly devoted to the role of feeling, Whitehead is through and through a modern rationalist in his faith in the role of reason: "Reason civilizes the brute force of anarchic appetition . . . . Reason is the special embodiment in us of the disciplined counteragency which saves the world."[9] This is indeed an important concept.

In the Organic Philosophy of Education these dual functions are emphasized as organically co-ordinate in the educational process. Proper balance is requisite throughout our educational theory. The reason of Ulysses equates with the pragmatic type of thinking in terms of short range emphasis. The reason of Plato involves the theoretic inquiry, the realm of reason. It has been said elsewhere that the educational process is at various times both of these; within the hemisphere of "ordinary experience" there is an emphasis upon the immediate pragmatic concerns of the learner; whereas the type of learning in the realm of reason is one of disinterested curiosity in the Greek sense of that term.[10] The former is immediate, purposeful, and pragmatic in character; the latter is scientific, theoretic, and unpragmatic in the objectivity of its spirit of inquiry.

This is consonant with what Charles Peirce has said about the relation of theoretical and practical pursuits to the effect that "personal interest in the sphere of scientific inquiry destroys the very objectivity of science."[11]

Education "in the cave" then typifies and exemplifies the reason of Ulysses with its short range, pragmatic emphasis. There is no disparagement of this function of reason here, for it is admittedly very important to the educational process. But it should not be without the complementary function—the reason of Plato. "Out of the cave" then educationally typifies that type of learning and inquiry which is more objective, scientific, and theoretic. The cycle of learning in the end involves passing through both of these functions of reason. With the *principle of reversibility* it becomes clear that both types of reason have an important role and must be nurtured in the totality of the educational process. Learning may well begin with a type of inquiry which is largely based on a personalistic interest— and it may well end in this same place. But in the interim of the cycle of learning there should eventuate the important function of objective learning and inquiry.

Several important implications for the Organic Philosophy of Education may be briefly indicated here. The recognition of the two types of reason, that of Plato and Ulysses, harmonizes with our treatment of various co-ordinates, such as the theoretical-practical, objective-subjective, structural-functional and logical-psychological elements. It is not contended that one can make a completely thoroughgoing equation between these two functions of reason and these various co-ordinates. This would be expecting too much. But by and large there is a general reinforcement of the bipolar field of learning experience in the realms indicated.

Recognition of the two functions of reason broadens and balances the aims, values, purposes, and curricula of organic education. The recognition of the contemplative function assures us of the legitimacy of aims, purposes, and curricular inquiry which go beyond the limitations of the functional, utilitarian, and practical criteria offered by some recent schools of thought. On the other side the recognition of the role of the prudential function of reason assures us that we shall not be completely academic and formalistic in our educational process. Theory eventuates in intelligent practice, and experimental practice requires the understandings of the theoretical. The educational process then embraces the pursuit of understanding and truth as well as its concerns with intelligent behavior.

The Co-ordination of Reason and Ordinary Experience

It has been suggested time and again that the organic doctrine requires the co-ordination of the hemispheres of reason and ordinary experience in terms of total learning. So-called "modern education" dwells upon the idea that all learning should be focused around *ordinary experiences* of "everyday living." There is a partial validity in this point of view. The realm of reason, which also implies systematic learning and inquiry, should be respected as such, and not subordinated to "everyday experience." Nor should it be omitted from the educational process. An adequate philosophy of education must necessarily indicate how both of these areas or hemispheres and their respective validities are to be reconciled.

In this sense "ordinary experience" means "the actual living through an event or events; participating in anything through sensation or feeling . . . the effect upon the judgment or feelings produced by personal and direct impressions as contrasted with descriptions or fancies."[12]

The realm of reason on the other hand, by way of contrast, places an emphasis upon objective, abstract thought and inquiry. Reason is of course a kind of experience too—intellectual or cognitive experience. Yet in its abstract character it is other than the immediate feelings and direct impressions connoted by the term "ordinary experience." It does not limit thinking to the realm of pragmatic or instrumental problem solving in terms of behavioral problems. Typical of the realm of reason are the disciplines of mathematics, logic, and dialectic.

Plato's Allegory of the Cave

The harmonization and utilization of the two spheres can best be understood in the light of Plato's famous allegory of the *Prisoners of the Cave.* (Book VII, Plato's *Rep.*) It will be recalled that in Plato's parable we are asked to visualize a cave in which the prisoners, who have been there for all time, sit on a bench with heavy chains about their heads and shoulders so that they cannot turn around. They sit and watch the flickering shadows cast on the inner wall, and as they do so they presume that the figures and voices which they "see" and "hear" actually come from the shadows on the wall.[13] A stranger visits the cave, and, finally seeing their predicament and dilemma, releases one prisoner from his chains and leads him outside into the light of the sun. He sees with difficulty at first for his eyes are unaccustomed to the brightness of the light. The stranger leads him about so that he may see the hills and valleys in their full actuality. He then takes him back to his accustomed place in the cave with his fellow prisoners. Socrates, the narrator, presumes that after such an experience this particular prisoner would look at the shadows differently than the others. He would have added insight into their actual nature. He would see the shadows as shadows. His former illusions would have been removed. "And if they were in the habit of awarding honors to the persons who were the brightest in such perceptions and distinctions," Socrates asks, "would he not excel?" The beautiful parable is one of the most profound of all philosophical literature.

Without trying to read metaphysical meanings into the parable at this point, let us utilize this figure in our reconciliation of the realms of experience and reason in the educational process. It seems that there is even more significance to the parable in an educational perspective, than the usual interpretation in terms of the ontological problem of *being* and *becoming*.

It is reasonably fair to say that we find our students as prisoners in the cave. The shadows on the wall are their unreflective observations of ordinary experience. They have been only half thoughtful. They "see" things in their own experiences, but not clearly—not with rational clarity and systematic penetration. They are engrossed in the "appearance" of the many things about them, and not with structural intelligibilities. Without the advantages of penetrating study we have only superficial notions of things as derived from "ordinary experience."

The student who has false knowledge based on ordinary experience and opinions, rather than upon real knowledge derived from penetrating study and inquiry, is very much in the cave. He has a welter of opinions but little real knowledge. He shares the views and false opinions or at least the limited opinions of those who have not benefited from deeper inquiry. In short he has ordinary lay opinion as contrasted with scientific insight. Since he has never been 'out of the cave' of ordinary experience, he is quite contented with his opinions and supposed understandings.

In our organic terms then 'being in the cave' is being in the functional realm of everyday experience. It is existential, problematical, and very much here and now. It is very real, but it is not an enlightened state. Its continuity is that of life experience. Here one follows the sequences of sleeping, waking, eating, working, playing, making a living, and solving problems of life. Problems emerge pragmatically. A kind of learning goes on. One learns in the cave through solving problems as they emerge. There is a kind of thinking which is fundamentally empirical and pragmatic. It involves the constant reconstruction of experience 'in the cave' in the parlance of modern education.

But learning 'in the cave' is not enough. It represents only one pole or sphere of the learning process. What is it then to move out of the cave educationally? *To go out of the cave in terms of the organic conception of the teaching-learning processes is to move into the light of reason, of scientific knowledge, of structural knowledge, of objectivity, of systematic inquiry, into the realm of the abstract, the realm of ideas, the realm of whole-part conceptual relationships.* Here we meet and discover the ideas, ideals, values, and concepts in their abstract intelligibility, which will later ingress into the actualities of the objects in our spatial and temporal cave.

Here the human intelligence finds its clearest objects of the cognitive interest. Here we find the satisfying clarity and distinctness which the intelligence craves in terms of conceptual relations in mathematics, logic, and dialectic. The diversity and confusion of the objects and shadows of the cave now become clarified in terms of the unity and diversity, or the whole-part relations, and the precision of ideal concepts.[14]

207

The fragmentary arithmetical relations, which one finds fused in the random experiences within the cave, now become abstracted into orderly and intelligible relations out of the cave. The confused sounds of music and dissonance which we experienced in the cave of everyday life now become intelligible in terms of mathematical harmonies, ratios, and proportions. The very welter of multiplicities and complexities compounded over and over in the cave of life experience now becomes separated and made intelligible through the prism of reason itself—that is, thought outside of the cave illuminated by the light of reason.

It is not required that the learner should stay in either realm. In fact it is part of the art of education to conduct the learner from the cave of ordinary experience to the realm of reason, and then back again into the welter of life experiences. Learning is not one-sided. It is both sensible and cognitive; it is emotional and intellectual; it is aesthetic and theoretic; it is functional and structural; it is experimental and speculative. Inquiry goes on both in and out of the cave. The reinforcement of learning acquired through the interweaving of learnings in and out of the cave results in the solid totality of what we maintain as organic learning.

Here then is the fundamental character of organic education. It is essentially bipolar; it requires the reciprocity of experience in both areas. But a singular one-pole-ism of "education as life experience" presumes that the business of education is to take place in the cave where we find the students. Reconstruction of experience is limited to the confines of the cave and its shadows, for to go beyond the cave itself is to commit the error of transcendentalism. Reconstruction of experience is pragmatically limited to the confines of the cave and its shadows. The very empiricism of this viewpoint carries with it as a rule the skepticism that there is anything outside of the cave corresponding to the light of reason. The organic doctrine contends that philosophically such a stand implies a failure to recognize the rational factor in human knowing and learning.

Contrariwise one commits the error of monopolarity if he insists upon an educational theory based upon an education which is carried on completely 'outside of the cave.' In other words 'schooling' would then omit the 'life experiences' which are necessary to balanced education. Organic theory does not endorse such a view which would amount to a one-sided formalism in education and pure rationalism philosophically.

By the same token organic theory makes no defense of dualism here. Since organic theory consistently embraces the spheres of ordinary experience and conceptual experience in a bipolar relationship, it follows that the spheres are interdependent as well as relatively independent, and therefore the relation does not constitute a dualism. There is an organic unity of the diverse experiences inside and outside of the cave. The educational process is incomplete without both aspects unified.

❋ ❋ ❋

The Logic of Subject Matter[15]

The modern psychological movement has resulted in a widespread belief in the incidental role of subject matter within the total educational process. Progressives usually reiterate that they do not want to reject subject matter as such; they merely want to teach it in the most effective mode, which is functional or psychological. In short, they reject systematic instruction of logically organized subject matter. This tendency raises an important question for the philosopher of education: What defense can be legitimately made for the study of logically organized subject matter?

The Logic of Subject Matter

So-called incidental teaching of subject matter has accompanied the rise of pragmatic educational methods, particularly the instrumentalism of John Dewey. This instrumentalism has indicated that human intelligence is instrumental in the sense that it utilizes the "means-end" relationship in all of its truly reflective activities. These activities are "goal-seeking" or "problem-solving" efforts; problems emerge from activities as aims are proposed. The solution of most problems educationally requires additional data, and this is where subject matter is said to arise incidentally. As the individual solves problems and utilizes data he reconstructs his experiences and thereby assimilates the subject matter functionally. The learner does something to the data in that he relates them to his ends and his experiences. The continuity of his learning follows his line of inquiry and doing. The learner's reconstruction of the subject matter is not congruent with that of the experts. The learner being comparatively immature can only approximate the order of subject matter laid out by the expert.

Now unlike many of his followers and interpreters, Dewey has said that functional processes of learning should terminate in an approximation of expert subject matter. Even back in 1910 when he wrote *How We Think*, he urged that in "Process and Product" we do our actual thinking in resolving a problem and then achieve logical order in the product of reconstruction of the experience. At least he did emphasize the logical product. But his emphasis was on the functional process. He said:

> Method means that arrangement of subject matter which makes it most effective in use. Never is method something outside of the material.[16]

Of course here his point is the inseparability of method and content. Still it does emphasize the functional order of things. Again he said:

> The subject matter of education consists primarily of the meanings which supply content to existing social life. . . . There is need of special selection, formulation, and organization in order that they may be adequately transmitted to the new generation. But this very process tends to set up subject matter as something of value just by itself, apart from its function in promoting the realization of the meanings implied in the present experience of the immature.[17]

Subject matter is therefore studied, for Dewey, within a means-ends context, and not in the older logical context, the logic of the relations of the subject itself as it exists in itself. In fact Dewey would not accept such a statement at all. It would appear that Dewey does believe in the approximation of the subject organization of the expert. But we may ask, "What is the organization of the content by the expert?" Although the writer does not find that Dewey has explicitly stated this fact, it would seem to imply that the expert, too, has organized his thought functionally and instrumentally. That the content should have a logic in itself would hardly be claimed by Dewey. Hence we should be a little wary of believing that Dewey's logic of subject matter is the same as the logic of a given content in itself.

There is no desire to extend this discussion on Dewey's point at this time. Suffice it to say that Dewey's instrumentalism and nominalism never quite allowed a genuine recognition of anything we might call an intelligible order in itself, be it reality or subject matter. Dewey never seemed to get outside of the circle of experience with its subjective emphasis.

This critique, however, is directed more toward those educational theorists who center their thinking in "education as adjustment" and the meeting of "child needs."

It seems that members of this group have taken an unnecessarily belligerent and contemptuous view of subject matter during the past few decades. There was a time when they loudly proclaimed that "we know no-subject-matter-set-out-in-advance!" The criticisms of the more moderate progressives and the conservative counterrevolutionaries in education did much to restrain the excesses of these theorists. Yet their voices are still heard today in some quarters. By and large, however, there has been a fresh awakening to the need for organized subject matter. Of course, the reaction has gone too far in some places and there has been a return to prosaic teaching of subject matter in many schools. This reaction, too, is unfortunate.

Thus far, then, we find the following "either-or" choice: (1) teaching subject matter directly in an old-fashioned manner; or (2) trying to follow Dewey's instrumentalism with the incidental teaching of subject matter in means-ends relations.

Intelligibility in Itself

If we adhere to principles of the Organic Philosophy of Education, we shall modify, reconstruct, and utilize both of the above as complementary relations. In place of the old approach to formal subject matter as content to be memorized, if this be true, we shall seek the intelligibility of the content in itself. With respect to Dewey's methodology we shall make at least two modifications: (1) include dialectical method (speculative inquiry) as valid as well as his preferred scientific method; and (2) relate shared means-ends relationships toward the understanding of the intelligibility of subject matter in itself.

Scientific method is accepted as one mode of procedure, but not as the only legitimate one. This writer presumes that scientific method includes the whole notion of the instrumentality of mind, problem-solving of emergent problems, and empirical verification after the mode of science. It is evident that such a method is applicable to a large area of life activities. It is not necessarily an appropriate method for nonscientific studies in the arts, humanities, or philosophy. Scientific and speculative methods are complementary.

211

Dialectical methods (or speculative inquiry) should be utilized in areas transcending empirical verification. Where thought cannot be reduced to observing, sensing, and verifying in an empirical or experimental manner, our teachers should not hesitate to use dialectic in encouraging the use of reason.

The pedagogical values of the means-ends participation is too well established to challenge its desirability. It should be used. Even here, however, we must insist on some reconstruction of the full significance and use of this principle. Participation by the immature raises the problem of intrinsic and extrinsic controls. Dewey placed his emphasis largely upon the intrinsic concept, almost too idealistically. The organic philosophy of complementary principles demands a prudent ratio of the intrinsic-extrinsic relationship on a sliding scale.

The defense of intelligibility *in se* can be argued and delineated on two different levels, the philosophical and the educational. The complexities of the former would involve us more than need be at this juncture with problems of metaphysics and epistemology. Let us examine the claim of intelligibility *in se* on the relatively simple level of elementary subject matters. At least we may see the point of the whole discussion.

Traditional elementary-school subjects, such as arithmetic, grammar, history, geography, reading, writing, and music, furnish us with ample examples. What is the logic *in se* of arithmetic or grammar? Does it have an intelligibility in itself which is relatively independent of the intelligibility of practical or functional usage?

Functionalists stressing incidental learning seem to believe that meaning is derived solely from seeing the functional relationships of such subject matters to their uses. Number is learned incidentally and functionally as related to games or work. Grammar is learned functionally as difficulties are encountered. Geographical facts are learned incidentally as social or historical problems are met. It is thus assumed that most of the traditional content will be learned in functionally needed situations.

But this is only one half of the intelligible process. The error lies in "psychologism" to the extent that only the psychological principle is stressed to the exclusion of the logical intelligibility of the content in itself. Some teachers, when asked why they did not teach the relations of a given subject matter, replied that they were not interested in the content itself. Or they may have replied that such content would be known functionally in the long run. More specifically arguments have centered about the "times tables" in elementary arithmetic or the "parts of speech" in grammar. Conservatives have defended the "memorization" of the parts of speech and also the "times tables" for future use. Propressives have frequently defended the omission of such "essentials."

Where do we stand on this argument? The answer seems to be that there are two kinds of defensible intelligibilities: *the functional and the intelligible relations of the subject itself*. We have said enough about the functional intelligibility. But let us see the intelligibility *in se*, which does not mean sheer "memorization" in the recommended context. The multiplication tables have a logical intelligibility in themselves. Systematic learning of the multiplication tables does not require memorization only; *real learning requires insight into the ideal relationships of these numbers in their logical sequence*. The progression of the "ones" and "twos" and "threes" provides a discernible and discoverable sequence which is intelligible in itself. "Dialectically" considered there is a problem, or a series of problems, within the field itself. The problems are comparable to what might on a higher level be called "pure mathematics" as opposed to "applied mathematics." The term "dialectically" is used pedagogically here for one can well imagine how a Socratic teacher might proceed to lead youngsters through the multiplication tables by asking questions. "Now that we have learned our 'threes,'" he might say, "How are we to discover our 'fours'?" "If three times one is three, and three times two is six, and three times three is nine, what then is four times one, and four times two?" The child is not at the moment interested in *functional application*. He is interested in logically intelligible relationships when he is being taught in this manner. He has shifted his thinking from the *level of practical thought* to that of *intelligible thought*. Or in terms of problems, he has ascended from a practical or particular problem to the level of problems in the intelligibility of a given field. He may descend to the level of practical problems again with new insight for his application. When he begins with a practical problem he is proceeding inductively; when he descends from the level of intelligibility to the level of practice he is proceeding deductively. Both are necessary.

The same is true with grammar. A child may make a mistake in the course of some activity in his speech. A correction may be made on the practical level. However, if the youngster is to understand

213

his error and correction, it will be necessary for the teacher to lead his thinking into the whole-part relationships of grammar itself, which possesses intelligibility in itself. Elevated to this level of study the youngster should be led into the problems of the field of grammar itself. What are the parts of speech? Why do we have them? How did they originate? What is the difference between a noun and a verb? An adjective and an adverb? Diagramming of sentences was at one time an honorable technique for learning the intelligible relationships of grammar. But why has this fallen into discard? Because "functional" or "incidental" learning theories have supplanted the traditional conception of "formalized subject matter."

Thus we see clearly two doctrines of educational theory in contrast. The modern instrumental doctrine stresses "learning through experience" which is usually interpreted in terms of "life problems" and "life adjustment." Perhaps one should say "frequently." School curricula should then revolve about "life activities." But we have illustrated and delineated a doctrine of *intelligibility in se*, within logically organized subject-matter fields, which provides another basis of curricular organization. Beyond the level of practical or prudential curricula is that level of curricula which has *intelligibility in itself* along subject-matter lines. One level requires the other in a total educational process. One level is that of understanding in logical relations, and the other level is that of practical application.

The Organic Philosophy of Education requires that we recognize both levels of thought and both curricula. They are complementary in their relationship. The intelligible level must be understood objectively, but the process of assimilation into the active personality of the learner requires particular application.

We must realize that the relationship between the psychological and the logical intelligibilities is that of organic polarity. Traditional or formal education made the error of reducing education to the monopolarity of the logical curriculum and logical procedure. The modern or functional education made the error of reducing education to the one-sidedness of the psychological curriculum and psychological procedure. These two errors can be corrected by the organic principle of polarity which recognizes the dependence, independence, and interdependence of the two necessary poles of psychological and logical intelligibility, curricula, and educational procedures; both must exist organically within our educational theory and practice.

214

Thus this means in effect that we must see that our pupils understand the logic of subject matter, whether in mathematics, science, or grammar, and that at the same time they must learn the functional intelligibility of these subject matters. Or in other words, they must achieve theoretical and practical understandings in an organic synthesis.

*　*　*

The Logical-Psychological Continuity

Hence one of the most crucial problems of educational theory is that of the continuity or sequence of the teaching-learning process.[18] This contention is illustrated by an observation made by the writer's esteemed colleague, Professor Frederick Eby, who says with respect to Pestalozzi's misunderstanding of the logical-psychological problem:

> In the attempt to follow out these principles in actual instruction, Pestalozzi encountered a subtle difficulty which never ceased to baffle his thought. The lack of psychological knowledge, together with his inability to express his ideas clearly, greatly misled him. He never perceived the distinction between the logical and the psychological order of subject matter.
>
> It was largely this failure to discriminate between these two methods of approach which made him constantly declare that "the art of instruction" depends "on the existence of physico-mechanical laws." It was this confusion which made him say that he would "mechanize instruction." His methods never got away from this grievous error.[19]

It is no exaggeration to say that Professor Eby's words apply to many contemporary teachers and educational theorists with equal force, for there appears to be "a subtle difficulty" which never ceases "to baffle our thought" on this perennial problem of the logical and psychological continuities in the educational process.[20] It has been the purpose here to arrive at a definite organic solution to this troublesome problem by undertaking thoroughgoing analysis and definition of the terms and application of our organic principles.

In effect the problems we are facing are quite familiar: In teaching should one follow a subject matter organization and continuity? Or should subject matters as such be used as resources and reference as the occasions arise in solving "life problems" as they emerge

215

"in meaningful activities" or in the "core curriculum" or "experience curriculum"?[21] In other words, should we follow the continuities of life experiences in our teaching? Should subject matters be taught incidentally rather than "systematically" in the older meaning of that term?[22] Should curriculum and instruction follow a subject matter organization, or should they follow the sequence of life experience?[23] Many more questions could be posed, but these no doubt suffice to focus our main problem here.

By and large it is true that traditional educational practices placed emphasis upon the subject matter organization with its corollaries which we might call *logical, formal, academic,* and *conceptual.* Since they were more concerned with intellectual training than "development of the whole child," they emphasized the logical aspects of subject matter. It appears clear in retrospect that the modern *psychological, sociological,* and *developmental* aspects of education were neglected.

With the rise of modern or progressive education the emphasis in theory and practice moved steadily away from the *logical aspects* of a subject matter curriculum toward a decided devotion to the *psychological, sociological,* and *developmental.* In a very real sense modern educational theory and practice have been "psychologized" in the sharp swing away from the logic of the older subject matter organizations.[24]

From the organic viewpoint both sides have erred in their one-sidedness. Traditionalists have committed the error of *logicism* by their adherence to the *logical and academic.* The modernists and progressives have committed an equal error in their over-emphasis upon the "experience curriculum" and the consequent *subordination* of subject matter "to life activities and experiences."

It is now clear that much of our existing confusion is the result of the constant warfare between these two conceptions. Conservative or essentialistic teachers tend to adhere to the logical sequences of subject matter organizations.[25] Progressive or modernistic teachers strive to achieve the continuity of life experiences, core curriculum, experience curriculum, or some approximation of these conceptions. In practice there are undoubtedly constant attempts to reconcile and harmonize the differences of the two conceptions. However, in the opinion of the writer there is no clearcut theoretical solution, which reinforces the intuitions of those teachers who try to combine the two systems, now in existence. There are many working hypotheses, no doubt, but no existing philosophy of education, which systematically resolves this problem of *logical* and *psychological continuity.*[26]

Using the bipolar conception of the organic field of learning, and the related principles, this writer is confident that a solid solution to this vexing problem can be achieved, and one which does justice to the validities in the respective viewpoints.

Modern educational theory and practice in this country has probably been influenced more by the thinking of John Dewey than any other person. His writings in *How We Think, Democracy and Education,* and *Experience and Education,* include chapters which bear directly on this problem of logical and psychological continuities. Therefore, the writer proposes to compare and contrast his own organic formulations and definitions of these terms with those advanced by John Dewey.

Organic Meaning of "Logical Order"

By *logical order* this writer means: *a systematic order or continuity inherent in the given premises of thought, expression, creation, or development; the logic of a given subject matter; rational or intelligible ordering; objectively determined order; order inherent in the object or field of study; related to structural and formal order; that order which is other than subjective or psychological order.*[27]

Thus one finds a certain *objective order* or *logical order* in the actual past events of history, in the field of mathematics, in grammatical and logical studies, in music theory, and in science. There is no intent here to maintain an "absolute" objectivity, for this would be inconsistent with the "objective-relativism" which is maintained in a *philosophy of organism.* Yet for all practical purposes there is such an *objective order* to be found in human organization of knowledge and experience. Furthermore, there is no contention here that a given *logic of subject matter* is absolute; it is freely admitted that human knowledge, organizations of subject matter, are constantly subject to

217

reconstruction. But for practical purposes of the educational process such imperfect subject matters do exist.

The Organic Meaning of "Psychological Order"

By *psychological order* this writer means: *that order of teaching-learning processes dictated by psychological considerations; order determined from the point of view of the psychology of the learner; order "subjectively" determined as opposed to "objectively" determined order of the logical; any order determined primarily by "psychological" as opposed to "logical" or "philosophical" considerations.*[28]

The chief distinction then between *logical* and *psychological orders* is that the former is determined by objective factors *relatively independent of the learner, while the latter is determined by direct concern for the learner in terms of psychological and developmental factors.* The *logical* has to do primarily with conceptual relationships while the psychological is concerned with such subjective factors as motivation, attention, interest, effort, control, maturation level, emotional stability, learning readiness, feelings, personal backgrounds, and the like.

It is contended here that the educational process is a very complex interweaving of many elements. In this context the teaching-learning process is not properly reduced to either the *logical continuity* or the *psychological continuity.* Actually the educational process is understood as a bipolar relationship; the *logical-psychological continuity,* as termed here, represents a bipolar interweaving of the *logical order* and *psychological order* as previously defined in this system.

Contrast with Dewey

Dewey's position on this issue was set forth in his *How We Think.*[29] As an "instrumentalist" he was primarily occupied with describing how the human thinks in the order of problem-solving, that is "actually" and "not in terms of the logic books." He held that real thinking occurs when one faces an indeterminate situation and must engage in reflective thought in order to resolve the problem.

Dewey equates "process and product" with "psychological and logical" respectively.[30] Logical forms are really the products of thinking, while "actual thinking" involves the "psychological process of problem-solving." "Process" implies the hard business of problem-solving, while "product" implies the orderly reconstruction or organization of one's solution to the problem. Even though he calls the process of problem-solving "psychological," he means a kind of dynamic logic. Both aspects are logical, according to Dewey, the one in form and the other in method. Form applies to product and method to process.

Dewey criticized the two extreme schools of thought, on one hand the school that believed the human intelligence to be so barren of native logical powers, that they would impose these logical forms through subject matters, and on the other hand the school of thought which holds that the mind is so averse to logical forms that it must resort to freedom of expression. He then observed that the two schools make the same error:

> Both ignore and virtually deny the fact that tendencies toward a reflective and truly logical activity are native to the mind, and that they show themselves at an early period, since they are demanded by outer conditions and stimulated by native curiosity. There is an innate disposition to draw inferences, and an inherent desire to experiment and test. The mind at every stage of growth has its own logic. It entertains suggestions, reaches conclusions, tries them in action, finds them confirmed or in need of correction or rejection.[31]

Process and product are connected for Dewey as are the "psychological" and the "logical."[32] His solution lies between the extremes of the two schools indicated. The main effort is to teach the young to think by leading them into "actual thinking," the "psychological," and to formulate their own product of learning, which is the "logical."

It is clear that there are theoretical and practical differences between Dewey's and the organic views here. It seems evident that Dewey's system is geared to the conception of education as a social process, a living process, in which learning occurs through the progressive solution of life problems and the reconstruction of experience. Organized subject matters are subordinate to the inquiry and problem solving which go on in the life process. There is a "progressive organization of subject matter" in retrospect by the student as a product of his instrumental line of inquiry.

The contrasting definitions of 'logical and psychological orders' between Dewey's views and those of the organic educational philosophy are as follows:

Organic definitions:	*Dewey's definitions*:
'*Logical order*': that order which is systematically derived from the sequence inherent in a given subject matter; or that order which is implicit in given premises or postulates; an 'objective' order of subject matter.	'*Logical order*': that logic which is expressed in the 'product' of 'actual thinking'; that logic used by experts in the organization of thought or subject matter.
'*Psychological order*': that order of teaching-learning processes dictated by psychological considerations; order determined from the psychology of the learner; order 'subjectively' determined, as opposed to 'objective ordering.'	'*Psychological order*': that order identified with natural processes of problem - solving, reflective thinking, order of inquiry, or order of experimentation.

In many respects this writer is deeply sympathetic with Dewey's contentions. His effort to avoid the extremes of the two schools of thought mentioned earlier is certainly meritorious. His contention that mind has its own native or innate logical forms is very laudable. In other sections where there are expressions on the problem of thought it will be seen that there are strong rationalistic convictions in the implicit powers and forms of human thought in the Organic Philosophy of Education. In fact it is likely that this organic doctrine comes closer to the thought of Plato and Leibniz on this score than did Mr. Dewey.

Dewey's reaction against the old memoritor approach to organized subject matter is very understandable, and in many ways laudable. His effort to replace the unimaginative imposition of organized subject matters with the process of purposeful and critical thinking is certainly all to his credit.[32] Education should be made as critical and reflective in its cognitive aspects as we can make it.

Despite all of these validities it is contended here that Dewey's strong reaction against the "logic of subject matter" has contributed to an educational movement which has erred on his side of the "psychological," the "functional," and the "experiential." Even though we have been reassured time and again by the followers that they do believe in the importance of subject matter, it does not change the fundamental conception that subject matters are *subordinated* to the pragmatic problems of human behavior.

Furthermore it is "idealistic" in the more popular sense of the word on the part of Dewey and his followers to assume that the immature can "progressively organize subject matter" out of their own experiences.[33] When subject matters are treated as so many reference materials for the solution of life problems, the complex whole-part structures and organizations of human knowledge are overlooked. The student cannot possibly reconstruct human knowledge during the years of his schooling, for the whole structure is the result of centuries of human experience and thinking.

The organic theory supports the co-ordinate role of organized subject matters along with the functional sphere of the total process. As indicated elsewhere this system recognizes the logic of subject matter; organicists believe in the *co-ordination* of *structural intelligibilities* with *functional intelligibilities*. We believe in the *co-ordination* or the *interweaving* of these *logical and psychological continuities*—not the *subordination* of one to the other.

The organic use of organized subject matters does not preclude an education which brings out an optimum amount of critical thinking in the learning process. Nor does the progressive rejection of organized subject matters in favor of an "experience curriculum" guarantee critical reflection and genuine problem-solving. *The contention here is that conceptual and critical thinking and learning can be promoted within the patterns of organized subject matters.* It is readily conceded to Dewey that there is a strong inclination for teachers and students to lapse into an uncritical type of learning when confronted daily with organized subject matters. Yet this need not follow automatically. Using the organic conception of the *field of teaching-learning* where there are co-ordinate spheres of *structural* and *func-*

tional intelligibilities, or realms of organized thought and action, teachers and students may enter into a *variety of modes of thought and learning.*

Organic Continuities and the Analogy of the Rope

These Organic continuities can be brought into sharp relief by the Analogy of the Rope. Let us assume that there are two strands which are interwoven to make a unified piece of rope. One strand represents the *logical continuity;* the other strand represents the *psychological continuity.* As separate strands they have their own individual identities, constitutions, and continuities; they are in one sense separable from the total rope and identifiable in this *separableness.* But to make a unified rope, they are *interwoven.* The rope itself is a kind of *unity,* but it is a unity of diverse strands or elements—which in turn are composed of many subordinate fibers.

Figure 8. *The Analogy of the Rope*

THE LOGICAL CONTINUITY: Strand No. 1

THE PSYCHOLOGICAL CONTINUITY: Strand No. 2

THE LOGICAL-PSYCHOLOGICAL CONTINUITY: The Strands
Intertwined

Explanation: The Organic conception of Logical-Psychological Continuity is analogous to a rope. The Logical Continuity is that order of subject matter determined by objective criteria; it is represented by Strand No. 1. The Psychological Continuity is that order of the teaching-learning process determined by psychological factors pertinent to the subject or learner. The Logical-Psychological Continuity is that order of the educational process achieved by the interweaving of the two strands.

The bipolar relations of independence (separableness), dependence (incompleteness *in se*), and interdependence (togetherness) are exemplified in the analogy. Conceptions of complementary and reciprocal relations are also exemplified. The identities of the two continuities are illustrated. The unity of diversities is also illustrated.

The Co-ordination of the two continuities is illustrated. One order is not subordinated to the other as we find in progressive and conservative theories of education.

The rope with its strands is analogous to our *principle of bipolarity* in general, or to our *principle of logical-psychological continuity* specifically. The bipolar relationships are illustrated in the *separableness* or independence of the strands; in the *incompleteness* or *dependence* of the strands (in terms of strength); and in the *togetherness* or *interdependence* of the strands in their *organic unity*. It is evident that the strands are complementary and *reciprocal* in their relationship to one another. Still the separate identities (or disjunctiveness) of the strands are not lost in the union.

The strands could be separated and used separately as two strands, but they would not be as strong. Note also that the analogy illustrates the *interweaving continuity*, which in the total educational process organically represents the fused continuity of the rope or both strands as a unity.

The analogy is particularly helpful with respect to *logical* and *psychological continuities* organically conceived. The question is frequently asked, "But which comes first the logical or psychological order?" Actually it is difficult to answer this question directly, for it involves the nurture of both continuities together. The togetherness, however, should not obscure the double continuities realized in the over-all continuity. The Rope Analogy provides the immediate insight into this relationship.

When we see that one strand represents the *logical continuity* and the other strand represents the *psychological continuity*, and that the *organic continuity* is the interweaving of these two strands, the problems virtually answer themselves. The question of priority of one strand over the other becomes academic. Since the strands go along together, there is no problem of priority in time. Since they are *coordinate*, there is no problem as to which of the strands is more important or more indispensable than the other. The strands again are identifiable in their own right. They are complementary and reciprocal; they are diversities realized in an over-all unity.

What is the significance of this analogy for organic teaching? It shows clearly then that the *logic of subject matter* must not be lost or obscured by too much singular devotion to the psychological factors and processes. There are objective continuities in history, grammar, logic, mathematics, physical sciences, chemistry, geology which must be respected in teaching. By the same token the effective teach-

223

er does not restrict himself to the strand of subject matter alone. He is equally concerned with the factors which contribute to the psychological order illustrated by the other strand. We are using psychological here in the broadest possible sense which includes development of the total personality as well as motivation, maturation, interest, effort, ability, and readiness. The psychological strand is interwoven with the logical strand; in their intertwined continuities they reinforce one another.

In other contexts we shall have much more to say about the continuities of single subject matters and those continuities of complex matters—those popularly referred to in educational literature as "interdisciplinary," "core," and "fused courses." This writer contends that both types of continuities must be maintained; single strands of subject matter are essential, but it is also important that interweavings of these identifiable strands in complex unification be attained. (See Figure 9.) The principle is still the same; the only difference is that this application of the analogy is applied to complex subject matters; the multiple strands represent (a) diverse strands of subject matter, and (b) the strands of the diverse psychological elements. Despite the increased complexity of this figure, it is evident that the same principles of continuity and interweaving of strands are applicable.

This analogy also helps the reader to see the contrast between the organic and other views of continuity in the educational process. The progressive continuity, for example, is largely in terms of the *psychological order*. Professor Kilpatrick as a representative of the progressive view contends that the logic of subject matter must be rejected; the order of learning must be in terms of the dictum "we learn what we live."[34] The order of learning is that of life activities, and not that of objective subject matter. As he says in his most recent book,

> But in getting these things done I shall not teach subjects, that is, not have textbooks in arithmetic or geography or history with daily lessons assigned. In time, suitable reference books will be published along these lines for the various age levels. Until that time comes pupils read existing textbooks as reference books.[35]

224

Figure 9

The Analogy of the Rope: Applied to Complex Subject Matters

(A) Single Subject Matters fused in Complex Units of Subject Matter. E.g. Social Sciences.

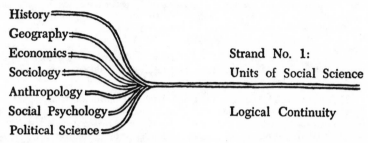

History
Geography
Economics
Sociology
Anthropology
Social Psychology
Political Science

Strand No. 1:
Units of Social Science

Logical Continuity

(B) Psychological Factors as they enter into the Psychological Continuity. Illustrative Factors only.

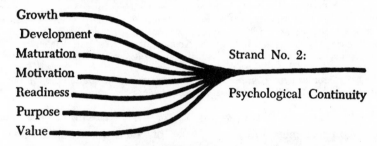

Growth
Development
Maturation
Motivation
Readiness
Purpose
Value

Strand No. 2:
Psychological Continuity

(C) The Logical-Psychological Continuity resulting from the intertwining of the two strands which in turn were the product of many other strands or elements.

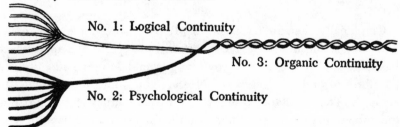

No. 1: Logical Continuity

No. 3: Organic Continuity

No. 2: Psychological Continuity

Explanation: In place of the previous Analogy of the Rope in terms of single subject matters, we here extend the Analogy of the Rope composed of many strands to units of complex subject matters. In Section (A) we note a graphic

225

illustration of single subject matters fused in complex units of subject matter. In this example we use some of the subjects which contribute to the social sciences. Each of the single strands of subject matter illustrated by history, geography, and the like, is to be objectively interwoven into the logical continuity of the units of social science. This task is objective in the same sense that the application of mathematics to physics is objective. Such a unification should be accomplished by professionals before entering into the teaching process: students should not be expected to solve problems of complex subject matters (a) without prior study in the courses contributing to the complex unity, and (b) without the assistance of their teachers in working through the prestructured units. These various strands become Strand No. 1.

In Section (B) we see the graphic illustration of illustrative psychological factors as they contribute to the psychological continuity. This continuity is the same as that presented in Figure 1. This is Strand No. 2.

Section (C) illustrates the Logical-Psychological Continuity resulting from the intertwining of the two strands which in turn were the product of the many other strands or elements. This analogy enables the reader to see the increasing complexity of the educational process as single subject matters are interwoven in complex unities and these in turn intertwined with the many factors which contribute to the psychological continuity.

*By and large the general rule should be that students engage in the study of simple intelligibilities (single subject matters) before they pursue studies of complex intelligibilities (fused courses and interdisciplinary studies). However, a strong case can be made for exceptions to this general rule in terms of certain Survey Courses and Introductory Courses of an Exploratory character. Still the Principle of Logical-Psychological Continuity is maintained. Exploratory courses in General Science, for example, present a general logical continuity which in later courses diffuses into the singular logical continuities of the contributing subject matters such as Physics, Chemistry, etc.

Kilpatrick's views illustrate the progressivist contention: the educational process must follow the order of emergent life activities with the incidental teaching of subject matter. This is the view which we termed monopolarity or the subordination of the objective logic of subject matter to the "psychological" order of life activities and "felt needs."

Graphically then in terms of the Rope Analogy, the progressive viewpoint is illustrated by a single strand of rope. The strand which has been called the *logical continuity* would have no identity, for its fibres would be fragments of the total rope, to continue the analogy. The inevitable result is the fragmentation of the order of the subject matter. Since there is no insistence on the continuity of subject matter as such, but only an incidental treatment, the whole-part relationships and resulting insights on the part of the learner are lost in such progressivist theory and practice.

226

Likewise the formalist or traditionalist in the sense of his one-sided devotion to subject matter *per se*, with little or no concern for the psychological factors in the educational process, would seem to believe in a single strand of rope—the *logical continuity*. In this case it might be said that the psychological factors were incidental to the formalistic teacher of subject matter. From the organic viewpoint this error is just as bad as that of the progressivist who teaches subject matter only incidentally.

Another analogy has been helpful to some of the author's students in grasping the organic notion of Logical-Psychological Continuities. (See Figure 10.) This is termed the Dot and Dash Analogy. If we ask this question, "What does the classroom teacher actually do in the order of time in her teaching?", this Dot and Dash Analogy may prove to be illuminating.

Figure 10. The Dot and Dash Figure

(A) Let concentration on the Logical Continuity be represented by: — — — — — — —

(B) Let concentration on the Psychological Continuity be represented by: ....

(C) Let the interweaving of both continuities be represented by: —. —. —. —. —. —.

The actual teaching procedure then is symbolized:

Emphases:

.... — — — — — — — — — . .... — — — — — . .... — — — —

Organic Continuity:

—. —. —. —. —. —. —. —. —. —. —. —. —. —. —. —. —. —. —.

Explanation: If dashes represent the logical continuity and dots the psychological continuity in terms of emphasis, actual teaching involves an interweaving of the two. Actually there may be alternating emphasis in terms of the teacher's deliberate attention to the procedures. See above in line termed "Emphases." The line labeled "Organic Continuity" illustrates the actual Organic bipolar interplay and overtones of the two continuities as one.

Let a series of dots (. . . . . .) symbolize the teacher's devotion to *psychological factors;* let a series of dashes (— — — — —) symbolize her concentration on logical factors. Further assume that the teacher faces her class at the beginning of a given hour of classroom teaching. What does she do in terms of the organic *logical* and *psychological continuities?* In the theoretical sense she will be furthering both continuities simultaneously, and in the practical sense she will be giving alternate attention and stress to logical and psychological factors. As the teacher introduces a unit of study, for example, and shares the discussion of prospective problems and subject matter, she contributes to both psychological and logical factors. This unified procedure might be symbolized by: $-\ -\ -\ -\ -\ -$. This unity is illustrated in daily conversation; when we tell someone about some thing or event, we utilize logical exposition, but at the same time our gestures, intonations, emotions, and concerns are reflected in a variety of ways and communicated simultaneously to our listener or friend in conversation. The conversation is both logical and psychological to be sure. It is both emotional and cognitive. So it is in teaching. Yet there are times when the teacher and the students become engrossed in the actual, objective logic of subject matter, be it mathematics or history. The emphasis is represented by $-----$ at this duration. If these logical aspects go smoothly it is because the psychological requirements have been attended to properly and they are in effect. That is, the teacher has nurtured factors of maturation, readiness, interest, purpose, and the like. But if the objective order of teaching-learning does not go smoothly at various points, the teacher must of course give immediate and direct attention to the psychological factors. Failure to learn may be caused by lack of conceptual understanding in the logical or rational sense, or it may result from a wide variety of psychological causes. Thus the teacher may for a duration shift to psychological aspects of the teaching-learning process, symbolized by .... at this point. It is important to note that although the teacher gives attention to psychological factors at this point, she does not abandon the conception of the logic of subject matter.

We must remember that the *logical components* of learning in themselves contribute to the *psychological components* and vice versa. The insights, comprehensions, and understandings gained factually and conceptually contribute to the satisfactions, feeling of progress, increase of interest, and perspective on purposeful activity. Likewise failure to learn the logical components and to make progress in the logical continuity has negative effects psychologically. By the same token the *psychological component* contributes to the logical progress in terms of interest, readiness, appreciation, motivation, desire, and the like. Both factors then have overtones of the other. The *logical-psychological* aspects of the teaching-learning process are bipolar in nature and manifest aspects of separability as well as *unity* and *togetherness*.

It may be objected that with the existent widespread differences between individuals in their intellectual capacities, it is impossible to maintain a logical continuity of subject matter. The rejoinder to this objection is as follows: The organic theory of the educational process has been based on the assumption that by and large humans are capable of learning subject matters under the proper conditions of learning. These remarks have not been directed toward that minority of persons who are genetically incapable of such learning. The exposition of the organic theory has been generic for the most part and concerned with the learning processes of man in the theoretic sense. Anything less than this becomes the province of Special Education, which although very important is not within the direct attention of this work.

We must not allow ourselves to be deceived by halfway measures in teaching. If we assume that a substantial percentage of our students cannot learn in terms of the order of subject matter, then it raises grave questions about their ability to progress very far in terms of *functional intelligibility* too. Also the easy assumption that they cannot learn the order of subject matter, all too frequently results in a fragmentation of the whole-part relations of learning.

It has been granted that learning in terms of the logic of subject matter cannot always be achieved on the level of understanding and knowledge (Episteme). Yet it has been contended that the logical continuity can at least be maintained on the level of instruction or "right opinion" (Doxa).[36] Degrees of maturity-immaturity may differ sufficiently that some learners will learn with understanding and others in terms of instruction alone.

Some Educational Implications

Hence in answering this question the respective roles of the philosopher of education and the specialist in the educational field of "curriculum and instruction" should be observed at the outset. The philosopher of education sets forth fundamental conceptions or basic principles of education which he derives from his study of systems of philosophy and their applications to the problems of education which are susceptible to the content and methods of philosophy. The specialist in fields such as administration, educational psychology, or curriculum and instruction, selects and applies those principles given in a philosophy of education to the problems of education as the concern of his special field. Although the philosopher of education can indicate possible applications of his principles to the various fields within education, it is not within his functions or required capacities to spell out the meanings of a given philosophy in the details of each special field. This would be an encroachment upon the functions of the educational specialist. By the same token it is not the task of the specialist *qua* specialist to formulate an over-all philosophy of education out of the experiences of his specialty. There are of necessity divisions of labor when we work with such a broad and complex field as human education.

The philosopher of education is obliged to indicate some of the implications of a given philosophy of education in broad concepts as they might be applied to special fields within education. In these terms then the writer will indicate briefly some of the implications which seem to follow from the organic conception of the logical-psychological continuity as previously described.

The organic field of teaching-learning provides a graphic background for the implications of logical-psychological continuity for curriculum and instruction. The field of curriculum in its broadest sense embraces the whole of this field as illustrated. Curriculum is here expressed in terms of the structural intelligibilities predominant in sphere 1 and the functional intelligibilities predominant in sphere 2. (See Figure 6.) The structural intelligibilities include patterns of organized subject matter in what has been called the logical order. These subject matters, of course, must be professionally selected and organized for maximum intelligibility on given levels of the educational ladder. American history, for example, can be written for elementary, junior high school, high school, or universities, and still maintain a structural intelligibility.

These patterns of pre-structured subject matter must possess coherent, whole-part relations, as units of study at a given grade level, and they must also have been designed professionally so that there are both longitudinal and latitudinal sequences of conceptual order. That is to say, for example, that units of study in the social sciences, such as history, geography, economics, and political science, must be professionally ordered and related in their conceptual relations in the vertical progression from grade to grade, but also horizontally in the interrelationships and interweaving of these strands of subject matter.

The sphere of functional intelligibilities is co-ordinated with the theoretic realm and involves the laboratory aspects of education in doing, making, creating, and the like. These activities and experiences involve the nurture of skills and habits in the actual utilization and assimilation of knowledge.

The logical-psychological continuity provides a resolution of the warfare between the proponents of systematic subject matter education and the devotees of functional education. It provides a rationale for curriculum and instruction in that a theory of continuity is offered. It shows that although subject matter continuity is important, it cannot stand alone. By the same token the continuity of life experience cannot stand alone without doing violence to the logic of subject matter. Thus following organic principles we must follow the co-ordinate principle of logical-psychological continuity, rather than over-emphasizing one against the other.

There is a repudiation of the idea that the whole curriculum should be set up as if education were only a social process. If the curriculum is formulated according to the progressive dictum that the content for the school curriculum is that of current social problems, then the logic of subject matter is defeated.

The organic curriculum is planned in terms of the *organic field of teaching-learning*. This includes the spheres of *reason* and *ordinary experience;* it embraces the content and experience called for by *structural, functional,* and *organic intelligibilities.*

In terms of *structural intelligibilities* there are pre-structured subject matter patterns and continuities. In terms of *functional intelligibilities* there are planned as well as emergent functional experiences. By and large organic education is systematic.

In the organic curriculum the logic of subject matter is respected as one strand of the continuity termed *logical;* the strand termed *psychological continuity* implies a constant concern with the psychological and developmental needs of the learner at every stage of the educational process. It is the art of teaching in large measure to interweave these two continuities into one, which we have called the *logical-psychological continuity.*

The crucial difference between organic curriculum theory and that of pragmatic or progressive curriculum theory is this: the progressive curriculum theory tends to *subordinate* subject matter to "socialization," "activity" and "behavior." The continuity is decidedly one-sided in its devotion to the "experiential sphere"; the organic curriculum, on the other hand, recognizes the equal and co-ordinate status of patterns and logics of subject matters. Thus organically the logical order is not subordinated to the psychological order, but is co-ordinate with it.

In reading these proposals some educators of progressive persuasion may protest, "But we too believe in the teaching of organized subject matters; we do not believe in the subordination of these subject matters to the emergence of life problems in our curriculum!" This writer would reply as follows: The organic theory seeks to correct the previous addiction to the 'emergent curriculum' or 'experience curriculum' by its insistence on the co-ordination of the structural and functional aspects of the curriculum. If the reader believes in the co-ordination of the structural and functional spheres of educational experience, along with the recognition of logical and psychological continuities as described here, then he is not a 'functionalist' as criticized here; he is an organicist. However, if he insists on the subordination of logical aspects of the curriculum to problem-solving and life activities, then he is a 'functionalist' or devotee of the 'experience curriculum.'

Summary. The organic philosophy here adheres to the classical conception of the functions of reason as being two-fold: (a) contemplative, or truth seeking, (b) practical, or prudential. Therefore, organic education is concerned both with inquiry and learning for purposes of securing truth and understanding *per se,* as well as the more pragmatic function of immediately purposeful learning. In this sense the Organic Philosophy of Education is different from recent behavioristic and pragmatic theories of education. This view reinforces my earlier contention that organic education requires the reciprocal learnings in the spheres of rational experience as well as ordinary experience. Hence organic learning requires the bipolarity of reason and ordinary experience, and thereby seeks to eliminate the respective monopolarities of formalistic and progressive theories of education.

Organic education requires 'the logic of subject matter' in contradistinction to progressive theories with their various polemics against organized subject matters. Education requires logical as well as psychological continuities. Logics of subject matter provide bases for whole-part patterns of learning and structural intelligibility. Recent reaction of progressivism against the logic of subject matter has resulted in a monopolarity of 'experiential curricula' and an unfortunate fragmentation and loss of logical continuity in the teaching-learning process.

Logical and psychological aspects of the educational process are in serious need of theoretical reconciliation. Recent educational theories of curriculum and instruction have been influenced largely by John Dewey's conception of 'logical' and 'psychological' orders of learning. Dewey equates 'psychological orders' with the natural processes of reflective thinking, or 'problem-solving,' as encountered in the continuity of life experiences. Hence the teaching-learning continuity should be in terms of life experiences rather than the logic of subject matter. Dewey equates 'logical order' with the logic expressed *ex post facto* in realizing the product of actual thinking, or that logic used by experts in the organization of their knowledge.

This writer's organic formulations of 'logical' and 'psychological' orders are to be distinguished from Dewey's and other progressives. By 'logical order' this writer means the *objective ordering* of subject matter in terms of logical or structural intelligibility. By 'psychological order' this writer means that ordering of the teaching-learning process according to the psychological needs or *subjective needs* of the learner. Progressive theories of education *subordinate* organized subject matters to emergent life activities and experiences. This organic theory insists upon the *co-ordination* of logical and psychological continuities into one continuity analogous to the interweaving of the separate strands of a rope.

This organic conception has important implications for the work of specialists in educational theory and practice. Specialists in curriculum and instruction (who accept this theory) are required to make professional determinations and organizations of the various logics of subject matters in terms of simple and complex intelligibilities at the various levels of intellectual maturation of the learner. They must determine systematically the longitudinal and latitudinal sequences of such objective, conceptual orders. In short, there must be determinations of the psychology of subject matters at various levels, as well as the psychology of human development. Teachers need to be trained in the discernment of the various logics of subject matters, and the psychological needs, and the co-ordination of these in the organic logical-psychological continuity of the teaching-learning processes.

FOOTNOTES

1. George S. Maccia, "The Epistemology of Charles Sanders Peirce and Its Implications for a Philosophy of Education," (Doctor's dissertation, University of Southern California, 1952). See also, George S. Maccia, "The Educational Aims of Charles Peirce," *Educational Theory*, Vol. IV, No. 3, (July, 1954), pp. 206-13.

2. Alfred N. Whitehead, *The Function of Reason* (Princeton: The Princeton University Press, 1929), p. 2. Reprinted with permission of the publisher.

3. A. N. Whitehead, *The Function of Reason*, p. 13. Reprinted with permission of the publisher.

4. A. N. Whitehead, *The Function of Reason*, pp. 17-18. Reprinted with permission of the publisher.

5. A. N. Whitehead, *The Function of Reason*, p. 21. Reprinted with permission of the publisher.

6. A. N. Whitehead, *The Function of Reason*, p. 22. Reprinted with permission of the publisher.

7. A. N. Whitehead, *The Function of Reason*, p. 23. Reprinted with permission of the publisher.

8. A. N. Whitehead, *The Function of Reason*, p. 26. Reprinted with permission of the publisher.

9. A. N. Whitehead, *The Function of Reason*, p. 28. Reprinted with permission of the publisher.

10. The pragamatic method of problem-solving is one of the many modes of learning which has its appropriate province.

11. See George Maccia, *loc. cit.*

12. See Webster's *New International Dictionary*, Unabridged, Second ed.

13. Plato, *Republic*, Bk. VII.

14. In Whitehead's terms, it could be said that 'in the cave' we are 'prehending' 'the actual objects' in time and space, while 'outside of the cave' we are comprehending the 'eternal objects' or 'forms of definiteness.' In the philosophy of organism it is also possible to prehend the pure potentials or eternal forms. In Charles S. Peirce's terms it is apparent that logically anticipated consequences or empirically verified consequences of abstract ideas might well be enlightened 'in the cave' of ordinary experience. Thus experience in and out of the cave yields its peculiar contribution to intelligibility.

15. Frank C. Wegener, "The Logic of Subject Matter," *School and Society*, Vol. 77, No. 2004, (May 16, 1953), pp. 305-08. Reprinted with permission of the publisher.

16. John Dewey, *Democracy and Education* (New York: The Macmillan Company, 1916), p. 194. Reprinted with permission of the publisher.

17. John Dewey, *Democracy and Education*, pp. 226-27. Reprinted with permission of the publisher.

18. James A. Turman, "A Comparative Study of Some Selected Solutions to the Problem of Logical-Psychological Continuity in the Educative Process," (Doctor's Dissertation, University of Texas, 1956).

19. Frederick Eby, *The Development of Modern Education*, 2nd ed. (New York: Prentice-Hall Inc., 1952, Copyright by publisher in 1934 and 1952), p. 452. Reprinted with permission of the publisher.

20. Frederick Eby, *The Development of Modern Education*, p. 452.

21. This reference is to recent progressive theories of curriculum.

22. One might cite Herbartian and Jesuit systems as examples.

23. The reference here is to Dewey's 'progressive organization of subject matter' through emergent experience.

24. No criticism of the legitimate role of psychological processes in education is meant; the reference is only to monopolarities or excesses of reliance on the psychological aspects.

25. The reference is to the error of monopolarity on the side of formalism.

26. James A. Turman, *loc cit.*

27. Excerpted from this author's other manuscript 'The Organic Philosophy of Education.'

28. *Ibid.* (See footnote 27.)

29. John Dewey, *How We Think*, New ed. (New York: D. C. Heath and Company, 1933), pp. 71-91.

30. J. Dewey, *How We Think*, pp. 71-91.

31. J. Dewey, *How We Think*, p. 83. Reprinted with permission of the publisher.

32. J. Dewey, *How We Think*, pp. 83-91.

33. John Dewey, *Experience and Education* (New York: The Macmillan Company, 1948), pp. 86-113.

34. William Kilpatrick, *Philosophy of Education* (New York: The Macmillan Company, 1951).

35. W. Kilpatrick, *Philosophy of Education*, p. 319. Reprinted with permission of the publisher.

36. Plato's distinction between *doxa*, 'right opinion,' and *episteme*, 'real knowledge.'

11

INTELLIGIBILITY

T H E organic philosophy is devoted to both feeling and thinking in the educational process. On the rationalistic side it is deeply concerned with the quest for *intelligibility* in the educational process. It will be seen shortly that the discussion of *intelligibility* and the educational process of this chapter is but a corollary of the previous delineation of the logical and psychological aspects of the organic educational process. The pertinent questions to which we need to address ourselves are as follows: What is meant by *structural intelligibility*? By *functional intelligibility*? By *organic intelligibility*? What is the *structure-function principle*? How are these conceptions related to the *organic field of teaching-learning*? What are some of the educational implications of these *intelligibilities*? What is meant by *simple and complex intelligibilities*? What are the educational implications? What is meant by *pure and mixed intelligibilities*? How do the *complex problems* fit into the organic conception of the educational process? What are the respective roles of knowledge and wisdom in the educational process? What are the roles of *theory and practice* in terms of organic principles?

Intelligibility and the Educational Process

Although the Organic Philosophy of Education is in thorough accord with Whitehead's emphasis upon the role of *prehension* and *feeling* in the *becoming* of any entity or organism, the role of apprehension with respect to the high grade organism should not be understressed. Whitehead has generalized in his philosophy to the extent that he is describing the relations of all entities, and not merely man. Since this writer is setting forth a philosophy of education

237

for man, he therefore insists on the objective of development of man's understandings as well as his feelings. Hence in this aspect we are very much concerned with the role of *intelligibilities* in the educational process.

Various *intelligibilities* are fundamental to the educational process. Three of these *intelligibilities* have been formulated here as (1) *structural intelligibility*, (2) *functional intelligibility, and* (3) *organic intelligibility*. They all exist as parts of the *total field of organic learning;* the interplay of *structural* and *functional intelligibilities* makes possible the emergence of *organic intelligibility,* or the integration of the *bipolar* elements of the learning process.

Structural Intelligibility

Structural intelligibility as formulated here refers to abstract or *theoretical intelligibility*. It emphasizes the comprehensibility of any object in its formal aspects. It might be termed conceptual comprehensibility. It refers to the *intrinsic knowability* of a given object. In Whitehead's terms it comes under the category of *symbolic reference*. Scientific analysis of an *object* or *objects* has its formal structure, or *structural intelligibility*.

In terms of the educational process *structural intelligibility* refers to the intelligible content of study in its abstract and theoretical form. The organized aspects of the curriculum as expressed in the conceptual patterns and relationships of such fields as the sciences, social sciences, humanities, and the like illustrate the organic meaning of *structural intelligibility*. In other words the logics of the various subject matters or disciplines, as well as the interdisciplinary patterns and frameworks of concepts, represent this type of *intelligibility*. Such learning is largely in terms of the *"what"* of such theoretical relationships. Here then is a contrast with what we have termed *functional intelligibility*.

Functional Intelligibility

The term *functional intelligibility* has been formulated here to mean operational intelligibility; the understandability of a process

238

or operation; knowledge in terms of *know-how* as contrasted with *know-what*. In general the relationship between the organic terms *structural* and *functional intelligibilities* is analogous to the respective understandings termed *theoretical* and *practical*.

Theory and practice. Theory and practice exemplify bipolarity within the educational process most clearly. It is apparent that theory and practice are partly separable, partly dependent, and relatively interdependent. Furthermore, theory and practice can be equated with knowing and doing, or the pursuits of abstract understandings and practical 'know-how.'

In terms of the educational process the organic philosophy defends the study and pursuit of these three aspects of the relations of theory: (i) empirical and practical experiences, (ii) conceptual and theoretical experiences, and (iii) experiences which interweave theoretical-practical experiences into a unity.

The student needs a type of curriculum and concomitant methods of instruction which permit him to grasp these three aspects in their diversity and unity. The 'emergent curriculum' or 'experience curriculum' is likely to obscure the abstract and patterned conceptual aspects of theoretical study in its subordination of theory to practice. The student should study theory separably as well as in the other relations so that he can clearly comprehend the whole-part relationships.

The student also needs clear-cut experiences and fitting instruction in terms of practice. The laboratory experiences of the physical sciences clearly illustrate the importance of the practical side of learning. Students need such practical experiences both in initial exploratory phases of learning and in culminating phases for application of abstract and theoretical learnings.

The student requires a third type of experience with respect to theory and practice, or those experiences which deliberately emphasize the interweaving and the integration in the concrescence of the learner. These three phases of theory and practice are equated with functional, structural, and organic intelligibilities in the educational process.

Organic Intelligibility

Organic intelligibility is defined here as the total comprehensibility of any significant unity of reality or experience for knowing or learning; theoretically it is the product of the partial intelligibilities. These intelligibilities include not only the structural and functional, but also what we have elsewhere referred to as *simple* and *complex intelligibilities.* It embraces knowledge as understanding of the *why* of a given structural-functional relation. It implies insight into wholeness and corresponding valuation.

Organic intelligibility then represents the ideal of the learning process. It represents a comprehensive intelligibility or synthesis which is the result of the integration of the other partial intelligibilities. In other words the *co-ordination* of the *bipolar spheres,* which may be symbolized by plus and minus, results in the *unification* of these diversities in over-all organic understanding and learning. It is also an integration of *conceptual* and *observational orders.*[1]

In practical educational terms then it is apparent that the discussion of these intelligibilities is entirely harmonious with what has been said elsewhere with respect to the educational process. Organic learning requires that teacher and students proceed systematically in the constant *interweaving* of *structural* and *functional intelligibilities* to attain *organic intelligibility. Doing* must not be *subordinated* to *knowing; knowing per se* must not be *subordinated* to *doing. We seek a co-ordination of education as doing, or education as a creative or art process, and education as gaining knowledge, that is, existent knowledge, by the artistic methods of the teacher which include instruction, problem-solving, dialectic, guided inquiry, and the like.*

It is clear that although *structural* and *functional intelligibilities* are separable in terms of different hemispheres of emphasis and form, we insist on their togetherness or interdependence. *Comprehensive intelligibility* cannot be attained without both of these intelligibilities working conjunctively as well as disjunctively. True learning is co-ordination of the 'know-*what*,' 'know-*how*,' and 'know-*why*.'

Some Educational Implications

The formulation of a few of the many educational implications at this point may well clarify the meaning and significance of these various intelligibilities in terms of the Organic Philosophy of Education. Enumerated very briefly they are as follows:

In setting forth a curriculum for the learning process there is planning in terms of these three intelligibilities. Pre-structuring and pre-planning of a professional sort are very necessary. One cannot assume that teacher and students will be able to construct a course as it emerges from *ad hoc* problems of the moment. Course content in terms of *structural intelligibilities* must be set forth in co-ordination with the planned *functional intelligibilities* and the resulting *organic intelligibilities*.

In the actual teaching methods utilized by the teacher there is recourse to the diverse methods which are most effective in respect to these three intelligibilities. The procedures and experiences required for developing the 'know-how' in certain stages may well be in some contrast to the experiences necessary for developing the 'know-what' and 'know-why.'

There is a constant effort to develop *transfer of learning* from one phase to the other; for example, the conceptual understandings of the theoretical realm are emphasized as applying to the specific skills and problems on the level of doing. Conversely specific efforts in terms of doing are viewed as intelligent exemplifications of general concepts and abstract principles of the understanding. Here again is the counterpart of the organic interweaving process, or what is here termed *reversibility* of the process.

Simple and Complex Intelligibilities

One of the tasks of an adequate philosophy of education is that of clarification and resolution of the problem of the role of subject matter in the educational process. Should subject matter be taught *per se,* or should it be subordinated to "life activities" and "problem solving"? Should various subjects be studied singularly and separately or should they be "fused" in various ways? Should we have the study of subjects largely or the "experience curriculum"? Stu-

241

dents of educational theory are familiar with these problems, for they permeate the literature of the field. It is in relationship to these problems that this writer has formulated the terms *simple and complex intelligibility.*

Simple Intelligibility

For the purposes of the Organic Philosophy of Education definitions of these terms are formulated as follows:

Simple intelligibility: That intelligibility which is found in single strands of subject matter; for example, the intelligibility of simple arithmetic as opposed to the arithmetic computations as found in complex situations; contrasted with *complex intelligibility;* more closely allied to *structural intelligibility* in other contexts. This means the kind of intelligibility and continuity found in single subjects of study, as opposed to fused courses of study, life problems, core curriculum, and interdisciplinary studies and problems. The latter represent *complex intelligibilities.*

Complex Intelligibility

Complex intelligibility: That intelligibility which is found in problems or situations requiring concepts, principles, and skills derived from two or more strands of subject matter or fields of knowledge; that intelligibility exemplified in the "fused curriculum," "core curriculum," "life situations," and "interdisciplinary studies." It is contrasted with *simple intelligibility* of single subject matters. Those problems and subject matters which are complex in character and exemplify the interweavings of various subject matters, or "cross cuts" of life itself are indicated as *complex intelligibilities.*

Educational Significance

Many of the progressive theorists have assumed, either explicitly or implicitly, that education should be a life process; that subject matters should be subordinated to life activities and life problems in some form of "fused" curriculum. It is the organic contention that the *logics of subject matters* or *structural intelligibilities* should not be subordinated to life problems and life activities in this fashion. It has been indicated time and again that the hemispheres of *ordi-*

nary experience and *the realm of the conceptual* should be *co-ordinated.* Any deviation from this theoretic position constitutes a *monopolarity,* instead of a *bipolarity.*

Efforts of some educators to establish the supremacy of the "fused curriculum" have been strenuous ever since the famous experiments of John Dewey at his Chicago Laboratory School at the turn of the century. Dewey's main hypothesis here was that learning activities of the early grades could be fused in terms of the basic "instinctive needs" of food, clothing, and shelter. The fusion of psychological and sociological modes of learning could then be executed in terms of these life activities and projects; traditional subjects were not to be taught directly or as separate subjects but subordinated to the actual processes of instrumental problem solving and purposeful behavior. Hence activities involving problems of securing, raising, transporting, manufacturing, selling, preparing foods, for example, would necessarily require the "fused" study of various subject matters such as reading, writing, speaking, computing, communicating, as well as aspects of contents of physical sciences, social sciences, and other subjects. In ordinary terms the "doing" of the "projects" would "cut across" the conventional subject matters and learning would be accomplished through "ordinary experience" rather than through "direct teaching of subject matters."

It is not the intention here to make a lengthy analysis of the differences here between the organic and instrumental theories of education. This whole book is in large part an endeavor to make this distinction. Particularly in our discussions of distinctions of *logical and psychological continuities* and in the *organic field of learning* there have been significant distinctions. However, it should be remembered that there is considerable agreement and overlapping in the two educational conceptions, particularly with respect to the hemisphere designated here as *ordinary experience.*

What is the point of *simple and complex intelligibilities* in this context? It is contended that those educators who subordinate all subject matters to "life adjustment" and "fused curriculum" are overlooking a simple fact of vast importance: *the problems of ordinary life experience are not simple but complex.* As a result of this error

243

they strive to set forth a fused curriculum and obscure the relatively simple and logical intelligibilities of subject matters. Thus we are faced with the paradoxical situation where immature students are expected to thrive on a fused curriculum which is composed of *complex intelligibilities*. Is it any wonder that students who are nurtured in the constant environment of problems which are interdisciplinary in character, involving *complex intelligibility*, are somewhat confused in the educational process?

One of the first principles of educational theory is that one should proceed from the simple to the complex. Yet how often this dictum is violated by overlooking the proper distinctions between *simple* and *complex intelligibilities*.

The organic contention amounts to this: *we must not overlook the fact that there is a logical continuity of given subject matters which is relatively simple compared with the "life problems" approach, which traverses diverse subject matters. The latter may be "psychologically" motivated; it may be "sociologically" needed. Yet the problems become very complex. They are perplexing to the expert and most perplexing and disturbing to the immature student.*

Single strands of subject matter constitute only a part of the organic learning process; yet they do offer something which is relatively compact and intelligible. There is a definite logical continuity, as well as the continuity of psychological development.

There is a place for interweaving single strands of subject matter into larger whole-part relations, for all subjects are related to all others ultimately. There is also a place for interweaving the logical with the psychological, and the *simple intelligibilities* with the *complex intelligibilities*.

Pure and Mixed Intelligibilities

In some places the writer has used the terms *pure and mixed intelligibilities*. The use of these terms here is virtually the same as *simple and complex intelligibilities*, just defined. By *pure intelligibility* is meant the kind of intelligibility found in logically ordered concepts and subject matters. One finds that *pure intelligibility* is best illustrated in mathematics. It might be argued that in the higher realms of mathematics, that the concepts are not very "simple" in their intelligibility. Here the term "pure" might better describe what is meant—that is, unmixed.

By the same token mixed and complex intelligibilities are equated. If a class in social science studies the "problem of war, its causes and cure," it is obviously one which is both *mixed* and *complex* in its intelligibility. It involves every field of human knowledge in its complex structure. In fact the problem is so complex that it becomes bewildering to both expert and student. It is not argued here that such problems should not be studied, for they are virtually indispensable to total education. Yet it is contended that relatively *simple* and *pure* strands of subject matter must be interwoven into the total fabric of the student's education.

Some Educational Implications

Complex problems involving *complex intelligibilities* do have a definite place in the over-all conception of the educational process as conceived organically. The continuities of the educational process are both simple (that is single strands of subject matter) and complex (diverse strands of subject matter intertwined).

Ordinarily simple continuities should precede complex continuities. However, for purposes of exploration and survey it is frequently necessary or desirable to move from a complex continuity back to the study of respective subject matter strands. Exploratory units of physical science may well precede more intensive study of the single fields which compose the single sciences.

Also some latitude and common sense judgment must be exercised in determining what constitutes a substantial strand of subject matter, for it too is composed of more elementary strands and *ad infinitum*. History in the general sense is a unity, but it too is composed of parts.

What is the role of *complex problems* in the organic educational process? *Complex problems* can and should be studied in conjunction with logical continuities, either simple or complex. Keep in mind the *bipolar co-ordinates* of *structural and functional, logical and psychological,* and *theoretical and practical.* A complex problem, such

245

as "the food problem," involves concepts from most every field of study. Thus the food problem could be studied *incidentally* with various single strands of subject matter contributing to the problem as they were encountered in the various strands of subject matter. Thus history, economics, sociology, and the sciences would contribute deductively to the "solution" of the problem. In other words this phase of the learning process would emphasize the movement from theory to practice, from conceptual understandings to practical applications, from *structural intelligibilities* to *functional intelligibilities.* It is deductive at this stage for it involves moving from patterns of ideas in their logical orientation to the level of application and practice.

In "core courses" or courses deliberately set up around "problem solving," the predominant mode of approach is reversed. A course in the study of "Critical Issues of Contemporary Living" might well treat the food problem with the instrumental approach—that is directly in terms of the problems faced. This would then presume that the contributions of the various subject matters would be instrumental and incidental to the main business of resolving the "food problem" in the course of inquiry. Hence with this pragmatic treatment the subject matters are subordinated to the problem solving inquiry.

In this case the method is primarily inductive. It begins with problems and searches for ideas, concepts, and significant data. It is just the reverse of beginning with patterns of ideas and making deductions to problems. Our view is that there is a place for both procedures. The educational process is characterized by *reversibility* and involves both induction and deduction and not either one exclusively. *Students must gain facility with all modes of thought.* By the same token we do not agree that the educational process is predominantly inductive and pragmatic. It is partly that.

Organically then we desire to co-ordinate functional problems with *structural intelligibility,* or the subject matter continuities. In the organic field of learning, units of study should contain *structural intelligibilities* and functional problems which involve *functional intelligibility.*

On levels of single subject matter strands there should be co-ordinate structural and functional problems. Theoretical problems should be matched by meaningful practical problems. The functional problems should be susceptible to resolution largely in terms of the maturity, background, and general understandings of the student, together with the utilization of the given subject matter under study. The selection of problems should include psychological factors of growth, development, maturational level, interests, values, purposes, and the like. Here again is the constant effort to co-ordinate logical and psychological factors.

What has been said about the continuities of single subject matters also applies to the continuities of complex subject matters. Where, for example, a teacher is teaching the core of social sciences, the conceptual pattern must exist to match the complexity of actual problems. Too often fused courses have been composed of complex problems which transcended the understanding of both teachers and students. This becomes a sad business of the blind leading the blind. With rare exceptions it should be laid down as a rule that problems should not compose the course of study if they are not susceptible to reasonably adequate solutions in terms of the understandings available in the resources of the class and teachers.

The Structure-Function Principle

The *structure-function principle* is derived historically from organically oriented philosophers. Philosophically it is a principle which holds that existent entities possess intelligible structure fused with dynamic function in bipolar, organic relationship. The intelligible structure is the embodiment of definite forms and patterns in an actual, processual entity; in the language of Aristotle it refers to the 'formal cause' in the 'four causes' of any actuality. The dynamic function of any entity has to do with its purpose or end, or the 'final cause' in the older philosophical language.

Even though the language of the ancient philosophers is used in speaking of formal and final causes, there is no intent to hold to the ancient metaphysics in so speaking. As Whitehead has so properly indicated, in the *philosophy of organism* it is necessary to reconcile

247

these older views with the modern doctrine of relativity. The use of the new language and the cosmology so well formulated by Whitehead is required.

Actual entities then do emerge in the *extensive-continuum* and do exemplify *eternal objects* or *forms of definiteness*. For all practical purposes these *actual entities* do persist temporarily before perishing; in this persistence they do exemplify forms of definiteness—that is, they have intelligibility. Chemical elements for example are composed of characteristic properties in definite ratios which can be known scientifically. They may not be eternally so, but at least they have this form of existence in our epoch. Hence these objects have definite structures and functions of their given natures; they portray the *structure-function principle.*

The structure-function principle is a well accepted principle of organic architecture, design, styling, and other applied arts. The so-called modern school of thought which calls itself "organic" in these arts illustrates what we term the *structure-function principle.* The design of a modern house or automobile is called organic when it reflects the form and design dictated by the harmonization of the object with its total environment. Its relationships are organic in as much as the functions of all the parts and the whole are harmoniously expressed in that structuralization which will give maximum utility and beauty. The organic relations do not stop with the created object; it is in turn harmonized with its environment. Thus the house of organic architecture exhibits functional structure in itself, and also harmonizes with the character of its surroundings.

Philosophically this is merely saying that the formal structure of a created object must be in harmony with its functions and purposes. Furthermore, this organic harmony not only results in maximum utility, but it also gives rise to beauty because of its exemplification of the right forms in right proportion.

Aside from the fact that this principle provides a sound undergirding as a philosophical foundation for our conception of education, it also has practical implications for the educational process and its attributes. It has been our contention that certain progressive philosophies of education, namely the pragmatic, have overemphasized the functional aspect. Structure has been sacrificed to function. The educational process has been distorted accordingly. Again there is the apparent error of subordination of structure to function.

Philosophers of organism acknowledge and welcome the respective roles of structure and function. But we must not become 'functionalists' in the sense that we become deprecative of 'structure.' The roles of structure ontologically and educationally are important to us. A philosophy of organism recognizes 'process' in the genetic becoming of an actual entity; it also acknowledges 'reality' (or structure) in the achieved 'being' of the actual object.

It is our fundamental tenet: *that organic structure always requires function, and organic function always requires structure.* Thus organic educational philosophy recognizes structure and function throughout the educational process. The organic curriculum, for instance, stresses its structure as well as its function. We can not agree with a 'core curriculum' which emphasizes 'function' at the expense of 'structure.' Neither can we agree with a 'formal curriculum' which neglects the functional side.

An emergent curriculum based upon the continuity of emergent, practical problems is not really 'functional' in our opinion. Structure here is subordinated to function. A truly organic curriculum requires recognition of the bipolarity of structure-function. The intelligibilities of theory must be preserved as well as those of practice. Hence it is clear that the bipolarity of structure-function educationally can be correlated with the logical-psychological principle of continuity in the educational process.

Knowledge and Wisdom in the Educational Process

Despite the various defenses of the role of knowledge in the educational process advanced here, there is no one-sided devotion to this aspect of learning. It is patent that knowledge should not be pursued in the spirit of pedantry, but that it should contribute to the development of wisdom in both teacher and student.

Although wisdom is a most illusive part of our education, it would appear that it results from the blending of one's vicarious learning with his own first hand experiences. Hence in the triadic schema of

249

the organic educational philosophy, wisdom is most likely as a product of the interweaving of the empirical and rational experiences in the third phase of our learning process.

We are all aware that wisdom itself comes with the ripeness of maturity and the full experiences of life; the possibilities of developing wisdom in the minds of the young in our schools are existent, but they are also limited. These remarks in favor of the attainment of knowledge should not be taken as a defense of pedantry. With Du Bellay this writer would say, "Of all things I hate pedantic learning." Or with Montaigne who in his essay, "Of Pedantry," expresses the idea so eloquently.[2] "In plain truth, the cares and expense our parents are at in our education, point at nothing, but to furnish our heads with knowledge; but not a word of judgment and virtue. Cry out, of one that passes by, to the people: 'Oh, what a learned man!' and of another, 'Oh, what a good man!' they will not fail to turn their eyes, and address their respect to the former. There should then be a third crier, 'Oh, the blockheads!' " The language of Montaigne is anachronistic, but the thought is still well expressed and pertinent. He says again, "We take other men's knowledge and opinions upon trust; which is an idle and superficial learning. *We must make it our own.*"[3] Is this not the essence of learning?

In this day and age when the great audiences of radio and TV programs listen to and watch intently their favorite question and answer programs in the foolish belief that they are witnessing examples of erudition and learning, we see the same pedantic error in mass phenomenon. Fragmentary factual questions and answers parade as learning and "knowledge." Unfortunately these same questions and answer games find their way into the classroom. Teachers who make a fetish of memoritor learning are the modern pedants. In actuality they are promoting neither knowledge nor wisdom when they follow these fragmentary practices.

The Organic Philosophy of Education does defend the teaching of organized structures of knowledge, or subject matter. But "structures of subject matter or knowledge" are structures and they do form intelligible patterns as objects of study; they are not constituted by isolated facts to be memorized. Biology as a field of study is not composed of fragmentary facts to be committed to memory; rather biology represents patterned knowledge to be understood in conceptual patterns and relationships. Yet even with this definition of knowledge, we cannot rest our case here; the conceptual knowledge of one hemisphere must be complemented by corresponding experiential intelligibilities in the other hemisphere. Through the increased insights and understandings of these two hemispheres, the teacher should be able to make headway with the students in terms of wisdom. Through the *principle of reversibility*, that is through the conversion of abstract knowledge into concrete applications, and a conversion of practical problems into abstract solutions, we should do much to avoid the error of pedantry and should nurture wisdom.

Formalistic schools are quite subject to the error of pedantry; "functionalistic" schools are on the other hand subject to the opposite error of utilitarianism. The recent revolt against logically organized subject matter is evidence of this latter error. Organic education recognizes the need for harmonization of structural and functional intelligibilities in terms of a constantly pursued aim of intelligent living, or the nurture of wisdom. Wisdom is not exclusively "in the cave" or "out of the cave," but it is rather the product of the joint enterprise.

Theory and Practice

The familiar terms *theory* and *practice* should provide us with the clearest and most intelligible explanation of the organic conception of *bipolar co-ordinates* as they operate in the educational process.

In the Organic Philosophy of Education *theory and practice* are considered seriously as *bipolar co-ordinates* with the characteristics we have repeatedly designated. Again one should envision the organic field of teaching-learning with the two hemispheres; theory is appropriately included in the realm of conceptual or structural intelligibility; practice is appropriately included in the realm of "ordinary experience."

Educational theory is separable, in one sense, from practice—not absolutely, but *relatively*. *Theory* in the sciences, arts, humanities, and professions is separable or independent in a qualified sense. The temporary and limited separation, for purposes of study, inquiry

251

and understanding, of theory from practice is here defended. Constant and relentless concern with practice commits the error of one-sidedness or monopolarity. As Charles Peirce argued, there must be a disengaging of the student's mind from preoccupation with problems of practice and utility to a concentration upon theory.[4] Constant concern about practice and consequences is destructive of genuine scientific or philosophical inquiry.

Our separation of *theory* and *practice* has been carefully qualified. There is a sense in which theory is dependent upon practice for meaning, significance, and application. There is also a sense in which theory and practice are interdependent, or display a necessary togetherness for their mutual intelligibility. In fact this is what we have said elsewhere about the relationships of (a) structural intelligibility (theory), (b) functional intelligibility (practice), and (c) organic intelligibility (mutual intelligibility).

Again stress on *co-ordination* as opposed to *subordination* is necessary. Some conservative conceptions of schooling tend to *superordinate* theoretical understandings in terms of formal education and thereby *subordinate* the practical and behavioral side of education. Some progressive conceptions of schooling tend to *superordinate* practice and behavioral activity and to *subordinate* the theoretical and the conceptual patterns of subject matter. Organicists believe both of these tendencies to be wrong. Instrumentalism, as one philosophical doctrine underlying much of modern educational methodology, errs by its very character of believing that intelligence is solely an instrument of action or behavior. With an unqualified acceptance of this instrumental doctrine it is inevitable that a progressive educational emphasis upon *practice* and the subordination of *theory* follows.

The theoretical realm of the field of learning experience emphasizes knowledge; it emphasizes the cognitive, and the quest for understanding. It is the product of our quest for truth and understanding in the intelligible realm. It does illuminate and guide our thinking and doing in the realm of practice. It has valuable utility, but it need not always be pursued in the immediate spirit of utility.

12

THE PROBLEM of OBJECTIVITY and SUBJECTIVITY

O N E of the most illusive problems of philosophy, psychology, and education pertains to the discernment of the objective and subjective elements of man's experiential relations to his total environment. Despite the admitted subtleties and difficulties which characterize this problem, it is contended here that Whitehead's philosophy of organism embodies a profound resolution to this modern problem. This resolution follows epistemologically from his ontology. Other philosophers have approximated Whitehead's line of thinking in their respective resolutions of the problem. Only the briefest outline of this vast problem is possible in this context, for our inquiry here is mainly concerned with the implications available for organic educational theory.

Some of the problems for our consideration in this chapter are as follows: What is the nature of this problem of objectivity and subjectivity? What are the respective problems raised by the philosopher, psychologist, and educator in this context? What is Whitehead's 'objective relativism'? What is his notion of the 'object-subject relationship'? What is Professor Urban's conception of 'Beyond Realism and Idealism'? What is Professor Hartshorne's proposed 'synthesis of realism and idealism'? What is the significance of these philosophical interpretations for organic educational theory? What is the organic principle of reversibility and how does it utilize the respective validities of objectivity and subjectivity? How has reversibility been formulated in terms of 'objectification-subjectification' in the context of the organic educational philosophy?

Problem of Objectivity and Subjectivity

The problem of objectivity and subjectivity is critical in such fields as philosophy, psychology, and education. The philosopher raises such questions as: Is objective knowledge possible? Is all knowing more or less subjective? If it is both objective and subjective, then in what respects does one's experience partake of each? Are the objects of knowledge independent of the knower? Are the objects of perception modified in the very act of experience? Is scientific knowledge possible? Problems such as these have been with philosophers through the ages, although modern philosophy has been particularly concerned with the epistemological problem.

The psychologist too has questions on *subjectivity* and *objectivity*. What are the psychological processes of knowing? What is the nature of perception? What is "consciousness"? What is the temporal sequence of knowing? What mental and physical factors are involved in perception and conception? In what respects are these processes "objective" or "subjective"? Is it a neurological process of conditionings resulting from sensory stimulations that explains our behavior in large part? These are only a few of the many questions that might occupy the psychologist on this topic.

The educator is interested in *objectivity* and *subjectivity* too. In what sense is learning an objective process? A subjective process? In what ways might objectivity and subjectivity interact in the learning process? What are the educational implications and consequences which might well follow from philosophical and psychological "resolutions" to these problems?

In this brief context we cannot enter into the various ramifications of the epistemological and related problems. Modern philosophy from the 17th Century has been occupied largely with the epistemological problem. Whitehead, for example, in his philosophical reconstruction of modern thought was very concerned with such philosophers as Descartes, Locke, Hume, Berkeley, Kant, Spinoza, and Leibniz. A thorough analysis would of course include Hegel, Peirce, Dewey, and many others of note.[1]

THE PROBLEM OF OBJECTIVITY AND SUBJECTIVITY

Whitehead's "Objective Relativism"[2]

It is clear that Alfred N. Whitehead's works are to a large extent concerned with this problem. Although his avowed ambition philosophically was 'to place absolute idealism on a realistic base,' he was constantly concerned with the distinct shift of modern philosophy from the traditional objectivism to the point of view of subjectivism. It might be said that his chief work, *Process and Reality*, is primarily concerned with the attainment of a delicate balance in a philosophy of organism between the contradictory claims of realistic and idealistic schools of thought. His analysis of Locke and Hume, and the philosophical developments from Descartes to Kant prove his concern with this problem. His "reformed subjectivist principle" is the outcome of his analysis.[3] Today his view is called *objective relativism* in as much as it fuses these contradictory viewpoints.

The object-subject relationship. Essential to Whitehead's resolution of this problem which has divided modern idealists and realists is his conception of the object-subject relationship. He objects to the usual tendency of philosophers to equate the object-subject relation with that of knower and known in explaining the structure of experience.[4] The relations of knower and known, although representing a subject-object relationship of a kind, are more of a cognitive relation on a high level of knowledge. Actually in the philosophy of organism all actual entities stand in object-subject relationship. In one sense an actual entity which is a datum for other subjects is an object; in another sense it prehends data from other entities in their role as objects—the prehending actual entity is itself subject, or percipient in this case. Although using the terms 'recipient' and 'provoker' in explaining 'subject' and 'object,' Whitehead is careful to emphasize that 'recipient' does not mean 'passive' reception of data, but rather an activity on the part of the 'recipient' in his feelings, prehensions, and intuitions in terms of his concrescence.[5]

Subject and object then are relative terms for Whitehead. Experience is explained from both the viewpoints of subjects or objects. Objects provoke and stimulate activity on the part of subjects and provide the data for prehensions and concrescence. That special activity which refers to the mode in which the subject responds to an object is termed an *occasion*. There are then three factors which constitute a *prehension*: (a) 'the object prehended'; (b) 'the occasion of experience'; and (c) 'the subjective form.' The latter involves 'the affective tone' of the subject in this experience.[6]

According to Whitehead the organic process then is to be explained largely in this interplay between actual entities as subjects and objects. This double subject-object role of actual entities constitutes his 'ontological principle.' All actual entities become as subjects by their prehension of other actual entities as objects; in turn all actual entities become objects and in a process of transition provide data for the becoming of other subjects. This is the sense in which actual entities enter into 'social process' ontologically or metaphysically.

In this experiencing, actual entities as subjects are constituted in their 'real internal constitutions' by their purposive interactions and shared feelings with other entities. In this sense it can be said that the philosophy of organism involves a kind of 'panpsychism'—that is, a community of feeling, empathy, and sympathy in the interactions of all actual entities in their respective roles as subjects and objects.

In this context we obtain further insight into organic creativity. Although the relationship of subject and object may sound as if the subject were passive, this is not the case. The actual world, which in itself is active, does provide the objective data for the subject or subjects of experience. Although subjects are abstractly termed 'passive,' they are really 'active' in their creativity as they interact with the objects of their experience.[7]

Urban's 'Beyond Realism and Idealism.' The doctrine of *objective relativism* as set forth in the philosophy of organism is substantially followed in this educational theory. It has been stated elsewhere that we are also very much in agreement with W. M. Urban's conclusion that the answer to the problems of reality and knowledge is not to be found *either* in realism *or* idealism alone.[8] The bitter argument between realists and idealists, Urban suggests, results in a philosophical impasse with neither side the victor. Each has a valid argument. The driving force of realism is its conviction that there is an external reality which is independent of the knower. In itself this argument seems to be irrefutable. However, the idealistic contention (and to a large extent the modern pragmatic position) that there can be no meaning or value of "some reality which exists in itself," and that such intelligibility and value is dependent upon a perceiving intelligence, is the "driving force" of idealism.[9] Organicists agree with Urban's contention that if we are to get beyond this philosophical impasse, we must formulate some kind of philosophy of "realistic-idealism" which goes "beyond realism and idealism." In my opinion this is exactly what Whitehead and other philosophers of organism have done: they have gone beyond the impasse of realism and idealism and beyond the respective principles of objectivism and subjectivism in a theory of organic experience. It is in this frame of reference that the Organic Philosophy of Education seeks a co-ordination of objective and subjective elements in the educational process.

Hartshorne's synthesis of realism and idealism. Professor Charles Hartshorne presents a very similar resolution to this same problem in a synthesis of realism and idealism which is substantially consistent with the lines of argument advanced by Whitehead, Urban, and our own viewpoint.[10] His line of argument may be summarized and restated as follows: there are two realistic and two idealistic contentions which can be fused to resolve the long argument between realists and idealists on the issue of the relation of subject and object, or the subjective and objective realms. The 'realistic principles' of 'objective independence' and of 'subjective dependence' are valid when brought into conjunction with the 'idealistic principles' of 'universal objectivity' and 'universal subjectivity.'[11]

It will be recalled that the 'principle of objective independence' holds 'that the object of perception is not dependent upon the percipient' or subject. Realists have vigorously defended this contention. The 'principle of subjective dependence' is a corollary of this principle and means that 'a subject in its perceptions or awareness is dependent upon objects.' This proposition is also defended by realists. Hartshorne, like other philosophers of 'realistic-idealistic' or organic persuasion, sees no incompatibility between these realistic principles and the idealistic principles of universal objectivity and universal subjectivity, or as he says 'panpsychism.' In fact, he holds that 'they are complementary and mutually supporting,' an observation with which we should fully agree. Hartshorne argues that 'objective independence and universal objectivity' are logically compatible because realistically the entity as object may be extrinsic in its relation to 'a particular subject,' and at the same time idealistically it may be admitted that the relations of the object to subjectivity 'in general' need not be extrinsic. Thus the idealistic contention of universal objectivity 'that any entity must be an object for some subject' is found to be a logical component of the "realistic doctrine."[12]

Hartshorne argues that although subject 1 may well know another subject 2, in this knowing relationship, it does not follow that this particular subject 2 depends upon the awareness of subject 1.[13] For example, a person may see a bird in flight; realistically the flight of the bird is extrinsic to a particular subject or observer; also, realistically this subject as observer in this relationship is dependent upon the awareness of the bird's flight; idealistically, the bird as an actual entity is bound to be an object for some other actual entities (as subjects). Also idealistically, any concrete entity is 'a subject in its awareness' of other entities, as is the observer in this case. Thus we see that the object-subject relationship makes realistic-idealistic relations feasible and compatible.

It is evident that the ramifications of this topic cannot be pursued further in this limited context. For the purposes of this chapter, however, the following conclusions may be stated:—

(1) A reconciliation of the realistic and idealistic doctrines is made possible through the organic interpretation of subject-object relationships.

(2) Actual entities are both objects and subjects in their respective relationships with other entities. When actual entities provide data for the prehensions of other subjects in their concrescence, they are objects. Actual entities prehending the data of other actual entities (objects) in concrescence are subjects.

(3) The realistic doctrines are in part correct in as much as actual entities do have an extrinsic relation to some other actual entities, that

is objects externally related to other objects. There is also the realistic validity of a subject requiring an object. However, the idealistic arguments are also logically valid in part in that each actual entity is subject for some other entities, and that an actual entity is also a subject aware of other subjects.

(4) The philosophy of organism achieves the necessary balance of objective and subjective factors in its exposition of the object-subject relationship. Thus Whitehead in his 'reformed subjective principle' has incorporated the valid elements of the modern philosophies (of Hume, Descartes, Locke, etc.) without at the same time sacrificing the validities of the 'objective world.' In other words the 'reformed subjectivist principle' fully recognizes the vital role of the experiences of actual entities in their interactions with other actual entities, but at the same time the philosophy of organism maintains the equally vital role of the real world in its 'causal efficacy' in a pre-Kantian conception. Idealism with its emphasis upon the subjective elements of experience is placed upon a realistic base with its respective objective elements of reality. There is thus a sense in which the world is objective in nature—but there is also an equally important sense in which the world is subjective in its experiencing. Looked at from one perspective the world is objectively real; when looked at from another perspective the world is subjectively real. Here then is the organic recognition of the valid 'driving forces' of both realism and idealism.

Significance in Organic Educational Theory

For purposes of practical application the Organic Philosophy of Education includes the following propositions with respect to the problem of objectivity and subjectivity:

(1) The principle of bipolarity, along with supporting organic principles, is applicable to the resolution of this problem for the purposes of educational theory and practice. Although the philosophical problem of objective and subjective relationships almost transcends human capacity, the analogous problem of the relationship of learner and subject matter is not quite so difficult. For all practical purposes the structural intelligibilities and conceptual relationships of estab-

261

lished subject matters for school study are "objective" in character. Of course they are subject to change.

(2) Both "psychological" and "educational" solutions to the objective-subjective problems in their respective fields are in large part rooted in philosophical presuppositions, either explicitly or implicitly. Various psychological theories, for example, are more or less rooted in philosophical conceptions which are realistic, idealistic, naturalistic, et cetera.

(3) Any adequate resolution of the problem, even for practical purposes, would require a co-ordination of objective and subjective validities with respect to reality, knowledge, and value.

(4) Certain existent philosophies, psychologies, and educational theories have committed the error of monopolarity or one-sidedness by (a) an excessive devotion to the factor or pole of "objectivism or subjectivism; or (b) by making an absolute bifurcation of these factors; or (c) by the subordination of one to the other.

(5) A sound educational theory is dependent in large part upon the underlying philosophical and psychological resolutions of the problem of the objective and subjective elements in a coherent and adequate system.

(6) These principles must be spelled out in terms of the practical meanings as applied to curriculum, instruction, role of the teacher, and the like.

In teaching and in guiding the learning process the teacher must be conscious of the alternating aspects of the educational process that we have called *objectification* and *subjectification* elsewhere. Schooling certainly is not merely an objective, intellectual process. In its subjective aspect it includes the feelings, prehensions, intuitions, emotions, values, biases, and unconscious drives of the learner.

The *psychological continuity* of the educational process requires the constant concern of the teacher with these *subjective factors* in the becoming of the learner. Subjective factors are closely correlated with psychological factors throughout this organic exposition.

Successful teaching then requires a concern with the learner's feelings as well as his intellectual understandings. His feelings of satisfaction or failure, of belonging or rejection, of progress or futility, his subjective aims—all these are illustrations of *subjective elements* in the developmental process.

In the psychological sense then, as differentiated from the logical, it is clear that vital problems of the teaching-learning process such as motivation, control, interest, and the like are bound up with the feelings and prehensions of the learner, or the *subjective* element.

This conception also harmonizes with the distinction which we have made between aesthetic and theoretic. Again there is no complete one to one equation of the terms, this would be expecting too much; but these many subjective factors tend to overlap with the aesthetic side of the individual and the educational process—in the broader meaning of the word aesthetic. That is to say that the term *aesthetic* includes feeling and *prehension,* and it is therefore closely related to our discussion of the *subjective.*

As the child develops through various maturational levels his individual perspective on *reality* and *values* and all things goes through successive changes and reconstructions. His views of God, parents, society, life ambitions, and the like, change, not only in objective understanding, but in the sense of his subjective, personalistic outlook.

The organic teacher then must be aware of these subjective and objective sides of the learner's development. The tendency to become overly zealous about the *subjectivity* of the learner and the educational process or the *objectivity* of the process should be curbed; we must not commit the error of *monopolarity* in terms of these *co-ordinates.* The teacher then has a balanced concern for objective and subjective aspects of the learner in the educational process.

The Organic Principle of Reversibility

Perhaps the question arises in the reader's thinking, "How is the teacher to co-ordinate the learning activities that have been delineated in the two hemispheres of the organic field of learning?" A large part of this answer is found in a conception of the educational process which I have termed the *principle of reversibility.* Since the writer has not found the explicit use of this term in educational literature, he must assume the responsibility for its meaning and justification.

The *principle of reversibility* means that the educational process is characterized by the reversibility of its contributing correlated principles or *co-ordinates,* namely *objectification* and *subjectification, intellectualization* and *individuation, abstraction* and *concretion, cognition* and *conation, comprehension* and *prehension,* and other terms enumerated in this organic context.

How is the *principle of reversibility* related to the organic notion of *interaction?* It is, of course, a fundamental proposition of any organic philosophy that the entity or organism is continuous with its environment; it is in one sense separable, but it is in a deeper sense continuous. Therefore, it is held by organicists that *interaction* is essential to the explanation of living and learning. We are heartily in agreement with this notion of continuity and interaction. However, *reversibility* in the educational process, as described here, is an extension of the notion of interaction. Although there is a constant interaction between the co-ordinates we have reiterated, the idea here is that the art of organic teaching requires the sustained and deliberate progression from one hemisphere to the other and back again. It is not a flitting "in and out of the cave" as it were, but rather a calculated process with shifting emphasis in modes of thinking and learning.

It is the organic contention that the teaching-learning process is essentially one which requires constant co-ordination of the *bipolar principle.* The *principle of reversibility* asserts emphatically and explicitly that the arts of teaching and learning involve the deliberate and sustained movement from one sphere to the other and back again and the utilization of the supporting principles of that sphere.

Thus logical and psychological continuities are interwoven by the constant use of these interweavings in terms of *reversibility.* As suggested in the metaphorical sense elsewhere, we find our students in the cave of life as it were; in this realm of ordinary experience we as teachers seek to further their experiences, personal growth and development in the many aspects of *psychological continuity* and functional experience. Here there is a sense of immediacy in the learning experiences of the learner. In this immediacy we find the factors which contribute to the psychological continuity in terms of perception, observation, and motivation, and in the here and now important problems and purposes. (We do not preclude psychological aspects from the realm of reason and form; it is merely a difference of emphasis and illustration.)

The art of the teacher then is to lead the student from the cave of life's ordinary experiences and problems into the area of *objective* and *structural intelligibilities*. Using the concept of *reversibility* **the** teacher then is leading from the psychological to the logical; she may well be in that phase of the educational process which we have called "objectification" of the subjective. The fragmentary experiences which the child has had, for example, in playing store, bank, or merchant, are gradually and systematically transformed into the cognitive insights of structural intelligibility. Limited personal experiences, problems, prehensions, and intuitions, are systematically converted into objective understandings, impersonal or scientific solutions, and cognitive comprehensions.

Thus far then we have described a process of *objectification*. The process is now to be reversed. We must return to the cave of life experiences and individual development by way of *subjectification*. It is that process in knowing or learning whereby the knower or learner interweaves or assimilates these objective understandings, valuations, purposes, meanings, and feelings up to that point of maturation. In short it means the assimilation and personalization of objective learnings. Subjectification involves the reconstruction of intellectual experiences in terms of one's unique personal processes of becoming and achieving a kind of being. It relates to one's self-determination—his own personal purposes and values.

Objectification and structuralization in teacher-learning processes are largely corollaries of the logical continuities. This does not mean in an exclusive sense, but in an emphatic sense. As the learner comes to realize the "logic of subject matter" he attains a high degree of objective or structural understanding. He comes to know the subject as delineated by professionals or experts. He knows history as history, mathematics as mathematics, and science as science. His personal experiences are extended and objectified.

Yet with *subjectification* and *functionalization,* or the *reversibility* of the other two processes, the personal aspects—or what we have called the psychological continuity—are realized. Thus by moving from outside of the cave and back to the personal and ordinary experience of the learner the psychological and logical continuities are reconciled. They are interwoven through *reversibility.*

Loosely interpreted those principles called psychological, functional, subjective, experiential, empirical, and personal are broadly synonymous. They represent those aspects of education which are centered in doing, making and problem-solving. Similarly, if one does not press the exact meanings or the diverse meanings too far, those co-ordinates, which we have called logical, structural, theoretical and the like, are also roughly synonymous in this context. Hence these elements are then utilized in the teaching process in terms of the principle of reversibility.

In summary then, our conception of the teaching-learning process is one of interweaving opposites through the deliberate use of the principle of reversibility. Some of the foremost co-ordinates which constitute the educational process are: (1) abstraction-concretion, (2) intellectualization-individuation, (3) impersonalization-personalization, (4) objectification-subjectification, (5) structuralization-functionalization, (6) comprehension-prehension, (7) externalization-internalization, (8) deduction-induction, (9) ratiocination-conation, and (10) generalization-application. Many other co-ordinates could well be included here; these are illustrative.

The reduction of the educational process to either side of these bipolarities, or the subordination of one to the other violates the conception of the *one and the many* which we have set forth as a metaphysical principle. Each set of co-ordinates represents an exemplification of the principle of unity and of diversity. Here then is the practical significance of the organic metaphysics as manifest in recommended solutions to the problems of the educational process.

Spelled out briefly these co-ordinates in terms of reversibility have this meaning for teacher and students: education is a sustained two-way process. It is the joint task of teacher and student to convert concrete experiences into abstractions; it is equally important that the abstractions of logical inquiry and organized subject matter be converted into the concrete and particular. The latter in Whitehead's terms constitutes the process of *concrescence.*

This organic conception also means that individual experiences of a non-cognitive sort should be systematically intellectualized; by means of reversibility the intellectualizations which accrue in schooling should be converted into individuated experiences.

Education commits the error of monopolarity if it adheres only to personalization in the educational process. Personalization of learning is a necessary part of total learning; but the unique personal feelings and prehensions should be deliberately guided into the common understandings of scientific and philosophical inquiry. Man learns *qua* man through objective reason, as well as through the uniquely personal experiences of life. Again the process is unending in that through reversibility the scientific and impersonal, or "disinterested learnings," are converted into meanings for self achievement. What is at one time learned in the spirit of dispassionate, scientific inquiry, may well be utilized at another time when one is deeply engrossed in problems of a pragmatic character.

We come close to the heart of organic educational theory when we realize that comprehensions and prehensions are constantly intermingling, and that educationally we systematically nurture these interactions. Organically, thinking and feeling are intrinsically related; at times in the educational process it is valuable to realize the separability of the two components; however, essentially in the living and learning organism the two are in constant and necessary interaction.

Some theorists in educational philosophy have emphasized the inductive character of the educational process. Others have been accused of being primarily deductive. Viewed as co-ordinates, subject to reversibility, it becomes clear that education is both inductive and deductive. In the organic field of experience the hemisphere of "ordinary experiences" illustrates the inductive aspect; the "logical hemisphere" represents the deductive aspect; movement from the concrete experiences of one sphere to the other is then largely inductive; the movement from organized fields of subject matter to practical problems and particular instances is primarily deductive.

With Charles Peirce we should say that *ratiocination* is an extremely important phase of the educational process.[14] Learning to think clearly and effectively is an important aim of education. Yet with Whitehead we seek an organic balance between the validities of thinking and feeling. Education should nurture both right thinking and right feeling as Plato and Aristotle indicated so long ago. It is clear then that we cannot be satisfied with an education which sees only "thinking" or "feeling." Elsewhere attention has been called to these components as the bipolarity of the *theoretic and aesthetic*. Here again reversibility and harmonization are important in teaching and learning. The teacher must make a deliberate and conscious effort to do justice to ratiocination and conation. The cognitions of music theory, for instance, are converted into feelings and strivings on the aesthetic level; inarticulate feelings on the other hand are to be converted into theoretic understandings.

Objectification-Subjectification

In formulating my conception of the educational process in the Organic Philosophy of Education I have improvised a term which embodies the notion of co-ordination, the *principle of reversibility*. We have described this principle elsewhere in this synopsis. The process of "objectification-subjectification" is an exemplification of reversibility. Although there are many other exemplifications of reversibility, this one is of outstanding importance with respect to organic educational theory.

Now by the notion of *objectification-subjectification* this writer means the application of the principle of reversibility to the separable components, objectification and subjectification. Through their bipolar relationships a unification of their opposite contributions is obtained. In other words the conversion of ordinary experiences into the structural intelligibilities of given fields of knowledge, and the reconversion of these conceptual understandings and skills into the fibre of one's personality constitutes the process of objectification-subjectification.

Considered separately *objectification* is here formulated to mean that process in knowing or learning whereby the peculiarly unique and personal understandings, conceptions, perceptions, appreciations, feelings, and valuations are developed into an objective status or level. The learner moves from personal constructions to a comprehension of objective constructions. These objective constructions may be interpreted as expert constructions of subject matter, human knowledge, or what we have called the logic of subject matter. Objective understandings and constructions are understood for the most part in such a form as to be intellectually shared with others possessing this knowledge.

Subjectification has been formulated in this organic context to mean that process in knowing or learning whereby the knower or learner formulates one's personal orientation in terms of understanding, appreciation, valuation, purposes, meanings, and feelings. In short it means the personalization of objective or external elements, forces, or symbols. It involves the reconstruction of experience in terms of one's unique and personal totality of being and becoming. It includes the assimilation of external data within the equilibrium of a given human organism.

In terms of the organic field of experience and learning then the process of objectification-subjectification can be understood very clearly. Using the Platonic *Analogy of the Cave* again, *objectification* is nurtured as the learner is deftly led from the realm of immediate and fragmentary experiences of the 'psychological order' into the realm of intellectualization of experience; here the rational and conceptual order which we have termed 'logical order' predominates. The youngster, for example, who has limited utilitarian and pragmatic experiences with arithmetical computation, 'in the cave' so to speak, is led into the conceptual realm of the logical relationships of mathematics itself. His limited personal experiences and perceptions of mathematics, of a subjective sort, are thereby extended and shared with others on an objective and abstract level. His personal understandings have been objectified—in a sense they have become scientific.

Using this same figure further it follows that after sustained progress has been accomplished in the conceptual realm, the learner is then led back 'into the cave' of actual experiences and the process of *subjectification* takes place. The learner faces such problems in the cave of life experience as: What do these abstract meanings mean to me? What is their significance to me? To what extent do they apply in my life or can they apply? What do they mean in terms of my ends and purposes?

Subjectification is complex; it has many manifestations educationally speaking. It involves assimilation, use, application, transfer, deduction, and personalization of abstractly conceived understandings.

As assimilation it implies the deliberate invocation of *ingressions of eternal objects* into the actuality of one's human being. Through interweaving processes the comprehensions of study are assimilated functionally into the working organism. When this is achieved there is no question of whether a person is going to use his knowledge; it becomes inevitable for it is part of his being.

In terms of use and application the ideas and understandings are deliberately invoked. Prudential problems may well be utilized to assist in the *subjectification process*. It is precisely at this point that the Dewey methodology of instrumental problem-solving becomes particularly appropriate. However, certainly one need not limit his methodology to this particular phase of the learning process.

We have said that we believe transfer of learning to be crucial to the organic educational process. Deductively applied through processes of *subjectification,* the abstractly comprehended structural intelligibilities play an important role, when they are converted into concrete and particular applications. Transfer of learning is not left to the chances of automatic application, but it is rather deliberately nurtured by the teacher and the learner at this stage of the process.

In this context it is clear that the educational process is both inductive and deductive co-ordinately in character, and that it is not predominantly one or the other as rival philosophies of education have contended. Formalistic and traditional theories of education have tended toward the deductive type of thinking and learning. Recent progressive theories of education have on the contrary emphasized the inductive character of the learning processes.

It is interesting to note that some of the exponents of classical or conservative theories of education have made striking concessions to the inductive character of the teaching-learning process, although for different reasons than those given by opposing schools of thought.

Professor Mortimer Adler, as a modern exponent of the Aristotelian Philosophy, emphasizes the difference between the order of knowledge and the order of learning:

> Today, in most cases, teaching proceeds as if the order of teaching should follow the order of knowledge, the objective order of knowledge itself, even though we know that this objective order cannot be followed in the process of discovery. In fact, it is completely reversed. Instruction which departs from the order of discovery also departs from the order of learning, for the way of discovery is the primary way of the mind to truth, and instruction merely imitates nature in imitating discovery. The objective structure of knowledge in no way indicates the processes of the mind in growth.[15]

Now it appears that Adler is arguing for the predominance of the inductive educational process, although he recognizes its distinction from the order of knowledge. His reasoning in defense of this position is as follows:

> Now the order of discovery is primarily inductive and dialectical, not deductive and scientific. Let me explain. The usual distinction between induction and deduction—going from particulars to universals or universals to particulars—has always seemed to be somewhat superficial, if, in fact, it is correct at all. Rather, it seems to me, the deductive order is going from what is more knowable in itself to what is less knowable in itself; and thus there is an objective foundation for less intelligible truths in more intelligible ones—the intelligibility being intrinsic to the object known, being *secundum se*, not *quoad nos*. In contrast, the inductive order is going from what is more knowable to us to what is less knowable to us. Thus, the deductive order is the demonstration of conclusions from prior principles, or where demonstration does not take place, the analytical expansion of prior truths

271

in terms of their consequences; whereas the inductive order is the discovery of self-evident principles, on the one hand, and, on the other, it is inferential procedure whereby every basic existential proposition is known— . . . . All *a posteriori* inferences are inductive, not deductive, and these are among the most fundamental inferences of the mind in the discovery of truth about the things. The other fundamental step is the intuitive induction of first principles.[16]

His conclusion is then as follows:

Therefore, the methods of teaching any subject-matter should be primarily inductive and dialectical, rather than deductive and simply expository, for the former method is a conformity of teaching to the order of learning, as that is naturally exhibited in the order of discovery, which teaching must imitate as a co-operative art; whereas the latter method is a conformity of teaching to the order of knowledge itself, and this is an order which should not determine teaching, for it does not determine learning.[17]

Before commenting on Adler's views let us determine what Jacques Maritain, the Neo-Thomist, has to say by way of concession to the progressive viewpoint:

As I pointed out above, the order of human virtues come to completion demands that practical action on the world and on human community superabound from contemplation of truth, which means not only contemplation in its purest forms but, more generally, intellectual grasping of reality and enjoyment of knowledge for its own sake. *But in the educational process, what we have to do with is not human life* as come to perfection; it is the very first beginnings of the lifelong movement toward such an ultimate stage. (italics added) Then the perspective is reversed. Action must come first—and concern for application, practical significance, and the impact of the things which are taught of man's existence—not for action itself as a final end, but in order to awaken progressively the child and the youth to seek and perceive truth for the sake of truth, to exercise their power to think, and to sense the joy of intellection. *From praxis to knowledge,* this is the normal method of education, especially in the first steps.[18]

It is not possible to enter into all of the implications of the arguments set forth by Adler and Maritain. These quotations illustrate that concessions have been made to the progressive emphasis upon the inductive process in educational theory. In making the needed recognition of the validity of the inductive process, educationally speaking, the necessity for placing equal emphasis upon induction and deduction is apparent in the organic theory of the educational process. Thus we find that progressive theories, and some conservative educational theories, are characterized by an overemphasis upon the inductive aspect. Certainly we must agree that the inductive aspect acknowledged by both of these schools of thought is a valid component, but it must not be superordinated to the deductive. In other words the deductive process must not be subordinated to induction. As we have indicated in our previous discussion, the process of subjectification and deduction is complex. It is also essential to the completion of the educational cycle.

Summary: The problem of objectivity and subjectivity of human experience is significant for educational theory as well as philosophy and psychology. The position adopted here is comparable to that of Whitehead's objective-relativism. Experience involves the relations of objects and subjects and may be viewed from either or both points of reference. Whitehead with his reformed principle of subjectivism retains the partial validities of realistic and idealistic theories in his ontology and epistemology. Charles Hartshorne has also formulated a synthesis of realism and idealism in dealing with the subject-object relationship. A similar resolution to the problem is to be found in Wilbur M. Urban's *Beyond Realism and Idealism* where he contends that there are respective validities in both realism and idealism with respect to the ontological and epistemological problem. The driving force of realism is its conviction that there is an external reality which is independent of the knower. There is also validity in the idealistic contention that meaning and intelligibility of external objects are dependent upon the percipient. The organic philosophy seeks to reconcile these respective validities through its principles.

The educational process requires the co-ordination of objective and subjective elements. Provision has been made here for the interweaving of objective and subjective elements within the organic field of experience through the principle of reversibility. The educational process requires both attention to objectification and subjectification; it requires the co-ordination of logical and psychological elements as well as impersonalization and personalization in the teaching-learning process.

'Objectification' here means that process whereby the peculiarly unique and personal feelings and experiences are converted systematically into objective understandings of common or shared knowledge. Subjectification here means the personalization of objective or external symbols, concepts, and abstractions. Education requires continual reversals of these processes in the harmonization and unification of these diverse aspects of experience and learning.

FOOTNOTES

1. See A. N. Whitehead, *Science and the Modern World* (New York: The New American Library of World Literature, Inc., A Mentor Book, by arrangement with the Macmillan Company, 1948), and other works.

2. A. E. Murphy, "Objective Relativism in Dewey and Whitehead," *The Philosophical Review*, XXXVI (1927), pp. 121-44.

3. A. N. Whitehead, *Process and Reality* (Cambridge: Cambridge University Press, 1929), copyright 1929 in U.S.A. by Macmillan Co., pp. 219-35.

4. A. N. Whitehead, *Adventures of Ideas* (New York: The Macmillan Company, 1933), p. 225.

5. A. N. Whitehead, *Adventures of Ideas*, p. 226.

6. A. N. Whitehead, *Adventures of Ideas*, p. 227.

7. A. N. Whitehead, *Adventures of Ideas*, p. 230.

8. Wilbur M. Urban, *Beyond Realism and Idealism* (London: Geo. Alen & Unwin Ltd., 1949), pp. 22-25.

9. W. M. Urban, *Beyond Realism and Idealism*, pp. 66-70.

10. Charles Hartshorne, *Reality as Social Process* (Glencoe, Illinois: The Press, 1953), p. 70 ff.

11. C. Hartshorne, *Reality as Social Process*, p. 70.

12. C. Hartshorne, *Reality as Social Process*, pp. 71-74.

13. C. Hartshorne, *Reality as Social Process*, p. 71.

14. See George S. Maccia, "The Peircean School," *Educational Theory*, Vol. V, No. 1, (Jan. 1955), p. 32.

15. Mortimer J. Adler, "The Order of Learning," *The Catholic School Journal*, Vol. 41, No. 10, (Dec., 1941), pp. 331-36. Reprinted with permission of the writer and publishers, Bruce Publishing Co.

16. M. J. Adler, "The Order of Learning," *The Catholic School Journal*, pp. 335-36. Reprinted with permission of the writer and publishers, Bruce Publishing Co.

17. M. J. Adler, "The Order of Learning," *The Catholic School Journal,* p. 336. Reprinted with permission of the writer and publishers, Bruce Publishing Co.

18. Jacques Maritain, "Thomist Views on Education," *Modern Philosophies and Education* (Chicago: The National Society for the Study of Education, 1955), *Fifty-fourth Yearbook,* Part I, Ch. 3, p. 67. Reprinted with permission of the publisher.

13

THE ORGANIC
THEORY of CONTROL

W E are now in a position to apply some of the organic principles to some of the most far-reaching problems of the
educational enterprise. The significance and meaning of *bipolarity*
and other organic conceptions can be better understood as we apply
these broad principles to specific problems of direction and discipline in the educational process. Some of the specific questions that
the writer will try to answer summarily are as follows: How does
bipolarity apply to the educational problem of human realization?
What do you mean by *proportionate bipolarity*? What is *the organic
theory of control*? What distinction is made between *human realization* and *self-determination*? How is education "a harmony of realistic and idealistic factors"? What is the organic conception of *reality*
and *freedom*? Of *authority* and *freedom*?

❊   ❊   ❊   ❊

The Organic Theory of Control[1]

Parents, teachers, and others concerned with the perplexing problems of the control of the behavior of the immature, require the
substantial assistance of a clearly formulated theory of control. Today we are confronted with conflicting theories of control, neither
of which is adequate nor sound in itself. For convenience we may
use the generic terms of "traditional" and "modern" conceptions of
discipline. The traditional conception is one of authority, while the
modern is one of comparative freedom.

276

The traditional conception has been characterized by the following beliefs: the immature are obedient to and respectful of the authority of their elders; they are under the direct control of parental and other institutional agencies; freedom of action is a prerogative of maturity and not of growing youth; hence the immature should follow the instructions of the duly established authority of their elders.

Concomitant with these disciplinary notions were the traditional conceptions of the school and the educational process as preparation for adulthood—a period of instruction and training, and a period of external discipline.

With the development of modern education came new philosophies of education and theories of discipline. Modern education, or recent progressive education, has been characterized by its emphasis upon freedom and the retreat from externally imposed authority.

Dewey says that control of the immature lies in the situation in which they participate, as opposed to the notion of external controls.[2] This position is certainly consistent with his conception of education as experience and social process. Furthermore, organically we should be quite agreeable to the large measure of wisdom and validity in this conception of control.

Yet we cannot devote ourselves as exclusively and completely to this notion as do the followers of Dewey, for we must acknowledge the external factors which are necessarily brought to bear upon the conduct of the immature and the mature. In addition to the modernists' "idealized" effort to achieve intrinsic and instrumental motivation and self-control through the meaningful situations in which the immature participate, we must acknowledge the necessity of proportionate degrees of instruction, training, and firm directional guidance concomitantly provided by the mature for the immature.

Thus we arrive at this foolproof proposition: *Opportunities for the immature to engage in learning activities which are intrinsically and instrumentally meaningful to them should be implemented through a process of sharing—to the optimum level of their actual capacities and abilities at any given stage in their development. Concomitantly, instruction, training, directional guidance, and the invocation of other needed external controls should be implemented by the best judgment of the mature authorities responsible for the immature—in direct proportion to the directional needs of the immature during those stages of their development when they do not have sufficient ma-*

277

turity and experience for self-controlling and self-directing insights, meanings, understandings, actualized capacities, and abilities.

In his now classical work, *Democracy and Education,* Dewey flatly rejected "education as preparation" and urged a conception of education as "life" or the conception of "education as growth and experience."[3] He criticized the older education with its emphasis upon education for the future as having to resort to external rewards and punishments in order to attain educational motivation. Rather than continuing this education for the future he urged that we recognize that all children proverbially live in the present—the significance of this shift being that the whole educational offering would then be turned to the "present interests" or concerns of the child or learner and thereby tap the resources of his immediate interests and intrinsic concerns. This movement has sometimes been called the "child-centered" idea in education.

Dewey's intent was laudable, for he wanted the young to learn through the motivation of intrinsic and instrumental values and understandings. Interest in terms of intelligent participation in meaningful activities and experiences would provide internal control and discipline, and thus obviate the distasteful compulsions and impositions of the traditional external discipline.

Quite skillfully Dewey elaborated a whole theory of democratic education in harmony with these conceptions. Concepts of growth, development, activity, experience, problem-solving, life adjustment are ingeniously interwoven with concepts of shared aims, instrumentally formulated means and ends, interest and effort, method and subject matter, responsibility and intelligent social living. Theoretically, democratic man emerges as a person who has learned to accept his responsibilities in a free society, because he has learned self-control, self-responsibility, and self-determination through the authority of his own internal and intrinsic insights, rather than that of authoritatively imposed controls on his behavior.

It is not an entirely new conception, for humanists throughout the ages have eulogized intrinsic as well as instrumental values. It will be recalled that in Plato's *Republic,* in the story of "The Ring of Gyges," that Socrates and Glaucon are deeply concerned with the conditions and nature of just action.[4] Gyges, the shepard, has found a magic ring which has the powers of making one invisible. Hence, the possessor of such a ring could behave quite immorally and still not be apprehended by defenders of law and order. With such a ring would one still act justly? Socrates contends that the truly just man would act truly and honestly with or without such a ring for his determinations of right action are intrinsic.

Dewey's moral philosophy is definitely different from that of Plato generally, but there is a kind of similarity with respect to the intrinsic factor. Dewey, although predominantly concerned with instrumental consequences in terms of action in his moral philosophy, does recognize intrinsic valuation and motivation.

The organic contention boils down to this: the traditional theory of control or discipline is inadequate because of its overemphasis on the principle of external control and a corresponding lack of emphasis on the principle of internal control, either intrinsically or instrumentally. The modern view errs by its overemphasis upon the principle of internal control and the consequent neglect of the principle of external control. According to the Organic Philosophy of Education each of the foregoing doctrines commits the error of one-sidedness. Human behavior should always be understood in terms of a *dynamic ratio* of external and internal principles.

The Organic Theory

The organic theory of discipline holds that each of these theories, the traditional and the modern, contains some validities and some invalidities. Yet it is not enough to merely assert a "both-and" solution to this problem; it is incumbent upon the educational philosopher to show precisely how this reconciliation is to be accomplished. By the same token it is slipshod thinking to say, "The truth is somewhere between these extremes." This is the kind of thinking which results in the present confusion. What then is the organic theory of discipline and control?

If we focus our attention upon the accompanying figure, we can discern how the organic theory works. Like all such graphic portrayals of complex conceptual relationships, one must not expect too much of it, nor push it too far. This is particularly true of this figure for it is actually the incorporation of mixed categories and concepts in the endeavor to present logical and developmental conceptions simultaneously.

Figure 11. *The Organic Theory of Control*
(and Human Development)

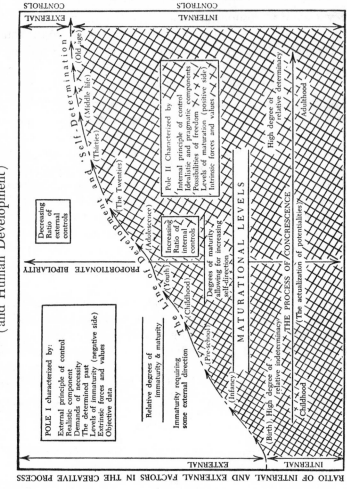

POLE I characterized by:

External principle of control
Realistic component
Demands of necessity
The determined past
Levels of immaturity (negative side)
Extrinsic forces and values
Objective data

Relative degrees of
immaturity & maturity

Immaturity requiring
some external direction

Decreasing
Ratio of
external
controls

Increasing
Ratio of
internal
controls

Degrees of maturity
allowing for increasing
self-direction

Pole II Characterized by:

Internal principle of control
Idealistic and pragmatic components
Possibilities of freedom (positive side)
Levels of maturation (positive side)
Intrinsic forces and values

MATURATIONAL LEVELS

THE PROCESS OF CONCRESCENCE
(The actualization of potentialities)

High degree of
relative indeterminacy

High degree of
relative determinacy

The Line of Development and 'Self-Determination'

(Infancy) (Pre-school) (Childhood) (Youth) (Adolescence) (The Twenties) (Thirties) (Middle life) (Old age)

PROPORTIONATE BIPOLARITY

INTERNAL CONTROLS   EXTERNAL CONTROLS

Childhood   Adulthood

(Birth)

RATIO OF INTERNAL AND EXTERNAL FACTORS IN THE CREATIVE PROCESS

INTERNAL   EXTERNAL

Explanation. The process of concrescence, or self-creativity, involves the gradual internalization of external factors in the becoming of the real internal constitution of the human organism. One moves from a high degree of dependency in childhood to a relatively high degree of self-control in adulthood. One moves from relative indeterminacy to relative determinacy. Thus there is a proportionate bipolarity of external and internal factors.

280

The rectangular figure represents a field of reality which is the matrix of human development. The curved line which bisects this organic whole is termed the "Line of Development." This line serves several purposes. It portrays the line of development of the individual human organism from birth to adulthood; it portrays theoretical levels of maturity and immaturity; and it serves as the concrescence of external and internal forces of control and influence. It further serves as a somewhat intermediate zone for analytical divisions between external and internal, extrinsic and intrinsic, realistic and idealistic, demands of necessity and possibilities for freedom.

Human control is a *proportionate bipolarity* existing between Pole I and Pole II; Pole I is characterized by the influences of factors termed external, extrinsic, realistic and necessary. Pole II is characterized by the possibilities for increasing degrees of internal control in terms of factors termed internal, intrinsic, idealistic, and liberal (in terms of freedom). The infancy stage of human development is characterized by the predominance of external controls and a minimum of conscious internal controls. The physiological and psychological processes of the infant provide certain internal controls, although certainly they are for the most part prehensive as opposed to apprehensive. The line of development depicts the theoretical and proportional increase of internal controls with increasing maturation (experience and education implied too) and the corresponding decrease in degrees of dependence upon external factors which accompany degrees of immaturation.

Thus middle youth exemplifies relative degrees of maturity and immaturity, partial development of powers and capacities, and corresponding fusions of external and internal controls. So-called adult maturity represents a continuing proportion of immaturities and maturities, external and internal controls. In one sense all of life can be divided into stages of kinds of maturation and immaturation. Controls are bipolar throughout life in the broader sense.

It is evident then that educators and parents responsible for the education of the immature must use their best judgments at all times in achieving the appropriate ratio of external and internal controls in their guidance of human development. It is comparable to the practical judgments which must be made in what Aristotle termed the "golden mean" of ethical behavior.[5] Only such precision of thought can be attained which the particular subject matter permits. The multiplicity of variables in human behavior permits a moderate degree of precision and calls for keen judgment on the part of the parent and educator.

We must recognize that the relations of principles frequently associated with the problem of discipline and control, such as authority and freedom, existence and value, externals and internals, and outer and inner controls, are not to be taken as bifurcations of actuality— but as bipolarities. All reality, according to organic philosophy, is connected and continuous. As human organisms we are continuous with all aspects of actuality—what might be termed nature, mankind, God, and Cosmos. Thus any sound theory of control must recognize the elementary truth of this togetherness of the factors contributing to human behavior.

Proportionate Bipolarity

Since human behavior is a dynamic thing, we must reinforce our previous *principle of bipolarity* by what this writer has termed *proportionate bipolarity*: bipolar or reciprocal relations of principles in varying proportions or ratios. In the context of human control, Proportionate Bipolarity means that with respect to the development of the human organism we find that the bipolarities shift their ratios or proportions during the processes of maturation and development. Normally a child of five needs a greater proportion of external control and direction, and a lesser degree of internal control and freedom, than he will realize or require at the maturational age of ten. At ten he will require a lesser degree of external control and will have realized a greater amount of self-control and self-determination, or increased internal control. Still there always remains the actual reciprocity of the two poles; this bipolarity is never eliminated.

At all times throughout the life of the human organism, there is this continuing tension between external and internal, realistic and idealistic, extrinsic and intrinsic, and outer and inner poles of human existence. The ratio of the principles in terms of human development is subject to modification through experience and education, and in addition reason.

Necessity and Freedom

Proportionate bipolarity applies also to the relations of necessity and freedom. Even with man's remarkable intellectual powers, he is never completely free. He has degrees of freedom through increase of his powers. As man's knowledge and skills increase he obviously gains in his freedom, yet he is only relatively free no matter how much he learns. The reason for this is that his knowledge largely refers to that which is actual or existential—whether in terms of facts or values. In short man cannot transcend reality itself, for his knowledge and his being are in relation to this reality.

Necessity implies the existence of fact, or the realistic component. Freedom implies the indeterminate components of life which can be altered through chance, will, volition, value and choice, or the idealistic component. Human behavior is to be understood as a bipolarity of the determinate and the indeterminate. Positive human development then implies a constant increase in the amount of internal control and a decreasing amount of external determination by outside forces. It implies increased self-determination and freedom, but always in relation to reality itself. Thus man may discover many of the secrets of atomic energy, and thereby increase his powers, but his discoveries are of actuality. He cannot by sheer will or wishful thinking banish the actualities of atomic nature. Here is the irrefutable valid element of realism. But by the same token, he can utilize atomic power for good or for bad ends, or value choices. Here he has some degree of valuation and self-determination. This then is the equally irrefutable argument of idealism, and some pragmatisms.

This is not meant to imply here that value choices are merely arbitrary and relative in nature. Certainly in one sense they are relational, and even relative; but, in a philosophical sense they may be considered immanent and transcendental. The proposition that humans ought to act justly might well be cited as an example of an ethical conception which in one sense is inherent in the nature of things, and in another sense is transcendent with respect to complete understanding and actualization, or exemplification in human life.

Internal-External Principles of Control

Humans are controlled by the subtle interactions of external and internal principles. External controls extend from the facts of physical existence which overtly operate upon us constantly to the more subtle influences which might be detected scientifically, biologically, sociologically, or psychologically. We are no doubt influenced unconsciously by atmospheric conditions, geographic factors, and such externals.

Other types of external controls are public opinion, institutional authority, or psychological factors. Such controls involve consciousness, but are not self-originating. There is a kind of external coercion. We comply with public opinion though we sometimes wish we might do otherwise. We consciously comply with the commands of the bandit when we are at his gunpoint, but not through choice. There is a kind of choice, but not what we should ordinarily term internal or intrinsic choice.

In the classroom we assert that certain controls are external. These include rewards and punishments of all kinds used to secure "discipline." Rewards may include honors, praise, recognitions, grades, and other approbations; punishments may include corporal punishment, demerits, poor grades, blame and other disapprobations. Yet we need not restrict our notions of external controls to these traditional notions. The laws of the community, the authority invested in the schools, administrators and teachers, school regulations, mores, customs, conventions, public opinion, parental authority, governmental authority—all of these may be classified as external controls.

The internal principle of control is synonymous with inner discipline, self direction, self discipline, and self determination. It presumes that our behavior in large part is being directed intelligently from inner choices. It presumes a relative degree of free choice which in organic thought is accepted as an intermediate judgment between the positions of extreme determination and extreme indeterminism. It is a mean between these views which shifts with the ratio of achieved intelligence, skill, and actuality. Actualized maturation of the young in their development opens the doors to increased emphasis and reliance upon the idealistic component in terms of internal direction, intrinsic valuation, and greater personal freedom of thought and action. Yet since the learner is always relatively mature and relatively immature, human behavior is always a ratio of these external and internal factors.

Control and the Educational Process

Control, then, turns out to be the proper ratio of the many bipolar opposites involved in the total educational process of human development. The child moves up the line of development from relative immaturity to maturity. At every stage he is relatively mature in some respects and immature in other respects. His actual and ideal potentialities are gradually actualized or exemplified in his person at each level of development.

To the extent that his actualizations have resulted in powers of conscious, intelligent, purposeful or intrinsic choices, he can be said to be determining his actions through the internal principle. In other words he has self control commensurate with his personal powers and their degree of maturation.

Yet this is only a relative kind of "self control" for the individual is relatively immature, hence to the extent of his immaturity he must have the direction provided by parents, schools, government, community mores and morals, laws and regulations.

Authority and freedom, like necessity and freedom, are bipolar in human behavior. External authority and internal freedom are bipolar. As powers mature in the individual the proportion of internal freedom and responsibility should be increased; to the extent that immaturity prevails, external control must be relied upon.

Educationally this means that until students are mature enough to gain real intrinsic insights into the complexities of human behavior patterns, they must be provided extrinsic directives or what Plato termed "right opinion." Genuine insight into the "whys" of moral behavior, for example, do not come as a rule without considerable experience and maturation. In the interim, human controls must be provided for the relatively immature in terms of instruction or right opinion.

In terms of the educational process in schools it means that the young cannot be controlled completely by the internal principle. Intrinsic motivations, although highly desirable, remain as ideals which are only partially realized. It is unrealistic to assume that youngsters or students can be wholly controlled or motivated by intrinsic motivations alone. It is precisely at this point that so-called modern education has over "idealized" the educational process with respect to motivation and control. The error results, it seems, from the singular devotion to the principle of internal control.

Many things must necessarily be learned in terms of right opinion rather than motivated by genuine insights and understandings.

✷   ✷   ✷   ✷

Summary. Conservative theories of education have been characterized by their reliance upon authority and external means of control of the immature. Progressive theories have conversely placed emphasis upon internal principles of control and the rejection of external controls. The organic theory of control stresses the proportionate bipolarity of such co-ordinates as authority and freedom, external and internal factors, with respect to the relative ratios of maturity and immaturity of the learner.

Dewey's philosophy of education rejected the concept of education as preparation and asserted a theory of education as life. External rewards and punishments were likewise rejected in favor of internal motivations. Organic theory assumes that Dewey's theory has partial validity, but that it was one-sided in emphasis. Education of the. young is both preparation and life experience; it requires external direction as well as gradually increasing amounts of internal direction and self-control. The young require direct control and external direction to the extent that they are immature; to the extent that they are mature, they require opportunities for increasing freedom, internal direction, and self-determination. Democratic sharing of means and ends in terms of personal development is a valid concept, as long as the limitations of the immature are recognized at successive levels of growth.

The organic theory of control can be depicted graphically as a proportionate bipolarity of external and internal controls. The line of development marks the gradual maturation of the learner, and demarcates external and internal controls required at various levels. Realistic and idealistic components are corollaries of these ratios, as are the demands of necessity and the possibilities of freedom, and extrinsic and intrinsic values. Authority and freedom are always correlated; freedom is always relative in human behavior. By and large youth may be accorded greater degrees of freedom with successive levels of maturation and development of powers of self-direction. Thus control of the young requires a judicious harmonization of external and internal principles at all times.

FOOTNOTES

1. Frank C. Wegener, "The Organic Theory of Control," *Educational Theory*, Vol. VI, No. 3, (July, 1956), pp. 170-76, and p. 191.

2. John Dewey, *Democracy and Education* (New York: The Macmillan Company, 1916), p. 47.

3. John Dewey, *Democracy and Education*, pp. 63-65.

4. See Plato, *Republic*, Book II, 359C.

5. See Aristotle, *Ethics*.

14

ORGANIC CONCEPTIONS of the CREATIVE PROCESS

I N the preceding chapters this writer has presented
some of his essential conceptions of the educational process. We
now approach the most critical problem of the educational process
and that is the nature of the creative process. All of the foregoing
aspects of the educational process are deeply affected by one's philosophy of creativity. Our conception of the educational process
would be very incomplete without a definite formulation of an organic theory of creativity.

It is thus the purpose of this chapter to inquire into the organic
conceptions of the creative process, largely at the philosophical
level. In the following chapter we see how these philosophical conceptions of the creative process reinforce and support the principles
and conceptions of the educational process which have already been
advanced in our movement toward the Organic Philosophy of Education.

Some of the underlying questions of this inquiry are as follows:
Is the educational process essentially creative? If so, where do we
turn for a sound philosophy of creativity? What is the present
need for a sound philosophy of creativity? Why should we turn to
Whitehead's philosophy of the creative process? What are some of
the sources of his philosophy of creativity? How are some of his
key conceptions related to the creative process? What are the stages
of *concrescence*? How might these phases of *concrescence* be illustrated in organic educational philosophy? What are some of the
implications of the creative process for development of the self in
terms of human development?

288

Creativity in Modern Thought

Apparently there are few educators today who would reject all kinds of *creativity* in the educational process. It is the contention here that despite the vast amount of lip service which is paid to the notion of *creative education* in recent educational theorizing, there has been insufficient attention given to the philosophical meaning of the term. *Creativity* is an honorific word of such prestige as to occasion little or no serious objection by the proponents of different schools of thought. Most educators will agree that 'education should be creative,' but precisely what is meant by this? Is it to be interpreted as the making of things? Is it a process of 'play' and 'self-expression'? Is it a process of 'unfolding' as Froebel suggested? Is it a process of 'social reconstruction'? Is it 'functional activity'? Does it mean what the progressives seem to mean: an education that is experiential, 'expressive of social self,' and 'socialization of character'? Or does it mean something else? In its generic form it is broad enough to occasion little objection. However, if and when spelled out in terms of definite conceptions of educational theory and practice, it is more likely that the real differences will be discerned.

Certainly there have been notable delineations of theories of creativity by general philosophers and by educational philosphers. American education of the 20th Century has been profoundly influenced by John Dewey's interpretations of the educational process with its experimental explanation of the creative process. One recalls also the profound contributions of idealistic thinkers such as F. W. Schelling, K. C. F. Krause, G. W. G. Hegel, F. Schiller, and F. Froebel, to name only a few who were concerned about creativity and its implications for man and education. This idealistic interpretation of creativity has exerted a profound influence on our thinking about this subject. As Herbert Read has reminded us, 'education as art' was first found in the writings of Plato. The Greek concern with the creative process is well known to students of the history of philosophy and education.

With the passing of the recent educational epoch, which was dominated by the educational philosophy of John Dewey, the question of 'what next?' in educational philosophy has become a matter of real concern.[1] The problem is pertinent here for it raises the question of

289

the adequacy of the experimentalistic conception of experience and creativity.

Educators are genuinely at the crossroads both with respect to an educational philosophy in general and a theory of creativity specifically. Where do we turn for an adequate philosophical grounding of the educational process? Where specifically do we turn for a theory of creativity? Idealists may turn back to Schiller and Froebel or some reconstruction thereof; pragmatists may endeavor to reconstruct Dewey's thought upon more adequate metaphysical grounds. It is a real impasse; it is a real problem of where to turn for adequate philosophical grounding to the problems of creativity and other concepts of educational theory.

It is the thesis of this organic educational philosophy that the most adequate theory of the creative process is to be found in A. N. Whitehead's philosophy of organism.[2] John Dewey's philosophy of experience is inadequate in that it does not provide sufficient metaphysical, ontological, or axiological grounds for an educational theory. Although Dewey's theory of experience and creativity contains numerous validities, it is too parsimonious and is metaphysically inadequate. By the same token idealistic theories of creativity in terms of self-expression and unfolding are likewise valuable up to a point, but they are inadequate in terms of the present need for a philosophical grounding of the creative process.

The task before us is the delineation of this organic theory of the creative process in its metaphysical sense, and the subsequent fusion of this conception with our other organic principles of the educational process.

Organic Education and the Creative Process

In moving toward the organic educational philosophy it is imperative that our stand on these problems of creativity be clearly and unequivocally stated. Thus in answering the first question pertaining to the role of creativity in human development, it is significant that the educational process is conceived here as essentially creative in the metaphysical meaning of the term *creativity*. Since creativity is accepted here at the metaphysical level, it is apparent that creativity is not merely incidental to the educational process; it is essential.

It should not be surprising to find that this position is advanced here, for any organic philosophy is by the nature of its inherent principles committed to some kind of creativity. It will be remembered, for example, that Plato's philosophy envisioned the world as an organic creature; he further held that 'the creative factors,' which included God, Pattern, Receptacle, and Good, combined in world processes to give birth to actual things which were 'mixtures.'[3] In Plato's language the metaphysical factors, known by dialectical inquiry into the realm of being, were manifest in the temporal realm of becoming. Thus philosophy itself was an attempt to understand these creative factors and their functioning in the temporal world.[4]

Although creativity as such may not be overtly expressed in Plato, it is at least implicit throughout his treatment of education. It will be recalled that his theory of education as art embraced gymnastics and music in the harmonized development of the individual. Gymnastics was not merely construed as good for physical development, but it ultimately contributed to the well being of the soul as well. Plato held a profound belief in the powers of music, both in metaphysical and literal meanings, to bring order and control into human experience. It was through music that man was to be educated because it had the power to penetrate to man's inner being in his feelings and thoughts.

We recall further that education was the chief means of bringing about the harmonization of the warring aspects of man's diverse nature—the attraction of physical pleasures, and the lures of the eternal forms appealing to man's spiritual being. These opposite attractions contribute to man's fundamental ambivalence, the lure of pleasures and of ideal ends. It was music (in its general sense of the nine muses and the literal sense) that was considered the main means of bringing about the harmonization of man's complex being, or the Greek ideal of *Sophrosyne*. All men must be educated in terms of the virtues, justice, wisdom, courage, and temperance, so that they may possess a right ratio of these virtues in conformity with their native endowments; since men are inherently different, like the various precious metals, they are destined to different educations in the realization of their individual capacities.

If space permitted we might well recall many illustrations of organic creativity implicit if not explicit in Plato's thought. Such an exposition would include his emphasis upon the *esprit de corps*, or the feeling of community with one's society; his belief in latent rational capacities of man, his concern with the development of man's aesthetic potentialities; his interest in intellectual and moral development as well as social; his recognition of the need of harmonizing the conflicting elements of man's complex nature; his deep concern for music, poetry, and literature; his perception of the togetherness of things; his perception, for example, of the relatedness of music, poetry, dancing, and gymnastics in terms of feelings for rhythm; his concern for man's pursuit of the good life in metaphysical perspective, and not merely within the confines of human society.[5]

We are all aware of the many shortcomings of Platonic thought in terms of our own political and social philosophy of democracy today. Yet there are those who are blinded to the many profound intuitions and truths in Platonic thought by their bitter attacks and denunciations of those aspects of his thought which do not accord with modern theory. It is to the everlasting credit of Whitehead that he was able to recognize lasting insights of Plato's thought as well as many of his limitations. In moving toward an organic conception of the creative process it is necessary to reckon with this rich heritage.

Aristotle, too, as a philosopher of organism anticipated principles which have been more recently expressed in a dynamic theory of creativity. Despite the fact that Aristotle's philosophy was grounded in the category of Primary Substance, he did formulate a principle which is now essential to a modern theory of creativity in process. His notion of entelechy, or the actualization of potentiality, is that principle. Some recent interpreters of Aristotle have held that he had never intended this notion to be taken in a restricted or static sense, but that he really meant a dynamic process of actualization of potentiality. Be this as it may, his educational theory was based largely on the principle that human development is a process of actualization of the potentialities of human nature. His conception of learning by habituation, through activities designed to achieve the golden mean in human behavior between habits of excess and habits of deficiency, contributed much to the organic conception of education.

Plato and Aristotle were in fundamental agreement on the function of education. They both recognized the high role of character education and its practical relationship to the life of the community. But they did not limit their conception of the aims and functions of education to the dimensions of society. They both say that education in its highest function goes beyond the practical life of society. We recall that it was Plato's dictum that the aim of education is to make us 'spectators of all reality.'[6] Eudemos, a follower of Aristotle, put it just a little differently, to help us "to serve and contemplate God."[7]

It is evident that an adequate theory of creativity as related to the educational process would necessarily represent a reconstruction of these ideas from Plato and Aristotle as well as an evaluation of other philosophers and educators. The reader will no doubt appreciate the fact that even the briefest survey of these many contributors to our modern thought is impracticable in this present context. Our purposes are better served by an immediate consideration of Whitehead's philosophical reconstructions as he moved toward the formulation of the philosophy of organism with its centering in the creative process.

Philosophical Reconstruction

At the outset it is to be recalled that Whitehead's conception of creativity results from a complete philosophical reconstruction. He faced the central problem of metaphysics—"the relation between the permanent and fluent elements of the world in a philosophy of process."[8] He had to explain the age-old problem of the relationship between universal forms and the facts of nature as they function in flux.[9] In moving toward the synthesis now known as the philosophy of organism, Whitehead began by his analysis and reconstruction of the original philosophical differences between the classical views of Plato and Aristotle and their contemporaries.

This synthesis was in large part achieved through Whitehead's bold transformation of Aristotle's long enduring metaphysical theory which was based upon the doctrine of Primary Substance as the primary category of metaphysics. The category of substance, which presumed a substratum in absolute time and space, and the consequent subject-predicate proposition about the nature of such objects, was transformed into a philosophy of process. The metaphysical theory of primary substance was rejected in favor of the organic metaphysical theory of 'process and reality.'

It is evident that such a task was a tremendous philosophical undertaking. It required a reconstruction of thought which retained certain validities of classical thought, the rejection of certain invalidities, and the harmonization of these elements with considerations drawn from the advances of modern thought in science, philosophy, and religion.

Reconstruction of Plato too

As part of his philosophical formulation, Whitehead, although profoundly indebted to Plato's philosophy, found it necessary to make reconstructions of his thought too. We cannot here go into these ramifications, but a few of these modifications can be mentioned briefly. We have noted already Whitehead's tributes to Plato's thought as being intuitions of the highest order and transcending most of the other philosophers. He is definite, however, in saying that Plato was wrong in a number of conceptions and beliefs.

It has been noted that Whitehead was frankly influenced by Plato's dialogue the *Timaeus* in framing his own cosmology. The genesis of the cosmos as intimated through the metaphorical language of Plato in the *Timaeus* appealed strongly to Whitehead in his own organic conception. Also, Plato's realm of being, or the eternal forms, become for Whitehead 'eternal objects' which are conceptual entities subsisting in the primordial nature of God. Instead of treating these ideal entities as 'reals' in themselves, Whitehead interprets them as 'possibles.' They 'subsist' eternally, but they are only 'possibles' for actualization in actual entities of the real world.

The old conflicts between Aristotelians and Platonists *in re* the nature of reality and the status of universals are in a sense resolved by Whitehead. We have raised the question earlier of whether Plato was 'dualist' or 'bipolar organicist,' noting that he has usually been interpreted as making a strong bifurcation between the ultimate reality of the ideal realm of being and the temporal world of becoming, or the distinction between reality and appearance.

We have noted further that Aristotle criticized his teacher for reifying the realm of the ideal, and making the universals the highest reality. Aristotle in his realistic emphasis, it will be recalled, insisted on the embodiment of forms in the actuality of substantial entities. Universals were conceptual abstractions from the essences of existing reality. Hence the problem of whether reality is to be found in the ideal realm of being or in the realm of actual things is created or recognized.

Whitehead's philosophy of organism alleviates this difficulty, according to the organic viewpoint, by its reconstructed explanation of the (a) nature of the eternal objects, (b) nature of the actual entities, (c) relationship between ideal entities and actual entities, (d) nature and function of God in this relationship, and, of course, many other related factors. We have already noted too that he contends that the formulation of any philosophy necessarily involves the Seven Notions, which Plato dealt with,—the Ideas, Physical Elements, Psyche, Eros, Harmony, Mathematicals, and the Receptacle.[10] All philosophy is an attempt to obtain coherence in terms of these seven notions. The genius of Whitehead's work is in large part manifested in his philosophy of organism in the reconstruction of these notions, in such a manner that the valid elements of classical views of organism are combined with the modern theory of relativity. Hence the theory of organism is centered in 'process and reality.'

Reconstruction of Modern Philosophies

We can only mention briefly Whitehead's task of the reconstruction of modern philosophies, particularly of 17th and 18th Centuries. The philosophy of organism is also in large part derived from his careful analysis of such modern thinkers as René Descartes, John Locke, David Hume, Bishop Berkeley, Immanuel Kant, Leibniz, and Spinoza. He finds validities and invalidities in all of these systems which he interweaves in his philosophy of organism.[11] If time permitted it would be most interesting to review his reactions to these great systems of philosophy. It should be noted that he objected to Descartes' dualism strenuously, although he does speak favorably of the Cartesian insight into intuition; he particularly is impressed by the formulation of the principle of subjectivity as one of the outstanding contributions of modern philosophy.[12] He is indebted to John Locke for his notion of the *real internal constitution* of entities. With certain reconstructions Whitehead finds this to be the central conception of entities as they become in a process of concrescence. Another notion, that of 'time perpetually perishing' was derived from Locke and, as reconstructed in Whitehead, it becomes one of the main ideas of organism.[13] Although at odds largely with the position of David Hume, Whitehead finds some merit to his thought too. He feels that he did emphasize process and the subjective element of experience. He scores Hume for his overemphasis upon 'presentational immediacy,' or sense perception, at the expense of the more profound intuitions of the massiveness and the causal efficacy in the order of nature itself.[14]

Whitehead is attracted by another great mathematical genius and philosopher, Leibniz. He approved of Leibniz's recognition of the subjective element of philosophy and its role, and the process of fusion of the many into one.[15] However, his theory of 'windowless monads' is less to the liking of Whitehead, for the monads lack the power of prehensive interaction and the double object-subject relations which Whitehead sees in actual entities in organic process.

Unfortunately we cannot review his views of many other philosophers of influence such as Berkeley, Bergson, Alexander, Bradley, James, Dewey, and others.[16]

Key Concepts and the Creative Process

It is our immediate aim in this section to learn more about the creative process philosophically for later fusions of creativity with the educational process. Unfortunately there is no easy way to understand Whitehead's theory of creativity nor his philosophy of organism. Use of his special terminology is absolutely necessary. Furthermore, creativity must be understood within the context of his whole philosophy. Hence we are faced with a dilemma of exposition within the severe limtiations of the space of this chapter.

In as much as it is not feasible to enter into lengthy expositions of the philosophy of organism, the discussion endeavors to relate a few of the key conceptions of Whitehead directly to the problem of the creative process. These conceptions include: definitions of 'creativity,' 'actual entities,' 'eternal objects,' and 'concrescence'; with the exposition of the stages of 'concrescence' other conceptions are included such as the 'actual world,' 'prehensions,' 'subject-object relations,' 'bipolarity,' 'eros,' 'subjective aims,' and 'God.'

Creativity in the Philosophy of Organism

'Creativity' is included within Whitehead's 'Category of the Ultimate.' As such it is associated with 'many' and 'one' as ultimate notions by which to explain the meaning of an 'entity' or 'thing.'[17] As we have noted elsewhere Whitehead recognizes the problem of the one and the many as the primary problem of philosophy. He also faced the problem of relating elements of permanence and those of novelty. Through these ultimate ideas of creativity, one, and many, we see his ingenious resolution of these perennial problems.

The 'many' is the principle of diversity, or 'disjunctive diversity.' The 'one' is the principle of unity, or 'conjunctive unity.' The actual world is in one sense conjunctive or one, and in another sense in 'disjunctive diversity.'[18] 'Creativity' is a necessary notion to explicate the dynamics of the one and the many, or the adventures of the world in its conjunctivity and disjunctivity.

> Whitehead defines 'creativity' as the universal of universals characterizing ultimate matter of fact. It is that ultimate principle by which the many, which are the universe disjunctively, become the one actual occasion, which is the universe conjunctively. It lies in the nature of things that the many enter into complex unity.[19]

It is important then to note that 'creativity' is an eternal object as distinguished from an actual entity. As an eternal object it is exemplified in the becoming of actual entities in concrescence and in transition. It is exemplified in the becoming of the universe. It is exemplified in God's activity as he weaves the extensions of his consequent nature upon his primordial conceptuality. In short God exemplifies 'creativity' in his own activity.

'Creativity' is also an ultimate principle in the philosophy of organism. It is the principle of novelty. That is to say the universe in its manyness achieves novelty in its creative advance through the exemplification of the principle of creativity.[20] Thus as the universe moves from disjunction to conjunction, or the creation of new entities, this ultimate metaphysical principle is embodied.

Creativity as exemplified in process is therefore the way in which the many become one; it is also the basis for the potential becoming actual.[21] As we shall see, 'creativity' is expressed in 'concrescence' or the becoming of actual entities, and in transition, or the perishing of some existents and the birth of other existents.

It is evident from these observations that 'creativity' in this context is a metaphysical principle.[22] It applies to all actual entities in their becoming. There should be no confusion then of 'creativity' in this context and some of the more popular notions of 'creativity' in educational theory.

Actual Entities and the Creative Process

Actual entities are the real things which constitute the world.[23] They are the actual occasions in the world of process. They are the real existents as they emerge from world process. They are born, they develop through a process of concrescence, and they die, or to use Whitehead's phrase, 'perpetually perish.' In his terminology they are *causa sui,* or self-determined.[24] This self-determination rests upon the conception that in their prehensions they may accept or reject the data made available by other objects. Hence in the becoming of an entity its being is determined by how it becomes: its feelings, intuitions, prehensions, and the character of its interactions with other entities. On the level of the human organism this self-determination implies a kind of autonomy in the creation of the self, or a discernible degree of free action or free will.

It is important to note that this developing entity is not a static substance floating in absolute time and space. The organic viewpoint rejects such a materialistic conception.[25] The entity is an event in as much as it is not static but fluent; it is in motion; it is in process.

This entity as an organic process repeats in its microcosmic structure and function what is in the universe macrocosmically.[26] Hence it is not merely a static material substance, but an organic entity which unifies the many in its process of concrescence or the process of self-creativity.

Thus we see that the story of process and reality is that of how actual entities come into existence and how they become or develop. The philosophy of organism is largely an exposition of how these actual entities unify the diverse forces and factors of the universe in their self-creativity. This process, however, cannot be understood in isolation, but requires the examination of many other factors and their relations.

Eternal Objects and the Creative Process

Eternal objects are ideal entities which are not necessarily involved in any actual entity, or what Whitehead terms 'a form of definiteness.' As such they are ideal conceptions subsisting beyond time as 'possibles' for actualization in entities temporally and spatially. Eternal objects are said to be internally related with one another, but they are externally related to actual entities.

Now as we have seen in other contexts, actual entities have a teleological aspect to their self-determination in their subjective aims. The process of becoming or concrescence is characterized by positive and negative prehensions of both actual entities and their data and ideal entities or eternal objects. Thus the eternal objects provide a lure for feeling and for the subjective aims. In other words these eternal objects are available for possible feeling or actualization in the developing organism, giving that entity more determination. From the side of the eternal object we may say that it has ingressed into the actual entity. Since the actual entity is in motion as an event it embodies the ideal form more or less imperfectly or in degree or ratio. Another way of saying this is that the developing entity participates in the eternal forms. Thus the developing subject exemplifies the 'eternal objects' in varying degrees in its movement. The diverse modes of ingression cannot be discussed here. From the viewpoint of the developing subject, forms can be prehended either from other actual entities or from the ideal entities.

Since the discussion of physical, conceptual, and hybrid prehensions requires detailed analysis, it will not be undertaken in this context.[27]

The Nature of Process

Whitehead's exposition begins with the dictum 'that all things flow.'[28] Yet all is not flux for there are elements of permanence; metaphysics must deal with reconciliation of these elements of permanence and flux. It has been noted that he has rejected any Platonic notion of a static heaven of Being, as well as his rejection of Aristotle's doctrine of primary substance. He is in agreement with Bergson to the extent that he believes there is a tendency of humans to 'spatialize the universe' and to think in static concepts.[29] At the same time he criticizes Descartes' dualistic solution of this problem.

Impressed with John Locke's exposition of two kinds of fluency which were only partly realized, Whitehead elaborated the creative process in terms of concrescence as the real internal constitution of an actual entity, and of the transition from one entity to another.[30] Whitehead's exposition of process on one side is the story of how concrescence takes place genetically. The other note of his exposition concerns transition—morphological in his concern with the formal aspects.[31]

The Process of Concrescence

It is impossible to review here Whitehead's twenty-seven Categories of Explanation.[32] It should be noted briefly that in the philosophy of organism these propositions are held:

(1) the actual world is constituted by the becoming of actual entities—or process;

(2) an actual entity is characterized by its unification of data derived from many entities in its becoming, or the actualization of many potentials;

(3) an actual entity achieves novelty in its particular unification of data;

(4) all actual entities are necessarily involved in this process of concrescence and objectification metaphysically; and

(5) the being of an actual entity is determined by how it becomes.[33]

Whitehead designates the complex process of becoming by the

term concrescence, derived from the Latin, *concrescere,* meaning 'growing together.' It appears to be a very well chosen term to indicate the becoming process of an actual entity as it moves from relative degrees of objectivity into the later phases of subjectivity, where the data are unified in the internal constitution and the subjectivity of the entity as product or superject. In other words it denotes the process whereby the many are realized in the unity of the concrete entity.

Three Stages of Concrescence

Concrescence can be understood best in terms of the various stages of development of the given entity or organism. Whitehead explains the becoming of 'the real internal constitution' of a given entity in three stages: (i) 'the responsive phase,' (ii) 'the supplemental stage,' and (iii) 'the satisfaction.'[34]

(i) The Responsive Stage

Whether we are speaking of concrescence in terms of a unit of experience within the life of an entity, or the entire life-cycle from birth to perishing, the creative process begins with the factor of activity. The initial situation is 'the preliminary phase of a new occasion.' That is to say the 'actual world' provides the 'real potentiality' for the becoming of an actual entity. The actual world provides the 'objects' which are necessary for the production of the new occasion. It provides the conjoint activity or the complex interactions of entities which constitute the primary phase of the new occasion. The actual world furnishes 'the primary phase with real potentiality.' Abstractly considered the emergent entity is a 'passive subject' which derives its activity 'from the creativity of the whole.'[35] However, actually the 'subject' actively experiences the data derived from other objects, even though such experiences are vague and largely undetermined during the primary or responsive stage.

The receptivity of the actual entity as subject in its concrescence is only relatively 'passive' and not actually so. Other actual entities which have reached their stage as determined 'superjects' are objectified in passing their available data to the developing subject, or actual entity in the primary stage. This seeming 'passivity' of the actual entity as subject in the primary stage should not be confused with the passivity of John Locke's *tabula rasa*.[36] Locke's theory required passivity in the process of sense experience on the part of the subject; these sensations were later the objects of reflection. However, the philosophy of organism is strikingly different at this crucial point. There is not merely the reaction of the actual entity to external substance. Rather the organic process of becoming is marked by the feelings of the emergent actual entity as subject in its reception and assimilation of external data. The response of the actual entity is in terms of positive or negative prehensions. Furthermore, these prehensions are not limited to 'sense perceptions' of data, or 'presentational immediacy,' but they involve the 'feelings' or 'intuitions' of the massiveness of the 'actual world' or what Whitehead terms the feeling of 'causal efficacy.' Pursuit of this problem here would take us too far from our immediate exposition.

The first phase then is marked by the pure receptions from the actual world as the objective data. It is characteristic of this stage that the feelings are engrossed in the reception of alien data. They have not yet been assimilated into the subjective aim or private immediacy of the actual entity. It is in the second stage that the private ideals begin to exert their influence on the process of becoming. There is a gradual organic transformation of feelings of alien data and sources of data into the immediacy and subjectivity of the evolving subject.[37] The aesthetic feelings gradually become private; the movement is from the indeterminate to the determinate, from the objective to the subjective, from external data to unification in the internal constitutions of the subject.[38] However, these movements are accomplished in the whole process of concrescence.

(ii) *The Supplemental Stage*

The second stage is marked by the conceptual reaction of the subject and the emergence of the private ideal. The physical prehensions of the initial stage are now met with conceptual reactions.[39] The many data of the first stage which were felt as alien are gradually transformed into subjective feelings of privacy. The subjective aims or private ideals emerge in the process and shape its further development. Thus the essence of this second stage is its re-creation of the previously alien elements into the subjectivity and privacy of the subject. It is here that there is an integration of physical and conceptual feelings, or the interactions of physical and mental poles.

In this immediate context it should be noted that all actual entities are constituted by a bipolarity of physical and mental poles in process. This fact has important significance for later understandings of creativity in terms of human growth, development, and schooling. The concrescence of the human organism is also characterized by the unification of physical and mental prehensions, or the interactions of the two poles. The physical inheritance via the physical pole is accompanied by conceptual reactions of the mental pole, which stresses 'emphasis, valuation, and purpose.'[40]

Whitehead divides the second stage, the supplementary, into two subordinate phases.[41] For the sake of simplicity we may refer to these two sub-phases as (a) 'the aesthetic supplement,' and (b) 'the intellectual supplement.'[42] In the aesthetic supplement there is the predominance of 'the feeling of contrasts and rhythms.' There is the re-creation of what was felt earlier as alien to the immediacy and privacy of the subject in its concrescence. Conceptual feelings blend with pure physical feelings in this sub-phase.

There is a certain 'blindness' and indetermination to the foregoing phase. In the intellectual supplement there is consideration of eternal objects and their acceptance or negation. If the eternal objects are dismissed this 'phase becomes trivial.'[43] However, if the eternal objects or 'pure potentials' are positively prehended there are resulting intellectual operations which are not trivial; the eternal objects are embodied in 'the actual occasion.' Whitehead says that pure potentials used in the determination of subjects are termed 'propositional feelings.'[44] These propositional feelings are forms of motivation in the becoming of the subject, for they represent 'vital contrasts of what is and what might be.' In other words as the subject becomes more aware of his self in increasing degrees of becoming, his envisionment of his own potentialities in terms of ideal aims contributes to the realization of the process of increasing determination.

303

Concrescence Illustrated by the Analogy of the Cave

The meaning and significance of concrescence can well be illustrated in terms of the analogy of the cave from Plato. Again may we remind the reader that our use of this analogy is not to be taken as endorsement of Plato's metaphysics or ontology. Throughout this work the utilization of this analogy is for strictly educational purposes—that is, to understand the educational process. The ontology here is rather in terms of the philosophy of organism.

The primary stage or 'responsive stage' of concrescence is comparable to the initial experiences of the learner 'in the cave.' There is the 'givenness' from the actual world as a datum. The prehensions of the physical pole are predominant in this stage and in this sphere. The prehended data are still alien in terms of feeling of their external derivation and in the sense of the self-identity or growing awareness of the self or learner.

There is a feeling of 'causal efficacy' of this experienced world, but it is not yet transformed into personal meaning and identification with the purposes and aims of the self. That is to say these experiences in the cave are vague intuitions of the world of actual objects. There is a kind of 'blindness' which characterizes this sphere of learning and this stage of concrescence. Yet as a second aspect of this primary stage, still in the cave, there is the 'presentational immediacy' or the immediate perception of sense objects. Thus experience in the cave is marked by the learner's indeterminate feelings amidst the realm of flux and the welter of things. He gives attention to things but his experience in this sphere lacks determinacy, purpose, perspective, and coherence.

The reader should bear in mind that these demarcations are sharply separated for analytical purposes, and that actually the organic educational process grows and develops in such a way as to make these divisions virtually imperceptible. The process of concrescence is completely fluent in its movement from indeterminacy to determinacy by successive degrees.

By and large Whitehead's 'supplemental phase,' or middle stage of concrescence, is analogous to the experience of the learner 'outside of the cave.' This second stage is represented by the experiences 'out of the cave' in the growing light of the 'conceptual reactions.' Perceptions of the 'observational level' are heightened by the conceptions of the 'conceptual level' of thought. The relative 'blindness' experienced in the first stage, 'in the cave,' gives way gradually to 'vision' and 'appetition' in terms of the learners 'subjective aims' and 'the lure of the eternal objects.' In Whitehead's terms there is 'an influx of conceptual feelings.'[45] As the subject or learner prehends the relations between his actual potentiality and the 'subjective aims' of what might be, there is a feeling of contrast or what Whitehead terms 'propositional feelings.' Thus this stage is marked by the increased self-determination through 'conceptual reactions' of the mental pole. The experiences 'out of the cave' in what Plato called 'the light of reason' provide illumination or 'insight' for the increased self-determination and the relationships between 'eternal objects' and the 'actual entities' previously experienced.

The third stage of 'satisfaction' is more difficult to equate with the analogy of the cave. Plato completes the original analogy by having Socrates observe that when such a prisoner returned to his old place in the cave, after having experienced the 'light of reason' outside of the cave, that he would see the shadows with new perceptiveness. The third stage of concrescence is marked by the determinacy of the learner's unit of experience, the resolution of the problem, and the restoration of his equilibrium psychologically. Analogously the original stage of relative indeterminacy and feeling of alien data in the concrescence of the learner has now through the experience outside of the cave in terms of conceptual reactions given way to the determinacy of the subject; this might be compared to a return from outside of the cave to inside of the cave; the learner has moved from objectivity to subjectivity. In another sense the earlier experiences termed 'causal efficacy' and 'presentational immediacy' are unified through what Whitehead terms 'symbolic reference,' or a 'synthesis into one subjective feeling.'[46] This movement from the two spheres inside and outside of the cave is what we have termed 'reversibility' in the organic educational process.

(iii) *The Stage of Satisfaction*

The final stage of concrescence is marked by the achievement of complete subjective unity—the indeterminate actual entity has become determinate; it has achieved its being. The many data have been unified in terms of the successive prehensions under the influence of the subjective aims and conceptual reactions. The creative urge has been satisfied and resolved through the realization of the original demands.[47] The tensions caused by the disequilibrium of the early stages of the becoming of the actual entity are alleviated and equilibrium restored to the organism.

Whitehead terms this final stage one of 'satisfaction.' His interpretation is somewhat different than one might expect. One might assume that he meant the feeling of satisfaction which comes with the realization of a goal. Although this notion sounds feasible, Whitehead speaks of 'satisfaction' in terms of what the completed entity now does as 'object' beyond its own concrescence as 'subject.' As he says, the entity as process has worn itself out; the 'satisfaction' is actually found in its 'effects.'[48] The actual entity as subject is now considered as superject. Its own internal constitution has been determined and achieved. It is now an object for the becoming of other entities. This is the stage of the 'superject,' although subject-superject are actually inseparable. Thus considered as 'superject' the entity becomes an object exerting influences transcending its own internal constitution in the formation of other entities in their becoming. It is in itself stubborn fact, settled and determined.

As Whitehead says, this phase is in one respect pragmatic because the actual entity as superject is considered in relation to its consequences, or influence on other entities. The stage of 'satisfaction' is one of the culminating effects of the actual entity as object.

In this context it might well be noted that the process has culminated in product—in 'substantial product.' The actual entity as product in its determined form is a 'substance' for all practical purposes. Such objects can be considered in terms of their 'substantial' forms and characteristics for they are determined fact. The 'substance' is not the same as Aristotle's 'Primary substance,' but nevertheless it is 'substance' in the context of the philosophy of organism.[49]

We see then that the primary stage of concrescence is characterized by: the conditions of the actual world as data for the emergence of a new subject; the interactions of prior entities that have
completed their process of concrescence with emphasis upon their
subjective achievement and are not placing emphasis upon their role
as superjects or objects for the creation and emergence of new entities as subjects. That is to say we must comprehend the overlapping
of the concrescence of entities as objects in their final stages with
the concrescence of other entities as subjects in their initial stage.
The perishing of certain entities in their culminating stage results in
their contribution of data to the birth of new entities in their initial
stage. The intermediate stage stresses the process of absorption and
assimilation of the alien data into the internal constitution of the
organism with an ever increasing degree of immediacy and feeling

Figure 12

Professor Craven's Interpretation of the Stages of the Creative Process

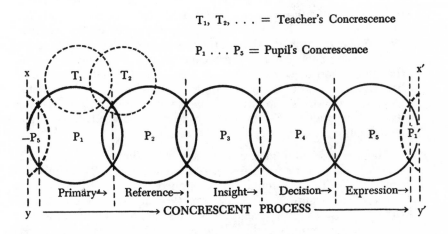

Fig. 1—Unit of Concrescent Process

307

of privacy in the self-determination of the entity. Physical feelings and prehensions are integrally constituted by interactions with conceptual reactions; subjective aims increase their intensity and in their influence upon the recurring prehensions, both positive and negative, in this process of self-determination. In the culminating stage the entity has achieved self-determination in terms of the strivings for realization of subjective aims and now passes into the phase of 'satisfaction' which we have noted as passing on into the objectification in other entities.

Professor Gus J. Craven's Figure, "Unit of Concrescent Process," provides us with an excellent schematic design of concrescence as applied to self-creation in the educational context.[50]

For the sake of precision and accuracy Professor Craven's own explanation of the figure is quoted extensively as follows:

> In Figure 1 the serial route of self-creation through a single unit of experience is diagrammed. P represents the self-identity of personality, the constant which does not change but 'becomes.' And the subscripts, 1, 2, 3, 4, 5, represent P's stages of becoming in a unit of concrescence the extensive limits of which are represented by the vertical axes, xy and x'y'. $-P_5$ is the closing phase of the immediate past which is presented in the primary stage of this particular concrescence as P_1. But according to Whitehead's doctrine of 'objective immortality,' $-P_5$ is also an object for the self-creation of other persons, which is P's transcendent creativity. Our interest here, however, is in the linear series of P's progress from P_1 on through P_5—the continuum between the vertical axes, xy and x'y'. Such a serial representation seems adequate also in the description of co-ordinates. But co-ordinate analysis, while it has the same sort of sequence, is a division of the concrete. Genetic analysis is the division of the concrescent process into its various stages of movement toward its objective, concrete actualization.
>
> There is also in Figure 1 the bare indication of the teacher's involvement in P's concrescence, represented at T_1, T_2. The continuation of T_1 on through T_5 is implied as a constituent in P_1 . . . P_5. This figure is, of course, greatly simplified. Were it possible to draw the other required circles without undue complexity in the diagram, we should be forced to represent the home, the community, and all the other influences which condition every concrescence of P.[51]

Outline of the Characteristics of the Five Stages of Concrescence as Derived from Craven's Interpretation

Reproduction of Dr. Craven's original exposition of his five stages of the process of concrescence is not practicable here. This is indeed unfortunate for the writer has found these interpolations very helpful and enlightening in understanding not only the complex subject of concrescence, but the numerous relations to psychology, religion, and education. In the interest of accuracy most of the following materials have been cited as direct quotations from Dr. Craven's dissertation.[52] It is believed that these outlined expositions elucidate the graphic portrayal of the five stages of concrescence.

I. The 'primary stage' is characterized by the following statements:

(A) There is a personal inheritance or 'givenness.'

There is always a 'givenness,' a set of the self, a personality gestalt acting as the conditioning datum of the primary phase of process. There can be no creation *de novo* in personality development.[53]

(B) The past is only partially a determinate of the future.

It is the determination of the present which defines the nature of the future.[54]

(C) The actual entity is receptive although not merely passive in this stage of concrescence.

What we are saying is that in a primary stage of experience a person is not an isolated entity with a conceptual feeling of himself as being wholly bound by his past: besides a prehension of his own self-identity, he has a felt awareness of being in the midst of a flux of things and events, and he is there in that particular welter as a rational person who can select the items to which he will attend. *It is this sense of self-determinateness that constitutes the primary stage with its initial creativity.*[55]

(D)

In the primary stage, P_1, the experiencing person is dimly aware of a set of feelings (prehensions) which define the mere fact of self-identity, the inherence of the past in the present, and a welter of other persons and things as situational data to which one is attending. As merely presented, these data are vague, incoherent, and purposeless. . . . The 'presentational immediacy' of the primary stage is to be characterized initially as mere attention.[56]

In each stage of concrescence Dr. Craven has summarized principles applicable to educational theory and practice. A few of these terse principles are presented here within the context of each stage of becoming. Illustrative of applications in the 'primary stage' are the following:[57]

(a) Each pupil brings into every unit of experience a personal inheritance as a basis for further self-creation.[58]

(b) The teacher's own inherited past and present personality structure enter as data into each primary stage of the pupil's self-development.[59]

(c) The pupil should be aware at the beginning of each unit of experience that he is entering upon a new adventure of self-creation.[60]

(d) The inherited culture of the race should be used critically as a basis for the pupil's aesthetic, ethical, spiritual, and social development.[61]

II. The 'reference stage' is characterized by these statements:

(A)

In the reference stage, this background of data begins to take on meaning as it conditions the subjective aim of the experiencing person for that particular concrescence. The reference function of that 'given' is to indicate how that body of data lends itself or, better still, points to the relevance of certain propositions as a means for the data to become operative in that process.[62]

(B)

Propositions are the introduction of potentiality into the concrescence as meaning. The reference stage is, therefore, the beginning of conscious organization of feelings presented in the primary stage. Through the operation of propositions, purpose as 'subjective aim' has its inception in the process. The subject, P, is referred by means of propositions to a conceptual end as the meaning of the present experience.[63]

Hence propositions define and by their nature as ideal lures initiate activity as a self-becoming.[64]

(C) The educational process moves from disequilibrium to equilibrium, or from dissatisfaction to satisfaction. In the reference stage it is necessary to stir the learners to an interest "from what is to what may or should be."[65]

Psychologically, it is the setting up of a condition of disequilibrium by the agency of psychogenic needs which initiate the drives

310

necessary for their satisfaction. When the needs have been satisfied, equilibrium is restored. Thus the organism lives rhythmically by these alternations of needs and satisfactions.[66]

The guiding principles of creative education for application to the 'reference stage' are illustrated by the following selections:

(a) The propositional value of curriculum materials is determined by their content of ideals for living.[67]

(b) Imagination should be cultivated for its illumination of the potentialities of propositions.[68]

(c) The reference stage in educational process should be utilized to develop unrest and dissatisfaction on the part of the pupil, but always in the light of what one is and may become.[69]

III. The 'insight stage' is characterized by these statements:

(A) In this stage the becoming is determined by conceptual relevance.

The insight stage is a clarification of the propositions presented in the reference stage. The whole concrescent process, $P_1 \ldots P_5$, is characterized by a progressive unification of feelings derived from the data by selection and rejection according to the subjective aim (purpose, objective) of the experiencing person. But the subjective aim itself is formed in the concrescence, as the meaning of the data becomes sufficiently clear to permit a choice of alternative goals.[70]

This illustrates the modern conception that purpose evolves in experience. Thus 'insight' represents that stage in the unification of a new self in which the concepts involved in the presented propositions achieve significant relevance.[71]

(B) Insight into the relevance of a proposition for the subject is not merely intellectual, but also involves feeling.

This conceptual relevance is what is meant here as 'insight.' But it is not purely intellectual in the sense of a mental operation, nor is it to be explained merely by adding the physical concomitants to the mental act. That the proposition is not purely mental is attested to by the fact that many propositions are accepted as true without persuasion by argument and proof as to their certain truth.[72]

(C) There is a sense in which propositions are admitted into belief without proof.

The notion is acquired that a judgment is inferential, because it admits a proposition into intellectual belief without certain proof. And the full truth of a proposition cannot be judged until it has been received and acted upon. Thus the expression of the unified self in its 'objective immortality' becomes *the* truth, the meaning, of that proposition as felt and thereby defines the tentative nature of knowledge—incidentally, it also reveals knowledge as a means and not a true end in itself.[73, 74]

(D) The 'insight stage' is closely related to the principle of identification. It is similar to a doctrine of interest holding: that when the data or contents of learning experiences are perceived by the learner as having relevance to his own objectives or subjective aims there is an 'added zest or interest' felt by the subject in terms of the process of concrescence. On the side of the genetic-functional, or psychological, aspects of concrescence there is a similarity to Dewey's genetic, 'means-ends theory' of experience; however, as we shall see in other contexts, the similarity ends here, for in Whitehead there is another aspect to the story of concrescence, the morphological side based upon the subsistence of the 'eternal objects' and the lure of the ideal forms. Thus there is a similarity on the psychological level, but there is a distinct difference on the level of metaphysics and ontology.[75]

Professor Craven explains 'conceptual relevance' as follows:

These propositions attain their 'intensive conceptual relevance' when the data-content are identified as having a place of interest —lying between the subject and its object as the means by which the subject may complete its own unification and thereby become the end of its concrescence. The material or activity characterizing the data-content then becomes 'interesting' and important because of its unique function as a means—and this is its meaning. This is the force of Dewey's statement that to set up an end in view is to have a like concern for the means of its achievement.[76]

This proposition also requires further exposition and amplification within the context of the organic educational philosophy in the next chapter.

The guiding principles of creative education for application to the 'insight stage' are illustrated by the following selections:

(a) Purpose evolves in a concrescent process as the experiencing person senses (sees, feels) the meaning of propositions for a novel self-creation.[77]

312

(b) Insight should not be conceived of as pure intellectual 'seeing' of relationships; some propositions can and will be accepted without logical proof of their truth.[78]

(c) Imagination should be stimulated as a means for the development of insight.[79]

(d) The insight stage in a concrescence should be utilized as a discovery of relationships between old and new values to prevent the habit of mere imitation.[80]

IV. The 'decision stage' is characterized by these statements:

(A)

The genetic analysis of a concrescent experience, involving self-formation of personality, requires by its very nature a 'decision stage.' In the diagram of Figure 1, P_4 represents the concrescent unity of P at the stage of decision. The primary stage, P_1, represents the person at the beginning of the process: he has a feeling of inheritance from his own past—sometimes called 'conformal inheritance'—and an awareness of other data being presented immediately. In the reference stage, P_2, these feelings of the given data (including the personal inheritance from the past) are felt as having a reference to the further stages of P's concrescence; they take the form of propositions which become ideal lures toward P's final unity. It requires a further stage, however, for these vague and diverse feelings incorporated into propositions to be clarified with enough 'intensive conceptual relevance' to be meaningful as choices. This is the 'insight' stage and is designated P_3. The decision stage, then, which follows serially as P_4, is the resolution of conflict, of incoherence, of indetermination into a determinate unity of feelings expressed objectively in the final phase, P_5.[81]

(B) In the 'decision stage' the indeterminate character of the subjective aims becomes determinate; the data of the 'reference stage' are admitted only as they conform to the subjective aims of the subject as he presides over self-formation. Former propositions that were clarified by insights finally become accepted at the decision stage.

This indetermination of the subjective aim persists throughout the concrescence until in the decision stage the process becomes fully determinate.[82]

(C) There is a sense in which the actual entity or person is *causa sui*, which here refers to the self-responsibility of the organism in terms

313

of its decision by which any lure for feeling is admitted for efficacy. (This follows from Whitehead's similarity to Spinoza's panpsychism, the notion that the actual entity is the locus of the universe, or a microcosmic exemplification of world processes.)[83]

(D) God is involved in human concrescence.

God in his primordial aspect is not before creation but with all creation . . . God leads the world by his lure of truth, beauty, and goodness.[84] . . .

The 'weaving' of his physical feelings is a reaction in experience to his conceptual lures by the experiencing person. Thus he saves the world by salvaging what he can from human decisions.[85]

(E) The creativity of the individual is related to universal creativity.

The second requirement needed to justify a free self-determination in a concrescent process is, to repeatfi a further clarification of the individual's relation to universal creativity. Since by the 'ontological principle' 'actual entities . . . are the final real things of which the world is made up,' there can be 'no going behind actual entities to find anything more real.'[86] Hence universal creativity itself must be described finally as relations between individuals. God is an individual entity and is therefore to be considered in his relations to creature individuals by the same metaphysical principle of ontology. . . . The 'principle of ontology' and the 'relative theory' thus combined to furnish the necessary basis of metaphysical logic for freedom in self-determination.[87]

(F)

Decision in a process of self-formation may properly be described in general terms of a 'will to form.'[88] . . . Decision as 'volitional assent' has, then, the character of a final, free determination to act upon the evidence, to accept an idea of the Self as true without intellectual or logical certainty. It also means self-determination as 'a *will* to form.' So that what was first 'attended to' and then as the proposition gained meaning was 'attended to' with *interest*, has now become desire. Imaginatively, decision is the compression of time, as past and as future, into the living present.[89]

The longer list of guiding principles for application to the 'decision stage' is illustrated by the following selections:

(a) The element of decision should have an important place in all learning experience.[90]

(b) Conscious self-formation should enter as an important factor into every significant decision.[91]

314

(c) When pupils are allowed to make decisions, their choices should be respected by the teacher.[92]

V. The 'expression stage' is characterized as follows:

(A)

The concrescent process enters its closing stage when by an act of decision the experiencing Self chooses among the prevailing alternatives . . . . P_5 adds to the feelings inherited from P_4, the decision stage, a definiteness not previously enjoyed by the concrescence. The vagueness and incoherence characteristic of the process in its initial stage have been progressively eliminated until in the stage of expression a final, determinate unity is achieved. This final unity of feelings in a definiteness of form is the meaning of Whitehead's 'actual entity.'[93]

(B) The potential entity of process becomes the actual reality.

In terms of an experiencing Self, the expression stage is realization of novel contrast under self-identity: the novel Self as potential has been transformed through process into reality. Concrescent unity is also to be described as integration of diverse feelings into one, final feeling of 'satisfaction.'[94]

(C)

As an objective expression, the process comes to a close; hence the genetic analysis is finished. But the end of one unit of concrescence is the beginning of another. The expression stage is also described as the 'objective immortality' whereby the closed unit of experience has 'perished' but lives on in creative advance of the world. This is its 'immortality.'[95]

The principles for the guidance of creative education at the 'expression stage' are illustrated briefly by the following selections:

(a) Every pupil should be encouraged to become a searching, inventive, expressive individual.[96]

(b) Every pupil should be helped to realize that he can be creative in developing a better Self.[97]

(c) Since education is a process, evaluation should ordinarily be considered as a sampling rather than as a final measure of achievement.[98]

It is hoped that the immediately foregoing section of this chapter devoted to Professor Craven's interpretation of the five stages of concrescence, as he has formulated them from his knowledge of Whitehead's philosophy of organism and related fields of psychology, religion, and education, has contributed to the reader's insights into the nature of the creative process and some of its implications for the educational process.

Although this writer is in substantial agreement with Whitehead's theory of the creative process, and also with Professor Craven's own interpretations of this process with its implications for creative education, there are some *apparent* differences in terms of amplification and interpretation of creativity with the Organic Philosophy of Education. However, this writer believes they are only 'apparent differences' and not real differences, for virtually all of the amplifications and interpretations within this educational philosophy with respect to the creative process can be substantiated at the philosophical level in Whitehead's philosophy of organism. There are questions, however, which this writer raises himself with respect to possible deviations from the philosophy of organism on other problems.[99]

There are several reasons for these apparent differences which the reader should understand clearly. In the first place Professor Craven's exposition of the five stages of concrescence is admittedly concerned only with one aspect of the process in his dissertation—that is the genetic-functional aspect of learning experience. Agreement at some points in this genetic-functional account of concrescence between Whitehead and Dewey, as we have noted in Craven's exposition, does not mean total agreement.[100]

Another explanation for seeming differences between creativity in the philosophy of organism and its interpretation in the Organic Philosophy of Education lies in the fact that Whitehead's concern with creativity is at the metaphysical level of exposition—relating to all actual entities. While this writer also accepts this interpretation of creativity at the metaphysical level, he has been concerned primarily with amplification of creativity at the human level of the educational process. Since Whitehead did not endeavor to make a direct application of his philosophical conceptions of creativity, one and many, and concrescence to the educational process, we have little or no evidence of what interpretations he might have made. This writer has been concerned with a fusion of his own educational conceptions and the main tenets of Whitehead's philosophy of organ-

316

ism. Hence he has sought to extend such conceptions as the creative process into the warp and woof of his own educational philosophy. Hence what may appear to be 'differences' of interpretation are for the most part enlargements or extensions of concepts from the philosophy of organism on the level of educational philosophy.

In the next chapter the meaning and significance of these organic conceptions of the creative process are delineated in the previously formulated principles and conceptions of the Organic Philosophy of Education.

Summary. 'Creativity' is generally accepted by educators; but the real problem is to determine the precise meaning of creativity and its role in education. Educators are at the crossroads with respect to an adequate philosophy of education and theory of creativity. It is the thesis here that by and large A. N. Whitehead's philosophy of organism provides us with an adequate theory of creativity. John Dewey's educational philosophy with its included theory of creativity has many merits, but it is philosophically inadequate in its parsimony.

This organic educational philosophy seeks to formulate an adequate metaphysical conception of creativity and its applications to the educational process. There are historical grounds for theories of creativity to be found in organic philosophers from the Greeks to the present. Both Plato and Aristotle were organic philosophers and expressed educational principles involving creativity. Modern educators and philosophers have certainly expressed a diversity of theories of creativity in terms of the educational process.

Whitehead's philosophy of organism and theory of creativity were accomplished by his tremendous reconstruction of many philosophical systems. These included reconstructions of such eminent thinkers as Plato, Aristotle, Descartes, John Locke, David Hume, Bishop Berkeley, Kant, Leibniz, Spinoza, and others.

Whitehead's philosophy of organism recognizes 'creativity' as an Ultimate Principle. It is an eternal object which is exemplified in the concrescences and transitions of actual entities. It is the principle of novelty; it is also the process whereby the many become one. It is clearly a metaphysical principle in the philosophy of organism.

317

The creative process is exemplified in the birth and development of actual entities and their 'perpetual perishing.' It is largely a story of how actual entities as subjects 'become' and how as 'superjects' or 'objects' they are objectified in the becoming of other actual entities. The 'eternal objects' are the pure potentials for the actualization of actual entities—providing them with 'forms of definiteness.'

Concrescence, meaning 'growing together,' has three stages as described by Whitehead, (i) 'the responsive phase,' (ii) 'the supplementary stage,' and (iii) 'the satisfaction.' The 'primary phase' is marked by the pure receptions from 'the actual world as the objective datum.' The supplementary stage is marked by 'the conceptual reaction of the subject and the emergence of the private ideal.' The essence of this second stage is its re-creation of the previously felt alien elements into the subjectivity and privacy of the subject by means of the subjective aims. The third and final stage of concrescence is marked by the achievement of complete subjective unity. The indeterminate actual entity in process has become the completed and determined reality. It is then a 'superject' or an object which contributes to the becoming of other actual entities.

These stages of concrescence can be understood in terms of the educational process by means of the analogy of the cave. The primary stage of concrescence represents the experiences 'in the cave' as vague and indeterminate. They represent primary intuitions of 'causal efficacy' and 'presentational immediacy.' The supplementary stage is represented by the experiences 'out of the cave' in the light of reason; this is comparable to Whitehead's 'conceptual reactions.' The fragmentary and 'blind' perceptions of the primary phase are now experienced in the light of conceptual forms. The 'visions' and 'subjective aims' of this stage experienced out of the cave guide and shape the process of concrescence. The return to the 'inside of the cave furthers the unity of the person in his becoming. That which was indeterminate has become determinate; the unit of concrescence is completed. This integration or unification of the developing person has been termed 'organic synthesis' in this educational philosophy; it accords with Whitehead's 'symbolic reference' in one sense, and in another sense with the fulfillment of the becoming process.

ORGANIC CONCEPTIONS OF THE CREATIVE PROCESS

There is a striking correspondence between Whitehead's three stages of concrescence and the organic educational process as depicted in terms of Plato's analogy of the cave in this work.

According to Professor G. J. Craven, Whitehead's process of concrescence can be interpreted in terms of five stages of development for purposes of the educational process. These five stages include: (i) 'the primary stage,' (ii) 'the reference stage,' (iii) 'the insight stage,' (iv) 'the decision stage,' and (v) 'the expression stage.' The 'primary stage' emphasizes the personal inheritance and the 'givenness' of the emerging subject. Each pupil has this 'givenness' at the beginning of a unit of experience. In the 'reference stage' this background of data begins to take on meaning as it conditions the subjective aim of the experiencing person for that particular concrescence. The pupil develops unrest and dissatisfaction in the light of what he is and might become. In the 'insight stage' the becoming is determined by 'conceptual relevance.' Purpose evolves in the concrescent process as the experiencing person or pupil senses the meaning of propositions for a novel self-creation. In the 'decision stage' the indeterminate character of the subjective aims becomes determinate. According to Craven there is a 'will to form' and a 'volitional assent.' The pupil enters into conscious self-formation at this point in his development. In the 'expression stage' the potential entity of process has become the actual reality. The pupil has reached the determined stage of his unit of concrescence.[101]

FOOTNOTES

1. Frank C. Wegener, "The End of An Educational Epoch: What Next?" Paper read at meeting of Southwestern Philosophy of Education Society, Fort Worth, Texas, Nov. 9, 1956.

2. This thesis is found also in the dissertation of Dr. Gus John Craven, "A Comparative Study of Creativity in Education in Whitehead and Others." (Unpublished Ed. D. dissertation, Department of History and Philosophy of Education, University of Texas, 1952.)

3. See Raphael Demos, *The Philosophy of Plato* (New York: Charles Scribner's Sons, 1939), pp. 3-7.

4. These descriptions of Plato's philosophy are not to be construed as necessary parts of the Organic Philosophy of Education. Whitehead's philosophy of organism is followed unless deviations otherwise are indicated.

5. Frederick Eby and Charles F. Arrowood, *The History and Philosophy of Education, Ancient and Medieval* (New York: Prentice-Hall, Inc., 1940, copyright by the publisher in 1940), pp. 367-81.

6. John Burnet, *Aristotle on Education* (Cambridge: The Cambridge University Press, 1903), p. 136.

7. John Burnet, *Aristotle on Education*, p. 136.

8. Dorothy M. Emmet, *Whitehead's Philosophy of Organism* (London: St. Martin's Street, Macmillan and Company, Limited, 1932), p. 174. Reprinted with permission of the publisher.

9. Dorothy M. Emmet, *Whitehead's Philosophy of Organism*, p. 175.

10. A. N. Whitehead, *Adventures of Ideas* (New York: The Macmillan Company, 1933), p. 188.

11. A. H. Johnson, *Whitehead's Theory of Reality* (Boston: The Beacon Press, 1952), pp. 119-51.

12. A. H. Johnson, *Whitehead's Theory of Reality*, p. 130.

13. A. H. Johnson, *Whitehead's Theory of Reality*, pp. 126-27.

14. A. H. Johnson, *Whitehead's Theory of Reality*, pp. 128-29.

15. A. H. Johnson, *Whitehead's Theory of Reality*, pp. 130-31.

16. A. H. Johnson, *Whitehead's Theory of Reality*, pp. 131-51.

17. A. N. Whitehead, *Process and Reality* (Cambridge: Cambridge University Press, 1929, copyright U.S.A. by Macmillan Co.), p. 28.

18. A. N. Whitehead, *Process and Reality*, p. 28.

19. A. N. Whitehead, *Process and Reality*, p. 28. Reprinted with permission of Macmillan Co., copyright in U.S.A., 1929.

20. A. N. Whitehead, *Process and Reality*, p. 28.

21. A. N. Whitehead, *Process and Reality*, pp. 28-29.

22. A. N. Whitehead, *Process and Reality*, pp. 28-29.

23. A. N. Whitehead, *Process and Reality*, p. 24.

24. A. N. Whitehead, *Process and Reality*, p. 122.

25. A. N. Whitehead, *Science and the Modern World* (New York: The New American Library of World Literature, Inc., A Mentor Book, by arrangement with the Macmillan Co., 1948).

26. A. N. Whitehead, *Process and Reality*, pp. 304-05.

27. A. H. Johnson, *Whitehead's Theory of Reality*, pp. 31-32.

28. A. N. Whitehead, *Process and Reality*, p. 295.

29. A. N. Whitehead, *Process and Reality*, p. 297.

30. A. N. Whitehead, *Process and Reality*, pp. 297-98.

31. A. N. Whitehead, *Process and Reality*, p. 309 ff.

32. A. N. Whitehead, *Process and Reality*, p. 30 ff.

33. A. N. Whitehead, *Process and Reality*, pp. 30-31.

34. A. N. Whitehead, *Process and Reality*, p. 301 ff.

35. A. N. Whitehead, *Adventures of Ideas*, p. 230.

36. Suggested by correspondence with Dr. Gus John Craven.

37. A. N. Whitehead, *Process and Reality*, p. 303.

38. A. N. Whitehead, *Process and Reality*, pp. 303-05.

39. A. N. Whitehead, *Process and Reality*, p. 301.

40. A. N. Whitehead, *Process and Reality*, pp. 25 and 32.

41. A. N. Whitehead, *Process and Reality*, p. 302.

42. A. N. Whitehead, *Process and Reality*, p. 303.

43. A. N. Whitehead, *Process and Reality*, p. 303.

44. A. N. Whitehead, *Process and Reality*, p. 304.

45. A. N. Whitehead, *Process and Reality*, p. 301.

46. A. N. Whitehead, *Process and Reality*, p. 252.

47. A. N. Whitehead, *Process and Reality*, p. 309.

48. A. N. Whitehead, *Process and Reality*, p. 310.

49. A. N. Whitehead, *Process and Reality*, p. 310.

50. From Dr. Gus John Craven's study, "A Comparative Study of Creativity in Education in Whitehead and Others." (Unpublished dissertation, Department of History and Philosophy of Education, University of Texas, June, 1952), Chapter VII, "Stages of Creative Process," pages 258-319. This writer is deeply indebted to Professor Craven for his kind permission to include his own original diagram and his interpretation of concrescence in the educational context. Since Whitehead did not apply his conception of concrescence directly to the educational process this adaptation and amplification is original.
Dr. Craven's five stages as depicted here are his own interpolations. This observation is confirmed as follows, "The writer believes that his organization of the genetic factors in experience into a sequential pattern of five stages is unique and may prove to be of some value to teachers. The validity of this belief will have to wait upon its application in practice." (Craven, *Op. cit.*, p. 329.)

51. Gus John Craven, *Ibid.*, pp. 269-70.

52. Professor Craven has read and fully approved this utilization of his materials.

53. G. J. Craven, *Ibid.*, pp. 260-61.

54. G. J. Craven, *Ibid.*, p. 261.

55. G. J. Craven, *Ibid.*, p. 267.

56. G. J. Craven, *Ibid.*, p. 272.

57. These principles have been selected at random from Professor Craven's much longer list of principles. Hence this listing is illustrative and not complete. The order cited here is incidental and does not indicate importance or sequence of application.

58. G. J. Craven, *Ibid.*, p. 270.

59. G. J. Craven, *Ibid.*, p. 271.

60. G. J. Craven, *Ibid.*, p. 271.

61. G. J. Craven, *Ibid.*, p. 272.

62. C. J. Craven, *Ibid.*, pp. 272-73.

63. G. J. Craven, *Ibid.*, p. 273.

64. C. J. Craven, *Ibid.*, p. 273.

65. G. J. Craven, *Ibid.*, p. 277.

66. G. J. Craven, *Ibid.*, p. 277.

67. G. J. Craven, *Ibid.*, p. 278.

68. G. J. Craven, *Ibid.*, p. 279.

69. G. J. Craven, *Ibid.*, p. 279.

70. G. J. Craven, *Ibid.*, p. 280.

71. G. J. Craven, *Ibid.*, p. 280.

72. G. J. Craven, *Ibid.*, p. 282.

73. G. J. Craven, *Ibid.*, p. 283.

74. It should be remembered that only one side of the creative process is being explained here—the genetic-functional aspect of concrescence. Further amplifications of this issue in terms of this organic educational philosophy are made in the following chapter.

75. See the discussion at the end of this chapter and footnote No. 100.

76. G. J. Craven, *Ibid.*, p. 290.

77. G. J. Craven, *Ibid.*, p. 293.

78. G. J. Craven, *Ibid.*, p. 293.

79. G. J. Craven, *Ibid.*, p. 293.

80. G. J. Craven, *Ibid.*, p. 294.

81. G. J. Craven, *Ibid.*, p. 295.

82. G. J. Craven, *Ibid.*, p. 297.

83. G. J. Craven, *Ibid.*, p. 298.

84. G. J. Craven, *Ibid.*, p. 299.

85. G. J. Craven, *Ibid.*, p. 300.

86. G. J. Craven, *Ibid.*, p. 300, in turn quoting A. N. Whitehead, *Process and Reality*, p. 27 f.

87. G. J. Craven, *Ibid.*, pp. 300-01.

88. G. J. Craven, *Ibid.*, p. 302.

89. G. J. Craven, *Ibid.*, p. 305.

90. G. J. Craven, *Ibid.*, p. 309.

91. G. J. Craven, *Ibid.*, p. 309.

92. G. J. Craven, *Ibid.*, p. 310.

93. G. J. Craven, *Ibid.*, p. 310.

94. G. J. Craven, *Ibid.*, pp. 310-11.

95. G. J. Craven, *Ibid.*, p. 315.

96. G. J. Craven, *Ibid.*, p. 316.

97. G. J. Craven, *Ibid.*, p. 316.

98. G. J. Craven, *Ibid.*, p. 317.

99. See Chapter 20, pages 449-52, of this text.

100. In a paper given as a presidential address, at the annual meeting of the Southwestern Philosophy of Education Society, (Fort Worth, Texas, November 9, 1956), entitled "Toward a New Philosophy of Education," Professor Craven set forth as the crucial difference between Whitehead and Dewey the fact that whereas Dewey's philosophy of creativity adheres to the genetic-functional account of experience, Whitehead's philosophy of creativity includes the morphological aspect as well. Thus Craven holds that Dewey's 'means-end' account of experience is inadequate because it neglects the morphological aspect which is found in Whitehead.

101. The reader is warned that those five stages of concrescence are not to be interpreted mechanically but organically.

15

CREATIVITY and the ORGANIC PHILOSOPHY of EDUCATION

T H E foregoing chapter presented 'creativity' largely in terms of Whitehead's philosophy of organism. Some interpretations and applications in terms of education were offered by Professor Craven and this writer. The problem of the meaning and significance of 'creativity' within the tenets of this particular Organic Philosophy of Education remains to be solved.

The fact that Whitehead was for the most part speaking and writing about 'creativity' on the highest level of metaphysical generality, and not delineating specific applications on the level of human beings in terms of their education, leaves considerable latitude for the re-interpretation of 'creativity' in terms of its educational meanings. Although he did write essays on education, he apparently did not make direct application of his conceptions of creativity, concrescence, and the like to the educational process. In fact historically his major philosophical writings, such as *Process and Reality* and others, came quite late in his life, whereas his educational essays were written much earlier.[1]

It is the contention here that one needs a philosophy of education in his interpretation or re-interpretation of Whitehead's philosophy of organism in general and his theory of the creative process in particular. That is to say that one does not simply transform Whitehead's general philosophy deductively into an educational philosophy. Rather it is a two-way process which is both inductive and deductive.

By and large there is an educational philosophy implicit in Whitehead's philosophy of organism. Yet in order to make this philosophy of education explicit, one must bring a knowledge of the unique problems and content of the field of education, realized from one's own study and experience, to the general philosophy in question. In addition he must bring a kind of philosophy of education—that is incomplete in its philosophical dimensions but at the same time possessing educational principles and conceptual structures. These principles represent the thinking and experience of the educational philosopher as he inquires further into the philosophical grounds of these tenets.

Thus a philosophy of education emerges both inductively and deductively, from educational study and experience inductively, and philosophical deduction. The 'philosophy of education' derived from experience requires completion by the conceptual level of philosophical grounding; the 'philosophy of education' implicit in a given general philosophy requires completion and grounding in educational principles born of experience and experimentation.

In moving toward an organic educational philosophy this writer began with his hypothesis of 'the school within a school' and proceeded to set out his own basic propositions and conceptions of the educational process. The development of this viewpoint has required inductive and deductive movements from his own educational and philosophical conceptions to and from the philosophers of organism.

In essence then the process has required a fusion of philosophical conceptions with this writer's own educational conceptions. It is not simply a matter of translating a given philosophy into its equivalent educational theory. This, of course, is in part the case, but only a part. Thus in this critical chapter we are faced with the task of fusing Whitehead's creative process from the metaphysical plane with our previously formulated principles and conceptions of the educational process in terms of this particular philosophy of education. It is in this sense then that amplifications and extensions of Whitehead's philosophy of creative process are necessary in this particular educational context.

It is the conviction of this writer that one of the main tasks of the educational philosopher is to formulate adequate philosophical grounds for an educational philosophy, and then to show how such principles are to be interwoven with basic conceptions of the edu-

325

cational process. This is the purpose of this chapter. The following discussions and expositions endeavor to show the interweavings of 'creative process' with the established principles of the organic educational philosophy.

The underlying questions of this chapter are as follows: What is the relation of Whitehead's 'creative process' to the Organic Philosophy of Education? What amplifications and extensions of 'creativity' occur in the applications to organic educational theory? How does the doctrine of 'self-creativity' embrace the educational development of 'man *qua* man' and as 'unique individual'? How is the education of man related to 'Process and Reality'? How does one reconcile 'pursuit of truth' with 'self-creativity' in terms of the functions of education? How is 'creativity' on the metaphysical level manifest as 'bipolarity' in terms of the educational process? How does 'creativity' reinforce this writer's 'principle of reversibility' in the educational process? How is 'creativity' manifest in 'the organic field of experience'? How is 'creativity' interpreted in terms of organic educational theory? What is the relation of 'creativity' to this writer's account of 'reason and experience'? How is it related to our 'multiple modes of experience and learning' conception? What is the relation of 'creativity' to the problem of 'objectivity and subjectivity'? How is 'the organic theory of control' reinforced by the metaphysics of 'creative process'? How is 'creativity' related to 'the pattern of organic education'? How does the organic theory of creativity differ from some other theories of creativity? Are principles of imitation, emulation, habituation, and the like inimical to 'creative education'? What are some of the other educational interpretations of 'creativity' within this educational philosophy?

Creativity of 'Man qua Man' and as a 'Unique Individual'

In Part IV the interpretations of the functions of man and the consequent functions of education are delineated more fully. However, within this immediate context of 'creativity' and the educational process, certain clarifications are requisite. More specifically we are concerned with the necessary amplifications and extensions of 'creativity' on the level of organic education.

It is quite conceivable that one might interpret Whitehead's accounts of 'self-creativity' solely in terms of the uniqueness of the 'self' or 'actual entity.' There is of course considerable emphasis on the relative freedom of the individual entity, or person, in his 'self-determination.' Some educational philosophers might then deduce that an organic conception of man and the educational process would necessarily be focused on unique individual development.

This writer has contended that the functions of education should embrace (a) the development of *man qua man,* and (b) the development of unique individuality. (See Part IV) Too many educational philosophies have regarded these as exclusive educational functions, whereas they are really mutually supporting. Now it is contended here that Whitehead's metaphysical conception of the creative process is entirely supportive of the foregoing educational conception. That is to say there are ample conceptions of the development of the individual actual entity within the locus of a species in Whitehead's notions of 'nexus,' and 'societies within societies within societies'—in the metaphysical sense. Thus the concrescence of a human being need not be limited to the actual person in his differences alone, but the concrescence is also within the 'nexus' or 'society' of the human species itself. Thus there is a relatively enduring pattern for the human species as a species, as well as the pattern of self-identity of the person in his concrescence. The immediate 'society' of the person as an individual becomes within the larger 'society' of the species which in turn is embraced by other 'whole-part' relations of 'societies.'

'Creativity' then in this particular educational philosophy means that 'self-creativity' of individual man must always be construed within the context of man as a member of the species *Homo sapiens.*

There is the stubborn fact of the 'inheritance' of the relatively sustained pattern of the 'enduring societies' (in the metaphysical sense of 'societies') of the species itself. We must not overlook the inherent structure-function organization of man's long evolved being. The whole of the species of man, as *Homo sapiens,* looked upon collectively, is a product, a superject, of millions upon millions of years of evolution. Thus the 'givenness' to any emerging member of the species in its 'self-creativity' is one of determined, stubborn fact. In a slow way the species itself is subject to evolution and creative advance. Yet we must not deal lightly with the nature of man as a product of this long evolution. He possesses remarkable flexibility and modifiability in his being. Yet, to the extent that *Homo sapiens* has been determined, there are persistent characteristics.

Hence as a matter of emphasis, with far-reaching implications for an educational philosophy, it is to be noted that our interpretation here is a double-sided one; man develops properly *qua* man, as well as in the creation of his own unique personality. The individual person in his concrescence receives a 'givenness' in the primary stage of two kinds. He receives the 'givenness' of the capacities and characteristics of the species 'Homo sapiens'; he also receives the 'givenness' of his own inherited capacities, and individual differences.

The common generic functions of man are described in a later chapter.

'Self-creativity' then is here emphasized within the context of the species, or man as man. The full force of concrescence as described by Whitehead is entirely applicable. It is, of course, very true that we must recognize the uniqueness of individuals and their individual differences in discerning the nature of the educational process. Yet it is to be fully understood that 'self-determination' for individual men is accomplished within the capacities and limitation of the species man. 'Self-determination' then means *that process of becoming this or that kind of a human being.* But in our enthusiasm for 'self-determination' as individuals, we must not overlook 'human development.' It is evident that in terms of our individual capacities, propensities, and aims, we do become particular kinds of human beings. We are more or less saints or sinners, leaders or followers, intellectualists or sensualists, thinkers or doers, autocrats or democrats, or various ratios of these particular things. Yet our becoming as individuals must not neglect the actualization of the potentialities of the species. There are capacities, appetitions, and propensities of man *qua* man, which must be considered deeply in the nurture of the individual in terms of 'self-creativity.'

This problem is also crucial because it involves the question of human values. The whole question of the universality or relativity of human values is involved here. If one moves completely to one extreme, say that of atheistic existentialism, (as distinguished from theistic existentialism) there is implied complete freedom for the individual to create his own values—his own norms or 'oughts.' Atheistic existentialists would seemingly hold that since there are no universal values or 'oughts' in the universe itself, no essences, then man is free to create his own values. Here then is an extreme form of individualism and 'self-creativity.'

On the other extreme it might be held that values are universal and absolute within the universe; that they are not created, but imposed by the creator or God. This carries with it the corollary that man possesses a fixed nature and the norms of his moral life are completely inherent in his being. This leaves little latitude for 'self-creativity,' or total 'creative advance.'[2]

Briefly stated, the position advanced here is in opposition to both of these extremes. We cannot agree that man has complete freedom in his choices or 'self-creativity,' because his concrescence in large part is based upon the 'givenness' of the actual world up to the point of his birth. This given datum includes both man as man and in his individual capacities. Ideal values subsist as possibles for actualization and as lures for man's subjective aims—for his moral choices. Actualized values also exist in things—in persons, institutions, and other entities, as products of past experience. Thus there are immanent actual values as well as the ideal values in the determination of man, both collectively and individually.

Individual man is involved in the philosophical enterprise of determining the status of these 'oughts.' He is called upon to make certain philosophical decisions with respect to the aims and values of life. There is the compulsion of the lure of the ideal objects which serve as a powerful persuasion toward the good life. Yet the very ambivalent character of man's being, with its many bipolarities, is such as to put man at war with himself, as Plato said. This is not alone an individual matter in becoming, although it is that. It is also

329

a collective enterprise—an inquiry into the good life for man as well as men. Hence we are equally concerned with human development as well as individual becoming. We are concerned with what is good for man as well as men.

The Education of Man in Relation to Process and Reality

Essential to the organic educational philosophy is the proposition that the education of man is not limited to 'social process' and that it is in terms of the process and reality of the universe. In this context of creativity it is important to understand the continuous relationship of human organisms as actual entities with all other entities. Whitehead and other organicists have emphasized the continuity of man with the world process and its actualized entities. Man is not to be dichotomized or bifurcated from nature, society, or the universe. Thus man's creativity of his own being in the process of concrescence is to be understood in continuity with and interaction with all other entities of the world—whether they be termed natural, social, or metaphysical. Frankly the organic viewpoint is anti-positivistic.

The phrase 'social process' needs clarification. In the philosophy of organism 'social process' refers to the experiences, feelings, interactions, and adventures of all actual entities of the universe; the phrase 'social process' is therefore not limited to the interactions of human society. Professor Charles Hartshorne, for example, in his recent book, *Reality as Social Process*, emphasizes this very point, that an organic world is one in which the actual entities influence one another in their becoming and being.[3]

Man then evolves in terms of the creative advance of the world. He is a microcosmic product of this 'creative advance' in which he participates. His matrix is metaphysical as well as social and cultural. It is for this reason that we have stressed the metaphysical 'creative factors' and their role in the education of man. Education cannot be properly restricted to 'social process' in merely the sense of human societies and the interaction of actual human entities. 'Social process' of course includes human interactions as well as the wider dimensions of the creative advance of the world.

It is commonplace today to assert that human development must be interpreted in terms of one's culture or his complete social environment both in and out of school. Or the statement is made that 'education must be culture-centered.' Surely this is a partial truth which must be recognized; education is a social process in a given culture or inter-culturally. But this viewpoint does not go far enough; it neglects the metaphysical dimension of 'social process.' The concrescence of the human organism involves its interactions with all realities and ideal possibilities of the universe. Man is formed too in his interaction with God as an actual entity and with the creative factors as exemplified in other actual entities, as well as with the more obvious human interactions of man's 'societies.'

It is this metaphysical aspect of the philosophy of organism with its conception of God as an actual entity which lifts it beyond the recent educational philosophies which are grounded and limited by non-metaphysical commitments to education and human society. God is essential to the organic conception of process, and to concrescence as depicted here in the educational process. Entities are self-formed in their process of concrescence by their subjective aims. These subjective aims in turn represent the feelings and strivings of the organism toward ideal values, which in turn are motivated by God's lure of the true, good, and beautiful, or by the ideal aspects of God's primordial nature. As Whitehead says, God is interweaving the eternal forms of his primordial nature upon the temporal extensions of his consequent nature. It is in this sense that we understand his saying that God needs the world and the world needs God; actual entities in their appetitions for self-realization strive through their becoming and subjective aims toward the ideal forms, while in turn these entities of the world provide the ground for the actualization of God's primordial conceptuality. God is not absolute in the sense of being completely independent of the world; he is partly independent in the sense of his primordial envisagement of the eternal forms, but he is dependent in part upon the actual world for realization of these ideal forms, and he is interdependent with the world in the sense of the shared interactions and prehensions in the creative advance— in the realization of the universe.

It should be noted in this context that the organic educational philosophy is not 'nature-centered,' 'man-centered,' or 'God-centered' in the older senses and implications of those terms. Again in the philosophy of organism there is the endeavor to achieve a higher synthesis. In other words there is no deification of nature as such; there is no deification of an absolute God in the sense that he is completely independent of the events of the world; nor is there a deification of human society to the exclusion of metaphysical and religious considerations.

Rather organic educational philosophy is centered in the creative processes of the world, more particularly in terms of man's own concrescence as part of the 'creative advance' of the universe. We are deeply concerned about the concrescence of man, not merely in the context of human societies, which of course are most important, but in the context of process and reality of the universe. We reject theories of education which are 'child-centered,' 'community-centered,' 'culturally-centered,' 'idea-centered,' and even 'God-centered,' as one-sided in their emphasis or limited in their conception. All of these, of course, have partial validities.

The Organic Philosophy of Education then is concerned with man and reality, particularly the concrescence of man in the context of world process. We are deeply concerned with the creative factors of the universe as they are exemplified in the becoming of entities, particularly in the concrescence of man. (See Propositions in Chapters 3-6 for further clarification.) This concern is expressed further in relation to the individual 'self' of man as realized in his concrescence. This self-realization in turn involves man in the most far-reaching problems of human existence.

Truth and 'Self-Creativity'

This writer has contended that the educational process should be directed toward the pursuit of truth as well as toward the modification of human behavior. Although it might appear to the reader that Whitehead's theory of 'self-creativity' would preclude the quest for truth *per se*, and a resulting emphasis on a pragmatic educational process, this interpretation does not necessarily follow. Such a narrow interpretation of Whitehead may result from seizing upon only one part of his philosophy.

It will be recalled from the previous chapter that according to Professor Craven's interpretation of Whitehead "the full truth of a proposition cannot be judged until it has been received and acted upon."[4] It was stated further that "Thus the expression of the unified self in its 'objective immortality' becomes *the* truth, the meaning, of that proposition as felt and thereby defines the tentative nature of knowledge—incidentally, it also reveals knowledge as a means and not a true end in itself."[5]

Now if these statements were taken in their isolation, or only in the context of the genetic-functional exposition of the process of concrescence, then it would appear that Whitehead's ontology and epistemology fall completely within the pragmatic meanings of knowledge and experience. Although there are pragmatic elements in Whitehead's philosophy of organism, he is not a pragmatist *per se* in general philosophy or educational consequences. When the whole of Whitehead's philosophy is considered, including the morphological and ontological elements, it is clear that he is not limited to pragmatism. Professor Craven concurs in this judgment.

The reader will recall the discussion in Chapter 10, "Reason and Experience," where it was pointed out that Whitehead apparently agreed with the two functions of reason set forth by the Greeks, the 'contemplative' quest for truth in terms of 'the Reason of Plato,' and the 'practical' function of intelligence in terms of 'the Reason of Ulysses.'[6] Whitehead did not believe in inert knowledge, it is true. But it seems evident that his frequent reiteration of man's pursuit of the true, good, and beautiful, would not lend itself to a narrow, utilitarian and behavioristic conception of 'self-creativity' within the educational context.

It will be remembered also that in Chapter 10, our agreement with Charles S. Peirce was indicated, to-wit: that the educational process embraces a two-fold function (a) to further man's pursuit of truth and understanding, and (b) to nurture man's personal behavioral development. Dr. George Maccia's research on this topic revealed that whereas John Dewey's educational philosophy focused solely on education as the nurture of intelligent behavior, Peirce's educational philosophy stressed this two-fold pursuit of truth and intelligent behavior.[7] In this connection it should be noted also that there is another striking similarity between the recognition of the relative separability of theory and practice in this organic educational philosophy and in Charles Peirce.[8] These diverse pursuits are included here as parts of 'self-creativity.'

It has been the contention here that pursuit of knowledge and understanding, or what Peirce termed 'ratiocination,' can be an objective quite apart from the immediacy of personalization, or 'self-creativity.'[9] This is consonant with our theory of the bipolarity of educational experiences and the relative separability of 'immediate, ordinary experience,' and 'rational, systematic experience.' With Peirce we believe in the relative separability of 'theory' and 'practice' in the educational process. This distinction is also entirely consonant with our earlier differentiation of 'contemplative inquiries' in terms of 'the reason of Plato,' and the more immediately 'purposeful activities' on the level of pragmatic or practical intelligence, or 'the reason of Ulysses.' As Peirce suggested, objective inquiry is destroyed if it is carried on in the immediacy of subjective purposes.

These conceptual experiences and resulting understandings from man's pursuit of truth as truth are a part of what this writer has termed 'objectification' in our educational meaning of that term. (Not to be confused with Whitehead's 'objectification' in concrescence.) This pursuit of truth and understanding results from the lure of the true, good, and beautiful, and, as Aristotle suggested, man's sense of 'wonder' about the world. This is man's philosophic impulse. There is an intrinsic quality about this pursuit of truth and understanding, quite apart from the pragmatic function of instrumental inquiry for behavioristic purposes.

Education should nurture this precious drive for the achievement of intrinsic value. This achievement of truth or 'objective understanding,' quite apart from the immediate psychological concerns of the individual in his 'self-creativity,' does make itself available for the process of 'personalization' or what this writer has termed 'subjectification.' Through the process of interweaving experiences of 'objectification' and 'subjectification,' through the organic principle of reversibility, the totality of the learning process is achieved.

This amplification of Whitehead's theory of concrescence as applied to educational theory is in essence this: *there is a recognition here of the relative separability of theory and practice in the educational process; there is likewise a recognition of the relative separability of the pursuit of truth and understanding per se, and deliberate behavioral modification.* Although the metaphysics of individual concrescence is such that there is a uniqueness to the development of the individual entity, whatever it may be, the educational interpretation of human development must take other complex factors into consideration.

It is important in human development to make allowance for 'disinterested curiosity' too. There is admittedly one sense in which the educational process should follow 'immediate interests' in personal development in the pragmatic sense. There is quite another sense in which educational inquiry should follow what the Greeks termed 'disinterested curiosity.'

This 'disinterested curiosity,' of course, is an interest in scientific and philosophical inquiry, not for immediate personal or practical application, but it is for man's indomitable quest for truth and understanding. The Greeks demonstrated that constant preoccupation with practical or immediate results yields less progress in the long run; the contributions of the Athenian Greeks in terms of philosophy, science, and art prove this. This viewpoint is, of course, essentially that of Plato and Aristotle. Hence, it has been the attempt here to show through the principle of reversibility that there must be an interweaving of objective, 'disinterested curiosity' in one sphere of learning, and the subjective, personal curiosity in the sphere of immediate experience.

It is feared here that a constant emphasis upon 'self-creativity,' without inclusion with objective learning and inquiry, would result in 'self-centered' personalities. It is the opinion of this writer that we seldom go directly to our goals in life. An Albert Einstein, for example, as one of the world's greatest scientists, was no doubt largely motivated by the spirit of scientific inquiry in the nonpersonal sense. Often in life the personal implications of arduous experiences are realized only in retrospect. It is the same with the

335

studies in school. Their far-reaching implications are not always within the grasp of the immature student at the time. Thus we advance these qualifications in the interpretation and application of 'creativity' to the organic educational philosophy.

'Self-creation' is interpreted here as personal development within the common structure-function constitution of *Homo sapiens*. As highly developed organisms with cognitive intelligence in addition to the basic capacities for aesthetic feeling and prehension, humans desire to know and understand in a way that transcends problems of immediate and practical behavior. It is for this reason that the spirit of inquiry found in science, philosophy, and other realms, is included in 'self-creativity.' Thus we include rational inquiry in the sense of the 'contemplative function' of man's intelligence. Constant concern with the 'self' as a unique individual can have bad effects on the personality. It is also true that the increase of one's understanding through objective inquiry is not without later practical value; in due time the 'subjectification' or 'personalization' of such objective inquiry and its resulting plane of understanding can and should be realized in concrescence.

It is in this sense that this organic viewpoint deviates from Dewey's notion that all inquiry and learning must be in terms of the means-ends context of pragmatic or instrumental inquiry. It is also at this point that Peirce deviated from Dewey according to Maccia's findings.[10]

Creativity and Bipolarity in Organic Educational Philosophy

Whitehead's 'creativity' is amplified as 'bipolarity' in terms of the Organic Philosophy of Education. It appears that what this writer has termed 'bipolarity' both metaphysically and on the educational level approximates Whitehead's 'creativity.' The 'bipolarities of the world' and the 'bipolarities of the educational process' which were set forth by this writer in Chapter 8 can now be understood as amplifications or extensions of Whitehead's 'creative process.'[11]

It has already been indicated that any actual entity is a microcosm in its exemplifications of the metaphysical principles of the universe as macrocosm.[12] The human being in his concrescence is an actual entity, or a microcosm exemplifying the great ideal opposites or bipolarities of the world. The human learner in his concrescence unifies the many in the one. The great ideal opposites of permanence and novelty, being and becoming, eternal and temporal, one and many, and sameness and otherness are manifest in the human microcosm. As indicated in the statement of foundational propositions, the educational process is necessarily one of the interweaving of these elements; it is one which necessarily endeavors to achieve a harmonization of these ideals in the actual person.

The bipolarities of the educational process are also involved in the process of concrescence of the learner.[13] The learner as a developing person exemplifies the bipolarities of objective-subjective experiences, logical-psychological experiences, structural-functional intelligibilities, and intellectualistic as well as aesthetic experiences. Creativity of the human being requires the interweaving of these co-ordinates and their many corollaries in the educational process.

Many other bipolarities might well be mentioned here in relation to creativity of the person. At least two should be noted. The human being like all other actual entities is constituted by the bipolarity of physical and mental poles. Since the human being is a high-grade organism it is capable of complex mental and intellectual prehensions and comprehensions. Still the physical aspect of man is of indispensable importance in feelings, intuitions, and emotions. Creative education must of necessity be constituted by the interactions of physical prehensions and conceptual reactions.

In a sense nature-nurture constitutes a fundamental bipolarity of process and reality. Man is a product of his personal inheritance and his concrescence into novelty, or nature and nurture. In a most profound sense human development involves the creative process in terms of this fundamental bipolarity of nature-nurture.

Again we must avoid one-sidedness. Educational creativity must not be predominantly centered in those aspects of education termed subjective, psychological, functional, personal, and practical. Neither should creativity be centered on those aspects of education termed objective, logical, structural, impersonal, and non-practical. By observing the basic bipolarities which have been advanced here, creative education in terms of human development can be kept in proper balance.

Creativity and the Principle of Reversibility

There is no basic conflict in Whitehead's creativity and the principle of reversibility formulated in this educational philosophy. It is a distinction between creativity on the metaphysical plane of interpretation and the principle of reversibility on the plane of human education.

The principle of reversibility was advanced originally here without reference to Whitehead's philosophy of organism. This writer advanced his own notion of reversibility as it emerged from the bipolar conception of the organic field of experience with its coordinate spheres. It seemed perfectly logical and necessary from the propositions laid down as a basis of this educational philosophy that the teaching-learning process should follow a principle of reversibility between the two spheres. Actually it represents an amplification of Plato's cave analogy in terms of the educational process.

Now Whitehead's conceptions and terminology pertaining to concrescence on the metaphysical level of all actual entities are essential to the organic educational philosophy. By and large they are applicable at the practical level of the educational process. However, additional conceptions and terminology are needed at the level of educational theory and practice in dealing adequately with the development of human beings. Some of these conceptions advanced here are: reversibility, objectification-subjectification, impersonalization-personalization, generalization-individualization, as expressions of bipolarity.

Since these conceptions have been explained elsewhere at some length, it will be unnecessary to repeat them here except as they exemplify education as a creative process.

To the extent that Whitehead's views of creativity are applicable to this educational formulation, it is clear that education is essentially creative in character. The learner is an experiencing agent; he is a high-grade organism, whose becoming may be conscious or unconscious. As any other actual entity, he enjoys the processes of

338

creativity without consciousness—but with feeling, as a high-grade organism within a deliberate process of education, his becoming should become more and more conscious.

The learner is at once both subject and superject; he is both the agent of becoming and its resultant product. As a high-grade organism his subjective aims may become conscious and deliberate, rather than dim intuitions. The ingression of ideal forms or values may well be encouraged and deliberately effected within this creative process by the learner himself and by others—presumably those concerned with his education. In fact, teachers, parents, schools, and all types of institutions are pertinent aspects of the environment with which the learner interacts, and which he accordingly prehends. It is apparent that Whitehead's large scale generalizations do lend themselves to a conception of creative education in the broader sense of that term.

How are these philosophical conceptions of creativity to be reconciled with the more specific notions advanced in this educational philosophy? More specifically, how is creativity related to reversibility and its related concepts?

The becoming and the being of any individual human organism involve the relations of that organism with all reality. As a subject it experiences other entities; as an object it influences the becoming of other entities. It is not a solipsistic situation; it is the emergence of self and the world; it involves not merely the experience of experience, but it involves the experience of actual entities, forces, and ideal entities.

In terms of the special terminology advanced here in respect to the bipolar educational processes, reversibility is essential to teaching-learning. Reversibility is expressed in terms of our notions of objectification-subjectification, impersonalization-personalization, and generalization-individualization. The becoming of the person as learner requires the two-way process of reversibility in his learning experiences.

Conversion of individualistic, fragmentary experiences into common or public understandings requires our 'objectification,' or the process of impersonal inquiry and generalization. When we reverse these processes these general understandings in the objective sense are converted into unique personal meanings for the individual as such. Thus they are then personalized or individualized. Both contribute to the total concrescence of the person. The reversibility or interweaving of the components results in the development of the total person in his capacities as man and in his unique individuality.

'Objectification' in terms of the organic educational process stresses the development of public understandings, appreciations, common skills, and values which are necessary to man as man. They are elements of a public philosophy which makes harmonious social living possible. They represent the things which we are able to feel and know in common as humans in a comparable stage of development. In educational terms they represent the minimum essentials of human development. They represent the answers to such questions as these: What minimal essentials of a public philosophy should be learned by humans in common? What knowledge should be held in common? What values should be held in common? In short, what are the essential elements of general education for man *qua* man?

'Subjectification' in terms of the organic educational process stresses the development of personal aims, values, interests, beliefs, and understandings. It represents the other side of the coin educationally. Men have individual capacities and differences within their common generic structures and functions. Creative education must do justice to man in his unique individuality as well as his common nature. In this aspect of the educational enterprise the process is reversed so that there is personalization. In effect, the learner then asks such questions as these: What does this knowledge mean to me? How do these understandings enter into my philosophy of life? How do they relate to my beliefs, values, purposes, and ambitions? How do they help me in answering the question of what I am going to be? In answering such questions the learner as unique self is building a personal philosophy of life. It is a very private philosophy of life which perhaps embraces his religious convictions, political beliefs, and personal morals and ethics.

Creative education must of necessity respect these two aspects of human development. An educational philosophy which stresses the role of individualistic self-creativity to the exclusion of the general education of man *qua* man becomes one-sided. A philosophy of education which sees only the common functions of man in terms of general education is one-sided. This is the enigma of educational theory. It has been this writer's constant effort throughout this writing to show what educational principles are necessary to the resolution of this problem. Hence in our application and interpretation of Whitehead's theory of the creative process we must not lose sight of our organic educational principles to-wit: bipolarity, reversibility, and interweaving in the organic field of experience. 'Self-creativity' in the organic educational philosophy then embraces general and special education.

Creativity and the Organic Field of Experience

The previous explanations of creativity and reversibility have in large part answered the question of this relationship between creativity and the organic field of experience. Some additional relationships of a revealing character can be observed at this point. The organic field of teaching-learning experiences provides the frame of reference for guiding creativity in school situations.

If the reader will keep Figure 6 well in mind, some interesting overlappings of various patterns of the educational process as set forth organically can be grasped quite graphically.[14] We can obtain a kind of unity from the diverse patterns which have been presented here.

The organic field of expèrience is marked by 'organic bipolarity' of two spheres of educational experience; one emphasizes 'ordinary experience,' or 'empirical experience,' or 'functional intelligibility.' The other emphasizes 'formal experience,' 'rational experience,' or 'structural intelligibility,' it will be recalled. The teacher interweaves or interlocks these two spheres of learning experiences through the principle of reversibility so that a synthesis or unification of these diverse experiences is achieved in the development of the learner. Thus there are really three phases of the organic field of teaching-learning experiences: (i) empirical, functional experiences; (ii) rational, structural experience; and (iii) synthesis of the experiences of these two spheres, or the inter-relating of the two spheres.

In one perspective there is an analogy which can be made between Whitehead's three stages of concrescence and these three phases of the organic field of teaching-learning experiences. This analogy again can be portrayed in terms of the parable of the cave.

The experience 'in the cave' is that of immediate, empirical experience in that sphere. This is analogous to Whitehead's 'primary stage' of concrescence. The prehensions of the physical pole are predominant initially. There is the 'physical inheritance' and the 'givenness' of the situation. There is a welter of experienced data which is vague, indeterminate, in its feeling. There is a feeling of 'causal efficacy' or an intuition of the external world as datum. There is a 'blindness' which obtains from these fragmentary experiences. Educationally there is lack of meaning, understanding, order, and purpose.

The experiences 'out of the cave' in the sphere of form, order, and structural intelligibility are a contrast to the other sphere. The prehensions here are predominantly of the 'mental pole'; they provide the 'conceptual reactions.' These prehensions and comprehensions provide an increased sense of order, meaning, purpose, and direction. This is what Whitehead terms 'conceptual analysis.' The 'blindness' of former experiences as indeterminate gives way to 'insight,' 'order,' and the understanding of former perceptions in the light of conceptual understandings. This is our sphere of 'rational experience.'

What this writer has termed the third phase of the organic field of teaching-learning experience, that of synthesis and integration of the other two spheres, is analogous to Whitehead's third phase of concrescence. Here is the unification of diverse experiences in the development of the learner. Empirical and rational experiences, functional and structural intelligibilities, and physical and mental prehensions are unified in the learner. The experiences have become determinate.

Another educational pattern from Whitehead fits this exposition. The rhythmic cycle of learning with its three phases, which were cited earlier, includes, (i) 'the exploratory or romantic stage,' (ii) 'the stage of precision or analysis,' and (iii) 'the stage of generalization or synthesis.' The exploratory stage fits by and large with the initial experiences of the empirical sphere; the precision or analysis stage conforms to our delineation of the formal sphere or rational experience; and the stage of generalization and synthesis corresponds to our synthesis of the experiences of the two spheres.

Creativity and Educational Theory

One of the most significant implications of this metaphysical conception of the creative process for educational theory is this: *it is a process which goes on in all actual entities, including human beings, despite our consciousness or unconsciousness of it.* As living organisms we have continuous experiences in terms of concrescence and transition, as subjects and objects, whether we give it deliberate attention or not. As living creatures we are constantly experiencing, feeling, prehending, and becoming as subjects, as well as exerting diverse influences as objects. The creativity of the person goes on despite anything we may do about it. This creativity is determined in large part by the type of experiences which the organism has.

The educational parallel is this: *the student or learner is undergoing the creative process whatever the educational situation may be.* The most formal and academic conditions imaginable may provide the matrix of the creative process for the becoming of some students. This is 'creative education' too. The most progressive and non-formal type of educational situation may also provide the matrix for creative education. *All kinds of education are creative to the extent that they influence the becoming of the student as a person.*

This observation brings us full circle to the question: What kind of education do we want? What kinds of experiences are appropriate to learning in the school situation? It is with this observation in mind that this writer suggested that one must have 'a kind of educational philosophy' in mind in order to reinterpret 'creativity' on the level of the educational process.

The answers to these questions for the Organic Philosophy of Education are given in Part IV, which presents our views of the functions of man and the functions of education.

343

This understanding of 'creativity' at its metaphysical level and its implications for the educational process is crucial. Thus the first implication has just been given, namely, *that the 'creative process' is broadly synonymous with life itself. The second implication is that creativity must also enter into the educational process in the deliberate or conscious sense through teacher and student.* Again this involves the creation of man as well as men. It is a broad interpretation of creativity as opposed to a narrow literal sense of 'creativity.'

This type of creativity then does not require the constant thought of making things in the educational process or even of being particularly 'inventive' at all times. A student, for example, is 'creative' when he studies a mathematics course, quite objectively, and feels that these understandings are a necessary part of his total development. Likewise a student can profit by the systematic writings and lectures of teachers and others in the 'creative' sense as long as he grasps the meaning and significance of the subject matter as a whole to his own development as a human being and as an individual. Modern education in practice has suffered much from this very misconception of 'creativity' as the notion that students must forsake organized, systematic, and vicarious learnings for an educational procedure based upon their own 'creations' and their own original productions.

'Creativity' and Its Different Meanings

In this immediate context the equivocal meanings of 'creativity' should be noted. Much of our trouble in education seems to arise over our failure to say precisely what we mean by 'creativity.' Perhaps a very brief review of some of these meanings would clarify our own stand.

The simplest and most popular meaning of 'creativity' is the dictionary definition: the act or power of bringing something into being; causing something to exist. This notion of creativity is so simple and so ambiguous as to apply to almost any use of the term.

'Creativity' is used also in the context of 'artistic production.' Thus 'creative education' in this sense becomes one of making and producing things in terms of the fine arts. This notion certainly has some validity but it is also patently limited in its scope as a basis for the educational process.

'Aesthetic creativity' has been expressed too in the idealistic philosophies of Friedrich Schiller and Froebel, both philosophically and educationally. According to Schiller man's development was accomplished by the artistic fusion of the realm of forms with the sensuous data of the world of matter in the quest for beauty. According to Schiller,

> The completion of man is the aesthetic reconciliation of the two natures which dwell within him; culture is to make the life of the individual a *work of art,* by ennobling what is given through the senses to full accord with the ethical vocation.[15]

Schiller's philosophy of creativity is one of the most formidable conceptions of this process. Art should not be limited to fine arts; rather it is the quest for beauty throughout life. Thus the person who deeply seeks to incorporate the forms of beauty in his personal existence is exemplifying aesthetic creativity. The quest for beauty carries with it the realization of the true and the good, too. A mechanical production of a painting or a musical composition will not of itself make a person good. However, true devotion to the quest for beauty, and its exemplification concretely in life, with the accompanying fervor of deep feeling for this beauty will increase goodness; these are the components of the quest for the good life. It is perhaps this view which some have when speaking of 'aesthetic creativity.'

Closely allied to this conception is that of Froebel's theory of 'education as unfolding.' Froebel was undoubtedly deeply influenced by Schiller. It is likely that many educators use the term 'creative education' in the light of the Froebelian doctrine of organic unfoldment. It should be noted that there are differences between this Froebelian theory of 'creativity' and that of the present organic educational philosophy.[16]

In another context 'creativity' is used by some to indicate a 'functional creativity' by which they mean the productivity of things in terms of instrumentality, utility, or practicality. This is the 'creativity' which is so often emphasized by pragmatists, experimentalists, in-

345

strumentalists, and functionalists in terms of 'socialized education.' This type of 'creative education' places emphasis upon the problem-solving procedure particularly in the realm of ordinary experience and personalized life problems. Again, although there is validity in this conception, it is limited in scope as the basis for an adequate philosophy of education.

'Creativity' is also frequently used as a synonym of 'inventiveness.' Inventive creativity apparently refers to the genuinely original and novel discoveries and creations of persons as contributions to society. The productions of our great scientists, inventors, composers, and artists might be cited as examples of this notion of 'creativity.' This notion of 'creativity' is also too narrow to form the basis of an educational philosophy.

There is a kind of 'creativity' which is identified with personal discovery or insight in terms of learning by the immature student, as contrasted with the former 'inventiveness' of genuine public discovery. The youngster, who 'discovers' that two and two are four for himself, experiences a kind of 'creativity.' This type of 'creativity' is exemplified both in the Dewey problem-solving type of learning characterized by emphasis upon purposeful inquiry and self-discovery, and in the Platonic dialectical method in education, or the 'Socratic method."[17] Again this notion of 'creativity' has considerable validity within the educational process. However, it does not have the depth and breadth philosophically to provide the groundwork of an educational philosophy of 'creativity.'

It is contended here that although these various notions of 'creativity' have some admitted validity in their particular contexts, they are inadequate metaphysically in scope and depth to provide an adequate conception of the creative process for a philosophy of education. It is for this reason that we have found it necessary to reconstruct 'organic creativity' in terms of this educational philosophy.

Creativity and the Multiple Modes of Experience and Learning

It was laid down as one of the educational propositions of this educational philosophy that the multiple modes of experience and learning should be recognized within the educational process.[18] Our discussions of creativity in general and concrescence in particular only serve to emphasize the fundamental importance of this proposition.

Creativity is largely a process of bringing together the many in the one. Concrescence involves the conversion of many indeterminate data into the very being of the one indeterminate form. Hence in the complex of human development there is the concrescence of the many into the one. Therefore, it is contended here that multiple modes of experience are required in the concrescence of the human being.

In non-school situations the becoming of the human being is constituted by all types of experiences, good and bad, pleasant and unpleasant, intellectual and emotional, and conscious and unconscious. In school situations the types of experiences afforded may be more deliberately planned and selected. Yet it is contended here that diverse modes of experience should be utilized, including the empirical, rational, intuitional, skeptical, authoritarian, and pragmatic. In the concrescence of the developing person these many experiences are to be unified.

Creativity in Relation to Objectivity and Subjectivity

There are several points of interest in the relation of the creative process to the problem of objectivity and subjectivity in education. The most important fact is that students are both subjects and objects.

As a subject in process of concrescence the student prehends other actual entities and ideal entities. That is to say he learns from his experiences with other persons and with the books and materials of schooling. As subject he passes through the various stages of concrescence: prehending, feeling, setting up subject aims, and actualizing these aims.

As object the student is the source of experience for other subjects, or persons. As object his being is objectified in its influence on the learning and experiencing of other persons, students, teachers, and parents, for example. In social relations and in classroom participation the student interacts both as subject and object.

Within the process of concrescence he is 'subject-superject.' The student in his development is actually both. As subject he continues his growth and development within units of concrescence; likewise within each unit of concrescence he becomes superject, and in that sense makes himself available as data for the becoming of other persons in their learning. In his process of change he is subject; at his level of maturation as actualized he is superject.

In this interplay between persons as subjects and persons as objects there is a sense in which 'education is a social process.' It has been indicated that in the metaphysical sense the interplay between all entities is 'social' to the extent that they prehend, feel, intuit, and experience one another in their becoming. Now in this ontological sense there is 'social process' in the interactions between persons as subjects and objects.

Another interesting parallel can be drawn between the problems of philosophy and education in this context. There is a sense in which all objects as such are objectively, or externally related. This is in the sense that they exist as realistic objects in their own right. However, there is also a sense in which all actual entities are subjects, and as such are internally related. These are the valid elements of realism and idealism. Now to the extent that persons, or students, are actual objects, in their own stubborn, factual existence, they are externally related. In this sense they are relatively independent in their atomistic being. Carrying the parallel further, the student as experiencing subject is dependent upon other persons, ideas, and entities for the data of his concrescence. As subject he exemplifies the principle of dependence and the principle of internal relations. Thus the Organic Philosophy of Education differs in part from realism, idealism, and pragmatism in its conception of the student or learner.

Creativity and the Organic Theory of Control

The organic theory of control was set forth by this writer largely out of his analysis of conflicting educational theories. It was an extension of the bipolarity conception. Further analysis reveals that this educational theory is really an amplification and extension of Whitehead's 'creative process.'

It will be recalled that the organic theory of control was set forth in terms of 'proportionate bipolarity.'[19] Human development is characterized by its actualization and unification of various bipolarities, namely external and internal factors. Through the progressive stages of maturational development and learning the person, or learner, moves from relatively small degrees of self-control, self-direction, and self-determination to greater degrees of self-control and self-determination.

If the reader will review the organic theory of control (in its graphic form) and at the same time keep in mind the theory of concrescence, he will note a striking correspondence between the philosophical two. It is clear that organic control is an amplification of the creative process on the educational plane. The contexts and terminologies differ somewhat, but the underlying principles are substantially the same.

In the process of concrescence, as in the theory of organic control, there are external and internal factors to be combined. The 'objective world as datum' in Whitehead is comparable to the 'realistic component' of this organic doctrine. The 'real internal constitution' in the philosophy of organism is comparable to the 'subjective factor' in organic control theory; the subject's 'real internal constitution' is the *quiddity* of organic development in terms of actualization of 'external and internal components.'

In the organic theory of control this writer contends that the learner gradually develops from relative degrees of immaturity and dependence to increasing degrees of maturity and relative independence. Creative theory reinforces this conception by saying that in the process of concrescence the learner moves from stages of indeterminacy to determinacy, or from potentiality to actualization.

Concrescence is another way of describing the process whereby external factors are gradually internalized in the developing constitution of the developing organism or person. Extrinsic values gradually become intrinsic values ideally in the educational process. External controls are gradually converted into internal controls. External principles of control gradually give way to internal controls— but not completely. The actual entity at the end of its concrescence, or the final stage, still operates in terms of its relations to other entities. This is the ontological principle.

349

In both conceptions then, in creative process and in the organic theory of control, human development proceeds from a state of relative indeterminacy to determinacy, from objectivity to subjectivity, from 'givenness' externally to an internally achieved unity, from the world as datum to the creation of the self, and from the state of 'vagueness and dimness' with respect to purpose, order, direction, or value, to the definite achievement of these conceptual reactions in terms of self-determination.

Thus although Whitehead's theory of creativity is conceived at the metaphysical level, it is exemplified in the organic theory of control as advanced here on the level of human education and development. The coincidence of these two theories perhaps lies in the common sources of organic thought—namely the Platonic tradition.

Creativity and the Pattern of Organic Education

Creativity is a process of unifying the many as we have reiterated. Yet educationally man in his relation to process and reality is so very complex as to require some definite pattern. Creativity within the context of a given philosophy of education needs the broad lines of some kind of pattern within which to express itself. The creativity need not be stifled by the existence of such a pattern, anymore than the painter need be restricted by the existence of his model.

The pattern of organic education offered here is composed of two sets of categories, which when set in juxtaposition, provide the necessary dimensions and outlines for creative education.

In one sense creative education is to be guided by the categories of Educational Needs, Values, Knowledge, Arts, Functions and Aims, and Institutional Responsibilities. The other dimension is provided in terms of man's ten basic functions, the intellectual, moral, spiritual, social, economic, political, physical, domestic, aesthetic, and re-creational.

Creative education then is to be accomplished by the interweaving of these two sets of categories. Human development needs the wide sweep of these categories in order to be comprehensive enough in its educational experiences. The magnitude and complexity of the educational task is realized when we see that these diverse facets of man's possibilities and capacities are to be unified in the concrescence of each individual.

Figure 13

The Organic Functions of Man and Self-Creativity

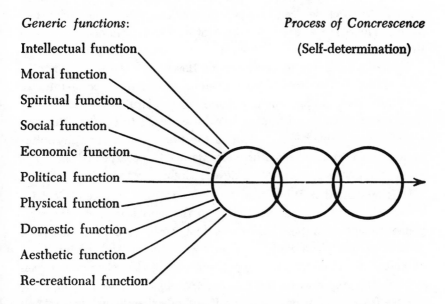

Generic functions:

Intellectual function

Moral function

Spiritual function

Social function

Economic function

Political function

Physical function

Domestic function

Aesthetic function

Re-creational function

Process of Concrescence

(Self-determination)

Explanation: Man has generic structure and functions as man. These given potentialities and capacities are developed under actual bio-social conditions. His functions are related organically and intrinsically. Through the process of concrescence the many functions are unified in the developing individual. This concrescence is largely one of moving from relative indeterminacy to a determinate condition of being. The individual in one sense is *causa sui,* or self-determining. In another perspective, of course, he is conditioned and influenced in his becoming by other factors. In terms of subjective aims it is evident that human purposes, values, beliefs, and ideals are of utmost importance in the educational process. It is also clear that the educational process is one which is basically philosophical in as much as concrescence involves one's self-determination in terms of beliefs and values.

Comparisons and Contrasts of Organic Creativity with Other Theories of Creativity

The organic philosophy of creativity both in Whitehead and in this organic educational philosophy is not to be confused with other historical or contemporary doctrines of creativity. The organic conception of creativity is not to be equated with idealistic, realistic, pragmatic, or existential theories *per se*. It is not to be equated educationally with theories of creativity in terms of the familiar notions of 'unfolding,' 'self-expression,' 'artistic creation,' or the 'socialized personality.' There are, of course, similarities and overlapping conceptions in varying degrees between organic creativity and other doctrines. There are also significant contrasts and differences between them.

The organic theory of concrescence flows from the principles of a philosophy of organism. In its exposition of concrescence or the creative process it is apparent that there are similarities and differences with other theories. There are realistic, idealistic, pragmatic, and even existential elements evident in the process as organically interpreted. Such cross-currents of elements are to be expected in a philosophy which endeavors to achieve a higher synthesis.

It is evident that Whitehead has put idealism on a realistic base in terms of metaphysical creativity. In the emphasis upon the emergence of actual entities from the actual world as datum there is a definite realism. The world of objects as stubborn fact, the intuitions of 'causal efficacy,' the ontological principle of the relations between entities, the emphasis on the existence of objects as well as subjects, the feelings, prehensions, and intuitions of other actual entities—all these aspects of creativity reveal realistic elements in organic creativity.

Yet these realistic elements are incomplete in themselves. There are many idealistic elements in organic creativity. The doctrine of internal relations, the reformed subjective principle, the panpsychic principle, the coherence of entities, the functions of the mental pole, the role of subjective aims, the lure of the pure potentialities or ideals, the intrinsic values, the emphasis on the self, the principle of equilibrium, the role of God, the force of *eros,* the pertinence of the ideal good, and many other conceptions which might be cited, are in large measure idealistic elements of organic creativity. These elements in themselves as idealistic, however, are incomplete from the organic viewpoint.

352

Elements of pragmatism and existentialism are also to be found in organic creativity. Such pragmatic elements as purposive behavior, personal development, process and product, means and ends relations, continuity of mind and body, continuity of man and nature, self-determination, the interactive process, 'interest,' 'the will to form,' problem-solving, the experiential process, and others are explicit parts of the organic conception of creativity.[20]

Such elements as the irrational as well as the rational, authenticity of personal experience, the stubborn facts of existence, the relativistic perspective of the person, a polarity of reason and actual existence, if they may be termed 'existential,' are also to be found in qualified form in the organic theory of creativity.[21]

Perhaps the most crucial difference between organic doctrine and these other theories of creativity is to be found in the bipolarity of the actual entity itself. Remember that the actual entity, or the person on the human level, is constituted in the process of concrescence by interactions of its mental and physical poles in 'the real internal constitution' of that entity. The organic self is not constituted by a 'dualism' of mind and body; it is not constituted either by a spiritual *psyche* or soul *in itself*; it is not constituted by an idealistic subjective ego. Neither is it constituted by physical relations or 'material entities' in a realistic or materialistic sense. Nor is the self constituted in merely a pragmatic experiencing of experience. Nor is the self in any existential sense completely devoid of any 'givenness,' 'oughtness,' or intelligible relatedness to the macrocosm.

The actual entity, or person, develops his being in a process of becoming which involves the integral relations and interactions of its mental and physical poles in bipolar relationship. Physical and mental poles require each other for their functions of constituting the self. These poles are only relatively separable, not absolutely so. It is in this conception of 'the real internal constitution' of the actual organism and its development in concrescence that organism differs from these other theories. Of course other conceptions, such as the subject-object relationship, are requisite to the organic theory of creativity.

So much for comparisons and contrasts philosophically; now let us note some contrasts in terms of educational theories of creativity.

Creative education as advanced here should not be confused with 'education as unfolding.' There are many valid elements of the theory of unfolding, if we had time to analyze them. Such notions as the 'inherent potentialities and capacities of man,' 'inner to outer development,' 'Schiller's aesthetic theory,' 'self-realization,' 'development into conscious relation to the cosmos,' and the like, have much to be said for them. They are indeed valuable ideas. Yet like many of the idealistic metaphysical conceptions, they are in need of reconstruction in terms of a higher synthesis educationally.

The reader should understand that the organic theory of creativity as applied to the educational process does not mean 'self expression' or 'artistic creation.' The popular and familiar notions of schools that practice 'creative education' by a curriculum which features 'self expression' and 'artistic creation' by having the children make things is far from what is intended here. These notions of creativity are misconceptions in as much as they emphasize the aspect of doing and *making things* to the neglect of the deeper and more serious business of 'human development' or the creation of persons.

Neither is the organic conception of creative education in full agreement with pragmatic theories of 'functional creativity' or 'creation of the social person.' Creativity of the person implies the fundamental relationship of man and the universe, or man and reality. Creativity which is restricted to the confines of 'reconstruction of the community,' or 'the development of the socialized person,' is narrower than the conception advanced here. Creativity requires the full development of man as man, as well as man as individual. It requires the exploration of man's relation to God and universe as well as to his immediate society.

To live is to create. Human existence requires becoming. When one ceases to create his being, when he ceases to become, he is no longer alive. Thus all human experiences are creative in one way or another, for good or for bad, for self-development or self-destruction. This is what is meant here by organic creativity.

354

Creativity and Some Supposedly 'Non-Creative'
Terms and Concepts

Persons who think about 'creativity' in some of the more popular senses of the term may be inclined to reject certain traditional terms and concepts in education as 'non-creative.' Time honored terms such as 'habituation,' 'association,' 'imitation,' 'emulation,' are examples of such concepts which are frequently discounted in the context of progressive or modern notions of 'creative education.' Hence they may seem to have no legitimate role in modern, creative education.

It is the thesis here that these terms and conceptions do have a very legitimate and important role in creative education when defined in their original meaning and in organic contexts. All of these terms date back to the Greek education in the long history of education. They were used specifically in the educational philosophies of Plato and Aristotle; their denotations and connotations were considerably different from the ordinary meanings which we usually accord these terms today.

'Association,' for example, today is thought of as a principle of psychology having to do with the mental processes whereby sensations, memories, ideas, and experiences are linked or 'associated.' The term 'habituation' today, by the same token, suggests psychological processes of conditioning, training, or inculcation. As such they seem to imply external controls as opposed to 'self-expression' and 'creative education.'

These terms frequently appear in behavioristic contexts in modern psychologies. However, Plato's uses of 'association' and 'habituation' were quite different from these contexts. His educational psychology, although perhaps behavioristic in some senses, appears in retrospect to have more in common with organismic psychologies in their wholistic emphases.[22] Platonism rejected mechanistic in favor of organic learning theory. According to Rupert Lodge, in his *Plato's Theory of Education*, 'habituation' was not used in a mechanical or behavioristic sense; his education was not merely 'a behavioristic conditioning process'; many of their learning activities in the social sense were 'freely chosen.' Plato realized that children enjoy such community festivities as marching, dancing, and singing. They gladly enter into

355

the spirit of holidays and religious observations.[23] 'Habituation' then should be interpreted in the broad, organic sense, rather than in a narrow, behavioristic sense. Habituation then denotes learning through meaningful activity rather than mere mechanical training.

The term 'association' for Plato apparently meant 'friendly companionship,' in what we would today term 'shared activities.' This notion of 'friendly companionship' carried over to the teacher-student relationship as well, according to Lodge. The student admired the teacher and desired to emulate him. This bond between student and teacher was one which has been commonly referred to as 'Platonic love.'[24]

With recourse to the original meanings of these terms, then, they appear to have an increasing relationship to the creative process as organically interpreted here. Instead of being 'non-creative' terms we find them quite compatible with creativity in the wider sense of the term, when they too are redefined in the original organic context of Plato's thought. In other words the learner in the process of concrescence is lured by his subjective aims and ideals of value as prehended purely or exemplified in a person idolized or loved. Whitehead's theory of concrescence then provides us with a new appreciation of the meaning of Plato's theory of education.

Professor Lodge's observation concerning the teacher and pupil relationship in Plato's educational theory takes on new meaning for us as he says,

> That is to say, behind the arts teacher the pupil glimpses the Muses and their leader Apollo, and behind the pedagogic association there is always a fluttering of the wings which indicates the presence of the spirit of Eros, guiding the pupils to the plain of Truth in that heaven beyond heavens where live the transcendental forms of beauty, goodness, justice, and ideality itself.[25]

In the light of Whitehead's process of concrescence, the pupil is drawn not only by admiration for the exemplification of virtue or excellence in his teacher, but he is drawn toward the pure forms themselves. As Whitehead suggests the *eros* is the drive toward perfection.

Likewise the term 'imitation' has a broad, organic meaning. It need not mean 'external mimicry' as so often connoted. In the Platonic sense, according to Lodge, it implied the appropriation of the ideals or the inner spirit of the teacher or person loved. The ideals of the person who is admired or loved are assimilated and become a part of the concrescence of the learner. In the present organic context it could be said that the learner prehends these feelings, values, and purposes in his close relationships with others whom he respects and admires. They become a part of his actual being through concrescence. This process is evident in our everyday observations of the experiences of the young. They seem to imitate and emulate their various idols and idealized personalities which they know from the world of arts, sciences, fashion, athletics, cinema, or other facets of society. Manners, values, styles, beliefs, and various patterns of behavior are both consciously and unconsciously imitated and assimilated. As Plato would say, *eros* enters into the educational process. We love that which we value and admire; we are drawn almost irresistibly toward the persons and things which we value and idealize. As Professor Lodge puts it, "We project ourselves into our 'otherness' . . . . into personalities which resemble our own and confirm us in developing into our full selves."[26]

This spirit of personality conversion through emulation has been illustrated convincingly throughout the history of religion; the disciples of a given religion apparently make every effort to emulate and walk in the steps of their leader or saviour.

Thus imitation can be a dynamic part of the concrescent process.

> The person who imitates projects his personality into a new merger of selves, and takes on the character of that which he imitates: acquiring from the enhanced principle of self-motion which thus comes to him all the capacities which the new principle is competent to initiate.[27]

Thus it is the inner spirit that is imitated and not the external manifestation; it is not the external Socrates, but it is the internal and essential character of Socrates that is emulated.[28]

The views of William James on *imitation* and *emulation* are pertinent at this point. He too was sensitive to the criticisms of *imitation* made by modern educators, even in 1892, saying,

> Among the recent modern reforms of teaching methods, a certain disparagement of emulation, as a laudable spring of action in the schoolroom, has often made itself heard.[29]

Although James was unusually enthusiastic about the imitativeness of mankind, and went much further than most of us would care to go today, he did state very forcefully the case for imitation in the educational process in these words,

> Each of us is in fact what he is almost exclusively by virtue of his imitativeness. We become conscious of what we ourselves are by imitating others—the consciousness of what the others are precedes—the sense of self grows by the sense of pattern. The entire accumulated wealth of mankind—languages, arts, institutions, and sciences—is passed on from one generation to another by what Baldwin has called social heredity, each generation simply imitating the last.[30]

In retrospect it appears that James overstated his case for imitativeness in saying that one is what he is "almost exclusively by virtue of his imitativeness." The point is that imitativeness is an aspect of concrescence and not the whole of the process. James, however, was not unaware of other elements in human development, such as inventiveness, for he said,

> Invention, using the term most broadly, and imitation, are the two legs, so to call them, on which the human race historically has walked.[31]

Thus the element of imagination and human ingenuity as expressed in the term 'inventiveness' is recognized as a part of the creative process along with 'imitation' in its broader, organic meaning.

James made further observations which have interesting implications for the educational process. He felt that imitation and emulation were closely related, stating,

> Imitation shades imperceptibly into *Emulation*. Emulation is the impulse to imitate what you see another doing, in order not to appear inferior; and it is hard to draw a sharp line between the manifestations of the two impulses, so inextricably do they mix their efforts. Emulation is the very nerve of human society.[32]

Again James has made an important observation, despite the fact that his statement is perhaps overly drawn.

It is significant too that he saw the important implications of the conception for the classroom with this observation:

> In the schoolroom, imitation and emulation play absolutely vital parts. Every teacher knows the advantage of having certain things performed by whole bands of children at a time. The teacher who meets with most success is the teacher whose own ways are the most imitable. A teacher should never try to make the pupils do a thing which she cannot do herself. "Come and let me show you how" is an incomparably better stimulus than "Go and do it as the book directs." Children admire a teacher who has skill. What he does seems easy, and they wish to emulate it.[33]

James is cited here, not because of our fundamental agreement with his psychology, but rather because his remarks on imitation and emulation do present a strong argument for some validity of these terms in an organic context. Imitation is seen to be a phase of concrescence. Imitation is in a sense the prehension of data from other entities; it is a part of the actual entity's receptivity. The important thing to note is that such imitation and receptivity are not really passive, but they involve organic assimilation into the inner constitution and purposes of the developing organism.

Creative education need not exclude such terms and conceptions then as we have reviewed here. Concepts such as imitation, emulation, habituation, and association, when interpreted broadly and organically, are legitimate aspects of the total creative process. The conscious process of determining one's own becoming includes the active prehension of ideals and values as they are personified and exemplified in historical or contemporary figures. In this idealization we need not think only of contemporary society; the world of literature, science, history, humanities, arts, religion, and philosophy provides a rich store of fact and ideas which may well stimulate the imaginations of the young with respect to the ideals and values which they want to emulate and create within their own becoming.

Brief Statements of Some Educational Implications of Creativity

In the interest of brevity as well as coverage of creativity and its educational implications the following observations are offered in outline form:

359

(1) Creativity need not imply that educational procedures will center only in the emerging problems of the individual. There are problems of the field as well as the problems of the individual. Problems of the field are the objective problems of such fields as biology, chemistry, history, physics, sociology, mathematics, or the like. Problems of the individual are subjective and involve the content of learning in relation to the learner's own means and ends. In educational objectification and subjectification both types of problems are legitimate.

(2) Creativity need not reject formal procedures for the informal and functional. Direct instructional procedures are needed to complement the direct experiences which students have in the total learning process. It has been suggested elsewhere the multiple modes of experience are required in the educational process; the same is true of the various educational methods.

(3) Creativity in the educational process is a shared enterprise. Teachers, parents, students, and all others involved in the business of education are jointly creative. Certainly the teacher exemplifies a kind of creativity in working with students as subjects. Of course the teacher is in a process of becoming too, and is rightfully stimulated to further growth through interactions with students and colleagues. The teacher does not create her students as the artist creates his painting, but the teacher does have a very influential role in the becoming of her students and in their 'self-determination.' With increasing maturity students are more and more consciously creating their own being.

Parents and others share the means and ends of their young people and in their various ways are creative. The method is that of persuasion rather than absolute authority, although there are degrees of authority too which must be exerted.

(4) Creativity does not mean that the educational process is to be interpreted completely in terms of direct experience. Students must of necessity learn vicariously through the experience of others, of the cultural heritage, as well as through direct and personal experience. In other words schooling as well as 'life experiences' is important in the education of the young. A large proportion of formal educa-

tion must be constituted by systematic and vicarious learning. Such systematic study is not incompatible with the broad conception of creative education advanced here.

(5) Creativity is also related to the important role of transfer of learning in the educational process. Transfer involves the perception of relationships of ideas and understandings. Emphasis upon creative intelligence in the educative process calls for an alertness on the part of the teacher and the student to see the many relationships as they occur in the process of concrescence. The process of interweaving the various components of the complex educational process requires the perception of such relationships. The movement from the primary stage of 'causal efficacy,' to the second stage of 'conceptual reaction,' to the final stage and 'symbolic reference,' particularly requires the transfer of learning.

(6) *Creativity and the Role of the Teacher*

In concluding this discussion the role of the teacher with respect to instruction and creativity should be noted briefly. In other places this writer has written of the dual role of the teacher. She has to assist the student both in his receptiveness of the objectivity of content and in the subjective aspects of interpretation and assimilation. The teacher must strive to employ the right proportion of direct teaching and nurture of receptivity and creativity.

The rule of thumb which is employed is that the teacher gives the instruction which is necessary, but strives to nurture and encourage the maximum amount of creative learning. Within the total process the teacher gives the amount of instruction and direct guidance that the situation demands, varying with individuals and classes. By and large we would agree that real learning in the best sense comes about when the individual learner is not told the answers to a problem, but when he arrives at the solution through his own efforts and insights. The gap between the problem and the solution is a closure made by the student. This is in the spirit of the Socratic Method, of Plato, and of Dewey.[34] The teacher in this sense is the midwife assisting the learner in the birth of an idea (insightful learning). In a sense this is creative learning for the learner gains insights through his own efforts as well as those of the teacher.

361

The point is that there is instruction (in various modes of experience) within the total educational process. The ratio of instruction, direct guidance, direct teaching by the teacher and the amount of learning termed self-experience, discovery, and genuine creativity vary with conditions and situations. Factors such as maturation, intelligence, background, motivation, relative difficulty of subject matter, and the like, enter into these ratios. The educational process, then, is not an either-or choice between these complementary factors; again it involves an interweaving of bipolar co-ordinates.

The art of teaching is characterized by creativity; it involves the teacher as a professional artist as well as the other sense of the learner as an educational agent creating his own being. The teacher in terms of his knowledge, philosophy, values, purposes, and skills is consciously creating in his professional capacity. His influences and teachings are potent in the determinations of the learner. Yet, it cannot be said that the learner is the total product of the teacher's own values, skills, and purposes. The learner is not an inert object of clay to be formed in that way; since the learner is a human organism the creative artistry of the teacher must be enjoined with the growing and developing creative powers of the learner in his increasing degrees of self-determination.

At this point our organic viewpoint is in approximate agreement with the educational theory of John Dewey. His contention that the means and ends of the educational process must be shared by teacher and students is very well taken indeed. Dewey has in a very real sense been the apostle of democratic sharing in the educational process. Our similarities are perhaps obvious; the dissimilarities are perhaps less obvious.

In brief the most significant dissimilarity is revealed in the organic theory of control and its concomitants.[35] The organic emphasis upon the proportionate relations of such bipolarities as immaturity-maturity, external-internal controls, authority-freedom, instruction-discovery, will be recalled. Whereas, Dewey's emphasis was on the side of maturity, internal and instrumental controls, freedom and self-discovery, our own emphasis has been on the necessary co-ordination of the opposites. Thus the organic view stresses the need for external and authoritative controls in proportion or balance with developing powers. Thus the creativity on the part of the teacher as a professional artist is perhaps as great or greater in the Organic Philosophy of Education than in the pragmatic.

Conclusion. We have noted that in Whitehead's philosophy of organism creativity is the ultimate of ultimates in his explanation of the process and reality of the world. Creativity embraces the processes whereby the creative factors of reality form entities through the appropriation of the many into the one, or a process of prehension and concrescence. In the light of the propositions advanced in this discussion of creativity in the Organic Philosophy of Education, it is evident that creativity is an ultimate principle of the educational process. The educational process is largely characterized by the deliberate harmonization and interweaving of diverse elements in the development of the human being. Creativity then is the organic principle which embraces the wholeness and the partness of these diverse harmonizations, interweavings of co-ordinates, and complementaries. Creativity in this sense is deliberate and intelligent fusion and integration of the diverse elements of the educational process in all of its many complexities.

Summary. Whitehead's delineation of the creative process is on the metaphysical and ontological level. A philosophy of education is not derived by simple deductive interpretation of such a given philosophy. It is constructed both deductively and inductively. Thus in moving toward the organic educational philosophy it has been necessary to fuse the organic theories of creativity with the principles of organic education. This fusion has demonstrated the proposition that a philosophy of education needs the rational elements of a general philosophy for its completion, and a general philosophical system needs amplification and extension grounded in a systematic educational theory to illustrate its adequacy and applicability.

Creativity in this organic educational philosophy embraces the development of *man qua man* as well as *unique individual*. Man possesses a relatively enduring nature which has developed objectively through evolutionary processes of concrescence. Thus the 'givenness' of individual man must be recognized both in the sense of *Homo sapiens,* and as individual inheritance. Common functions as well as individual differences and propensities have their respective roles in organic education.

Education is in a limited sense a 'social process'—that is within human society. In the philosophy of organism the creative advance of the world is 'social process' in the metaphysical or ontological sense. All actual entities are both objects and subjects, and as subjects 'experience' one another in becoming. Thus human development must embrace man as an actual entity who experiences all other actual entities and ideal entities. This interaction includes God and the creative factors in a dimension which transcends the ordinary limitations of education confined to human societies and their interactions.

In contrast to philosophies of education centered in nature, man, God, the child, community, culture, or ideas, this organic educational philosophy focuses upon the development of man in relation to process and reality.

Objective and subjective aims of education are both embraced within this theory of creative education. Human development organically envisioned includes the pursuit of truth in the intrinsic sense as well as the purposeful pursuit of subjective aims in terms of personal creativity. Objective inquiry requires a kind of 'disinterested curiosity' within the learning process. This objective type of inquiry should not exclude those phases of the educational process which require subjective interest, or purposeful self-development. These two types of 'interest' are complementary in the educational process.

The Organic Philosophy of Education has been worked out largely in terms of the bipolarities of the educational process. As such it represents an amplification and extension of Whitehead's theory of creativity on the ontological plane. The learner as a developing person exemplifies the intersection of educational bipolarities as well as metaphysical bipolarities.

Creativity is carried on in the educational process largely by recourse to the principle of reversibility. In essence this means the interweaving of the various educational bipolarities such as objectification, and the like. It represents the method for developing man as man as well as in his unique individuality.

Creativity is expressed in the organic field of experience in triadic pattern. Using the analogy of the cave these three phases of the educational process are apparent. Experience 'in the cave' is immediate and empirical. By and large it is comparable to Whitehead's first phase of concrescence. Experiences 'out of the cave' involve the light of reason; they imply increasing degrees of order, structure, and form. They compare with Whitehead's second stage, or 'conceptual reaction.' The third phase of Whitehead's determination or 'satisfaction' is comparable to the organic notion of synthesis of the two previous experiences in and out of the cave through reversibility.

Creativity has important implications for educational theory. Creativity in the broadest sense implies that all human beings are becoming as long as they live. Thus 'creative education' broadly includes any kind of education in the sense that it provides experiences for the concrescence of the learner. Both formal and informal types of education are 'creative.' However, we may further and nurture 'creative education' by increasing our attention to the means and ends of human development. Education in this sense becomes deliberately or consciously creative and involves weighing the respective values of various types of experiences.

Since 'creativity' is an equivocal word, attention should be given to its intended meaning. Although other conceptions of 'creativity' admittedly have partial validities for education, they are recognized here as too limited for providing an adequate basis for a philosophy of education.

Creativity requires the utilization of the multiple modes of experience and learning in the educational process.

It has been said that organically considered all actual entities are both subjects and objects in different perspectives. It follows that students in their educational development are also both objects and subjects in different perspectives.

The organic theory of control is an amplification of the theory of creativity on the educational plane. In both theories there is the recognition of the movement from indeterminacy to determinacy, from relatively little self-determination to increased or actualized self-determination. In both theories there is recognition of the unification of external and internal factors in the concrescence of the organism.

Organic educational philosophy provides a broad pattern for educational creativity in terms of its categories of needs, values, knowledge, arts, functions, and institutional responsibilities, and the ten basic functions of man. The many functions of man are to be unified in terms of individual concrescence through appropriate experiences.

Creativity in the organic educational philosophy is in partial contrast with philosophies termed realistic, idealistic, pragmatic, and existential, as well as in contrast with educational theories termed 'unfolding,' 'social reconstruction,' 'self-expression,' and the like.

Some supposedly non-creative terms and concepts are quite compatible with the organic creative theory when broadly defined. Such terms as habituation, association, imitation, and emulation can be broadly defined in organic terms. They need not imply narrow conceptions of drill, training, and mimicry; they imply organic concrescence and assimilation in terms of purposeful activity when broadly and organically defined.

Many other educational implications of creativity might be cited. Creativity need not imply that educational procedures will center only in the emerging problems of individuals; there are also problems of the field. Creativity need not reject formal procedures for the informal and functional. Both can be creative. Creativity is also a shared enterprise; this need not overlook the necessity for the firm guidance by the teacher. Systematic schooling as well as direct life experiences are both legitimate parts of creative education.

The teacher in terms of creative education has broad responsibilities. The teacher teaches as well as guides development. The teacher exerts her influences on the development of the student, as well as nurturing his own increasing degrees of self-determination. Creativity is deliberate and intelligent fusion and integration of the diverse elements of the educational process in all of its complexities.

FOOTNOTES

1. Some of Whitehead's essays on education were derived from lectures given as early as 1912, 1917, and 1922.

2. See the critique of 'the law of imposition' in A. N. Whitehead, *Adventures of Ideas* (New York: The Macmillan Company, 1933), p. 154.

3. See Charles Hartshorne, *Reality as Social Process* (Glencoe, Illinois: The Free Press, and Boston: Beacon Press, 1953), p. 29 ff.

4. See Gus John Craven, "A Comparative Study of Creativity in Education in Whitehead and Others," (Unpublished dissertation, Department of History and Philosophy of Education, University of Texas, Austin, Texas, 1952), p. 283. In this book see discussion on 'insight stage' pages 312-13.

5. See G. J. Craven, *Ibid.*, p. 283.

6. See Ch. 10, "Reason and Experience."

7. See earlier discussion of Maccia's study *in re* Peirce in Ch. 10, "Reason and Experience," pages 202 ff.

8. See George S. Maccia, "The Peircean School," *Educational Theory*, Vol. V, No. 1, (Jan., 1955), p. 32 f.

9. See G. S. Maccia, *Ibid.*, p. 32 f.

10. See G. S. Maccia, *loc. cit.*

11. See Figures 4 and 5, pages 171-72.

12. See philosophical proposition number 24. See page 111.

13. See Figure 5, page 172.

14. See Figure 6, page 183.

15. See Wilhelm Windelband, translated by James H. Tufts, second ed., *A History of Philosophy* (New York: The Macmillan Company, London: The Macmillan Co., Ltd., 1893, copyright by the publisher, 1893, 1901), p. 602. Reprinted with permission of the publisher.

16. 'Creativity' has a different ontological base here in the philosophy of organism and it does not amount to a theory of 'unfolding.'

17. See Frank C. Wegener, "The Dual Task of the Teacher in Guiding the Learning Process," in *Problems and Principles of School and Society: An Outline* (Dubuque, Iowa: Wm. C. Brown Co. Inc., 1953), p. 6.

18. Eee educational proposition number 15. See page 62.

19. See Figure 11, page 280.

20. The phrases 'interest' and 'the will to form' are quoted from G. J. Craven, *Ibid.*, p. 302 ff.

21. See Karl Jaspers, *Reason and Existenz* (copyright 1955 by the Noonday Press).

22. See Rupert Lodge, *Plato's Theory of Education* (London: Kegan Paul, Trench, Trubner & Co., Ltd., Broadway House, 68-74 Carter Lane, E. C. 4, 1947), pp. 114-23.

23. See R. Lodge, *Plato's Theory of Education*, p. 114. Reprinted by permission of the publisher, Routledge & Kegan Paul, Ltd.

367

24. See R. Lodge, *Plato's Theory of Education*, p. 119.

25. See R. Lodge, *Plato's Theory of Education*, p. 119. Reprinted with permission of the publisher.

26. See R. Lodge, *Plato's Theory of Education*, p. 119. Reprinted with permission of the publisher.

27. See R. Lodge, *Plato's Theory of Education*, p. 123. Reprinted with permission of the publisher.

28. See R. Lodge, *Plato's Theory of Education*, p. 123.

29. See William James, *Talks to Teachers* (London, New York, and Bombay: Longmans Green & Company, 1900), p. 51. Reprinted by permission of Henry Holt and Company, Inc.

30. See William James, *Talks to Teachers*, p. 48. Reprinted by permission of Henry Holt and Company, Inc.

31. See William James, *Talks to Teachers*, pp. 48-49. Reprinted by permission of Henry Holt and Company, Inc.

32. See William James, *Talks to Teachers*, p. 49. Reprinted by permis- of Henry Holt and Company, Inc.

33. See William James, *Talks to Teachers*, pp. 49-50. Reprinted by permission of Henry Holt and Company, Inc.

34. See F. C. Wegener, *Problems and Principles of School and Society: An Outline*, p. 6.

35. See Figure 11, page 280.

PART IV

The Functions of
Man and Education

16

THE TEN BASIC FUNCTIONS
of MAN [1]

ESSENTIAL to any philosophy of education is a clear-cut presentation of its stand relative to the all important problem of the nature of man. Much of educational theory and practice hangs upon the particular theory of man expounded in any given philosophy of education. Whether one's view embraces a conception of man termed naturalistic or supernaturalistic, realistic or idealistic, secular or religious, or a higher synthesis of these components, the educational consequences are of inevitable import.[2] The writer has tried to state his conception of man as forthrightly and as clearly as possible in the confines of a very short essay. Some of the questions which are considered in this essay are: What is the organic view of the nature of man? In what sense does man have a common nature? What are the organic views of the functions of man? What then is the organic view of the task of education?

*   *   *

Educational theory needs a philosophical clarification of that much used and abused phrase, "the education of the *whole child.*" Nominally there is no real dispute here. Most of us are for the education of the "whole child" in the same sense that we are for the "good life" and "against sin." It is only when we begin to question the meanings and consequences of this concept that we encounter serious controversy. Do we mean only the now familiar "psychological needs" of the whole child, such as "sense of belonging," "security," "feeling of well being," and the like? Or does it mean all physical, emotional, and mental needs? Does it include the "spiritual needs" of the child, or are these alleged needs foreign to the concept of wholeness? One

371

can easily envision the violent controversies that might be engendered by a penetrating discussion of such questions.

The Nature of Man

The Organic Philosophy of Education[3] postulates the following propositions with reference to these foregoing issues.

(1) *The meaning of "the whole child" can be resolved only by the delineation of the nature of man, for the child is actually the potential man.* The education of the whole child is a part of the entire process of developing man. When we inquire into the nature of the whole child, we inadvertently raise the philosophical question of the nature of man. Educational theory, at this very point, extends its inquiries into the realms of philosophy. Our inquiry then turns to questions such as the following: What is the nature of man as man? Is he only nominally *Homo sapiens*? Or shall we conceive of man as a species as a fiction? Shall we think of the education of the whole child only in terms of the now popularized psychological notion of "individual differences"? Should we not realize that education must be primarily concerned with the common denominators of the whole person and secondarily with the unique capacities and aptitudes termed "individual differences"?

(2) *Mankind, qua Homo sapiens, possesses a common nature.* This common nature is best understood in terms of the proper functions of man. These functions are common potentialities inherent in man which may or may not be developed. They may be thwarted and undeveloped. As potentialities they are universal and generic capacities of *Homo sapiens*. They are not 'instinctive' in the older sense of rigidly predetermined patterns of human behavior. Rather, they are latent capacities, needs, or drives within the inherent structure of man. In short, these functions are immanent in man's common nature.

Since they are not "instinctive" modes of behavior, but rather universal and generic capacities within man, they are capable of diverse cultural realization. The generic capacities are indeed universal, but their actualizations in specific individuals in diverse cultures may be varied. Universal potentiality does not mean uniform actualization. All men must eat, to be sure, but all men do not subsist on the same diet. All men must reproduce their kind to survive, but this does not mean they must all possess the same identical conceptions of the family. All men may feel the spiritual drive, but they need not agree upon the same actualizations in terms of overt religious orthodoxies.

372

The postulation of common functions of man, universally and generically, is not necessarily incompatible with the established anthropological conceptions of cultural diversity. Cultural diversity is no doubt a fact—granting certain common manifestations. Metaphorically, the identical seeds may yield modified products when nurtured in diverse soils. Scientific proof of cultural diversity does not destroy the philosophical conception of common capacities and hungers.

The Functions of Man

(3) *The Ten Basic Functions of Man are postulated as follows*:

(i) *Intellectual,* (ii) *Moral,* (iii) *Spiritual,* (iv) *Social,* (v) *Economic,* (vi) *Political,* (vii) *Physical,* (viii) *Domestic,* (ix) *Aesthetic,* and (x) *Re-creational.*

Although it is necessary to set these functions sharply apart for purposes of analysis, they are actually organically and intrinsically related. There is a sense, of course, in which they are *independent,* but they are also *dependent* and *interdependent.*[4] In analogy to the organic body of man they are related very much like the organs and parts of this body to create a whole. Brain, heart, lungs, stomach, limbs, and nervous system are all in a sense independent parts, but they are structurally and functionally related. The organic conception of the whole man, and therefore the "whole child," includes the *ten basic functions of man.*

(i) *The Intellectual Function.* If a man is to become truly man, he must develop his intelligence. As Aristotle advised us long ago, we cannot realize our proper natures unless we develop this intellectual virtue or function. Now, when we say this, we do not feel compelled to defend all that is included within the Aristotelian philosophy *per se.* The technical questions of philosophy as to the qualitative differences between man and animal are important, but need not detain us in this particular context.

Even in the most modern context, it must be admitted that man is at least a creature capable of symbolic learning and thinking. We need not deny the remarkable manifestations of animal learning and thinking to establish the unique quality of man's thinking. The vast accomplishments of man as expressed in all aspects of his culture— industry, art, architecture, music, science, humanities, mathematics, and all such creations—assert evidences of his mental powers.

Without the actualization of intellectual powers these accomplishments would not be possible. Where these powers have not been nurtured, man's cultures languish. Educationally we must develop man's intellectual powers both (1) prudentially, and (2) theoretically or contemplatively. The practical problems of life cannot be resolved without a developed prudential intelligence. The search for truth and understanding, despite our limitations, must be nurtured in what might be termed "theoretical" or "contemplative" areas of inquiry. Creative intelligence, too, must not be neglected.

Neither the "whole child" nor the "whole man" can be realized educationally without the nurture of the Intellectual Function. It should be noted that the Intellectual Function is organically and intrinsically related to the other nine functions.[5] They cannot be adequately developed without the intellect. They are properly conceived as *complementary functions.*

Although the Intellectual Function is universal as a potentiality, it is realized through the specific instruments and agencies of any given culture. The generic function may then be developed in diverse languages, mathematical systems, symbols, literatures, and habitual modes of thinking; without proper nurture it may never be actualized to any significant degree.

(ii) *The Moral Function.* Co-ordinate with the Intellectual Function of man is the Moral Function. They form the major virtues of mankind. Hence, one cannot be a human being in the full meaning of the word without the development of his moral capacities. One must achieve this development in terms of moral understanding, ethical sensitivity, and the practical moral powers of judgment and decision.

Universally and generically this means that humans, normatively considered, are inherently capable of executing moral powers. We say normatively, because some individuals may be born without the individual capacities for realizing the moral power. For example, individuals born with defective mentalities, such as imbeciles, would never develop enough intelligence to have real moral comprehension.

Normatively, then, human beings are capable of moral responsibility. Through the nurture of their generic powers they can become actual moral agents; they can learn to make genuine moral judgments of right and wrong, good and evil, legal and illegal, and social and anti-social. They have this potentiality and moral power

374

uniquely, because they do not share it with animals. As far as we can ascertain, at least, animals other than man do not appear to be capable of genuine moral responsibility.

Again we must assert an inherent unity and an overt diversity. Although *Homo sapiens,* as a species, is inherently capable of becoming moral, such capabilities are manifest in diverse cultural institutions. It is a fact that mores, morals, and ethical codes differ in the various cultures and even within cultures. This fact merely demonstrates that the generic powers may be channeled into different specific forms of action. Likewise, as our own mores and moral conceptions change with time, it does not necessarily mean that our moral powers are changing, but rather that the overt modes of manifestation are changing.

The Moral Function may be singled out for identification; it is intrinsically related to all of the other functions. For example, it is organically and reciprocally related to such functions as the Intellectual, Spiritual, Social, and Aesthetic. The education of the whole child demands attention to all of these functions of man if substantial integration is to be achieved.

(iii) *The Spiritual Function.* Very closely allied with the Intellectual and Moral Functions of man is the Spiritual Function. Analogous to man's material need for food is the inherent spiritual drive for integration with the real. Philosophy, history, and even anthropology indicate that the philosophical pursuits of man have been associated with this spiritual drive toward the real. Where men have speculated about the nature of being, of reality, of values, morals, ethics, and the nature of God, these speculations have furnished much of the content and motivations for further strivings into the realm of the religions and theologies.

Within the nature of man there appears to be a universal desire for communion with a spirituality which transcends the purely sensuous experiences of man. The articulated conceptions of what constitutes such a reality and even substitutions for the reality are many. Whether the *Nous* of the Greeks, the Nirvana of the Buddhists, the God of the Christians, the Yahweh of the Hebrews, the Allah of the Mohammedans, the Eternal Spirit of the Mystics, the Great Spirit of the American Indians, the Over-Soul of the Emersonians, or the God in Nature of the Pantheists, in all of these manifestations of belief there seems to be a spiritual hunger underlying this eternal quest.

It is not asserted here that man is a *religious* animal, *per se*. Rather, man has a *spiritual* hunger or drive. He has a yearning to belong to reality or to be in community with man, nature, and reality. This assertion is difficult to prove scientifically. Perhaps it is only through experience, feeling, or intuition that we can know the truth of such an assertion. Yet the psychologists frequently assert that man "wants to belong." He feels "insecure" if he does not belong. They mean this socially; but isn't this drawing a very fine line between wanting to belong in a social sense and our statement here that man's urge is to belong to what is real in our universe?

The postulation of a universal, Spiritual Function or drive, inherent in mankind, does not commit one to any specific religious orthodoxy. It has not been implied that man *must* believe in a spiritual substance, a personal God, an immortal soul, an orthodox religion, or an eternal heaven or hell. The varieties of crystalized religious beliefs are many. The channeling overtly of our spiritual powers is guided by many persons, factors, and institutions, and in the end amounts to personal belief. The person who willfully destroys his spiritual powers through ignorance or perversity thwarts an important dimension of his total personality.

Spirituality is not necessarily a supernatural concept. Plato spoke of the tripartite division of man's nature; spirit for him referred to that "soul" or "division" intermediate between the vital functions of the body and the rational functions of the intellect. Proverbially, the spirit of man is the heart which symbolizes a deep feeling which is intermediate between rationality and sensuality. Without nurture of this hunger of the heart, mankind would be dismally hollow indeed.

(iv) *The Social Function.* Man is immanently a social creature. Without benefit of social participation, directly or indirectly, he cannot develop his proper functions. His Social Function is organically and integrally related to the other functions. Yet it is an error to regard the Social Function as the singular end of man's activities. It is only one of the basic functions and as such provides a means of developing the other propensities.

That man becomes human through social participation is agreed upon by ancient philosophers and modern scientists of social thought. The social, economic, and political institutions, for example, are requisite to man's realization of his potential nature. Individual man in isolation from all social influences could not conceivably actualize the full potentialities of his nature; he would be little more than Rousseau's "noble savage" at best.

In underscoring the importance of the Social Function of man, we should not make the error of setting it up as the end of man's activities. There is a sense in which man strives to create a good society; to this extent it is one end. Even more important is the use of society as a means toward the actualization of man's capacities both individually and collectively.

Much has been said of education as a social process. We must accept the truth of this notion, but not exclusively. In addition to the social process, education is a process of inquiry, thought, and contemplation. Through dialectical inquiry, for example, the individual in pursuit of truth and self-realization may transcend the limited connotations of the social process.

(v) *The Economic Function.* Man is an economic animal. Since he must eat to live, this proposition becomes the most evident of all of his functions. Like all animals, man faces economic problems on the level of survival. Despite the fact that man shares this necessity with other animals, there are unique aspects of man's economic nature. As societies become more complex, the problems of production, distribution, and consumption of goods become intricately involved in the whole cultural milieu. The welfare of the society is intimately related to successful economics. Man's full powers are required in wrestling with the fluctuations of the economy. Thus, in addition to vocational competence, man must comprehend the problems of economics intellectually. Man is an economic creature both in a primitive and a complex sense.

In the recognition of the fundamental role of economics, some scholars have made extravagant claims to the effect that economics is the key to our successes and failures. The complex social problems of our modern societies are frequently explained in terms of "economic determinism." From the organic viewpoint, this is but a reversal of the error of the ancient philosophers who looked with contempt upon the economic. Since the Economic Function is only one of the Ten Basic Functions of Man, it is a gross error to explain the whole of man and society by one of its parts.

The Economic Function is manifestly related to the other functions. Prudential intelligence must solve its problems. Moral intelligence must regulate its human relations. Spirituality must prevent its grossness. Political science must regulate its manifold activities. Each function of man contributes to the organic totality.

(vi) *The Political Function.* Man appears to be a political animal both by nature and necessity. By nature he is gifted with the potentialities of sociability, intelligence, and speech. As Aristotle indicated in his *Politics*:

> Hence it is evident that the state is a creation of nature, and that man is by nature a political animal. And he who by nature and not by mere accident is without a state, is either a bad man or above humanity; he is like the "Tribeless, lawless, heartless one," whom Homer denounces—the natural outcast is forthwith a lover of war; he may be compared to an isolated piece at draughts.
>
> Now, that man is more of a political animal than bees or any other gregarious animals is evident. Nature, as we often say, makes nothing in vain, and man is the only animal whom she has endowed with the gift of speech . . . . And it is a characteristic of man that he alone has any sense of good and evil, of just and unjust, and the like, and the association of living beings who have this sense makes a family and a state.[6]

Whether or not one accepts or rejects the precise intention of Aristotle's *Politics*, it is clearly evident that man is of necessity a political animal—particularly in a democratic society. Without a successful political system supported by an intelligent citizenry, it is axiomatic that man cannot maintain his political rights and freedoms. The development of the proper functions of man demands an education which will guarantee the realization of the political being of man, which in turn relates to all the other functions. In order to become human in the fullest sense, man must be a political being, and education must work toward this end; but in working toward the function of citizenship and politics, the emphasis upon this facet of man's nature should not obscure the greater objective of the development and cultivation of man's total personality and his community with the very essence of all reality. This is merely another way of saying that man is not singularly a social being. Man in his total personality has all of these other dimensions.

(vii) *The Physical Function.* The Physical Functions of man are perhaps the most evident of man's functions. They are actual, or existential, as well as normative, universal, and generic. Physical nature demands at least minimal care of the functions if survival is to be a fact. Bodily processes cannot be totally neglected. This is in contrast to the functions that are developed only with effort and nurture, such as Intellectual, Moral, and Spiritual Functions, which can be sadly neglected.

Whereas some of the historic religions and philosophies tended to disparage and minimize the importance of the Physical Functions of man, we today realize their pervasive importance. Such functions are not evil, but good; unless, of course, they are perverted, distorted, or exaggerated.

The organic philosophy views man as a complex organism whose organic being is not reducible to the physical category alone, but as an organism composed of these various powers or the ten basic functions. The endeavor to explain man in purely physical terms commits the error of reducing whole to part. This is true, also, of the attempt to reduce man's organic being to any other of his ten functions.

True health is to be obtained through the harmonious co-ordination of all of these functions. Education of the whole person becomes intelligible in view of this desired end.

(viii) *The Domestic Function.* In one sense the procreation and nurture of children, or the Domestic Function, is the most essential of all. In the physical category, it is a biological function. In the social category, it is a sociological function. Organically considered, the generation and education of human offspring should properly embrace all ten of the categories. In fact, all of the other functions become more significant as related to the Domestic Function.

The organic philosophy recognizes the family as the proper agency for the procreation and nurture of children. This does not mean that the other institutions of society, such as school and church, are excluded from their contributions to the development of the whole child. It does mean that the family is the fundamental unit of society, and that the potentialities of all members of the family are best developed originally in a home which provides affection, love, belonging, security, and guidance.

The creative principle is essential to the Organic Philosophy of Education. Although creativity is embodied in other functions of man, it is most profound in the Domestic Function. Man participates in the creation and preservation of life. Man and wife become human actualizations of the veritable Male and Female Components of reality itself. Together they become the progenitors of actual human life in all of its dimensions; they are the actualizers of vast potentialities. In a sense, they participate in the divine act of creativity.

(ix) *The Aesthetic Function.* Complementary to the Intellectual and Moral Functions of man is the Aesthetic Function. Co-ordinate with the intellectual object of truth, and utility, and the moral object of the Good is the aesthetic objective of the Beautiful. Comparable to the organic relatedness of the True, Good, and Beautiful is the co-ordination of the Intellectual, Moral, and Aesthetic Functions. Again they are all diverse manifestations of an organic unity.

In one sense of the term aesthetic, man's freedom is the discovery and creation of beauty. Fundamentally, man is capable of real art. He is a creator and appreciator of beauty. Again we find the all important principle of creativity. Art need not be limited to the fine arts, of course; in fact, man's arts could be considered in the ten categories of function.

There is another sense of the term aesthetic which means perceptive, especially feeling. As used by Baumgarten in *circa* 1750, it meant the science of sensuous knowledge, whose goal is beauty, in contrast with logic, whose goal is truth.[7] It is used by some modern philosophers to mean "prehension," "feeling," or the "aesthetic component" of knowledge. The latter is expounded by Professor F. S. C. Northrop,[8] for example, as complementary to the "theoretic component" of man's knowing process. The "aesthetic component" provides man with a direct intuition of existence, while complemented by the "theoretic component" which furnishes the cognitional aspect of thought.

Man's Aesthetic Function includes, then, these two meanings of the aesthetic, (a) the pursuit of beauty and (b) the "prehensive" component of the knowing process.

(x) *The Re-creational Function.* We have spoken of man's creative functions. Man also has a Re-creational or Renewal Function. Organically considered, man should re-create his total being intellectually, morally, spiritually, socially, economically, politically, physically, domestically, and aesthetically. Athough man can be re-created in the activity of his vocation, his true re-creation comes through the proper utilization of his leisure—his freedom.

In this light we see leisure activities as the opportunities for achieving the ends of the whole man. Specific activities such as reading, writing, studying, thinking, contemplating, inquiring, praying, and creating are modes of recreating one's being. Creation and re-creation go hand in hand. The true artist creates and re-creates at the same time. Just as surely as the cells of the physical body must be re-plenished and re-created in the cycle of generation and corruption, so must the renewal of man's intellectual ideas, his moral convictions, spiritual feelings, social relations, economic well being, political strength, domestic felicities, and aesthetic insights be accomplished.

Since the term 're-creation' is so easily confused with the popular connotation of the term 'recreation' as amusement or relaxation, this writer proposes a special term in its place. 'Recrescence' from the Latin, *recrescere*, meaning to grow anew, seems much more appro-priate to our organic meaning. Thus where the term used by White-head, 'concrescence,' is used to indicate the fundamental creative process itself, we may use the term 'recrescence' to emphasize the process of renewal or 'growing anew.'

The Whole Organic Man. Within the dimensions, then, of these Ten Basic Functions of Man we can obtain an adequate concep-tion of the education of the "whole child." It is the task of education to assist each individual in the actualization of his potentialities into the whole organic man.

We have spoken of common, universal, and generic functions of man. This does not mean that man is without very important dif-ferences. The point is that our individual differences are manifest in our individual capacities and aptitudes in these common cate-gories.

Our analysis has accentuated the ten functions as separate. It should be remembered that they are organically related. They func-tion in harmony. A single activity involves the whole organism. Thus, a musician manifestly uses intellectual, physical, and aesthetic func-tions simultaneously. Organic education may draw upon one or two functions predominantly, in a given activity, but involves the whole person.

The Organic Philosophy of Education views the problems of aims, functions, values, curricula, general and special education, and the nature of the educational processes in education through these postu-lated ten basic functions of man. Through the unity of this frame-work the diverse problems of educational theory and practice can become more intelligible.

* * *

These ten basic functions of man serve to emphasize the rich diversity and many-sidedness of man's nature. Yet these many functions do not exhaust our conception of man's nature. Elsewhere it has been indicated that the organic educational philosophy views man as a microcosmic exemplification of the bipolarities of the world in the macrocosmic sense. Man in this bipolarity is fundamentally ambivalent. This proposition does not mean that our view is 'dualistic.' Man like all other actual entities is constituted by the integral relationships of physical and mental poles and their related functions. The physical and mental poles are essentially interdependent; likewise man's body and mind are integrally interdependent; they are not casually related as are the dualistic substances of the Cartesian philosophy. Body and mind are in such intimate, intrinsic relationships as to be inseparable, except in the qualified sense of 'separableness' which we have expounded about the relations of bipolarities in other contexts.

This bipolar conception of man represents another effort within the organic educational philosophy to go beyond some of the traditional 'either . . . or' views of man as either good or evil, man as a complete product of his culture or of nature, man as either possessing inherent qualities or being a 'neutral substance.' The organic contention advanced here is that man's bipolar nature exemplifies positive potentialities. He is not merely a 'neutral substance' to be conditioned by his culture; rather he is a product of long evolutionary concrescence with accumulated, positive characteristics and potentialities for further actualization and determination in his interactions with all other entities (actual and ideal) in and beyond human society in 'the creative advance' of the world. Good in man is the actualization of ideal values in man's concrescence in terms of his actual potentialities in the achievement of right proportion and harmonization of opposites. Evil results from the failure to achieve right proportions, or justice, or the failure to harmonize opposites, and the wrong proportion of the elements in one's becoming and being.

Summary. Educational theory needs to be grounded in a conception of man which is comprehensive, coherent, and adequate. This educational philosophy holds to the organic nature of man. *Homo sapiens* possesses a relatively persistent common nature which is the product of the creative advance of man and the world. Man's common nature is expressed here in terms of his basic functions. These basic functions are generic potentialities and are actualized in terms of the variations of the many existent cultures. There is no necessary incompatibility in the theoretical designation of man's common functions, of individual differences within those functions, and of reckoning with the specificities of cultural variations and diversities.

The ten basic functions of man are: Intellectual, Moral, Spiritual, Social, Economic, Political, Physical, Domestic, Aesthetic, and Recreational. These functions are parts or aspects of the whole man; although in a sense separable, they are organically related like the organs of the body. Although the development of these functions may be emphasized separately, they necessarily and intrinsically involve one another and the whole organism in continuity with the world.

These ten basic functions provide the framework or pattern whereby the diverse problems of educational theory and practice can become more intelligible.

FOOTNOTES

1. Frank C. Wegener, "The Ten Basic Functions of Man," *Educational Theory*, Vol. V, No. 2, (April, 1955), pp. 110-17. Reprinted with permission of the publisher.

2. James N. Brown, "Educational Implications of Four Conceptions of Human Nature, A Comparative Study," (Washington, D. C.: The Catholic University of America Press, 1940), a published dissertation from The Catholic University of America.

3. Throughout this writing this author has referred to his educational philosophy in capitalized form as follows: 'The Organic Philosophy of Education.'

4. Professor Archie J. Bahm, University of New Mexico, has expressed his views on 'Organicism' in relation to eight other viewpoints in his book, *Philosophy: An Introduction* (New York: John Wiley & Sons, Inc., copyright 1953 by publishers), p. 241.

5. See Figure 13, page 351.

6. *The Basic Works of Aristotle*, ed. Richard McKeon (New York: Random House, 1941), *Politics*, Bk. I, Ch. 2, p. 1129. Reprinted with permission of the publisher, Oxford Univ. Press, Inc.

7. See Webster's *New International Dictionary of the English Language*, Unabridged, 1950 Edition.

8. See F. S. C. Northrop, *The Meeting of East and West* (New York: The Macmillan Company, 1946).

17

THE FUNCTIONS of EDUCATION

IN large part the functions of education are implicit in one's conception of man and reality. Admittedly there are important considerations in virtually every branch of philosophical thought—conceptions of reality, knowledge, and value. Yet for our purposes, it is important that we move from the previous chapter on the functions of man to the present consideration of the functions of general education. The logical structure established should be helpful in our delineation of the functions of education.

The most pertinent questions for our subsequent consideration are: What is the organic meaning of the functions of education? In what sense are there universal functions of education? In outline form what are the functions of education? What is meant here by "education of man *qua* man" and "education as individual"? What is the organic conception of conservative and progressive functions? What is the function of education with respect to individual and society? What is the obligation of education with respect to the ten basic functions of man?

"Functions of education" are interpreted here as the most general conceptions of the tasks of education, while "aims of education" refer to the more specific objectives in the subordinate sense. In later contexts our discussion of aims and objectives or organic education will clarify this distinction further.

The functions of education as delineated here are not arbitrary or eclectic, for they grow out of the philosophical conceptions of reality, knowledge, value, and man as described in the Organic Philosophy of Education. The functions of education are inseparable from the *ten basic functions of man* and our contention that man is a *micro-cosm*, or a *concrescence* of the *macrocosm*. The purposes and functions of education are undeniably a restatement of the purposes and functions of man as related to all reality.[1]

In the following delineation of the organic conception of the functions of man and education it should be noted that our view is not exclusively in agreement or disagreement with the classical or modern positions on this argument. The modern argument so often advanced that man is a product of his culture as behavioristically determined, and that therefore the purposes and functions of education should be culturally determined, has only partial validity. Pushed to its logical conclusion this view negates the *doctrine of immanence* as advanced in a *philosophy of organism*, and cultural behaviorism becomes sheerly a form of cultural relativism.[2]

We cannot agree, then, that man is simply a neutral substance to be conditioned by cultural determinants of "right and wrong" in the exclusively social context. Nor can we agree with the idea that the aims and functions of education are strictly relative to the variant conditions of time, place, and situation, and that therefore there can be no universal aims or functions of education.[3]

On the other hand it has been argued by those of the classical persuasion that education does have its universal aims of education.[4] Therefore, it is argued, the aims and functions of education have little or nothing to do with a given culture, or the demands of time, place, and situation.

It will be seen in the following discussion of the functions of education that organically we believe that this is not necessarily an "either-or argument." Rather we need to ask *"In what respect* are there "universal" functions of education?" *"In what respect* are there culturally determined functions of education in terms of the given epoch?"

By and large our position is this: Man as *Homo sapiens* has evolved through successive epochs over millions of years; therefore man as man as he exists on this planet does possess a *form of being* which has resulted from a concrescence of forces in his *becoming*. Despite differences of race and individual differences man as man possesses common structural and functional characteristics which we have described in terms of *the ten basic functions of man.* Although man in his long evolution is realized in *process,* he does possess as a species an "enduring society" of forms or a relatively continuing pattern in this *epoch.* We need not defend "man as man" in terms of Aristotelian primary substance; man as realized in process does have an achieved form which for all practical purposes is subject to slow change and evolution and he does have "a nature" in this sense.[5]

Hence man conceived in organic terms of process is not just a neutral substance to be conditioned and determined by social forces.[6] Man contains the real forces, forms, and potentialities and actualities of the universe in its metaphysical proportions as well as in the cultural dimensions. Man's fundamental ambivalence, for example, is not merely socially acquired, but is an incarnation of the very metaphysical bipolarities of the physical and mental, the irrational and rational, fact and form, aesthetic and theoretic, the primordial and the consequent, and the other great ideal opposites or contrasts.

Yet it is not a one-sided argument; there is much to be said for the cultural determinations of man's becoming. The generic potentialities which we have termed the *ten functions of man* are susceptible to diverse cultural modes of nurture and development. The generic functions of man cannot be developed in general without recourse to the specific content of a given culture. Therefore, the functions of man as expressed in terms of functions and aims of education in various cultures must be developed through the specificities of the given languages, beliefs, religions, social schemes, ideologies, and other aspects of culture. The over-all functions of man, as we have set them forth, will inevitably be viewed and interpreted through the prism of a given cultural context and philosophy.

Here again then is an application of the principles of *unity* and *diversity.* We cannot evade these all pervasive metaphysical principles. With the classical tradition then we see the unity of man's generic functions in life and in education; with the modernists we see the principle of diversity as it expresses itself in cultural variations; organically then we see the functions of education as a *unity of opposites*—a bipolarity of his functions in *unity and in diversity.*

Outline of the Functions of Education

Before the exposition of the functions of education is given, it will be of some value to see the whole pattern in brief outline form.

I. Development of Man's Commonality and Individuality

It is the function of education to contribute to the development of each person toward his maximal potentialities and possibilities in the *intelligent pursuit of the good life;* in short, education should assist the individual in his process of becoming and creating the best person of which he is capable.

(A) To the extent that human beings have generic functions and potentialities of a common nature, education should seek to develop man *qua* man; in terms of the principle of unity *Homo sapiens* possesses generic functions which should be developed universally; admittedly these generic functions will have to be realistically developed in the diverse, existent cultural patterns.

(B) To the extent that each individual represents a unique concrescence of potentialities and propensities, education should cooperate with the individual in his own process of self-determination or self-creation in terms of his becoming and being; the principle of diversity recognizes the "otherness" in human beings, or individual differences, and therefore education has the additional responsibility and function of assisting the individual in the realization of his uniqueness.

II. The Co-ordination of Conservative and Progressive Functions

It is the organic function of education to progressively seek coordinations and integrations of opposite forces as they fuse in man and society; education should fuse the education of man *qua* man, and man as unique individual; it should likewise contribute to the progress of humanity in given societies by maintaining the inevitable ideal opposites, flux and permanence, actual and ideal, necessity and freedom—in short a harmonization of the *progressive-conservative functions* of an *enduring society.*[7]

(A) On the side of the conservative function of education the following responsibilities are embraced: (1) Stabilization of human progress through the systematic transmission of the wealth of human experiences from the past; (2) Maintenance of the cultural continuity in terms of past, present, and projections into the future; (3) Continued animation of the knowledge, experiences, lessons and wisdom from the cultural heritage so that each succeeding generation does not have to begin anew and thereby to learn the trial and error learnings of mankind only through "experience"; (4) To provide elements of permanence and stability; (5) To conserve that which is best as selected from the total human heritage.

(B) On the side of the progressive function of education to execute the following responsibilities: (1) Contribution to the *creative advance* of humanity through constant inquiry, reconstruction of human knowledge and institutions, and the recognition of the novel aspects of human life and reality; (2) Counterbalancing the previously indicated stabilizing function by asserting the need for dynamic and progressive efforts toward increased human knowledge and vision and conversion into actual exemplifications in thought and action.

III. *The Co-ordination of the Individual and Society*

Education has a joint responsibility to the individual and society; from the interest of the individual education must assist him in his development *qua* man, and *qua* individual; from the interest of society, education must safeguard the welfare of society as realized in the development of the many individuals; in short, the interests of the individual and society must be developed so that they are of mutual benefit, or negatively stated, they must be developed so that their interests are not inimical.

(A) In one sense then it is clear that education has the function of individual development of the person; the significance of this function is that education serves the individual in a manner that transcends the orientation of the needs of society and of citizenship —here the concern is with the quest of the good life in *the dimensions of man and reality*. In other words, although the education of man must in one sense be concerned with the social dimensions of man, education in the fullest sense embraces man's quest for the most complete realization which has dimensions that are philosophical, religious, aesthetic, intellectual, and indeed cosmic, which conceivably transcend "education as a social process."

(B) In another sense, however, it is also clear that education has an *obligation to society* as well as to the individual; a stable society is necessary with its many institutions in providing the milieu within which man may develop his ten basic functions; modern complex societies cannot sustain themselves without the reciprocal services of its individual components, for after all a society is fundamentally organic in nature; there is a fluency of beliefs, values, ideals, and purposes that forms the very mentality of a given society which is intrinsically operative; society then must depend upon education to insure the development of human potentialities so that they will be of value rather than detrimental to the welfare of the whole society.

IV. *The Creative Advance of the Individual and Humanity*

It is the function then of education to assist man individually and man as humanity in the *creative advance*. Education is inseparable from the problems which man faces in his quest for the good life; education must not attempt to restrict man to the arena of "social life" or "cultural pattern," even though his life must operate in and through such societies. Education must be concerned with *man and reality*, and must not be limited to "man and society." The problems of man are as wide as the feelings and apprehensions of man, and therefore include the broad scope of philosophy, religion, science, and everyday human experiences.

It is the organic function of education progressively to seek co-ordinations and integrations in just proportions between the relationships of man's development as man and his development as an individual, between conservative and progressive functions, between man and man, man and nature, and man and all reality. Education in its highest form is that of organic creativity. It is the creation of man. Within the over-all creative advance of the world the diverse entities of men, societies, institutions, values, ways of life—all these are in the process of becoming and being. In the words of Whitehead they are at once "subject and superject." Education is rightfully one with this very process of life and creative advance. Each one of us is in a very real sense the product of all that has gone before in our world. We shall contribute to our own being and to the creative advance of the world before we have expired. Education in this sense is *concrescence*. It is a unification of the many possibilities in the one. It is the deliberate fusing of the ideal and actual possibilities in the actual entities and objects of life in the time-space continuum.

As a deliberate process, as well as a natural process, we must educationally seek to go forward with balance, proportion, right ratio, and justice; the perennial ideal opposites of "Joy and Sorrow, Good and Evil, Disjunction and Conjunction, Flux and Permanence, Greatness and Triviality, Freedom and Necessity, God and the World," of which Whitehead speaks, must be philosophically recognized in our execution of the organic function of this complex business of education.[8]

V. *The Development of Man's Ten Basic Functions*

We have described in very general terms the functions of education as viewed from the Organic Philosophy of Education. These functions of education can be spelled out further in terms of the ten basic functions of man. These ten basic functions of man provide an intelligible framework for the formulation of *educational values, aims, curricula,* and *functions*. To the extent that mankind possesses a nature, we are able to find norms for the education of man; we are therefore emancipated from the current notion that education must derive its aims and functions entirely from the shifting opinions and needs of the individual and community. In part we derive norms and values from the society or culture where education is to take place, but it is also maintained that there is a metaphysical immanence which is exemplified in the nature of man as it exists today as a product of all the creative forces of the past and present. Again we invoke the principle of the unity and diversity of man as previously explained.

Synopsis of the Functions of Education

(A) Education and the Development of the Intellectual Function

It is the universal function of general education to develop the intellectual function of man. The intellectual function should be developed in *man qua man* and in man in his *unique self-determination*. Since there are diverse cultural manifestations in terms of languages, symbols, mathematical systems, and the other necessities of the intellectual function, actual educational procedures will have to be accomplished within these given contexts. Although there is an underlying unity of all human thought processes, there are diverse modes of expression in the various disciplines and in the many cultures. General education should embrace diverse modes of thought and their respective contents and objectives. The intellectual function, although partly separable for educational purposes, is organically related to the other nine functions of man and requisite to their harmonious development.

(B) Education and the Development of the Moral Function

It is also the universal function of general education to develop the moral function of man in both of the senses we have previously delineated. Such moral education must be geared to a given morality of a given culture or philosophical orientation. The specific moral feelings and habits provided to youth can be led gradually into adult philosophical inquiry into the complexities of value problems. Education must include the nurture of moral responsibility and the formulation of values within its primary responsibilities. This is especially true in a democracy where individual freedom and responsibility are at a maximum. Habits and feelings of right doing are to be coordinated with right understandings as maturity permits. Gradual conceptualization of values should mark one's philosophical growth. Although the moral function is distinguishable in a sense, it should be developed organically and intrinsically through a process of concrescence with the other nine functions of man.

(C) *Education and the Development of the Spiritual Function*

It follows that it is also a universal function of general education to develop the spiritual function of man as far as a secular institution possibly can. Schools can sensitize persons to their need and hunger for spiritual realization. The history of philosophy shows that the quest for the true, good, and beautiful has brought the philosophical quest very close to the search for spiritual solace. Profound intellectual, moral and aesthetic inquiries cannot help but bring one into what might be called spiritual experiences. Spirituality has been linked with man's heart metaphorically and his innermost and most profound feelings. In a sense it is identified with *eros* or the constant urge for the ideal or perfection.[9]

Although definitions and conceptions of spirituality differ greatly with philosophies and religions, we cannot help but associate spirituality with one's identifications and harmonies with the cosmic sources of values, goodness, order, beauty, and meaning. As Whitehead indicates the source of these values is God.[10] One feels these values in the aesthetic experience of a profoundly stirring symphony or work of art; one cognizes these values in his philosophical contemplations. Recognizing the almost insuperable complexity of human beliefs about spiritual matters, this writer is not asserting that all men can agree on particular solutions to the problem; he is asserting that there is enough evidence to show quite conclusively that man does have a spiritual hunger, and that education should encourage each person in his own self-determination to satisfy this hunger in his own way.

(D) *Education and the Development of the Social Function*

It is commonplace to state that man is a social being and that he develops in a social environment. Classical and modern philosophers and educators agree on this dictum. It is clear that it is a universal function of general education to develop man's social function. An education which neglects social philosophy, science and practice is incomplete. Although agreeing upon the social aspect of education, we cannot agree with those modern theorists who would reduce education itself to "a social process." This is an oversimplification; it amounts to reducing the complex whole to one of its parts. As stated elsewhere this is one of the unfortunate errors of modern educational theory. It is true that society is essentially organic in character; still all other entities of our world are organic. Just because society is organic, there is no reason to presume that the individual must be completely subordinated to that society. The organic philosophy respects the individuality of the human personality. The individual in part realizes himself in and through society; he contributes to that whole society. But a philosophy of organism is not completely limited to the social context; man must find his being in the context of the cosmos as well as society. Hence the teacher encourages the individual as an individual to go beyond the cave of social life in his quest for self-realization and self-determination. In one's quest for the good, true, and beautiful he may well transcend social limits as an individual; but with his insights and understandings gained outside of the cave he can return to the social scene to make his contributions to his fellow men in their common society. Youth must be introduced to their own given society; with increasing maturity they can probe comparative social theories with philosophical acumen. Education in terms of the social function is not an isolated thing, but it is intrinsically related to the whole of man's being and his other nine functions.

(E) *Education and the Development of the Economic Function*

The force of what has been said about the social function also applies to the economic function, which is again a universal function of education. The economic function of man is existential—it is absolutely indispensable for the most primitive existence. In complex modern societies and with world-wide economic tensions and problems, the economic base of human problems must be understood by modern man. Yet even here we cannot go as far as economic determinists and other enthusiasts of economic theories who would reduce the problems of man to an essence of economics. Again such reductionism amounts to conversion of the complex whole to one of its parts. Economic problems are intertwined inextricably with man's other functions and problems as we have consistently maintained.

Education must be concerned with economic education both in theoretical and practical terms, and in our role as consumers and producers. The formulation of intelligent life values and philosophies for practical action cannot afford to neglect the economic sphere. A stable society, or a stable world, requires that we deal most intelligently with the economic problems too. Our responsibilities as men and as citizens require this kind of understanding. But even aside from our common concern with the problems of economics, we as individuals in our self-determination must be concerned with economics. Frequently our life vocations, partly determined by economics, provide the main avenue of personal development.

(F) *Education and the Development of the Political Function*

It is a universal function of general education to develop the political function of man. With Aristotle we can agree that man is a political animal. We need not and do not restrict the political function of man to the few, but in terms of our modern democracy extend it to all men. It is clear that without political science and a citizenry educated in terms of their political function, there cannot be the kind of free and stable society which can provide the cultural environment within which to nourish the ten basic functions of man in his pursuit of the good life. A democratic ethos with carefully balanced freedoms and responsibilities is essential to the kind of human development envisioned in the Organic Philosophy of Education. Education for political responsibility by the masses of mankind is a tremendous undertaking. It assumes man's political function and his educability for the execution of this function. It is a function for the many and not the few, although even within a democracy leadership of the most capable in this area is required.

It is within the study of political science that man comes to grips with problems of law and order; through the study of human law, man pushes into the philosophical questions of the laws of the cosmos.[11] It is quite apparent that the political function cannot be properly developed in separation from the other organic functions of man. Finally it should be noted that the schools as such are not supposed to determine the ultimate political affiliations of the students which they will assume in adult life; rather the schools are responsible for the adequate preparations and beginnings of philosophical inquiries which will eventuate in political affiliations and participations. Thus the spiritual function in the educational program is not completely unique in this respect.

(G) Education and the Development of the Physical Function

The Organic Philosophy of Education is quite in agreement with the ancient Greek ideal which emphasized the education of the physical and mental aspects of man's nature. Gymnastics and music were co-ordinated in the harmonious development of man's whole nature. It is the universal function of education to develop man's physical function. This development is of course not limited to a narrow concept of gymnastics; rather we are concerned with the whole complex business of man's existential, physical functions. No organic philosopher minimizes the importance of the body in all of its varied functions and what it contributes to the beauty and utility of life. The body is no mere "prison of the soul" to be treated with contempt; rather it is the existential receptacle through which man integrates the varied functions of his very being. Man's relationship with all other real entities and forces is through the prehensions, feelings, emotions, hungers, drives, and comprehensions of his organic psychosomatic structure. Man's physiological and psychological structure is the product and end result of millions of years of evolution. These deeply entrenched experiences of the human race cannot be ignored in the educational process. It is perhaps unnecessary to emphasize again that the physical function of man is intimately and intrinsically related to all of his other functions. They are interactive. Organic philosophers from Plato through Pestalozzi and Whitehead have acknowledged this fact. With Pestalozzi's dictum of the necessary education of "head, heart, and hand," we can heartily agree.

(H) Education and the Development of the Domestic Function

It is the function of education universally to be concerned with the development of man's domestic function. The human family is the veritable matrix of our social life and most of our social values.

Ideal values find their highest exemplification in the home; by the same token evil and human tragedy find their exemplification in the failures of the home. It is clear that the success of family life is so vital to individuals and to society that its operation cannot be left to chance. The role of the members of the family and their relationships to themselves and to the other institutions of society must be studied scientifically, humanistically, and philosophically. The success or failure of the family is one with the progress of mankind. It is clear that the domestic function of man is closely identified with all of his functions. Education should contribute substantially to man's success in the domestic function.

(I) *Education and the Development of the Aesthetic Function*

It is a function of general education to develop the aesthetic function of man. Broadly speaking man embraces aesthetic and theoretic components. In his aesthetic component he is a creature of feeling, sensation, emotion, intuition, and prehension; in his theoretic component he is a creature of reason, cognition, and abstract intelligence. These two components in their reciprocal relations make man. The Organic Philosophy of Education contends that education is to be composed of a balance of feeling and thinking.

Organic education is not confined to the intellectual aspect. Human capacities for feeling, intuition, emotion, and aesthetic experience must be nurtured in co-ordination with the intellectual aspects of learning and experiencing. Aesthetic and theoretic components of human experience must be nurtured in harmony.[12] Or more specifically, the aesthetic function of man must be nurtured along with the other nine functions of man.[13]

(J) *Education and the Development of the Re-creational Function*

Perhaps it is unnecessary to point out at the outset that "re-creational function" refers to the renewal or re-creating function of man. "Recreation" in the popular sense is only incidental here. In this broad sense then we hold that it is the universal function of general education to develop man's re-creational or renewal function. Education should not only be concerned with the fostering and guiding of man's creativity but his re-creativity. Man is capable of re-creating himself in terms of all of his functions separately or together. His re-creation may well be intellectual, moral, and spiritual, or physical, social and aesthetic. The business of re-creation inevitably involves man's values. Much has been said about the necessity of education for intelligent use of leisure time. The question of how one is to use his leisure really begs his system of values. It is in this sense primarily that we argue for the universality of the re-creational function of education. We cannot afford to ignore the potentialities for good and evil latent in the problem of leisure and re-creation. The way that mankind uses its leisure time is significant in terms of its progress or decline. People who have learned how to re-create themselves in the fullest sense of that word have learned how to live. Furthermore intelligent re-creation exemplifies the values, purposes, and understandings as well as accomplished abilities of persons. The organic interplay of the re-creational function of man with his other functions is too evident to require further elaboration.

Summary. The Organic Philosophy of Education sets forth the following functions of education: (I) It is the function of education to contribute to the systematic development of each person toward his maximal potentialities and possibilities in the intelligent pursuit of the good life. This task requires the two-fold development of man in his commonality and in his individuality. (II) It is the task of education to co-ordinate the progressive and conservative functions of an enduring society; the great ideal opposites such as permanence and novelty, necessity and freedom, stability and reconstruction, should be exemplified in the functions of education. (III) Education also has a two-fold obligation to serve the individual and society. Education in organic terms embraces man and reality, and is not limited to the recent emphasis upon man and society. Education must be devoted profoundly to man's quest for an adequate philosophy of life and its realization in his own becoming and being. (IV) Education has the responsibility of giving man systematic assistance in the development of his whole being in terms of the ten basic functions. Since these are universal and generic functions of man, it is the universal function of education to develop organic man

THE FUNCTIONS OF EDUCATION

intellectually, morally, spiritually, socially, economically, politically, physically, domestically, aesthetically, and re-creationally.

FOOTNOTES

1. See Figure 14, page 400.

2. Alfred North Whitehead, *Adventures of Ideas* (New York: The Macmillan Company, 1933), pp. 143, 145, 165, 166, in which he discusses *Doctrine of Immanence* and qualifications.

3. The organic philosophy of relativity need not be limited to the context of cultural relativity.

4. See Mortimer Adler, "In Defense of the Philosophy of Education," *Philosophies of Education* (Chicago: The National Society for the Study of Education, 1942), *Forty First Yearbook*, p. 238.

5. The reference is to Whitehead's transformation of the category of substance to one of process and creativity. Entities or *substances*, then, exist only as events in process; however, they may well possess enduring patterns during the epoch.

6. Many modern social scientists hold that man is a *neutral substance*, neither good or bad inherently; man acquires characteristics which society terms 'good or bad.'

7. In Whitehead's special sense of 'enduring society.'

8. Alfred North Whitehead, *Process and Reality* (Cambridge: Cambridge University Press, 1929, Copyright U.S.A. by the Macmillan Co.), pp. 482-83.

9. A. N. Whitehead, *Adventures of Ideas*, p. 189.

10. Alfred North Whitehead, "Religion in the Making," *Alfred North Whitehead: An Anthology*, selected by F. S. C. Northrop and Mason W. Gross (New York: The Macmillan Company, 1953), pp. 504-06.

11. A. N. Whitehead, "Laws of Nature," *Adventures of Ideas*, pp. 131-51.

12. See F. S. C. Northrop, *The Meeting of East and West* (New York: The Macmillan Company, 1946), pp. 436-79.

13. See Figure 13 and 14, page 351 and page 400.

18

THE PATTERN of ORGANIC EDUCATION

Analysis of the Functions of Education in Terms of Needs, Values, Knowledge, Arts, Aims, and Institutional Responsibilities

T H E ten categories have been stated in general form as functions of education. It is now important that we realize the extensive scope of these ten categories in terms of (A) Educational Needs, (B) Values, (C) Knowledge, (D) Arts, (E) Functions of the School and Aims of Education, and (F) Institutional Responsibilities. In a synopsis of this character only the briefest of interpretations and applications can be given here; more adequate and extensive explanation will be given in a later work on this subject.

I. *Education and the Intellectual Function*

(A) *Intellectual Needs.* Human beings have intellectual needs in terms of symbols, language, instrumental intelligence, truth seeking intelligence, understandings, knowledge, wisdom, communication, cognition, articulation, self-expression and cultural intercourse. In order to realize our human potentialities and capacities we are in *need* of these intellectual tools, skills, habits, and understandings. Complex civilizations cannot operate without a high degree of development of human capacities and cultural advancements which necessarily depend on intellectual development. Neither can the individual attain his human realization or adequate individual realization without meeting these needs. Without the development of man's powers to meet his cognitive needs he is bound to remain relatively primitive, inhuman, thwarted, and undeveloped in terms of his human functions and capacities.

Modern man needs the tools of thought and a mastery of symbols. His symbols are found throughout the fields of human knowledge.

Figure 14. *The Pattern of Organic Education*

	(A) Needs in terms of education*	(B) Values in terms of education*	(C) Essential knowledge*	(D) Arts and experiences
I. Intellectual function	Intellectual needs	Intellectual values	Intellectual knowledge**	Intellectual arts and experiences
II. Moral function	Moral needs	Moral values	Moral knowledge	Moral arts and experiences
III. Spiritual function	Spiritual needs	Spiritual values	Spiritual knowledge	Spiritual arts and experiences
IV. Social function	Social needs	Social values	Social knowledge	Social arts and experiences
V. Economic function	Economic needs	Economic values	Economic knowledge	Economic arts and experiences
VI. Political function	Political needs	Political values	Political knowledge	Political arts and experiences
VII. Physical function	Physical needs	Physical values	Physical knowledge	Physical arts and experiences
VIII. Domestic function	Domestic needs	Domestic values	Domestic knowledge	Domestic arts and experiences
IX. Aesthetic function	Aesthetic needs	Aesthetic values	Aesthetic knowledge	Aesthetic arts and experiences
X. Re-creational function	Re-creational needs	Re-creational values	Re-creational knowledge	Re-creational arts and experiences
Note: These functions are organically related.	*Note:* Those needs susceptible to educational treatment.	*Note:* Values which can be nurtured in schools and through experience.	*Note:* *Structural — functional curricula co-ordinated. **Knowledge of tools of thought, e.g. grammar, logic, mathematics, etc.	

400

Figure 14 (continued)

(E) Functions of General Education	(F) Institutional Responsibilities
Development of the intellectual function systematically and universally*	The unique function and responsibility of the schools
Development of the moral function systematically and universally	Responsibility shared with other institutions*
Development of the spiritual function systematically and universally	Responsibility shared with other institutions
Development of the social function systematically and universally	Responsibility shared with other institutions
Development of the economic function systematically and universally	Responsibility shared with other institutions
Development of the political function systematically and universally	Responsibility shared with other institutions
Development of the physical function systematically and universally	Responsibility shared with other institutions
Development of the domestic function systematically and universally	Responsibility shared with other institutions
Development of the aesthetic function systematically and universally	Responsibility shared with other institutions
Development of the re-creational function systematically and universally	Responsibility shared with other institutions
*Note: 'Systematic' rather than random or 'ad hoc' education; 'universal' for all humans, but specific in cultural adaptation. Develop functions both in terms of man's common functions and individuality.	*Note: Although the school shares these responsibilities with other institutions, it has primary responsibility for the systematic development and interweaving of these functions of man.

He needs to master the arts of reading, writing, speaking, and listening.[1] He needs to learn the diverse modes of thinking and knowing. Man needs to learn the diverse arts of effective thinking.

(B) *Intellectual Values.* Corresponding to these needs are positive values in the intellectual category. The intellectual life makes possible an ever increasing amount of truth and understanding for man. He learns more and more about himself, society, nature, life, reality and the entire cosmos. He gains values of understanding and of appreciating his world to the extent of his limited human intelligence. Also he gains instrumental values as well as intrinsic values in terms of his intellectual powers. Instrumentally he increases his prudential powers in terms of the "means-ends" activities of life as John Dewey has described them. The increase of human excellence intellectually makes possible advances in science, philosophy, religion, and the various fields of human endeavor and study. The increase of man's intelligence wins him greater freedom in his ability to cope with the problems of life. He learns to manipulate nature and reality more successfully. He gains values in terms of his ability to act intelligently as well as the contemplative values of appreciating truth, beauty, and reality.

He attains values of purposeful endeavor and the concomitant satisfaction which accrues with the realization of intellectual progress. With knowledge and wisdom man attains greater degrees of freedom and with that increasing degrees of responsibility. The values are by no means limited to the instrumental and prudential; they are also intrinsic in character.

The values which flow from the development of man's intellectual capacities are so manifold as to defy any brief summary. The intellectual values are not exclusively intellectual; they are manifest in the moral, spiritual, social, and other functions and values of man.

A brief cataloging of values directly associated with man's intellectual function are: powers of reason, levels of understanding, appreciation of theoretical and practical, the cognitive, logical, mathematical, symbolic, scientific, contemplative, prudential, creative and problem-solving.

In a word the values of the intellectual functions are the evident values of literacy as contrasted with illiteracy. They are the values of an intelligent life as opposed to the limited values of an unintelligent life—or of civilization as opposed to primitive existence.

The problem of intellectual values was raised by Socrates when he asked, "Is the un-examined life worth living?" In other words how valuable is a life which neglects the whole realm of intellectual development. It is likely that most of us would shrink from a flat either-or choice between intellectual life and no life at all. Life on various non-cognitive levels certainly seems worthwhile to us. Yet as human beings would we not agree with the sentiment of Socrates that life must be intelligent if we are to live fully?

(C) *Organized Knowledge.* Man's intellectual expressions are so varied as to be found in virtually all fields of organized knowledge. No one field has a monopoly on knowledge necessary for intellectual development. It has been our thesis that, despite the underlying unified character of the thought processes of *Homo sapiens* in its potentialities, there are diverse modes of thought as expressed in the different fields of human knowledge and action. The physical sciences, the social sciences, the humanities, the arts, and the many applied fields of human study and endeavor exemplify these diverse modes of thought and understanding in their own way.

In terms of what we have called *structural intelligibility* man needs knowledge to successfully execute his intellectual function. He needs the tools and content of thought as provided in these diverse disciplines.

Man needs the conceptual tools of thought; these include a knowledge of basic use of symbols and ideas as expressed in the language of mathematics on one hand and the language of words on the other. The intricate problems of modern life and the great masses of facts and experiences require that man possess the conceptual tools for handling these unwieldy elements of experience. The understanding of the tools and instrumentalities of the intellectual life must be understood not only in themselves as tools, but they must be understood in the context and content of the great fields of human knowledge, physical and natural sciences, social sciences and humanities, the arts and the various professional and applied areas. The tools and concepts of scientific method, for example, should be understood within the context of scientific studies. The precise tools and concepts of mathematics should be understood grammatically, logically, and structurally in themselves, as well as in the studies of history, literature, philosophy and the humanities which provide their context.

(D) *The Intellectual Arts.* Man's intellectual function should be developed in terms of *structural intelligibility,* as we have just indicated, but also in *functional intelligibility.* Education is in one sense a process of gaining insight into knowledge, or science; on the other hand education is a process of creating or doing, which is education as art. At advanced stages students may through research do creative work in the theoretical realm. However, at less mature levels, education as art and creativity will of necessity take place in the realm of "experience." Hence education organically involves the intellectual function as an art too. The student must not only gain understanding of knowledge about the intellectual function, he must develop creative and practical skills in the utilization of intellectual arts through experiences. The sciences of the intellectual function then must be converted into intellectual arts. There should be laboratory experiences in the various ways of thinking. The formal knowledge of scientific method, philosophical inquiry, literary analysis, problem solving, language, logic, mathematics, and semantics must be complemented by experiences designed to develop effective skills in what might be called intellectual arts. Without giving way to a complete and exclusive doctrine of "education as creativity" we can well allow for creative experiences. It is precisely in this way that the Organic Philosophy of Education seeks to avoid a one-sidedness in educational theory and practice.

It is here that we would teach for transfer of general understandings to levels of practical application. Likewise abstract understandings can well be turned into particular skills. In this sense we should be following our principles of actualizing the ideal and making the abstract concrete. Intellectual knowledge is to be expressed in the intellectual arts.

(E) *Functions and Aims of Education.* It has been stated that it is the universal function of general education to develop the intellectual function of man *qua* man, and as unique individual in self-determination. Under this broad categorical function there are numerous aims and objectives. Some of these aims and objectives in this category might be stated as follows: (1) To teach ways of thinking; (2) To nurture diverse habits and methods of thinking; (3) To foster understanding of the intellectual heritage; (4) To develop the intellectual arts; (5) To develop both the contemplative and prudential functions of man's intelligence; (6) To develop both theoretical and practical intelligence; (7) To realize intellectual values in life; (8) To develop intellectual capacities of all students to their optimum level; (9) To develop the intellectual function in harmonious and organic relationships with the other functions of man in the educational process.

(F) *Institutional Responsibility.* It is a problem of school and society to discern the respective educational responsibilities of school, home, church, and other social agencies and institutions. It is the organic view that the development of the intellectual function of man is primarily the responsibility of the schools. The systematic development of intelligence or the intellectual function is the unique function of the schools. It goes without saying that intelligence is also developed in other ways in addition to what the schools may do; yet it is primarily a school function on lower, intermediate, and higher levels of education.

II. *Education and the Moral Function*

(A) *Moral Needs.* Man as a social and moral creature needs moral and ethical guidance. Man needs an education which will develop his moral potentialities; he needs to formulate a set of moral and ethical beliefs which he can follow throughout life. It is not enough to have intellectual knowledge and skills in the manner just described; the problem of what constitutes the good life is a perennial philosophical issue which faces man. The growing child needs a developing conception or knowledge of right and wrong, of justice and injustice, and of moral and immoral. Furthermore he needs nurture in terms of right habits and right moral feelings during his most formative years. With the increase of maturational powers he should more and more come to realize his moral capacities and responsibilities as a human being. These moral needs are not necessarily limited to a relativistic social context; moral needs in the broadest sense require grounding in one's philosophical and religious conception of man and reality. Adequate satisfaction of moral needs from the organic point of view includes a need for social adjustment, but it penetrates to problems of man's relation to God, cosmos, and reality as well as society. In classical terms one of the virtues of man is his moral function; he needs an education which will develop this moral function.

(B) *Moral Values.* Education has to do with the increase and realization of values in individuals; moral values are crucial to the whole educational process. With Plato we should say that education should make the young love the good and hate that which is ugly and evil.[2] With Whitehead we should agree that evil is constituted by our pursuit of lower experiences in place of higher experiences; the good life then is conversely constituted by our pursuit of higher experiences in place of lower experiences.[3] In the creative process of realizing man's moral values as man and in self-determination as an individual it is the responsibility of education to give firm guidance in the process. These values are inherent in the nature of man and reality; all such values are positive, only there are higher and lower values available to human experience.[4] Choosing lower values instead of higher values only degrades man from what he might have been in Whitehead's organic view. Man is capable of choosing strictly animal values instead of higher human values. Still it is the responsibility of education to nurture the systematic actualization of moral ideals in the concrescence of the individual's development as he actualizes existent potentialities. In short, actual capacities for moral development are blended with the ingression of ideal values. This is the creative process of moral development.

(C) *Moral Knowledge.* Since persons in a democracy have the freedoms and responsibilities of moral values and actions it is imperative that education should provide for adequate moral knowledge. The issues and solutions to man's moral problems should constitute a substantial part of general education. Youth must be carefully and thoroughly nurtured in the ideals and moral knowledge of their given society and culture. With maturity, however, historical and comparative dimensions of the moral issues should be thought through. Historical perspective on the sources of our moral values should be systematically studied. Likewise mature study should take the student into comparative systems of value. The sustained inquiry throughout the educational program from earliest to most mature years should have as its objective the individual's formulation philosophically of his own, genuine moral values. As the existentialists say, he should be stimulated and guided into his own 'authentic values'—not into a mere passive recitation of the values of others.[5]

(D) *Moral Arts.* With Aristotle we may say that knowledge alone does not make man good. Education has fulfilled only half of its obligation to the moral function when it has provided moral knowledge. The golden mean of Aristotle's *Ethics* is not achieved by the mere recognition of it as an ideal; diligent efforts both by teacher and students must be directed toward the actualization of this moral ideal. Conceptual knowledge must be converted into personal experiences and functional skills in the moral arts. Objective moral knowledge must be subjectivized; abstract moral insights must be concretized through intelligent experiences.[6] Ideal values are to be incorporated in the self-determination of the person's becoming through creative experiences. Conversely the moral perplexities of the student's ordinary experiences are illuminated by the sustained inquiry into moral knowledge. The moral arts are to be learned in co-ordination with moral knowledge.

(E) *Moral Functions and Aims of Education.* General education has the responsibility of nurturing man's moral function. Some of the aims of professional education in this respect are as follows: (1) To provide youth with moral training and understanding in terms of the ideals of their immediate culture; (2) To develop moral virtue; (3) To develop understanding of the great moral doctrines historically; (4) To encourage mature students in their study of comparative doctrines of moral values; (5) To guide students in their constant quest for higher moral experiences over lower experiences; (6) To encourage the formulation of authentic values; (7) To insure the philosophical inquiry for the attainment of moral values as a sustained element of general education throughout all the years of formal education; (8) To co-ordinate and harmonize moral knowledge and moral arts; (9) To harmonize the moral function of man with his other functions.

(F) *Institutional Responsibility.* It is true that other institutions of a democratic society share the responsibility for the development of the moral function of man. The home, church, community, and other agencies of society have a vital interest in man's moral development. To the extent that moral values are a private matter in terms of one's religious and philosophical orientations, the family and church have a very direct concern. However, the fact that moral development is shared by many institutions does not relieve the school of its essential function in the moral sphere. The matter is so basic to the development of man, it is so complex and vital, that it cannot be left to other institutions. Moral education must be systematically carried on in the complex dimensions we have described.

III. *Education and the Spiritual Function*

(A) *Spiritual Needs.* Contemporary psychologists have emphasized man's social needs in terms of belonging, approval, and adjustment. Many educational philosophies stop here within the social scene. A *philosophy of organism* insists on interpreting man in relation to the cosmos. As a product of the cosmos, rather than merely a society, man has spiritual needs. Man needs a sense of belonging to all reality; he needs a faith in the ultimate nature of reality by which he can order his life. As Whitehead indicates it is this ultimate religious faith which largely determines how one's character is to be developed. Spiritual development has to do with one's inner development. Or as Whitehead has put it so succinctly, "Religion is what one does with his own solitariness."[7] Spirituality in this sense goes beyond the social dimensions. Spirituality relates to the innermost feelings of man as related to God and universe. Man needs an affiliation and communion with world consciousness as well as his social consciousness. Man in his most personal feelings and thoughts in his solitariness has need for an "at homeness" in the world. Man's inner resources and their derivations from the creative factors of the world are in a word spiritual. Man has need for cultivation of these spiritual resources and affiliations.

(B) *Spiritual Values.* The foregoing discussion has already suggested spiritual values in terms of needs. Spiritual values are those which go beyond physical values. When spiritual hungers are adequately satisfied by rational religions or intuitions one gains a feeling of personal serenity and security. One feels less dependent upon persons and things and becomes more secure within himself. There is the spiritual value of identification with objective reality itself; there is the value of the feeling of elements of permanence in the universe of process. The sickening feeling of lostness and homelessness is replaced by the feeling of at-homeness in the world. One feels that his personal resources of emotion, prehension, intuition, reason, value and purpose in living are not without foundation; they are personal manifestations which are in turn grounded in the reality of the universe. One does not then fear solitariness, for he is not really alone.

(C) *Spiritual Knowledge.* Within the historical and cultural dimensions of the whole curriculum of general education, students should study world religions and world philosophies. To understand the peoples of the world we must understand their beliefs; many of their most fundamental beliefs are rooted in established religions. These religions in turn are closely identified with basic philosophies. The study of world religions and philosophies would include those of East and West, such as Hinduism, Buddhism, the ethics of Confucianism and the religion of Taoism, Islam, Judaism, and Christianity.

The study of these world religions and philosophies should be studied as objectively as possible in the realm of inquiry. The attempt should be to obtain understanding of the ways that people have interpreted such perennial problems as cosmic forces, God, soul, immortality, authority, good and evil, and the way of life. The study should include all shades of religious and philosophical expression from the most supernatural faiths to the most naturalistic philosophical expressions. The Stoic "life of reason," the Epicurean "limitation of desires," the Socratic self-knowledge, Rousseau's "democratic way of life," Nietzsche's "will to power," Pasteur's "scientific quest for value," and finally "self-realization as value" should be included as deviations from orthodoxies of religion.[8]

It is clear that we cannot truly understand the peoples of the world without the basic religions and philosophies which they hold. They should be studied in complex cultural and intercultural contexts which include the ideologies and beliefs in all of the other functions of man, such as moral, social, economic, and aesthetic and the like. It is the task of professional educators to arrange these vast materials in intelligible form for study at various levels of maturation and understanding.

(D) *Spiritual Arts.* Complementing the cognitive study of religious and philosophical knowledge are the spiritual arts. The spiritual aspect of life involves creative doing as well as knowing. If teachers are to assist in the cultivation of spiritual development, there must be a concerted effort to complement cognitive knowledge with experiences, feelings, and intuitions. That indispensable creative factor in life, *love,* must be nurtured and sensitized in the quest for ultimate meanings of the cosmos and of man. Since the spiritual arts are so personal in nature, it poses a most difficult problem for the procedures of general education. The art of solitariness, for example, as a spiritual expression, is something which the individual must work out for himself in the end.

It is at this point that the Socratic dictum of "know thyself" becomes most significant for the educational process. Spirituality is not gained through imposition of external facts; spirituality and philosophical insights are derived from the testimony of the inner life. Rightness and wrongness are known within. As Flewelling summarizes it,

> Thus it was that Socrates arrived at the great and liberating principle of freedom. There is no just law against the good man or of which he may be afraid. Neither law of God nor of man.

This inner witness of the spirit also is the gift of every man, 'the light that lighteth every man cometh into the world.' In this discovery of Socrates we have the true basis of education and democracy. It is not necessary to consult the law, the magistrate, the priest, the institution, or even public opinion. Look within! *gnothe seauton!* Know thyself![9]

As Plato also knew, there is a point in the educational process when the eye must be turned inward from external things.[10] The light of reason must illuminate the way. Philosophy has been the handmaiden of the spiritual life throughout history. Its objective problems in the end become personal faiths. Education should then endeavor to provide philosophical and spiritual experiences which will contribute to the individual's ultimate self-determination.

(E) *Spiritual Functions and Aims of Education.* In the development of the spiritual function of man, the preceding observations may be restated in terms of these aims of education:

(1) To impress students with the needs and values of man's spiritual life;

(2) To provide students with an understanding of world religions and philosophies;

(3) To encourage students to make their own individual self-determinations in terms of the spiritual function of man;

(4) To co-ordinate spiritual knowledge and spiritual arts in organic unity;

(5) To encourage the formulation of the individual's authentic spiritual values through the dialectic of Socratic inquiry;

(6) To harmonize one's formulation of spiritual values with those values and understandings which obtain in the other nine functions of man in philosophical unity and diversity, or "the unity of opposites."

(F) *Institutional Responsibility.* It is frequently asserted that since we have separation of church and state in our country, home and church shall have total spiritual responsibility, while the schools are to assume strictly secular responsibilities. The problem of religion and education is consequently one of the most divisive of modern times. Our views have been indicated in the foregoing pages. You cannot split up organic man and his functions. An adequate education requires the formulation of beliefs to live by; these in turn require the harmony of functions, particularly philosophical and spiritual. In the philosophical approach to the nurture of intellectual, moral, and spiritual values, that we have recommended, there is no necessary infraction of law. Laws prohibit the teaching of sectarian religion *per se*. They do not prohibit philosophical inquiry into the ultimate problems of the nature of man and the universe. "Spiritual development" does not necessarily mean sectarian indoctrination.

The schools should do all that they can to carry out the aims listed above. They must encourage the kind of philosophical inquiry that historically has eventuated in spiritual and religious identifications or expressions by the individual. Nurture of the spiritual function in this philosophical sense is a function of general education and the schools. It is to be hoped that the individual will have derived enough insight into the need for his further spiritual development that he will of his own accord and through his own self-determination make whatever religious identification which he may choose as an individual outside of his formal education in schools. The very character of the spiritual function makes it a shared responsibility between home, church, school and other institutions of society. Spirituality may or may not be developed in established religions and churches. What sometimes goes on in the name of "religion" in churches is far from religion or spiritual development.

Our conclusion is that home and church may nurture spiritual development through their own sectarian or non-sectarian expressions of religious faith and philosophy. The schools which have the responsibility for general education also have an inherent obligation to nurture the *spiritual function* of all persons within their jurisdiction without recommendation of particular sectarian or secular solutions *qua* "religions." Nurture of the spiritual function by the schools therefore takes the form of philosophical inquiry and experience in non-sectarian terms; nurture of the spiritual function by certain homes and churches may well be in the forms of chosen sectarian expressions of that function. All in all it is a shared enterprise by various institutions of a democratic society. In the end it is a matter for individual self-determination. Since the matter is of such importance, educators must walk the tight rope between the error of sectarian influence on one side and the error of neglecting the moral and spiritual functions of man on the other side.

IV. *Education and the Development of the Social Function*

(A) *Social Needs.* Both ancients and moderns agree that man is a social animal. He has indispensable social needs which should be met through education and social living. Man has need for family, friends, and society with its diverse offerings. We do not agree that all education is "a social process," but we do agree on the basic character of social needs to be met through human experiences and relations. Spiritually man needs an at-homeness in the cosmos; socially man needs belongingness in the human community. He needs the love, warmth, and stimulation of human relationships. Although much of individual determination can be an inner reflection, the individual certainly needs the contributions of other members of society. Through cooperative creative efforts man achieves social progress; he consolidates the gains made individually and collectively. One has only to contemplate what it would be like to live alone completely insulated from society to realize the many advantages and services of society. With all of its shortcomings and problems, human society is a vast improvement over primitive existence in inadequate or anti-social forms. For total development of his functions man needs society.

(B) *Social Values.* A discussion of social values would take us far beyond the limits of this synopsis. Suffice it to outline just a few of the social values for purposes of illustration:

(1) The enjoyments and benefits of family, friends and social groups;

(2) The values of belonging and being needed by others in social groups;

(3) The values of human love and affection;

(4) The values accruing from the organized structure and processes offered by society;

(5) The values culturally derived from social institutions such as education, security, protection, languages, arts, etc.;

(6) The values derived from human progress and human solidarity;

(7) The values derived in individual becoming by interaction with persons, ideas, institutions, etc.;

(8) The values derived from the talents of other persons in law, education, medicine, business, arts, religion, politics, economics, etc.

In moments of sentimental romanticism one might day-dream about the idyllic life of a Robinson Crusoe in the spirit of Rousseau's "back to nature" philosophy; however, calm and dispassionate reflection about the many values of social living would more than offset the more romantic reveries.

(C) *Social Knowledge.* In actualizing man's social function it is necessary that education include the broad scope of social knowledge. We should perhaps not go so far as August Comte and his positivistic followers in making the social sciences the core of education. Certainly it is beyond debate, however, that social knowledge and socialization shall be accomplished in the adequate educational program. Early education should educate youth in terms of his given society; with increasing maturation the gamut of social sciences, humanities, and related subject areas should be studied in historical perspective and in intercultural perspective. Understanding of contemporary societies and how they developed genetically is essential. Although one should be thoroughly educated in terms of his own society, the demands for world understanding today require comparative study of societies and cultures.

(D) *Social Arts.* Modern education has placed considerable emphasis upon the role of socialization in the educational process. Much has been done to encourage group activities and social dynamics. Although we cannot agree with the over-all philosophy of education as a social process, we can agree with the importance of providing social experiences and social skills to accompany social knowledge. Socialization is fine as a part of the total educational process. Although it might be argued that youngsters have plenty of social life outside of the school, it is also true that many of them lack the proper social experiences which can be given by the school under controlled circumstances. Social skills, customs, mores, and manners are some of the social arts which should be co-ordinated with more

414

formal and abstract studies of society. Then, too, there should be the actual nurture of *feelings* for fellow humans and the benefits of co-operative endeavors in work and play.

(E) *Social Functions and Aims of Education.* In the development of man's social function the Organic Philosophy of Education would emphasize the following aims:

(1) To assist the individual in a process of socialization in order to meet his social needs and capacities;

(2) To nurture the individual's realization of social values;

(3) To co-ordinate social knowledge and understandings with the social arts and skills within the learner;

(4) To harmonize social development with the other functions;

(5) To assist the individual in maximum self-determination and development through the social function;

(6) To educate the individual in terms of his rights and responsibilities as a member of society;

(7) To educate the individual as far as possible toward the realization of intelligent social living and social progress.

(F) *Institutional Responsibility.* It is of course true that individuals in a democratic society derive their dispositions, attitudes, beliefs, and values in reference to the social function from their varied experiences and complex responses and interactions in society. One learns social responses and attitudes incidentally in the diverse social processes. Yet it is largely the responsibility of the schools to embrace *systematic development* of man's social function in terms of the previously cited aims. Other institutions throughout society are vitally concerned with the development of this function; despite their concern their contribution to this development is not systematic but incidental. The well regulated home is ordinarily expected to assume responsibilities in the rearing of children in terms of this function as far as they can; nevertheless, it is quite evident that most parents are not in a position where they can assume the larger educational responsibility of systematic development of the social function in the dimensions described. At best it is a shared responsibility between various institutions, but with substantial reliance upon the school for sustained and coherent development of social functions with the other correlated functions.

V. *Education and the Development of the Economic Function*

(A) *Economic Needs.* It is clear that man and society have indispensable economic needs for minimal existence. Man shares this existential need with all other animals and forms of life. The uniqueness of man's economic function as distinguished from other animals is found in the organic complexity of the interdependence of this function with others. Man is not satisfied with minimal existence in economic production; he desires an economic system which will provide a high standard of living, of luxuries as well as necessities, and which will make possible the kind of society in which there is stability and leisure for the development of his many other functions and freedoms.

Some of the advocates of economic determinism are so imbued with the idea of the centrality of economic needs that they find the cause and cure for most of mankind's ills and social problems in the economic matrix. As we have stated elsewhere we believe this is another form of reductionism and is accordingly untenable for it reduces the totality of organic life to economic causation and value. Although economic needs are indispensable to man, we cannot agree that virtually all of our problems are ultimately economic.

With the development of more and more complex societies man's needs actually and educationally have become accentuated. Increases of world population, for example, despite technological advances in the Western World, have accentuated the world food problem. Man has need for enough knowledge, understanding, and know-how to solve this crucial problem along with the many other economic problems. These problems are of course not simply economic but multi-sided and multi-faceted.

Man in different roles has needs for economic values and economic education. As human being, as citizen, as consumer, as producer, and as vocationalist he needs economic education. As a person he needs economic experience and education for his own self-realization and

416

self-determination; as citizen he needs understanding for intelligent political and social participation; as consumer and producer he needs both theoretical and practical understanding of economics; it might be added that psychologically and morally man needs the values which can be derived from human production in the broad category of the economic function.

(B) *Economic Values.* Economic values are perhaps more obvious than the values in some of the other categories. There are, however, some economic values which are less evident on the surface. In brief outline form some of the economic values which should be realized through education and human experience are as follows:

(1) The obvious values of economic production to provide minimal human existence;

(2) Economic values instrumentally interpreted as they help humans to achieve other ends and purposes;

(3) Intrinsic values derived through satisfaction of economic production as well as consumption;

(4) Psychological and moral values derived from the enjoyment of the creativity and productivity of economic goods for human welfare;

(5) Values gained through an increased security due to economic progress and a relative degree of freedom from poverty, starvation, suffering, and the rigors of uncontrolled nature;

(6) Derivative values in terms of increased leisure time and the release of human energies into the development of man's other functions;

(7) Values derived from increase of economic powers and resources as they contribute to the total creative advance of mankind;

(8) Values to persons as one of the means of self-determination and personal realization both as a human being and as an individual.

(C) *Economic Knowledge.* Economic knowledge is necessary in the educational development of man's economic function in theoretical and practical dimensions and in scientific and philosophical contexts. It is essential that each individual should attain understanding and insight into the specific structure and problems of his own society's economic system. Education cannot stop here. Adequate economic understanding requires historic perspective on the genesis and development of economic systems and problems; it requires comparative study in the contemporary world of contrasting economic theories and ideologies; it requires inquiry into the science of economics and into philosophical interpretations. Intelligent participation in modern problems requires this kind of extensive economic knowledge in close co-ordination with other functions and understandings.

(D) *Economic Arts.* Co-ordinate with the conceptual inquiry into systematic economic knowledge are the experiences and skills developed through applications of principles and understandings. This amounts to an application of various organic educational principles. Abstract economic knowledge needs to be made concrete; objective understandings need to be realized in personalized experiences; scientific knowledge needs to be realized through functional intelligibilities which might here be termed economic arts. I refer here to economic arts *qua* man, citizen, consumer, producer, and perhaps as professional. Certainly what can be done in schooling is problematic and no doubt limited; yet the point is that such experiences and creative activities need to be carried on co-ordinately with conceptual inquiry if *organic intelligibility* is to be achieved.

Other educational values may accrue at this stage of the educational cycle. Deliberate teaching for transfer is called for at this point; such teaching in this context will be predominantly deductive. There is also the important business of assisting the individual in the formulation of his own *self-determinations* in terms of his economic beliefs, values, and interpretations. Our sustained contention that the total educational process should have as one of its aims the encouragement of the individual's formulation of his own philosophy of life, his beliefs and values, is extended here into the economic sphere. Also, despite the fact that we have been discussing economic knowledge and arts largely in terms of general education, it is important to realize the possible influences on the individual's thinking and planning as he looks forward to his vocational determinations.

(E) *Economic Function and Aims of Education.* General education has a universal responsibility with respect to the development of the economic function. From the organic viewpoint this function should be developed in terms of these aims:

(1) To meet the economic needs of the learner educationally in the varying contexts of man, citizen, consumer, producer, and as an individual;

(2) To nurture the student's understanding and appreciation of the economic values;

(3) To develop a conceptual understanding of essential economic knowledge; to develop personal abilities and skills in the economic arts through educational experiences; and, to co-ordinate conceptual understandings and functional skills in the person of the learner;

(4) To further the individual's formulation of his own philosophy of life with his authentic beliefs and values in the economic sphere;

(5) To provide some guidance in the economic sphere in the individual student's own "self-determination" prospectively in the economic sphere of life and in the economic function;

(6) To harmonize the learnings of the economic function and the other functions of man.

(F) *Institutional Responsibility.* The responsibility for the development of man's economic function educationally in systematic co-ordination with his other functions as described here is one for the schools, or general education. That is to say the educational preparation for economic participation in the life of the community is formally the responsibility of the schools in terms of general education. The totality of the socio-economic milieu of any community certainly provides experience and training in practical economics and in the experiential sense. The community itself, with the interactions of individuals, groups, and various institutions vitally interested in economic life, provides a living laboratory for economic experiences and stimulations. Business, industry, agriculture, home and government all have stakes in the economic intelligence of the individual. Professionally and commercially they may well offer educational experiences and programs and share in the development of the individual's economic intelligence and ability.

FOOTNOTES

1. Dr. Mortimer Adler has spoken frequently of these arts in terms of liberal education.

2. Frederick Eby and Charles F. Arrowood, *The History and Philosophy of Education, Ancient and Medieval* (New York: Prentice-Hall, Inc., 1940, Copright 1940 by publisher), p. 422.

3. See Howard W. Hintz, "A. N. Whitehead and the Philosophical Synthesis," *The Journal of Philosophy*, Vol. LII, No. 9, (April 28, 1955), p. 228.

4. H. W. Hintz, *Ibid.*, pages 228 ff.

5. See Ralph Harper and Robert Ulich, "Significance of Existence and Recognition for Education." *Modern Philosophies and Education* (Chicago: The National Society for the Study of Education, 1955), Fifty-Fourth Yearbook, Part I, pp. 215-58.

6. Note the importance of the organic principle of reversibility here.

7. Alfred N. Whitehead, "Religion in the Making," *Alfred North Whitehead: An Anthology*, selected by F. S. C. Northrop and Mason W. Gross (New York: The Macmillan Company, 1953), p. 472. Reprinted with permission of the publisher.

8. Ralph Tyler Flewelling, *The Things That Matter Most* (New York: Ronald Press, 1946, copyright 1946 by the publisher), see table of contents.

9. R. T. Flewelling, *The Things That Matter Most*, p. 278. Reprinted with permission of the publisher.

10. Plato, *Rep.* Bk. VII, Part IV.

19

THE PATTERN of
ORGANIC EDUCATION – Continued

IN this chapter we shall continue our analysis of the Needs, Values, Knowledge, Arts, Functions and Aims, and Institutional Responsibilities in terms of VI, The Political Function, VII, The Physical Function, VIII, The Domestic Function, IX, The Aesthetic Function, and X, The Re-creational Function.

VI. *Education and the Political Function*

(A) *Political Needs.* Although man may well seek the good life in a conception of good that transcends his given society, the good society is essential as a means to the attainment of man's highest ends. With Plato and Aristotle we can agree that man needs organized education to develop his proper functions as man; that furthermore both man and his requisite educational accompaniment require the functioning of the good society to sustain this many sided educational development of man. Man is essentially a social and political animal with the needs of such an animal. The proper nurture of his ten basic functions requires a society with enough organization, stability, and freedom to permit sustained development of his complex functions. Such a society requires intelligent government; man in turn requires a system of law and order to contain and nourish his activities in a careful balance of authority and freedom. He has need of political science and political arts so that he may participate as citizen in the maintenance of such a society. He has a need for social justice; he has need for the protection and security which such a society can provide in his quest for self-determination and the good life.

(B) *Political Values.* The political values have already been suggested in the foregoing. In summary form these values might be described as follows: (1) Values of self-government and self-control; (2) Values of law and order; (3) Values obtained from just executive, legislative, and judicial functions of government; (4) Values of human association and cooperative endeavor in solving common problems; (5) Values in the protection of human rights and freedoms; (6) Values in the consolidation of human progress; (7) Values for providing a relatively stable environment for the development of man's functions; (8) Values obtained for the realization of the highest human and individual ends in life; (9) Values prehended and felt as the organically exemplified ideals of life in human organization.

(C) *Political Knowledge.* The development of the political function in man requires political knowledge. It is evident that the citizen must understand the structure and function of his own government and legal system. The child, for example, must be gradually inducted into an understanding of the political system of his own country. With maturation, however, it is essential that political knowledge be attained both historically and comparatively. One should understand the cultural backgrounds and historical developments which gave rise to his country's political philosophy. In a world of ideological conflict it becomes more and more essential that political science be understood in terms of the comparative philosophies undergirding them. As Aristotle indicated, the true understanding of political science requires maturity.[1] He believed that students should be twenty-one before serious study of politics.

(D) *Political Arts.* Students need to attain *functional intelligibility* or "know-how" in political arts in co-ordination with political knowledge. As increasing maturity permits, students should be provided with experiences which will develop political skills on the practical level. Laboratory experiences are important in the political sciences as well as in the physical sciences. Actual participations in school government and student organizations where increasing degrees of self-government are permitted complement formal knowledge. Participation in community functions as maturity permits is also desirable—although naturally limited in scope. Practical action is not always required to develop the political arts in overt fashion. Vicarious

422

participation can be attained by seeing the relationships between political knowledge as taught in classes and as related to the actual current affairs of politics. Practical insights are attainable through analysis of current papers and journals describing political events when related back to problems and principles of political science.

Mastery of the facts of political sciences by the student is not enough. The teaching-learning process should engender genuine reflective inquiry so that the individual gradually (with maturity) formulates his own political philosophy in harmony with his philosophy of life. The subject must come alive through reflective inquiry. Students must be allowed the rights of dialectical inquiry within the realm of the political arts.

(E) *Political Function and Aims of Education.* In the development of the political function of man as man and in the individual in his self-determination the following aims along with others reflect the organic emphasis:

(1) To engender understanding and appreciation of man's quest for law and order as expressed in political sciences;

(2) To develop understanding of one's rights and responsibilities as man and as citizen;

(3) To develop an understanding and appreciation of the many political values available to man;

(4) To co-ordinate political knowledge and political arts in the individual through the organic educational process;

(5) To assist the individual in his study of political philosophies toward the gradual formulation of his authentic political philosophy and beliefs for action;

(6) To fuse and interweave the values and understandings of the political function with the other functions of man;

(7) To assist those persons especially who have the capacity and desire to realize their own becoming and self-determination largely through the political function of man in this endeavor.

(F) *Institutional Responsibility.* It is evident that in a democracy we obtain our political views, biases, and preferences from a wide range of experiences and sources in our society. Educationally, however, these influences are eclectic and incidental for the most part. The school is the institution which has the primary responsibility for the systematic development of the political function of man. Because the responsibility is so great and far reaching in its importance, it follows that the schools should be as objective as possible in political teaching. Complete objectivity here is, of course, impossible. Particularly in a democracy is it true that students (with maturity) should be given every opportunity to inquire into all sides of these fundamental political issues, both perennial and contemporary.

VII. *Education and the Development of the Physical Function*

(A) *Physical Needs.* It is well known to students of the history of education that the Athenian Greeks of antiquity idealized the harmonization of the body and the mind in the educational process.[2] Gymnastics and music were essential to the blending and development of sound body and sound mind in the pursuit of the Greek ideal, *Sophrosyne,* or the balance of ideals as actualized in the individual. Plato acknowledged that gymnastics were not merely for physical development alone; they, too, as blended with music were to contribute to the goodness of man's soul. The organic philosophy of education heartily agrees with the Greek ideal with respect to body and mind and its education in organic unity.

The actual physical needs of man and the conjoint knowledge necessary to meet these needs are too well known to require description here. Recognition of the fact that man is an active human organism which has evolved over millions of years should remind us of his physical functions and their importance. In short, education in the systematic development of man's physical function should be geared to man's biological, physiological, and psychological needs along with the other functions. Man has need for habits and understandings which will be productive of health and physical welfare. Educationally, he needs the knowledge and appreciations which science, philosophy, and other disciplines can provide with respect to his physical welfare. Although we are here separating the physical function and physical welfare from the other aspects of man, it is understood that any organic philosophy emphasizes the totality of the per-

424

son's well being as a product of all of the functions of man and their relationships in turn with man's total environment. Education must be in terms of the whole person; physical, mental, and moral welfare, for example, are interactive.

It is difficult to separate physical and psychological needs. In the development of man's physical function his needs in terms of emotions, feelings, prehensions, intuitions, hungers, drives, desires, appetites and the like should be dealt with considerately and intelligently.

(B) *Physical Values.* In the idealization of intellectual, moral, and spiritual values in man's pursuit of the good life, it is possible that we may underestimate the concomitant values of the physical function. Briefly stated some of these values are as follows:

(1) There is the intrinsic value of health and physical welfare; that is to say there is the joy and satisfaction which accompanies such well being as opposed to the sorrow and unhappiness which is experienced in a state of poor health or disease;

(2) There are the instrumental values of strong and healthful physical functions as they provide the physical and psychological energies, drives, emotions, feelings, and desires to carry on the intellectual, moral, social, domestic, and other functions of man;

(3) There are both intrinsic and instrumental values to be derived from proper satisfaction of man's biological, physiological, and psychological needs;

(4) There are personal values of a non-cognitive sort which accompany the proper satisfaction of human feelings, emotions, prehensions, intuitions, hungers, drives, desires and appetites.

(C) *Physical Knowledge.* Intelligent and deliberate realization of these physical values requires considerable physical knowledge. It is apparent that the whole program of activities and studies that we know of as "Physical Education" is essential; studies of physiology, biology, and psychology, as well as the other physical sciences and social sciences, are also important in the over-all understanding of man's physical welfare. It could be argued quite cogently that philosophy, religion, and the humanities in general contribute to man's understanding of himself even in relation to the physical function. Since the physical function of man is organically interdependent with the other functions no absolute division of functions can be made; therefore, it follows that we cannot expect sharp demarcations in the delineation of the various segments of human knowledge which would contribute to human welfare in terms of the physical function.

(D) *Physical Arts.* It is most evident in the case of the physical function of man that this development cannot be accomplished through an education which adheres only to conceptual knowledge; therefore it follows that man's physical function in co-ordination with other functions requires appropriate experiences, habits, and skills which might be called the physical arts. It should not be assumed by the reader that because of our analysis of the ten functions separately, that it necessarily follows that the curriculum and the educational process should be divided according to these ten categories. It will be recalled, for example, that the Athenian Greeks of antiquity nurtured the physical arts in close conjunction with such arts as music, singing, choral recitation, dancing and poetry.[3] The physical arts may well include formal and creative experiences and skills extending through formal gymnastics, informal gymnastics, games, sports, athletics, play, dancing, military training, and related arts. Constructive activities requiring co-ordination of intellectual, physical, aesthetic, and re-creational functions are entirely feasible in the Organic Philosophy of Education.

(E) *Physical Function and the Aims of Education.* In the development of man's physical function as a universal function of general education, the following aims of education are suggested:

(1) To provide an educational program which will prepare the individual for the actualization of his physical function and which will assist him in the gradual satisfaction of his biological, physiological, and psychological needs;

(2) To assist the individual in the achievement of physical values, both in terms of educational understandings and appreciations, and in actual realizations;

(3) To provide adequate conceptual understandings of the physical function of man in terms of organized knowledge; to nurture arts of

426

physical expression through appropriate experiences and skills; and to blend such understandings and abilities in the person;

(4) To nurture the development of the physical function in harmony with the other functions of man;

(5) To develop the potentialities of the physical function of each person to optimal capacity not only for his own good but for the performance of his social responsibilities in war or in peace;

(6) To assist the individual as an individual in the realization of his own peculiar capacities and propensities in the physical function as it pertains to his "self-determination";

(7) To assist the individual in the formulation of his philosophy of life as it includes the problems of physical values and their place in relation to other values.

(F) *Institutional Responsibility.* Since we have postulated the physical function as a universal responsibility of general education, it follows that the formal institutions dedicated to general education have this responsibility. Development of the physical function in harmony and co-ordination with the other functions requires a comprehensive, systematic educational program that only the schools could perform adequately. The broad military educational programs might come more nearly to an approximation of this task than any other institution. However, as conceived here, the development of the physical function is so fundamental and so essential to general education that it cannot be left to halfway measures. Many agencies and institutions of our society can contribute to such development but the schools must accept the major responsibility with respect to this function of man and education.

VIII. *Education and the Development of the Domestic Function*

(A) *Domestic Needs.* We have contended that the domestic function is essential to man's happiness. The domestic needs within this function are patent; all persons need the warmth, love, affection, security, sense of belonging, the congeniality of close human relationships and interdependencies that the family is capable of producing. So much has been written psychologically and philosophically about the important role of proper nurture of the human personality in the home that we need not amplify these descriptions in this synopsis. The family as the nucleus of social relationships can be a positive force for good in the educational process, or it can be a most devastating force for evil in the creation of the personality.

Man needs family functions to realize his own capacities fully; men and women need the institution of marriage with its primary function of procreating and rearing children. It is clear that the institutions of society itself are largely in existence to serve the basic social needs of the family. Parents need the responsibilities and the joys which accompany the care and nurture of the young; the children need the love, affection, security, and guidance which the parents can provide. The close relationships of the family allow the possibility for the finest exemplification of the moral, spiritual, social, and other functions of man.

Elsewhere we have called attention to the organic belief in the bipolar forces of the cosmos expressed classically as the male and female components. The union of man and woman in marriage exemplifies this metaphysical principle of bipolarity biologically, sociologically, and psychologically in the continuation of human society. The male and female components are complemented in this family union and in the procreation and nurture of their children. Here is the need for "union of opposites" and participation in the "creative advance" of the cosmos in the most vital and intimate of human relationships.

Educationally there is need for intelligent preparation for parenthood and the responsibilities of family life. There is so much at stake in the responsibilities of home life that these things cannot be left to chance. Nor can it be assumed that one's ordinary experiences of family life are adequate in preparation of the oncoming generation for such responsibilities. Learning through experience is not enough. There is a real need for systematic preparation of the individual for prospective responsibilities in the family; the vast knowledge and experience which we have available in the sciences, humanities, and the arts should be focused upon the important business of family living.

(B) *Domestic Values.* In discussing domestic needs we have already suggested domestic values. Some of the most apparent values available to man through the institution of the family are:

(1) The values of love, affection, belonging, security, and close human relationships which nurture the well being and joy of living of the whole person;

(2) The values which accrue from the actualization of one's biological, sociological, and psychological potentialities through the procreation and nurture of children;

(3) The values which are contributed to society as well as to the individuals of the family;

(4) The values educationally which are derived from the family environment; the values derived from the child's earliest beginnings in human expression, in language, understandings, feelings, beliefs, and affections;

(5) The values afforded by the family in the creative advance of mankind.

(C) *Domestic Knowledge.* Not too long ago schools provided "domestic science" in the preparation of young women for their prospective home responsibilities. These sciences centered largely in the problems of food, clothing, shelter, and care of infants. In recent decades schools have widened their offerings for "Family Living" and they now include courses which probe the psychological and sociological dimensions of home life. It is inevitable that education for the development of the domestic function of man will expand in scope and depth.

If complete and systematic development of the individual for the domestic function is envisioned, then the contributions of the physical sciences, social sciences, humanities, and arts will surely be needed. The problems of the home are the problems of man; the rights and responsibilities of the members of the family in a process of self-determination call for all the knowledge and wisdom that can be derived from education and human experience.

More specifically, students should understand the rights and responsibilities of family living in cultural perspective; they should understand the problems of family living as compared with past and present in different cultural contexts. It is not enough that students be taught the "how-to" aspects of home making; it is a part of the preparation, but not the whole. In terms of intellectual inquiry young people should study the problems of the home in philosophical context; they should see the problems of man and his endeavor to secure happiness as expressed through the family itself.

(D) *Domestic Arts*. The domestic arts are manifest in the individual's abilities and skills in intelligent family living. The abstract character of the foregoing "domestic knowledge" should be complemented by the development of abilities and skills through experience. Laboratory experiences in the various phases of the domestic function should be afforded the maturing student. The abstract character of intellectual inquiry should now be personalized and rendered concrete. The individual should be encouraged and guided in the formulation of his own ideals, values, and beliefs with respect to the domestic function and other functions. In other words the Organic Philosophy of Education holds that abstract inquiry should eventuate in the gradual formulation of a living philosophy and the exemplification of ideal understandings in the very existential character of the person as learner.

(E) *Function and Aims of Domestic Education*. In the development of the domestic function of man through educational preparation the following aims are suggested:

(1) To develop understanding and appreciation of the domestic function of man in all students;

(2) To nurture the comprehension and the sensitivity of all students to the vital needs and values to be realized in intelligent family living;

(3) To provide adequate intellectual grasp of knowledge necessary to the intelligent utilization of rights and responsibilities of democratic family living;

(4) To develop functional intelligibilities and skills in terms of the domestic arts;

(5) To blend these domestic understandings and abilities in the *organic intelligibility* of the learner;

(6) To prepare each individual for the satisfactory performance of his obligations to society through the domestic function;

(7) To fuse and interweave education in the domestic function with the other functions;

(8) To nurture the individual in the formulation of his own philosophy of life in terms of values, beliefs, and purposes in the domestic function and other functions.

(F) *Institutional Responsibility.* The school and home are obviously the most deeply concerned institutions about the problem of institutional responsibility for the development of the domestic function. It is also quite evident that it is not an "either-or" solution, but rather it is a conjoint responsibility of both school and home. In this division of labor the school is in the best position to develop the domestic function systematically in the diverse ways that we have suggested; the home, on the other hand, provides the actual and existent environment for experiential development of the individual. Since the domestic function is virtually inseparable from the other functions of man, the schools cannot afford to neglect this responsibility. The development of the domestic function then is a conjoint responsibility of school and home, of professional educators and laymen, of teachers and parents, of teachers and students.

IX. *Education and the Development of the Aesthetic Function*

(A) *Aesthetic Needs.* We have held that it is a universal function of education to develop man's aesthetic function. In the broadest sense of the term the aesthetic function of man embraces the whole realm of feeling, prehending, intuiting, and sensing; the aesthetic component in this sense complements the theoretic component. Man has need for nurture of this aesthetic component. In another sense of the term man has need for aesthetic education in learning the arts of human expression. The fine arts are the most evident mode of such aesthetic expression; but all intelligent and purposive creativity as conceived in the categories of man's functions can be realized as aesthetic modes of expression. To create humanity, man must express himself through all the channels available to man. Man then needs to be taught how to express himself in the intellectual arts, moral arts, spiritual arts, political arts, and the other arts. Man's latent potentialities must not be bottled up, but they must receive educational guidance and instruction in forms of legitimate expression. Then too, as we have stated elsewhere, man needs the nurture of right feeling and the quest for beauty. Music, as Plato realized, is one of the great media for penetrating to the very core of man's being in the development of the aesthetic function.

(B) *Aesthetic Values.* Aesthetic values correspond to the foregoing aesthetic needs. It is the task of general education to assist each individual in the understanding and realization of the following aesthetic values:

(1) Values derived from the aesthetic component of life in terms of "right feeling," "enjoyment of life's beauties," and what Bergson has so well called the "élan vital";

(2) Values that are realized in the creative powers and modes of human expression in terms of all of man's functions;

(3) Values derived from art through expression of beauty and truth;

(4) Values of art in a self disciplining influence (as suggested by Whitehead);

(5) Values in terms of personal development through creative experiences;

(6) Values to the human personality in aesthetic responsiveness;

(7) Values realized through increased appreciation of all aspects of living;

(8) Intrinsic values of finding beauty in life and reality;

(9) Values of aesthetic experiences as they complement the theoretic component in the totality of man's learning.

(C) *Aesthetic Knowledge.* It may seem paradoxical to speak about the role of aesthetic knowledge in the educational program when the aesthetic component has to do with the realm of "feeling" as contrasted with *ratiocination.* Still there is certainly the legitimate use of aesthetic knowledge as it refers to human knowledge about theories of aesthetics, theories of feeling and perception, psychological and philosophical interpretations of aesthetics and art, and certainly the fields called liberal arts, fine arts, practical arts, and the like.

There seems to be no shortage of books and references offering knowledge of "arts" or "how to do things" in the many fields of human endeavor. Within the broad category of aesthetic knowledge then we have the "arts" in virtually all of the functional categories of man. Knowledge is wanted of the intellectual arts, moral arts, spiritual arts, political arts, and the like.

Aesthetic knowledge would then seem to include (a) the realm of aesthetics proper (in which various theories and problems of beauty might well be delineated), and (b) knowledge of creative arts (as manifest in the various categories of human functions).

The whole field of aesthetics and arts should be studied in cultural contexts of past and present. Again may we remind the reader that in our delineation of these functions of education it does not necessarily follow that the curricula should have these same divisions. Although it is conceivable that some aspects of aesthetics and arts will be studied separately, it is more likely that aesthetic knowledge will be obtained within the contexts of the various fields of study.

(D) *Aesthetic Arts.* Aesthetic knowledge as previously outlined must necessarily be complemented by the "aesthetic arts" throughout the educational process. In the experiential sphere experience must be provided which will develop the individual's creative powers and capacities. Keeping in mind the several meanings of the term "aesthetic" we may turn first to its broadest meaning. Where "aesthetic" refers to the whole realm of feeling as opposed to the realm of ratiocination, it is apparent that experiences must be provided in the aesthetic realm which will complement the theoretic or intellectual component. Opportunities for the exercise of the judgments of taste, feeling, observation, sensory experience, prehension, and intuition are called for; experience of relations to other persons, things, objects, and events complement the abstract aspects of the learning process.

The aesthetic experiences in their various modes are necessary in the actualization of the "aesthetic values" we have previously outlined. Experiences which will generate personal powers and skills in specific modes of expression in the ten categories of man's functions are called for in a thoroughgoing educational philosophy. Experiences which personalize aesthetic intuitions and understandings fall within this realm.

The ideal values or ideal possibles can be fused with actual potentialities and propensities through creative experiences. Friedrich Schiller in his essays on *The Aesthetic Education of Man* advanced the thesis that the realms of form and matter should be actualized through the aesthetic process. With some reservations there is certainly much to be said for this thesis. However, as we have stated elsewhere, the totality of the educational process is so complex that we should not reduce it to one of the functional categories of man.

To summarize the aesthetic arts we suggest that various experiences should be provided. (1) Aesthetic experiences which complement the theoretic and intellectual understandings; (2) Experiences which will generate personal powers and skills in specific modes of expression; (3) Experiences in the fine arts; (4) Experiences which personalize and individualize more general aesthetic understandings and appreciations; (5) Experiences designed to develop aesthetic responsiveness throughout life's diversity; (6) Experiences which heighten the individual's love and appreciation of beauty in contrast to ugliness and deformity.

(E) *Aesthetic Function and Aims of Education.* Aesthetic education is not for the few but for all human beings; the aesthetic function of education is universal. Some of the important aims of aesthetic education might well include the following:

(1) To promote a sensitivity to beauty in the lives of all persons;

(2) To meet the aesthetic needs of man through the educational process as far as possible;

(3) To assist man as man, and the individual as individual, in the realization of aesthetic values;

(4) To increase aesthetic understandings and insights throughout the various fields of human knowledge;

(5) To develop the individual's powers of expression by means of aesthetic experiences in the ten functional categories of man;

(6) To fuse and harmonize aesthetic understandings and aesthetic powers of creativity and expression within the individual organism;

(7) To harmonize the aesthetic function of man with the other functions;

(8) To give special assistance to those who find the aesthetic function of man as their primary mode of self-determination;

(9) To assist the individual in the formulation of his philosophy of aesthetics as a part of his over-all determination of beliefs, values and purposes.

(F) *Institutional Responsibility.* If it is true that the aesthetic function is a necessary and universal function of man, then it follows that general education has the obligation to assume this developmental function in the education of man. It is clear that the totality of man's environment provides the over-all laboratory for aesthetic experience and development. However, the Organic Philosophy of Education holds that the systematic development of the aesthetic function of man, as well as the aesthetic component of man's experience, in harmony with the other functions of man, requires the sustained professional teaching and guidance of an educational institution organized and designed for the acceptance of such institutional responsibilities.

Aesthetic education is not a mere addition or appendage to the education of man; it is an indispensable part of the whole man and his development in relation to the whole of reality. Aesthetic education is organically and intrinsically related to the whole man throughout all of his functions. Aesthetic feelings, prehensions, intuitions and experiences permeate the very existence of man, so that no other function is *completely separable* from these experiences. They are, however, *relatively separable* organically as we have indicated in other places. Since aesthetic experiences are an integral part of the education of the whole man and his development, it follows that schools must accept the institutional responsibility for the systematic development of this function with the other functions.

X. *Education and the Development of the Re-creational Function*

(A) *Re-creational Needs.* We have maintained that man has a re-creational function as man. By "re-creational" we mean the necessity for the constant organic re-creation of man himself in all of his facets and functions; "re-creativity" is but "creativity" in the progressive and successive stages of man's organic development throughout his life. Perhaps the synonym best expressing our desired meaning is "renewal." Man must renew his whole organic being. We emphasize "recrescence" and "renewal" in this more profound sense, for the term is not intended here to be restricted to the more popular vernacular meaning of activities carried on merely for fun or amusement.

What are man's re-creational needs? In brief they might be outlined as follows:

(1) Need for recrescence as renewal of his whole being;

(2) Need for experiences which are novel and refreshing;

(3) Need for leisure in which he can carry on renewal;

(4) Need for knowledge of the meaning and significance of re-creational activities;

(5) Need for life values and understandings which will make possible the intelligent use of leisure;

(6) Need for an adequate philosophy of life which will motivate and guide the individual's re-creational activities and pursuits;

(7) Need for understanding the real scope of renewal activities in terms of all of the functions of man;

(8) Need for educational assistance in one's self-determination and self-realization through the re-creational and other functions of man.

(B) *Re-creational Values.* The whole question of human values and their realization becomes sharply focused when we come to formulate the re-creational function of man. Why? We believe the problem of value comes into sharp focus because we are forced to consider intrinsic values as well as the more evident instrumental and practical values. Recrescence involves the utilization of leisure time as well as the time which is absorbed in the necessities of the work-a-day world in terms of economics, politics, domestic life, and the like. The practical demands of everyday living make these instrumental values quite obvious. But it is only when we ask the question, "How should I best use my leisure time in re-creation or renewal?," that the problem of value in life is seen so clearly. If the necessities of practical living were taken care of, what then would we do with our lives? When you have answered this question adequately you have also set forth the answer to the problem of re-creational values. In short, you have a philosophy of value.

Re-creation of the whole man is realized through all of the categories of man. Man certainly needs renewal intellectually, morally, and spiritually, quite as much as he does physically. It is the very character of organic entities to renew themselves; hence man as a high grade organism requires this all around renewal and re-creativity. Again it is apparent that although we indicate the separate functions as categories of distinctive renewal, the various functions are conjoint in their interactions. But even admitting this observation has some truth, it is also evident that there are striking differences between the qualities of physical re-creation through athletic participation, and let us say, the meditations and prayers of spiritual renewal.

The re-creational values might be outlined briefly as follows:

(1) Intrinsic values felt through the renewal of one's whole being;

(2) Values obtained from experiences carried on for non-practical purposes;

(3) Values to be obtained from intelligent use of leisure time;

(4) Values derived from insight into the real meaning of leisure time;

(5) Values realized in the becoming of one's being;

(6) Concomitant values derived from the development of all of man's functions;

(7) Values in terms of one's self-determination;

(8) Values which are obtained as a by-product of a unified philosophical approach to life's varied activities and experiences as contrasted with an unphilosophical and fragmented approach to life;

(9) Values derived from contrasts of renewal activities with ordinary and perhaps monotonous requirements of life.

(C) *Re-creational Knowledge.* What would constitute "re-creational knowledge" in the sense that we have interpreted man's renewal function? Since we have interpreted the renewal function in terms of all of the categorical functions of man, it follows that such knowledge would include all of the descriptions of knowledge we have surveyed in the other functions. In a narrow and vernacular sense of re-creational knowledge one might indicate knowledge of such familiar recreations as literature, amateur science, painting, music, crafts, hobbies, sports, gardening, and other domestic activities. However, in the broader sense that we have indicated, knowledge for man's total renewal is virtually congruent with the requisite knowledge and arts of intelligent living. Although we do ordinarily think of renewal activities as associated with leisure time pursuits, it is entirely conceivable that even our everyday tasks might be partially re-creational if approached in the right spirit.

It is not so much practical knowledge that is needed by the developing student as it is the need for an adequate philosophial comprehension of the re-creational values and leisure values of which we have spoken. If the educational process has been conducted successfully throughout the student's schooling, he will have gained such a philosophical insight into the real values of life and the consuming desire to develop these values in his own life. If the other functions have been harmoniously developed both in understanding and in personalized experiences, the problem of one's proper use of leisure and the execution of the renewal function will be solved.

(D) *Re-creational Arts.* Most of what has been said about the topic just preceding on "re-creational knowledge" is applicable to "re-creational arts." The person who has gained proficiency and experience in what we have called intellectual arts, social arts, domestic arts, physical arts, aesthetic arts, and the others, has obtained the interests and abilities requisite to the re-creational arts. Assuming that each student has met minimal requirements in his educational program in each of these other categories, it then becomes a matter of his own self-determination, or an assertion of his own preference as to how he shall best use his leisure time in the re-creational function.

438

(E) *Re-creational Function and the Aims of Education.* Granting that education should assist the individual in the development of his renewal function the following aims of education in this category are suggested:

(1) To assist the individual educationally in the realization of his renewal function and in the realization of re-creational needs;

(2) To cultivate an understanding and appreciation of the values to be obtained through renewal;

(3) To provide each person with requisite knowledge and skills to carry on the renewal function;

(4) To blend the renewal function with the other functions;

(5) To assist the individual in the realization of an adequate philosophical comprehension of the good life so that the values realized might be expressed in the re-creational function.

(6) To guide and assist the individual in his self-determination and realization through the renewal function and other functions.

(F) *Institutional Responsibility.* Again it is apparent that the rights and responsibilities of the individual's re-creational activities lie largely with the individual himself. Under our democratic way of living the individual has maximum freedom with the way he spends his leisure time and the way he conducts his life. One's renewal, whether in physical, social, political, or spiritual realms, is a matter of individual rights and preferences. Nevertheless, the Organic Philosophy of Education holds that the schools in terms of general education do have an institutional responsibility for the systematic development of the renewal function of man in harmony with the other functions we have delineated. While students are in school attendance, educators in coöperation with other interested institutions of the society should exert all of the influence which is commensurate with the rights and powers of the schools upon the students for their own good and the good of society. Much is at stake both for the individual and for society with respect to the manner in which one uses his leisure time. An occasional individual may decide to waste his life, but a society composed of wastrels will be necessarily weak. It is our conclusion then that the schools of general education have a major responsibility with respect to the systematic development of this and other functions.

Summary. The pattern of organic education is formed by the conjunction of Educational Needs, Values, Knowledge, Arts, Functions and Aims, and Institutional Responsibilities, as one set of categories, and the Ten Basic Functions of Man as the other set of categories. These categories in conjunction provide two dimensions of the educational pattern. They may be graphically visualized as horizontal and vertical dimensions of the educational enterprise.

It is the universal function of education to develop systematically man's intellectual function in terms of intellectual needs, values, knowledge, arts and experiences, functions and aims, and through various institutional experiences. By the same token it is the universal function of education to develop systematically all of the basic functions of man in terms of these categories. Although it is apparent that these functions of man must be nurtured and developed in terms of organic togetherness, there are good reasons why separable emphasis must at times be placed upon the development of these functions. Again they are both conjunctive and disjunctive for our educational purposes.

If we view the organic pattern of education vertically, we see that man's basic needs can be catalogued successively throughout the ten basic functions. Needs are comprehended more comprehensively as intellectual, moral, spiritual, and so on. In this context also we are able to see man's values as correlated with basic functions and needs. Furthermore, this perspective shows clearly the relationship between these functions, needs, and values and the organic curriculum, which in turn is comprised by the co-ordinated categories of knowledge, arts, and experiences. We see that the structural and functional intelligibilities discussed in other contexts of this book are manifested here in the correlated categories of knowledge, arts, and experiences. Thus the organic contention, that spheres of knowing and doing, or reason and experience, or theory and practice, are to be co-ordinated in the educational process, is exemplified here in terms of the two-dimensions or sets of categories in the educational pattern. The curriculum of knowing and doing, or knowledge and arts, then is integrated with the organic conception of the ten functions of man and their systematic development.

From this vantage point we see also that the functions and aims of organic education are here harmonized with needs, values, and organic curriculum, as well as the functions of man. Functions and aims of organic education are cited here within the context of these categories, and not in isolation.

The same perspective is provided in terms of the problem of institutional responsibilities with respect to education. We see that from the organic viewpoint the schools have a unique responsibility for the systematic development of man's basic functions in relation to needs, values, knowledge, and arts. The development of the intellectual function of man is primarily that of the schools. The schools share the development of man's moral function with other institutions of society. Yet the schools have a deep obligation to carry on the systematic nurture of man's moral and ethical functions in relation to his total development. The schools share the development of man's spiritual function with other institutions. The schools have a definite obligation to carry on spiritual development of all individuals. Nurture of the spiritual function in the schools need not be sectarian but in the form of philosophical inquiry and experience in non-sectarian terms. The schools share the development of man's social, economic, political, physical, domestic, aesthetic, and recreational functions with other institutions. However, again we must note that the schools have special obligations in terms of the systematic development of understandings and abilities in these aspects of the human being and the life about him.

FOOTNOTES

1. See Aristotle, *Politics*.

2. See Frederick Eby and Charles Flinn Arrowood, *The History and Philosophy of Education, Ancient and Medieval* (New York: Prentice-Hall, Inc., 1940, Copyright 1940 by the Publisher), p. 228.

3. See F. Eby and C. F. Arrowood, *The History and Philosophy of Education, Ancient and Medieval*, pp. 228-30.

20

A CRITICAL REVIEW

IN concluding this book it might be well if we summarized the line of thought which has been advanced in *The Organic Philosophy of Education*. It may be of some assistance to the reader if the logical continuity of this educational philosophy is indicated briefly in retrospect.

The chapters are set forth in four parts. I. The first chapter presents the original conception of "The Proposal . . . The School Within a School" as an initial hypothesis. Its purpose is to present the reader at the outset of this inquiry with the basic conception of an educational theory constituted mainly by the co-ordination of two hemispheres of the educational enterprise. It also presents the organic conception that education conceived only within the social context is too narrow, and that educational theory must be conceived in terms of man and all of reality. There is a psychological as well as logical reason for beginning the book with this particular article; it demonstrates to the reader the necessity of a philosophical foundation for such an educational theory of co-ordinate hemispheres of educational activity, and it further illustrates the need for systematic elaboration and formulation of such an educational philosophy into its various ramifications. Chapter 2 completes this introduction by its overview of the emerging Organic Philosophy of Education. Some of the sources are reviewed, and the term 'organic' is briefly defined. It was shown that organic philosophy, as expressed here, is not a form of dualism, nor eclecticism, nor a philosophy of expedience. By way of introduction this educational philosophy is categorized in the generic classification of organism, as differentiated from categories of realism, idealism, and pragmatism *per se*.

II. Part II follows logically with its synopsis of the foundational propositions of this educational philosophy as it has been developed thus far. Since we are moving *toward* the formulation of an educational philosophy of systematic character, it is necessary to indicate the foundational educational propositions which have been determined at this point of progress. These propositions are comprehensive in scope and provide the reader with a quick overview of this educational orientation. The educational propositions are given first in order only because it was felt that most of the readers might be primarily concerned with the educational concepts and principles, and secondarily interested in the philosophical foundations. Chapters 4 and 5 deal only with these propositions in brief and general treatment with no attempt to expound or defend them at any length. Our purposes would not be furthered by such an attempt in such a synopsis. Chapters 5 and 6 provide a review of the foundational philosophical propositions which in turn undergird the foregoing educational propositions. There is no attempt to give lengthy exposition of these propositions in this brief context. Many of the propositions are enlarged in later chapters.

The educational propositions state in various ways that the educational process is essentially one of harmonization, integration, coordination, and blending of the contrasting elements as they are realized in the concrescence of the individual organism. Education in its most profound sense is an exemplification of creativity in human development and self-determination. Educational theory is not properly based upon 'either . . . or' choices between elements termed progressive or conservative, practical or theoretical, psychological or logical, functional or formal, experiential or conceptual, or the like, for education in its larger sense is viewed as an organic co-ordination of these and similar components which are complementary and reciprocal in nature.

Chapters 5 and 6 provide the philosophical propositions for supporting the foregoing educational propositions. The educational process as described organically is shown to be an exemplification of organic philosophical propositions. Thus the educational propositions advanced here are not merely expedient compromises at the level of practice, but they are manifestations of a philosophy of organism with clearly defined metaphysical and cosmological roots. This philosophy of organism, as derived from ancient organic thinkers to such moderns as Whitehead, Bergson, Peirce, Montague, Alexander, Hartshorne, Urban, and many others, represents the recent philosophical endeavor to arrive at a higher synthesis beyond the older dichotomies of naturalism versus supernaturalism, realism versus idealism, relativism versus absolutism, and science versus metaphysics.

The logic of the book then is clearly this: just as a higher synthesis is required in general philosophy, and is according to our belief expressed in a philosophy of organism, a higher synthesis is requisite in philosophy of education; the continuation of arguments about educational philosophies in terms of the older dichotomies of realism versus idealism, naturalism versus supernaturalism, modernism versus classicism, and the like, is now anachronistic, for we are in serious need of transcending these older issues. This work, *The Organic Philosophy of Education,* represents a deliberate effort to go beyond these former issues.

III. Chapters 7 through 15 are directed toward the application of organic principles to the educational process in the articulation of an organic educational theory. Chapter 7 places the principle of bipolarity in historical perspective. It is evident that bipolarity as it is realized today has had a long and illustrious historical development throughout the various philosophical epochs. Chapter 8 shows how 'polarity' and 'bipolarity' have been variously interpreted and formulated by contemporary philosophers and educators largely of an organic persuasion of some type. The meaning of bipolarity is then delineated in terms of this educational philosophy. It is not to be construed that bipolarity is the only significant principle of organic philosophy; on the contrary it is only one of many organic principles; it is, however, a most essential principle in this educational philosophy in elucidating our conception of the educational process and the means of resolving our key issues.

The conception of bipolarity embodies the essential contentions of organism. The great ideal opposites of the world are exemplified in the process of nature. Our world is both one and many, eternal and temporal, containing elements of permanence and novelty in its creative advance. Thus the eternal object *creativity* is expressed in the world of process as the many becoming one, both in emerging entities and in the world collectively.

The principle of bipolarity embodies the respective truths of the principle of unity and the principle of diversity. Althought it represents a formidable rejection of dualism *per se*, it protects the valid aspects of the principle of diversity or 'duality' as well as the validity of the principle of unity. In chapter 9 the principle of bipolarity is expressed in terms of the organic field of experience *in re* the teaching-learning processes. It is now evident that the familiar dichotomies of reason versus experience, logical versus psychological continuities, objective versus subjective conceptions, structural versus functional elements, organized subject matters versus behavioral experiences, progressive versus conservative conceptions, are not necessarily conflicting doctrines of education, but they are complementary and reciprocal principles when qualified by means of the organic conceptions.

Chapter 10 shows how the two-fold functions of reason and experience are both complementary and reciprocal within the organic conceptions of the educational process. Neither classical over-emphasis on academic reason, nor modern-pragmatic emphasis on prudential problem-solving, needs to dominate our educational theory, if the bipolar theory is applied. It was also shown that structural intelligibility requires a logic of subject matter, and functional intelligibility requires a recognition of psychological needs; both require interweaving in order to achieve organic intelligibility. These various intelligibilities are described in Chapter 11. We see that logical continuities are necessary to the educational process as well as psychological continuities. When these two strands of continuity are maintained like the strands of a rope they are complementary and reciprocal in what we have called the logical-psychological continuity of the educational process.

In Chapter 12 we see the importance of the philosophical resolution of the problem of 'Objectivity and Subjectivity' as related to

the educational process. It is precisely here that we see the importance of 'going beyond realism and idealism' and pragmatism in the
organic conception of the object and subject relationships. Chapter
13 outlines the organic theory of control as formulated here. The
contrasting factors of external and internal, extrinsic and intrinsic,
authority and freedom, and immaturity and maturity, were shown
to be related in terms of proportionate bipolarity.

In Chapter 14 various organic conceptions of the creative process
are set forth largely on the philosophical level. Whitehead's philosophy of organism is recognized as possessing the necessary and
adequate conception of the creative process at the ontological and
metaphysical level. The conception of creative process described here
is applicable to all actual entities. For our purposes this theory of
creative process was reinterpreted in terms of the analogy of the cave
for educational amplification. The philosophical and educational
meanings were further amplified in a presentation of Professor Craven's description of the five steps of concrescence in the educational
process.

In the opinion of this writer Chapter 15 represents the heart and
core of the book. Here the conception of the creative process from
the metaphysical level is amplified and extended in terms of the principles of the Organic Philosophy of Education. Here is the critical
fusion of ontological notions of the creative process with those on an
educational level. Here we find an integration and an interlocking
of creative process with previously formulated principles of organic
educational philosophy such as 'the two-fold development of man,'
'education and process and reality,' 'truth and self-creativity,' 'educational bipolarity,' 'Organic theory of control,' 'reversibility,' and the
like.

IV. Chapters 16 through 19 present the functions of man and education as formulated in this educational philosophy. It is presumed
here that an adequate conception of the nature of man is essential to
any systematic philosophy of education. The organic conception of
man set forth here endeavors to go beyond the older categories of
the native goodness of man, the inherent depravity of man, the de-
privation of man, the dualistic conception of man, or the more recent

bio-socio-psychological conception of man as a neutral substance to be formed by his culture. In keeping with the principle of bipolarity and other organic principles man is viewed as a product of the creative advance of the world; he exemplifies the profound bipolarities of the world; he is fundamentally ambivalent in his relatively stable but evolving nature.

Man in one perspective can be described in terms of this essential ambivalence and bipolarity of his nature. It is also true that man is very complex and many-sided in his potentialities and functions. These generic and universal potentialities of man have been formulated here as the ten basic functions of man. In their generic and universal potentiality these functions emphasize man's unity; in their specific individual and cultural capacities and nurture they exemplify the principle of diversity.

The organic conception of man leads to the denial of the progressive doctrine 'education as a social process.' Education is more than the immediate factors of man and society. Education really has to do with man and all of reality in its metaphysical and cosmological dimensions as well as physical, social, and psychological dimensions. This follows from the contention of the philosophy of organism that all entities of the world prehend one another in feelings, purposes, values and interactions, and that man is a product of this total creative advance of the world. It has been explained elsewhere that there is an important semantic distinction between 'social process' as referring to human societies, and the term 'social process' as used by some philosophers of organism to indicate the metaphysical and cosmological sympathies and interactions of all entities of the world. The critique here is directed at the narrower use of the term as pertaining to human societies, and it is not meant to criticize the organic use of the term in its broader sense.

Having outlined the organic conception of man and his functions, it was then shown how these human functions logically gave rise to the functions of education. Again it seems necessary to go beyond some of the older issues which have plagued us with questions of educational aims and functions, such as, "Should education make us more alike or different?," "Should education be progressive or conservative in its functions?," "Should education serve the individual or society?," and "Should education have universal aims and functions or ones which are relative to the individual and culture?." The organic principles and conception of man make it possible to achieve a higher synthesis in terms of these questions of educational functions: (I) In one sense education develops our common functions of man *qua* man, while in another sense it assists man in the development of his individuality; (II) education organically conceived performs both progressive and conservative functions co-ordinately; (III) education serves both the individual and society; (IV) education has a universal responsibility to develop man's basic functions, although such development must take place in the specifics of various cultural orientations.

Chapters 18 and 19 concluded this logical development of the organic educational philosophy by their delineation of the pattern of organic education. This pattern was formed by the conjunction of two sets of categories forming the two dimensions graphically. The ten basic functions of man furnished one set of categories for viewing the educational enterprise. The other dimension was furnished in terms of these categories: Educational Needs, Values, Knowledge, Arts (Experiences), Functions and Aims, and Institutional Responsibilities. The interweaving of these two sets of categories then provides us with the pattern of organic education and the necessary perspective for the complex business of the education of man.

This logical development of *The Organic Philosophy of Education* is arbitrarily terminated at this point. It is not fully arbitrary for the initial objectives set down for the writing of this book have been achieved for the most part. Although there is much more to be done by way of extending and deepening this educational philosophy, perhaps enough of the structure has been presented to convey the meaning and significance of this viewpoint.

In other works this writer intends to develop organic theories and conceptions of school and society, education and social progress, democracy and education, curriculum and instruction, the role of the teacher, as well as further inquiry into the educational implications of the philosophical and scientific considerations of the problems of reality, truth, value, man, ethics, morality, and religion. If this present work has served to move us positively toward a more adequate and coherent philosophy of education, it has achieved its purpose for this necessary first step.

Some philosophical questions. Numerous questions remain for inquiry both at the level of general and educational philosophy. Those questions which pertain to the nature of human thought are especially important in their implications for learning theory. Further inquiry is needed on the nature of thought, the inherent aspects of thought, the universality or relativity of modes of thought, and related questions. Whitehead's writings provide us with organic explanations both genetically and morphologically, but there are still intriguing questions to be pursued further.

This writer is particularly interested in the old argument precipitated by the writings of John Locke and Leibnitz in their respective essays on human understanding representing empirical and rationalistic viewpoints. Locke's *tabula rasa* theory has been generally interpreted and accepted as a rejection of traditional notions of 'innate ideas' as derived from the Platonic origins. Too often this interpretation of 'innate ideas' is very naïve and unfair to the rationalistic position. Leibnitz's reply to Locke in his essays is considered as a defense of the rationalistic position on the innate aspect of human thought. Modern educational philosophies seldom consider the rationalistic side of this argument. In fact much of modern psychological, sociological, and educational theory assumes a Lockean type of psychology and epistemology, if not a Humean viewpoint. Thought itself is most frequently interpreted as the relativistic 'product of a given culture.'

Although Whitehead has reconstructed much of modern ontology and epistemology to the satisfaction of this writer, there are problems of interpretation still. Are there universal aspects to human thought? This writer tends to believe that this question can be answered in the affirmative. Are the categories of thought universal to man's inherent capacities as man, or are they formed by and relative to specific cultures? What is the present status of Plato's categories of thought? Are these categories expressions of a universal bipolarity in human thought processes as well as expressions throughout nature? It is the feeling of this writer that there is much to be said on the side of the universal character of the potentialities of human thought, which has not been said by modern empirical psychologies.

Plato's doctrine of reminiscence is frequently pushed aside today as an absurd and obsolete theory. Too often it is interpreted in terms of theories of reincarnation of the soul or other spiritualistic beliefs. Plato's doctrine can be interpreted very realistically. It is quite possible that his insights, explained metaphorically in an age when scientific knowledge was very limited, can be elaborated much more convincingly in terms of our present knowledge of biological evolution. This writer believes with A. E. Taylor that there is much more to this theory of reminiscence than the usual all too literal interpretation. It is not necessarily a theory of reincarnation, but a metaphorical explanation of the rational potentialities of human thought.

Thus there are important questions to be pursued further with their educational implications. What is the status of the 'eternal forms' or 'eternal objects' with respect to human thought? Are not Whitehead's 'eternal objects' as they 'subsist' in the primordial conceptuality of God really strong arguments for the side of universality in the potentiality of human thought? What are the implications of the 'great ideal opposites' of which Whitehead speaks? Is it not likely that there is universal bipolarity latent in the very nature of thought? In short, to the extent that humans think conceptually, do they not think inevitably in terms of the bipolar categories of one and many, true and false, same and other, and being and non-being? Isn't this why Whitehead is forced to observe that we cannot think of 'one' without also thinking of 'many'? Regardless of cultural differences of symbols and language isn't it plausible that the members of *Homo sapiens* in their potentiality for conceptual thought possess these bipolar categories?

Granting the subsistence of 'eternal objects' other problems occur. One such problem pertains to the relative status of 'forms' or 'eternal objects.' Is there a hierarchy of forms from the most trivial and unnecessary level of conception to the most important and necessary? Are there not some 'eternal objects' which have a metaphysical status

450

of inevitable manifestation in the world process, while others have only 'possibility' for exemplification in actual entities?

Creativity, for example, is an 'eternal object' and an 'ultimate principle' in the philosophy of organism. The 'one and many' are also ultimates. As 'eternal objects' they would be considered only as 'possibles' for actualization; but as metaphysical entities they would be inevitably manifest in actual processes of things, for metaphysical principles never take a holiday, as Whitehead reminds us. It is entirely possible and likely that these questions are fully and clearly expounded in Whitehead's vast writings. However, since this writer makes no claim to extensive scholarship with respect to these writings, this question does appear to have importance for further consideration and inquiry.

There is also the question of the double aspect of the 'eternal objects' and their respective 'lures.' If there are an infinite number of 'eternal objects,' then for every possible positive 'form of definiteness' there must be a negative one. Thus there must be conceptions of good and evil, true and false, beautiful and ugly, and similar opposites *ad infinitum*. Empirically it is apparent that humans are attracted or lured by opposing sets of values. The 'subjective aims' are not always noble and good, but they are real aims. Evil events must exemplify evil forms. Now does this double aspect interpretation of 'eternal forms' reduce the whole notion of such lures to a verbalism and return us to our original and perennial problems of good and evil?

Many other questions might well be raised. Some may well ask, Why is Whitehead's God the one exception to the metaphysical principle that all actual entities come to be and then perish? If God is an exemplification of metaphysical principles, as Whitehead contends, then why is he an exception on this score? Defenders of the philosophy of organism can no doubt make a strong defense of Whitehead's position, but it still remains an interesting question.

The casual reader of Whitehead also gets the notion frequently that the philosophy of organism is one-sidedly devoted to 'process' as contrasted with 'structure' or 'substance.' One might ask, Why isn't there more emphasis on the aspect of relatively enduring 'structures' or 'substances' in Whitehead's philosophy? Again the followers of White-head might well reply that he does adequately explain and defend 'actual objects' as 'substances' in his philosophy of process and reality. This question remains an important one, despite one's interpretation of Whitehead.

These questions are raised in the spirit of philosophy and continuous inquiry. Despite our great indebtedness to Whitehead for his magnificent contribution in his philosophy of organism, these questions and many more remain for our inquiry. He would undoubtedly be the first to commend critical inquiry in the spirit of philosophy rather than blind discipleship and unthinking devotion to an established viewpoint. It is in this spirit that we hope to pursue these philosophical questions further and their important implications for education in *The Organic Philosophy of Education* in subsequent writings.

GLOSSARY OF WHITEHEAD'S TERMINOLOGY

Note: In the development of his philosophy of organism, White-head has deliberately formulated a new and appropriate terminology. For the older language of philosophy based upon 'primary substance,' he provides the new terminology of *Process and Reality.* The writer here is faced with a dilemma in setting forth a glossary of White-head's terminology for the convenience of the reader who may not be familiar with his terms or philosophy. An attempt at simplification and restatement of his key terms runs the danger of misrepresentation and inaccuracy. Still, exact reproduction of Whitehead's definitions, out of context, runs into the difficulties of presenting abstruse definitions which only require further definition for the reader. The writer, therefore, tried to approximate Whitehead's definitions briefly and directly as closely as possible without exact reproduction of his entire definitions. (F. C. W.)

✿   ✿   ✿   ✿   ✿   ✿

Actual entities: The real things which constitute the world; the actual occasions in the world of process; real existents.

Actual world: The temporal-spatial world of actual entities.

Beauty: The reciprocal adjustment and adaptation of the multiple factors constituting an occasion of experience.

Bifurcation: Dualistic division of nature or reality; a violation of the organic principle of relativity and connectedness, and/or the principle of sufficient reason, by absolute separation of entities properly conceived in organic relationship.

Bipolarity (or *Dipolarity*): Indicates Whitehead's contention that all entities are constituted by the possession of mental and physical poles and their organic relations; the structural unity of experience by which the becoming or self-formation of an organism is realized through concrescence; organic bipolarity emphasizes the interdependence of the mental and physical poles which are interactive in the creative integration of the organism; thus organic bipolarity is essentially different from the dualistic philosophy which holds to the absolute independence of two substances, mind and body, which are merely in casual association, e.g., Cartesian dualism of mind and body. Bipolarity is also in contrast with philosophies which are essentially monopolar in their reduction or subordination of one pole to the other, or their neglect of the conjunctive and disjunctive, organic relationships of the two poles.

Categories: Whitehead's basic categories which include (I) The Ultimate, (II) Existence, (III) Explanation, and (IV) Obligations.

Categoreal scheme: His basic entities which include (I) actual entities, (II) eternal objects, and (III) God as eternal and consequent entity.

Causal efficacy: The real internal powers within entities and in a nexus of entities; vector forces of actual entities.

Coherence: The relationship of a given system of thought whereby the ideas or propositions presuppose and require one another.

Conceptual prehension: A prehension by an entity of an ideal or eternal object; the conceptual activities which constitute the mental pole of an entity.

Concrescence: Derived from the Latin verb, *concrescere*, meaning "growing together." Used by Whitehead to indicate the "becoming process" of an actual entity; the complex unity realized by the coming together of prehended data from many sources; it denotes the realization of the many in concrete unity. Or, that process whereby an entity appropriates or absorbs data from other entities through prehensions and unifies or integrates these diverse prehensions; the concrete bringing together of the many into one.

Conjunctive: Used by Whitehead to indicate an entity's organic relatedness and connectedness with other entities, as distinguished from their respective disjunctive relationships, or individualistic existence.

Correspondence theory of truth: Ordinarily the theory which holds that the truth of propositions is determined by the existence of some one to one correspondence between the terms of the proposition and the elements of some fact. In Whitehead, it refers to his acceptance of the conformity of subjective forms to the objectified nexus. In other words, the correspondence of mental and physical prehensions.

Creativity: Whitehead's universal of universals; the ultimate principle of the organic process whereby the many become one; the actualization of potentiality; the principle of novelty.

Disjunctive: Entities exist both atomistically and organically, relatively speaking; 'disjunctive' refers to the relatively atomistic or individualistic existence of the actual entity.

Dogmatic fallacy: The error whereby we presume that abstract propositions or terms are adequate in describing or reproducing the complex relations of concrete reality.

Dualism: Any absolute division of the elements of reality; philosophical bifurcations of the continuities of reality.

Endurance: The temporal-spatial existence and persistence of a given entity or entities.

Entity: A thing or existent; for Whitehead, there are both temporal actual entities and timeless eternal objects or 'forms of definiteness'.

Essence: Loosely identified with Whitehead's "eternal objects" or "forms of definiteness," although he objects to "essence" in the sense used by "critical realists"; Whitehead's "eternal objects" are not "vacuous entities" floating in nowhere; they are construed by some interpreters as "envisagements" in the primordial nature of God.

Experience: The feelings or prehensions of an entity encountered in its becoming and being. "Experience" in Whitehead emphasizes the subjective emergence of the entity from the data of the external world in contrast to Kant's objective world arising as a construct of subjective experience.

Eternal object: An ideal entity, not necessarily involved in an actual entity in its conceptual recognition; "a form of definiteness"; an ideal conception subsisting as a "possible" for actualization in actual entities; Whitehead's term which approximates Plato's "ideas" or "eternal forms"; also called "pure potentials."

Event: A variant for "actual occasion" or "actual entity," emphasizing the ongoing character of its existence in process and in interacting relations with other entities and events.

Exemplification: A term used to indicate the embodiment or con-cretion of ideal forms or eternal objects in the becoming of actual entities; the realization of the ideal in the actual entity.

Extensive continuum: The general relatedness of all entities of the world in temporal-spatial and processual becoming and being; the community of entities in the space-time continuum.

Feeling: A synonym for positive prehension, physical or mental; a process by which many data are absorbed into the one entity in its becoming; "feeling" involves the generic operation of passing objective data to the subjectivity of the becoming entity.

God: An actual entity, possessing a bipolar nature which in one pole is eternal and primordial, while in the other pole a temporal, consequent nature; both transcendent and immanent in this bipolar nature; the source of importance, value, and the ideal beyond the actual for the world; "God" in the panentheistic sense of incorporat-ing both transcendent theism and immanent pantheism in a bipolar nature; God is the only eternal actual entity.

Good: An "ideal object" or "eternal form" which obtains exempli-fication in actual entities which then possess the value of "goodness.'" The ideal good is a "possible"; it becomes completed or actualized by its embodiment in concrete entities; exemplification is partial and imperfect.

Ideal opposites: The great bipolarities which characterize the world processes. Whitehead emphasizes the "final opposites" of "joy and sorrow, good and evil, disjunction and conjunction, flux and permanence, greatness and triviality, freedom and necessity," and "God and the World." (See *Process and Reality*, p. 483)

Immanence, doctrine of: A cosmological doctrine emphasizing the "immanence" of the "laws of nature"; a doctrine opposed to "imposi-tion," and one which insists on the action and reaction of internal constituents, as the explanation of the world. Whitehead speaks of "the mutual immanence of actualities"; in short it is a doctrine which holds that present entities are objectified in entities of the future through prehension and concrescence, or the many becoming one and the one many.

Ingression: That process by which "pure potentialities" become realized in actual entities.

Internal relations: The metaphysical doctrine that the characters of entities of nature are the result of their interconnections and the interconnections the result of characters.

Intuition: Any immediate and direct experience of data for understanding; such intuitions may be of many types including sensuous, non-sensuous, religious, moral, et cetera.

Macrocosm: The world as process in contrast with particular entities as microcosmic; the world in its massive perspective or perception.

Many: This term presupposes the "one"; it conveys the notion of "disjunctive diversity"; the principle of diversity.

Mental pole: Since all entities have two poles, the physical and the mental, the mental pole consists of the activities of mental prehensions which involve emphasis, valuation, purposing, et cetera, as conceptual reactions to the data prehended by physical feelings.

Microcosm: An actual entity which embodies in process what the universe is in macrocosm.

Misplaced concreteness, fallacy of: Whitehead's term for the persistent error of one's mistaking the abstract for the concrete; any neglect of the degree of abstraction involved in the description of concrete entities; or simply, taking words or symbols too seriously in their reference to concrete entities as finalities with respect to those entities.

Negative prehension: A decision which rejects or negates the data of a prehension by an entity.

Nexus: Particular facts characterizing the togetherness of actual entities; the connectedness of groups of actual entities.

Object: Any entity with the potentiality of entering into the internal constitution or concrescence of other entities.

Objectification: The realization of the data of one actual entity in the becoming of another entity or entities; it really refers to the mode or way of such realization of one entity in others; also the transcending by an actual entity of its own subjective immediacy.

Objective immortality: The realization of an entity in the creative advance of the world through its passage into other entities; the realization of an entity or its parts in the creation of a new entity; in perishing an entity becomes part of the data for the becoming of another entity or entities and thereby achieves "objective immortality."

One: Singularity of an entity, not the number one; the correlative of 'many'; principle of unity.

Ontological principle: Whitehead's principle of efficient and final causation; the principle of "being" in the philosophy of organism designating the focus of reality on the processes of actual entities.

Organism: A living entity; existence in terms of organic as opposed to materialistic conceptions; a living world as opposed to dead or inert nature; mutual immanence of entities.

Panentheism: Bipolar conception of God as embracing both a primordial, transcendent nature and a consequent, immanent nature in one being; the term is used as a mediating term between Pantheism with its extreme immanence and a Theism of the type which tends to extreme transcendence.

Permanence: The element of endurance in things which is inseparably linked with its ideal opposite, flux or novelty; for Whitehead, the world is neither permanence nor flux; it is composed of both.

Physical pole: Since all entities possess physical and mental poles, the physical pole consists of those concrete data prehended physically.

Physical Prehension: The reaction of one entity to another concrete actual entity, as contrasted with conceptual prehension; the appropriation of physical data; however, this must be qualified by Whitehead's "hybrid" category. A hybrid physical prehension involves the physical prehension of an actual entity, with the added involvement that the contents are derived from the mental pole of the prehended entity. "Physical" as used by Whitehead does not always mean "physical" in the sense of material.

Potentiality: Ordinarily an inherent power or capacity for passing to a different state of being. Whitehead uses "potentiality" in his theory of creativity; actual entities possess "real potentiality" in terms of their own creativity.

Prehension: Whitehead's special term for the way an entity appropriates data from other entities, to distinguish the process from the mental or cognitive process suggested by the ordinary term "comprehension"; the process of "feeling" whereby data are grasped or "prehended" by a subject; the relatedness of entities in terms of concrete facts; "feelings" as differentiated from "comprehensions."

Presentational immediacy: One type of perception emphasizing the immediate experiencing of clear-cut data; perception of objects in the ordinary sense of "sense experience"; contrasted with "causal efficacy" which involves the feeling of time.

Process: The way of becoming of actual entities.

Real internal constitution: Term derived from Locke by which Whitehead indicates the powers of actual entities in their self-functioning and self-creativity.

Relativity: The doctrine that each entity in the universe is necessarily involved in the concrescence of all other entities.

Satisfaction: The determinate feeling experienced by an actual entity in the final phase of its process of concrescence.

Simple location: The error of locating an object as a substance or bit of matter in a specific location at a given time and neglecting the larger relationships to other regions of space and other durations of time.

Society: According to Whitehead, it is a nexus with social order. The term "society" is not to be confused with or restricted to the ordinary vernacular meaning of society. He uses the term to indicate the patterned relationships or forms of an enduring object or creature. Organic reality is composed of larger societies. Molecules, cells, membranes, organs, bodies, human beings, human societies, nature, et cetera, are examples of enduring objects of "societies within societies." He refers to the enduring form of a given object in time.

Speculative philosophy: An enterprise involving the formulation of a system of general ideas which are coherent, logical, and necessary, by which all of our experience can be interpreted.

Subject: Refers to any entity when its internal constitution is being considered.

Subject-superject: Whitehead's terms for designating an actual entity in its double aspect, that of an experiencing subject, and also as an object involved in the experience of other entities.

Subsistence: Commonly refers to that mode of being attributed to "ideas" or "forms" beyond a temporal frame of reference; however, in Whitehead it refers to the mode of being of the "eternal objects" as envisagements in the primordial, conceptual nature of God.

Superject: An entity as an influential datum in the becoming of other entities; an entity in its potentiality for objectification in other entities.

Subjective aim: Whitehead's term for "the lure for feeling"; the emotional, purposive, and appreciative feelings of an actual entity which are not necessarily intellectual; ideals, aims, or purposes as felt by an entity in its becoming.

Subjective form: Refers to the inner life of an organism; the way a subject prehends a datum.

Subjective principle: An alternate statement of the principle of relativity; the relatedness of all entities; the recognition of the fact that all entities are potentialities for the becoming of other entities.

Symbolic reference: Refers to that part of experience which is interpretative, or more technically the mixed mode of perception which embraces (a) presentational immediacy, and (b) causal efficacy; in short, symbolic characterizations of objects in experience.

Truth: "The conformation of appearance to reality."

Unity and diversity: Principles of the one and the many.

Vacuous actuality: The postulation of entities or objects existing independently of other entities or without relations.

Valuation: The decision made by an actual entity with respect to acceptance or rejection of the ingression of an eternal object; decisions made in terms of the purposes of an actual entity.

INDEX

Abelard, 138
Activity movement, 20
Actual entity,
  and bipolarity, 156-57
  and creativity, 50
  and eternal objects, 248
  and objects, 76
  are *causa sui*, 298
  definition of, 99, 107
  (See Entity)
Actual potentialities, 194-95
Actual reality, 315
Adequacy, 32
Adler, Mortimer J., 18
  and inductive process, 271
  and methods of teaching, 272
  and order of learning, 271
Aesthetic arts, 433-34
Aesthetic function, 431
  and music, 432
Aesthetic knowledge, 432-33
Aesthetic needs, 431-32
Aesthetic supplement, 303
Aesthetic values, 432
Aesthetics, 380
Aims,
  subjective, 310, 313
Aims of education, 405, 407, 408, 411,
    415, 419, 423, 426, 427, 430, 434,
    435, 439
  Platonic and Aristotelian, 293
  (See Education)
Alexander, S., 35
Analogy of the cave, 30, 42, 205, 207
Analogy of the rope, 222
Anaximander, 133
Anselm, 138
Applicability, 32
Aristotle, 27, 35, 40, 42, 53, 378, 407
  aim of education, 293
  and contraries, 136 ff
  and creative process, 292
  and human development, 293
  critique of Plato, 137, 295
  ethical behavior, 281
  philosophy, 271
  substance, 153, 292 f
Art,
  education as, 289
  of teaching, 362

Arts,
  aesthetic, 433-34
  domestic, 430
  economic, 418
  intellectual, 404
  moral, 407
  physical, 426
  political, 422
  re-creational, 438
  social, 414
  spiritual, 410-11
Association, 355-57
Authority, traditional, 276, 277
Authority and freedom, 77 f, 164, 285
Avicenna, 138

Bahm, A. J., 27, 149, 150 ff, 152
  on rationalism, 154-55
  on substance, 153
Beauty, 434
  quest for, 345
Becoming, 77
Being, 197
Bergson, H., 35, 42, 99, 300
Berkeley, 35
Bidney, D., 27, 149
Bifurcations, 39, 97, 101, 155
Binary wheel, 134
Bipolar relations, 169
Bipolarity, 8, 13, 28, 29, 34, 36, 40,
    44, 50, 101, 150, 155 ff, 261
  and categories of thought, 449
  and continuity, 222
  and creativity, 336 ff
  and God, 120
  Breed's views, 163-64
  Dewey's viewpoint, 166-67
  educational significance, 173-75
  organic, 27
  proportionate, 197-98, 281-83
  Sheldon's views, 159-60
  sources, 27
Breed, Frederick, 12, 27, 149, 165
  and bipolarity, 163-64

Categories, 27
Category of the ultimate, 298
Causa sui, 298, 313
Causal efficacy, 185, 261, 302, 305
Causation, 202

461

INDEX